BIOETHICS AND BIOPOLITICS IN ISRAEL

Although the "Israeli case" of bioethics has been well documented, this book offers a novel understanding of Israeli bioethics that is a milestone in the comparative literature of bioethics. Bringing together a range of experts, this book's interdisciplinary structure employs a contemporary, sociopolitical approach to bioethics issues, with an emphasis on empirical analysis, that will appeal not only to scholars of bioethics but also to students of law, medicine, humanities, and social sciences around the world. Its focus on the development of bioethics in Israel makes it especially relevant to scholars of Israeli society – both in and out of Israel – as well as medical practitioners and health policy-makers in Israel.

Hagai Boas has published on brain death, organ transplantations, and bioethics. Since 2012, he has been the program director of the Edmond J. Safra Center for Ethics at Tel Aviv University. Beginning in October 2017, he will be the head of the Science and Technology section at the Van Leer Jerusalem Institute.

Yael Hashiloni-Dolev is a sociologist of health and illness, a professor at the school of government and society at the Academic College of Tel Aviv-Yaffo, and a member of Israel's National Bioethics Council. Her areas of interest include new reproductive technologies, genetics, gender, bioethics, contemporary parenthood, and posthumous reproduction. She has authored two books: *A Life (Un)Worthy of Living: Reproductive Genetics in Israel and Germany* (2007) and *The Fertility Revolution* (2013, in Hebrew).

Nadav Davidovitch is an epidemiologist and public health physician. He is a full professor and director, school of public health, Ben-Gurion University of the Negev. His current research deals with health policy, health inequities, health and immigration, environmental health, and public health history and ethics.

Dani Filc is a professor at the Department of Politics and Government, Ben-Gurion University. He is the author of *Hegemony and Populism in Israel* (2006, in Hebrew), *Circles of Exclusion: The Politics of Health-Care in Israel* (2009), and *The Political Right in Israel* (2013).

Shai J. Lavi is a professor of law at Tel-Aviv University, where he is also the director of the Edmond J. Safra Center for Ethics. He is also the executive director of the Van Leer Jerusalem Institute. His book *The Modern Art of Dying: A History of Euthanasia in the United States* won the 2006 Distinguished Book Award in sociology of law from the American Sociological Association.

Bioethics and Biopolitics in Israel

SOCIO-LEGAL, POLITICAL, AND EMPIRICAL ANALYSIS

Edited by

HAGAI BOAS
The Van Leer Jerusalem Institute

YAEL HASHILONI-DOLEV
School of Government and Society, The Academic College of Tel-Aviv-Yaffo

NADAV DAVIDOVITCH
School of Public Health, Ben Gurion University of the Negev

DANI FILC
Department of Politics and Government, Ben Gurion University of the Negev

SHAI J. LAVI
The Van Leer Jerusalem Institute and Buchmann Faculty of Law, Tel Aviv University

CAMBRIDGE
UNIVERSITY PRESS

University Printing House, Cambridge CB2 8BS, United Kingdom

One Liberty Plaza, 20th Floor, New York, NY 10006, USA

477 Williamstown Road, Port Melbourne, VIC 3207, Australia

314-321, 3rd Floor, Plot 3, Splendor Forum, Jasola District Centre, New Delhi - 110025, India

79 Anson Road, #06-04/06, Singapore 079906

Cambridge University Press is part of the University of Cambridge.

It furthers the University's mission by disseminating knowledge in the pursuit of education, learning and research at the highest international levels of excellence.

www.cambridge.org
Information on this title: www.cambridge.org/9781108714105
DOI : 10.1017/9781316671986

© Cambridge University Press 2018

This publication is in copyright. Subject to statutory exception and to the provisions of relevant collective licensing agreements, no reproduction of any part may take place without the written permission of Cambridge University Press.

First published 2018
First paperback edition 2019

A catalogue record for this publication is available from the British Library

Library of Congress Cataloging in Publication data
NAMES: Boas, Hagai, editor. | Lavi, Shai Joshua, editor. | Hashiloni-Dolev, Yael, editor. | Filc, Dani, editor. | Davidovitch, Nadav, editor.
TITLE: Bioethics and biopolitics in Israel : socio-legal, political and empirical analysis / edited by Hagai Boas, Shai Lavi, Yael Hashiloni-Dolev, Dani Filc, Nadav Davidovitch.
DESCRIPTION: Cambridge, United Kingdom : Cambridge University Press, 2018. | Includes index.
IDENTIFIERS: LCCN 2017029979 | ISBN 9781107159846
SUBJECTS: LCSH: Bioethics – Israel. | Bioethics – Government policy – Israel. | Bioethics – Law and legislation – Israel.
CLASSIFICATION: LCC QH332 .B51526 2018 | DDC 174.2–dc23
LC record available at https://lccn.loc.gov/2017029979

ISBN 978-1-107-15984-6 Hardback
ISBN 978-1-108-71410-5 Paperback

Cambridge University Press has no responsibility for the persistence or accuracy of URLs for external or third-party internet websites referred to in this publication, and does not guarantee that any content on such websites is, or will remain, accurate or appropriate.

Contents

List of Contributors — page vii

Introduction: Bioethics in Israel — 1
Hagai Boas, Yael Hashiloni-Dolev, Nadav Davidovitch, Dani Filc, and Shai J. Lavi

PART I: BIOETHICS AS BIOPOLITICS — 21

1 Securitization of Public Health Preparedness in Israel and Palestine: A Challenge for Public Health Ethics — 23
Nadav Davidovitch and Benjamin Langer

2 Republican Bioethics — 41
Dani Filc

3 Force and Feeding: From Bioethics to Biopolitics in Recent Israeli Legislation about Force-Feeding Hunger-Striking Inmates — 56
Yoav Kenny

4 A Cognitive Dissonant Health System: Can We Combat Racism without Admitting It Exists? — 76
Hadas Ziv

5 Nothing about Us without Us: A Disability Challenge to Bioethics — 97
Sagit Mor

PART II: FAMILIALISM AND REPRODUCTION — 117

6 The Effect of Jewish-Israeli Family Ideology on Policy Regarding Reproductive Technologies — 119
Yael Hashiloni-Dolev

Contents

7   "Quiet, Dependent, Nice, and Loyal": Surrogacy Agencies' Discourse of International Surrogacy   139
    Hedva Eyal and Adi Moreno

8   Palestinian Fertility in the Israeli Sphere: Palestinian Women in Israel Undergoing IVF Treatments   160
    Himmat Zu'bi

9   Childbirth in Israel: Home Birth and Newborn Screening   180
    Margherita Brusa and Yechiel Michael Barilan

10 "Life after Death": The Israeli Approach to Posthumous Reproduction   202
    Vardit Ravitsky and Ya'arit Bokek-Cohen

    PART III: IS THERE AN ISRAELI EXCEPTIONALISM?   221

11 Reckless or Pioneering? Public Health Genetics Services in Israel   223
    Aviad E. Raz

12 The End-of-Life Decision-Making Process in Israel: Bioethics, Law, and the Practice of Doctors   240
    Nili Karako-Eyal and Roy Gilbar

13 Organ Donation, Brain Death, and the Limits of Liberal Bioethics   258
    Hagai Boas and Shai J. Lavi

14 Toward an Israeli Medical Ethics   277
    Michael Weingarten

15 Tilting the Frame: Israeli Suicide as an Alternative to Suicide in Israel   295
    Haim Hazan and Raquel Romberg

Index   313

Contributors

Yechiel Michael Barilan, The Sackler Faculty of Medicine, Tel Aviv University

Hagai Boas, The Van Leer Jerusalem Institute and The Edmond J. Safra Center for Ethics at Tel Aviv University

Ya'arit Bokek-Cohen, Achva Academic College

Margherita Brusa, University Hospital, Padua, Italy

Nadav Davidovitch, Department of Health Systems Management, Ben Gurion University of the Negev

Hedva Eyal, The Federmann School of Public Policy and Government, The Hebrew University of Jerusalem

Dani Filc, Department of Politics and Government, Ben Gurion University of the Negev

Roy Gilbar, School of Law, Netanya Academic College

Yael Hashiloni-Dolev, School of Government and Society, The Academic College of Tel-Aviv-Yaffo

Haim Hazan, Department of Sociology and Anthropology, Tel Aviv University

Nili Karako-Eyal, School of Law, College of Management (COMAS)

Yoav Kenny, The Edmond J. Safra Center for Ethics, Tel Aviv University

Benjamin Langer, Schulich School of Medicine, Western University, Canada

Shai J. Lavi, The Van Leer Jerusalem Institute, The Edmond J. Safra Center for Ethics and the Buchmann Faculty of Law, Tel Aviv University

Sagit Mor, Faculty of Law, University of Haifa

Adi Moreno, Department of Sociology and Anthropology, Tel-Aviv University

Vardit Ravitsky, Bioethics Program, School of Public Health, University of Montreal and Director, Ethics and Health Branch, Center for Research in Ethics

Aviad E. Raz, Department of Sociology and Anthropology, Ben Gurion University of the Negev

Raquel Romberg, Independent Scholar

Michael Weingarten, Faculty of Medicine in Galilee, Bar Ilan University

Hadas Ziv, Physicians for Human Rights Israel

Himmat Zu'bi, Department of Sociology and Anthropology Ben-Gurion University of the Negev

Introduction: Bioethics in Israel

Hagai Boas, Yael Hashiloni-Dolev, Nadav Davidovitch, Dani Filc, and Shai J. Lavi

Consider the following scenes: Early morning at an IVF clinic at a public hospital in a city in northern Israel: two women sit silently next to each other, both waiting for an ultrasound and a hormone adjustment protocol. Their weary eyes disclose that both have already had their share of ups and downs with these tiresome fertility treatments. The emotional roller coaster is clearly taking its toll; exhausted from the ongoing dance of hope and despair, the two are lying back on their chairs, motionless, staring at the clock in front of them. Who are these women? What are their stories? Is there any significance to the fact that both are Israelis? Grueling fertility treatments burden women everywhere who turn to them to fulfill their common wish to bring a child into the world. However, learning that one woman is undergoing her tenth cycle of treatments, subsidized by the Ministry of Health, and that the other is to be impregnated with the sperm of a dead man she had not known while alive, one could certainly attest to Israel's unique reproduction policy as a major factor in this scene.

Spring 2006: the global outbreak of avian influenza (H5N1) has become a clear public health menace. The Israeli army joins private contractors to cull infected poultry flocks, but collaboration on a regional scale is needed. Without cross-border partnerships with the Palestinians and the Jordanians, the Israeli efforts to combat the outbreak are not sufficient. Facing infectious diseases obliges preparedness at the international level. Indeed, rephrasing the "diseases know no borders" maxim, the head of foreign affairs at the Israeli Ministry of Health declared that "birds know no borders." But how can this necessary collaboration be attained in a region as conflict-ridden as the Middle East? Can public health be separated from politics? In a prolonged state of conflict threatened with the potential of unconventional warfare and terrorism, is preparedness against emerging infectious diseases different from biosecurity?

July 2015: the Israeli parliament, the Knesset, has enacted a law allowing a judge to sanction the force-feeding of hunger-striking prison inmates if there is a threat to an inmate's life, even if the prisoner refuses. In response, the chairperson of the Israeli

Medical Association declared the law unethical. "Doctors should follow the rules of medical ethics which are independent of political coalitions," he argued (Efrati and Lis 2015). Both critics and supporters indicated that the issue of force-feeding hunger strikers mixes together the ethical and the political spheres. "Hunger strikes are a new type of suicide terrorism," claimed the minister of public security, thus conceding that the law was more concerned with addressing Israel's security than with saving the strikers' lives. Ethicists who supported the law tried to camouflage its political aspect by adhering to the adage of the "sanctity of life" as the supreme rule in medical ethics. Both supporters and critics of the law on force-feeding referred to its ethical aspect as the professional framework for the debate. But focusing on only the medical ethics aspect of what is also a highly political question actually served to emphasize how interconnected the issues of bioethics and biopolitics are.

Taken together, these three scenes illustrate bioethical reality in Israel. The first scene introduces a bioethical issue of Israel's very well-known liberal reproductive policy. The second scene raises questions of how the geopolitical setting demands the development of an ethics of cooperation. The third scene relates to the Israeli–Palestinian conflict as a key factor in discussing bioethics. Whereas consensus is easily achieved regarding the bioethical nature of the first scene, the second and surely the third are often relegated to the realm of politics rather than that of ethics. However, we argue that all three cases represent important elements of current Israeli bioethics and all three cases illustrate the mixture of the bioethical and the biopolitical. Further, this sampling suggests that Israeli bioethics is indeed distinguished by some singular characteristics, but that it nonetheless reflects the current general concerns of the entire field of bioethics, particularly the shift from concentrating on medical ethics alone to focusing on political issues that are inherent in the field.

Israeli bioethics has attracted the attention of local and international scholars for more than two and a half decades (Prainsack 2015). In this respect, the studies in this collection represent another attempt to satisfy the growing curiosity about how Israel developed its bioethical regimes. However, in contrast to the majority of previous accounts of Israeli bioethics, the perspective of most studies in this volume does not pre-assume that the Israeli case is an exception to liberal bioethics. Instead, they present a thorough study into the meeting points of the bioethical and the biopolitical in the local setting of Israeli society, and suggest the Israeli case as a case study for the global concerns of bioethics today.

This introductory chapter will develop our main argument by presenting two analytical axes. The first will consider the theoretical and methodological position that bioethics is always biopolitics, a proposition that mainstream bioethical discourse often ignores or hides. The second will explore our position that Israel's bioethical landscape serves as a useful example for discussing the challenges of bioethics today. The introduction concludes by presenting this volume's structure and chapter outline.

EXTENDING BIOETHICS BEYOND MEDICAL ETHICS AND LIBERAL THINKING

Although bioethical concerns moved beyond conventional doctor–patient relationships already during the second half of the nineteenth century with the emergence and development of social medicine and the public health sector, it was not until the second half of the twentieth century that criticism of the medical profession became more prevalent. Attacks on the medical profession were varied and originated from numerous sources: social and political – the rise of the civil rights movement, feminism, anti-psychiatry, and other critical approaches against biomedicine; legal – an increase in medical lawsuits; economic – the need to restrict the use of expensive medical technology; alternative medicine – criticism of conventional medicine (Davidovitch and Filc 2006); and from patients who started to no longer blindly trust doctors and their motives. In addition, immense ethical breaches, two glaring examples being Nazi medicine and the infamous Tuskegee syphilis study, fueled the growing mistrust in the medical profession and its ethics (Reverby 2000; Rubenfeld 2010).

It is within these contexts, particularly the social, political, and economic ones, that the growth and development of bioethical discourse and practice should be examined. It is therefore not surprising that many medical practitioners have perceived bioethics as another antagonist force, or at least a foreign entity to be resisted (Rothman 1992). In contrast, some doctors who joined jurists, religious officials, and philosophers in supporting new trends in bioethics viewed bioethics as a tool that could be used to set guidelines that could help save the medical profession, which had been subject to serious criticism for quite some time (Filc, Davidovich, and Gottlieb 2016). Others (Evans 2002) considered bioethics a way for professions, including the medical profession, to maintain their control over decisions rather than opening up the decision-making process to others.

As mentioned previously, the impact of the Holocaust played an important role in the development of bioethics. The Nuremburg doctors' trials are considered a watershed in the development of bioethics, especially as it emerged in the United States. One central outcome of the trials was the creation of the "Nuremberg Code," which is quoted to this day in every bioethics textbook. The code was written by American doctors and jurists in an effort both to avoid the recurrence of such medical atrocities and to clearly differentiate between the crimes committed by Nazi doctors and ordinary medical research (Rothman 1992). Nonetheless, there has been debate about the role of the Holocaust in the development of bioethics, particularly in light of the rather late adoption of the Nuremberg Code in research ethics, not before 1964 in the formulation of the Helsinki Declaration.

Since its emergence as a recognized field, bioethics began developing in different directions. In its early stages, when questions of biomedicine's responsibility for social impacts and future generations were raised, bioethics emphasized ethics within medical research clinics and laboratories. Later, thinkers in the field became interested in questions of doctor–patient relationships and examined the balance of power between medical professionals and patients from a liberalist viewpoint (unlike traditional medical ethics, which considered these relations legitimately paternalistic). Bioethics also began to be applied to additional medical professions, such as nursing, pharmacology, physical therapy, and public health.

While theologians and analytic philosophers joined bioethical discussions from the earliest stages of the field, members of other disciplines, including historians, sociologists, and anthropologists, only later joined bioethical debates, expanding discussions in the field to subjects ranging from feminist criticism of the medical world and bioethics to critical bioethics. Initially flourishing as a new discipline in the United States, the study of bioethics later spread throughout the world, influencing various nations and cultures differently. On one hand, today international bioethical codes exist and influence both international and local discourse in various fields, including clinical medical practice, doctor–patient relations, medical research, public health, and health policy. On the other, opinions on how to use this tool are quite diverse and expressions of bioethics diverge widely according to locale.

While bioethics has expanded and become more pluralistic, both disciplinarily and geographically, mainstream bioethical thinking is still strongly embedded in the classical liberal worldview. By *liberal bioethics* we refer here to the hegemonic mode of thought in bioethics that has developed mainly in liberal democratic societies.

Mainstream bioethics is mostly influenced from the disciplines and intellectual traditions of liberalism, analytical philosophy, and biomedicine that have made central contributions to mainstream bioethics, while also depoliticizing the field. Without negating the essence of bioethical thinking, liberalism and analytical philosophy's presumption of universal rationality, together with biomedicine's assumption of the professional's role as neutral due to its scientific and value-free character (Beagan 2000; Keshet and Popper-Giveon 2017), facilitated the de-politicization of mainstream bioethical thinking. Notwithstanding the depoliticizing influence of liberalism, analytical philosophy, and biomedicine, bioethics remains inherently political, with many layers to its political character.

First, at the most visible and recognizable level, the political nature of bioethics arises from the political discussions surrounding "traditional" topics of bioethical thinking, such as beginning- and end-of-life decisions. Second, mainstream bioethics is political precisely because of the assumptions it holds as certainties, such as the universal validity of liberal assumptions. One example of such an assumption is that liberal bioethics, like liberal legal theory, incorporates in its model the claim that there is a clear-cut distinction between law and politics (Altman 1990). In fact, it can be argued that bioethics' efforts to depoliticize the field by depicting its liberal values, which are in their essence political, as rational and universal and bioethics' claim that it is possible to detach interpretation from political discussion, are, paradoxically, political acts. Third, bioethics' actual field of activity, including its determination of what topics are to be discussed and what topics are outside its scope of study, render the field inherently political. Even bioethics' method of phrasing its questions and issues, greatly influenced by its strong link with liberal legal theory, is inherently political. According to liberal legal theory, the goal of the rule of law is to secure a wide zone of freedom (Altman 1990), and in consonance with this goal, mainstream bioethics asks whether a specific procedure should be forbidden. Only if it should not be forbidden does mainstream bioethics inquire whether it should be allowed. Fourth, bioethics is political because of its role as the *ethics of bio-capitalism* (Rose 2007). And, finally, bioethics is political in the Foucauldian understanding of biopolitics as the management of life (Foucault 2003, 2004).

According to Salter, mainstream bioethical thinking "presents itself as a neutral technique that uses 'tools for measurement that transcends culture'" (2007: 273). However, it is difficult not to recognize the political nature of discussions over issues such as prenatal screening, stem cell research, assisted suicide, or euthanasia. With regard to bioethics' first layer of politicization by discussing essentially political issues, Bishop and Jotterand argue that bioethics is being increasingly politicized, and "one's 'bio-ethical views' will reflect one's *political* assumptions concerning the nature, goals and values that should guide the biomedical sciences" (2006: 205; italics in the original). Consequently, discussions on the aforementioned issues have confronted both Democratic and Republican administrations in the United States, as well as secular and religious political parties in Israel with challenges to traditional liberalism from religious worldviews.

Regarding the second issue, that bioethics' efforts to depoliticize are actually political, Callahan argues that bioethics presents "a set of essentially political and social values ... not as a formal theory but as a vital background constellation of [axiomatic] values" (2003: 298). These values combine the assumption that the discrete individual is superior and has greater value than the society as a whole with "a more or less utilitarian perspective as an operative principle in ethical decision making" (Koch 2006: 253). According to Beauchamp and Childless, autonomy, non-maleficence, benevolence, and justice emerge as the four basic principles of mainstream bioethics. The order of the four principles is not arbitrary but lexically deliberate, and individual autonomy, liberalism's central value, outweighs the other three. It must be said that during the past decade, mainstream bioethical thinking has become more pluralistic, and the combination of individualism with a more or less utilitarian perspective has been enriched by other voices and approaches.

Mainstream bioethics' assumption that liberal core values and conceptions about human nature and society are universal has been challenged not only by religious thinkers, but by conservative viewpoints (Koch 2006; Smith 2000; Trotter 2006), communitarian ethics (Callahan 2003; Etzioni 2011), feminist philosophers (Leach et al. 2010; Nyrövaara 2011; Tong 1998; Wolff 1996), and critical disabilities studies (Newell 2006). Conservatives argue that bioethicists' approach is far from universal, that there is an alternative sanctity of life ethic, and that the "older value of a blanket valuation of protected human life" should overcome liberal principles (Koch 2006: 263).

In contrast to liberalism's methodological and axiological individualism, communitarian thinkers posit that human beings are social animals that always exist and operate within a network of other people and social institutions; that the public sphere is important and is not clearly separated from the private one; and that the welfare of the whole must be taken into account (Callahan 2003). Thus, communitarians argue that the first, or at least an equally important ethical question to be raised in bioethics should address the potential societal and cultural impact of decisions (Callahan 2003; Etzioni 2011).

Feminist thinkers have been also very critical of mainstream bioethics (Bowden 1997; Gilligan 1982; Held 2006). Feminist thinking presents several objections to mainstream bioethics, criticizing several aspects: its abstract approach instead of one that is more contextual or relational or that takes into account differences; its assumption of human separateness instead of connectedness; its preference for the right over the good; its marginalization of women; its assumption of man as the universal category; its disregard for gender differences; its embrace of individualism; and its disregard of unequal power relations (Tong 1998; Wolff 1996).

Thinkers from the field of critical disability studies argue that mainstream bioethics is characterized by "disabilism," which classifies different types of impairments under a single universal category of disability (Newell 2006). They further contend that disregarding the perspectives of the disabled depoliticizes issues and that considering the person as a discrete being rather than relational and part of a group of others discriminates against those who are harmed by a lack of care (McBryde Johnson 2003).

As demonstrated, other bioethical traditions pose significant challenges to mainstream bioethics. However, with the exception of feminist bioethics and certain scholars within disability studies, the other approaches to bioethics address only the first two political dimensions presented earlier: the discussions in which it engages, and the assumptions under which it operates. Neither conservatives nor communitarians criticize the scope of issues discussed by bioethics, the political economy that frames its discussions, or bioethics' role as part of biopolitics.

The third political dimension in the field of bioethics refers to how bioethics frames its field, the scope of issues covered by bioethicists, and the institutional settings in which bioethical discussion takes place. In reference to how bioethics frames its field, Guido Berlinguer rightly notes that "[B]ioethics... has been focused almost exclusively on recent developments in biomedical sciences – on extreme cases that were, up to now, infeasible and sometimes almost inconceivable" (2004: 1086). The cases referred to include organ transplantation, stem cell research, genetic therapy, cloning, assisted ventilation, and more. These discussions, important as they are, address biomedicine's cutting-edge practices that are performed mostly, if not solely, in developed countries. These practices generally remain distant from the experience of the overwhelming majority of humanity that nevertheless must confront issues of disease, illness, treatment or lack thereof, and death. Bioethics seldom addresses the ethical issues "raided by the mundane, routine, global depredations of illness and premature death" (Rose 2007: 16). Still working within a "principalist" approach, Berlinguer identifies equality, not only the equal dignity of every individual, but equity of life, disease, and health, as a principle that re-politicizes bioethics and broadens both its scope and the character of its practice (2004).

The fourth political dimension of bioethics is that of political economy. As Cooper (2011) claims, life has become a commodity. Indeed, it could be argued that since the emergence of a class society and extraction of labor, human life has become a commodity. However, until the advent of the biotechnological revolution, life as a commodity existed as human labor, and its extraction was mediated by social forms that allowed for the exploitation of human labor. The biotechnological revolution enables life to produce surplus value in much more immediate forms and bioethics plays a significant role in supporting this revolution. Bioethics plays "a crucial function in market creation, as biotech companies seek to commoditize DNA sequences, tissues, stem cells" by legitimating the extraction of surplus from life, and expanding the commodification of bare life (Rose 2007: 16).

The fifth and last political level in bioethics is that of biopolitics. As Bishop and Jotterand have argued, "bioethics has always been a bio-politics" (2006: 205). The other three political dimensions of bioethics analyzed previously refer mostly to power understood as sovereignty. Considering bioethics as part of biopolitics relates to biopower understood as "bio-politics of the human race" (Foucault 2003: 243). Biopolitics is "the acquisition of power over man insofar as man is a living being," i.e., man as a mass and the biological processes, such as birth, illness, and death, that affect it (Foucault 2003: 243). From this point of view, bioethics can be considered as an essential knowledge and as a technique of power over man as a living being. In this sense, Schicktanz and colleagues (2012) illuminate the way in which bioethics developed as a field of "expertocracy" in which "ethic experts" achieved influence and legitimization due to what is understood as a "superior and/or exclusive form of knowledge" (Schicktanz et al. 2012: 130). It is even possible to assert that the very emergence of bioethics as a discipline and a practice is a reaction to and a form of biopolitics (Schicktanz, Schweda, and Wynne 2012), since major bioethical breaches, such as Nazi medicine and the Tuskegee syphilis study, are examples of power exerted over man as a living being. In addition, bioethics can also be seen as a form of biopolitics, since bioethics evolved into a practice that is part of the "conduct of conducts" that characterizes biopolitical governmentality. Consequently, bioethics, representing ethical thinking related to life in general, but especially to human life and human health, plays a central role in contemporary biopolitics.

In contrast to the dominant liberal approach to bioethics, which obscures bioethics' political character, we argue that the Israeli case throws light over this political character. The very publication in 2015 of a book including reflections on bioethics from a number of Israeli specialists from different disciplines and entitled *Blue and White Bioethics* highlights the closeness between bioethics and the polis (as blue and white are the colors of the Israeli flag and serve as a metaphor for the Israeli state). The political character of bioethics in Israel is conspicuous in each of the political dimensions discussed in this volume. Much, if not all, of bioethical thinking and discussion in Israel consists of confrontations among a variety of political actors, such as health care professionals, lawyers, academics, political parties, etc., defending or opposing liberal and orthodox religious views. Bioethical decisions and legislation in Israel express a constant tension between liberal, individualist positions and conservative, communitarian ones. The political role of bioethics in framing the field of discussion and excluding certain topics is particularly evident in the Israeli case, where issues such as the health consequences of the neoliberal commodification of health care, accusations regarding the abduction of Yemenite and Balkan babies,[1] power relations between Jewish and Palestinian Israeli citizens, or the serious health consequences of the prolonged occupation of the Palestinian population in the West Bank and the Gaza Strip have been systematically excluded from Israeli bioethical thinking. Finally, we can witness in Israel the role of bioethics in the emergence and development of a "somatic" ethics. Because Israel is a biocapital power, especially in the med-tech and repro-tech sectors, it plays a central role in the ethics of the flourishing of biocapitalism (Rajan 2006). In addition, the political nature of bioethics in Israel can arguably be discerned from the field's silence about the issue of how, because of the Israeli occupation of the Palestinian territories, the lives of Palestinians are transformed into bare, unprotected lives, lives left to die (Agamben 1998).

ISRAEL AS A CASE FOR BIOETHICS ANALYSIS

The alleged divergence of Jewish-Israeli bioethics from prevailing Christian-Western norms and culture has elicited different reactions. On a normative plane, some leading scholars in the field have criticized Israeli bioethics for not meeting the minimal standards of liberal bioethics, such as medical autonomy at the end of life, and for violating the principle of doing no harm in the excessive use of reproductive technologies at the beginning of life. In contrast, prominent Israeli bioethicists have endorsed Israeli exceptionalism, arguing against what they perceive as the dominance of Anglo-American bioethics in Israel and calling for a local, autonomous Israeli bioethics (Kasher 2015; Siegal 2015).

---

[1] In the 1950s, several babies born to new immigrants from Yemen and the Balkan countries were reported as dead. However, the number of cases, the lack of parental involvement in the decision to transfer the babies from one facility to another, and the lack of transparency related to questions about treatment and cause of death aroused strong suspicions that these babies were abducted from their biological families and given up for adoption. Notwithstanding public activism, investigations were not thorough and lacked transparency. Despite the extremely high public profile of the issue decades later, Israeli bioethical thinking mostly did not address the matter.

On a descriptive plane, scholars have directed their efforts at trying to elucidate the distinct Israeli bioethical approach in light of its special mixture of religious, political, legal, and historical traditions. Some scholars have attributed Israeli exceptionalism to the influence of the Jewish religion (Kahn 2000). Others have emphasized the unique cultural history of Jews and non-Jews in Israel, including the impact of the Holocaust. Others have turned to demographic and political explanations and to the Israeli–Palestinian conflict (Birenbaum-Carmeli and Carmeli 2010; Kanaaneh 2002). Most scholars, whether from a normative or a descriptive perspective, share the prevailing presupposition about the singularity of Israeli bioethics.

Prior to the 1990s, what is now commonly referred to as *Israeli bioethics* was mostly perceived as Jewish medical ethics or Jewish bioethics (Prainsack 2015). However, since the turn of the century, significant growth has taken place in the number of English-language scientific publications discussing bioethics in Israel. They have been examining the leading bioethical topics of our times, such as assisted reproduction, organ donation, stem cell research, genetics, and end-of-life decision making, all topics about which the Israeli point of view and public policies have appeared to be unique. Specific Jewish medical ethics of course remained relevant in this discourse, but it has been acknowledged that the State of Israel and its policies, as well as Israel's medical and popular cultures, do not rely solely on Jewish medical ethics, despite its strong and comprehensive influence.

Since the 1990s, scholarly curiosity about Israeli bioethics has been stimulated by the surprising fact that some highly contested topics in Western bioethics, most notably abortions and selective abortions, stem cell research, cloning, and community genetics, have been easily accepted in Israel, without raising public and expert debate. However, regarding end-of-life issues, Israeli law has remained adamant in its opposition to withdrawing life-sustaining support even upon the explicit request of the patient. Israeli law has also imposed a very stringent definition and limited acceptance of brain death. Israel's proclaimed exceptionalism has been explained by different culturally specific factors such as: Judaism's teachings regarding the beginning and end of life (Lavi 2010); the sanctity of life and the role of human beings as God's partners in creation (Wahrman 2002); the extraordinary pro-natalism and pro-family characteristics of Israeli society (Hashiloni-Dolev 2007; Rimon-Zarfaty 2014); the effects of demographic and militaristic threats, as well as the trauma of the Holocaust, leading to an emphasis on survival (Kasher 2015); and a positive attitude toward science and technology as part of a Zionist legacy that views them as crucial for achieving progress and ensuring the survival of the community (Prainsack and Firestine 2006).

The academic emphasis on explaining the exceptionalism of Israeli bioethics has led to the neglect of examinations of similarities between Israel and other nations as well as of internal contradictions in Israel, such as its more open attitudes toward beginning-of-life issues in contrast to relatively restrictive attitudes toward end-of-life issues. In addition, by stressing the novelty of Israeli regulations, scholars have occasionally overlooked the more traditional features of Israeli bioethics. Indeed, the field of bioethics in Israel exhibits both modern and more dated elements. Equally misleading is that even in areas where Israeli bioethics seems exceptional, such as in the cases of artificial reproduction technologies, brain death criterion, or posthumous sperm retrieval, its exceptionality is often merely a matter of degree and not of kind. If this difference of degree rather than kind was recognized, Israel's variations from accepted practices in other countries could be more easily understood.

In their seminal paper discussing Israeli exceptionalism, Prainsack and Firestine anticipated two possible future scenarios:

> With regard to normative analysis and policy recommendations, we consider two different paths as equally worthy of consideration: first, Israeli policy makers may take on an identity of what we call "positive difference." This consists of the conviction that the liberal Israeli regulatory framework of biotechnology is no less moral than elsewhere, but less "inhibited" by religious moral objections (which do not exist in Judaism to the same extent as in Christian teachings) and guilt feelings from the past (such as in the German case, see Gerhardt (2002)). This attitude is prevalent among many stakeholders in biotechnology in Israel: it manifests, among other things, in the portrayal of Israeli biotechnology policy making as "doing it the Israeli way." ... The other possible path could be that Israeli policy makers will eventually give in to pressure from the international community. (2006:42)

However, there is another option, not raised by Prainsack and Firestine and congruent with the technological determinism theory (Marx 1994) that suggests that once technologies are available, all societies will eventually adopt them if they have the means to do so. While this theory suffers from oversimplification, it is time to ask a number of questions raised by the Israeli case. Has Israel's permissiveness and/or recklessness, depending on one's moral perspective, continued in its unique direction or has it restrained itself in light of international views and pressures? Or has the Western world moved in the direction of Israel's less inhibited bioethical standards? The answers are obviously not clear-cut, as will be demonstrated by the different chapter in this volume. During the past decade, Israel has been zealously regulating bioethical issues, sometimes downplaying its radical positions and sometimes serving as an instructive example for other countries.

Outline of Chapters

This collection of studies is comprised of three sections. It opens with a set of works that discuss different aspects of the connections between the political and the ethical in Israeli bioethics. The first five chapters cover issues that are less common in the discussions on bioethics in Israel, as they are considered "political" and are not included in the usual analytical axes of understanding bioethics in Israel. If we understand bioethics as having a strong political aspect, then the focus of interest of bioethics lies not only in the clinic, but also in the social, economic, and cultural contexts that frame, condition, and define the content of what is considered a medical issue and what is not. The implication of the chapters in this section suggests that medical care cannot be separated from social processes and should serve as a reflection of the political agenda of a given society.

The first chapter is devoted to Nadav Davidovitch and Ben Langer's account of developing regional preparedness for infectious diseases, introducing public health as a central bioethical concern. Confronting global pandemic threats necessitates regional cooperation even in a state of prolonged conflict. Davidovitch and Langer argue that the persistent state of conflict significantly affects the preparedness mode of health agencies in both Israel and Palestine. In Israel, health preparedness is swiftly translated into terms of national security and is then managed by military agencies. In Palestine, with a much more fragmented and weak health system, health risk preparedness lags far behind that of Israel.

In the second chapter, Dani Filc elaborates on the entanglement of bioethics and political thought by suggesting a new perspective dissociated from the liberal understanding of bioethics, which focuses on individuals, their autonomy, and their best interests. Instead, Filc argues for an ethical approach that gives precedence to the embeddedness of individuals in communities engaged in conflicting relations rather than to an abstract set of principles. Filc terms his approach "radical egalitarian republicanism" in order to emphasize his normative perspective that a community-oriented ethical system needs to go beyond particular groupings and seek an all-inclusive, egalitarian approach to defining the common good. The debate on force-feeding hunger strikers is used to demonstrate how the radical egalitarian approach departs from conventional ethical understanding. Unlike liberal approaches that conclude that force-feeding is unethical as it violates strikers' autonomy, or Jewish bioethical attitudes that force-feeding accords with the highly valued principle of the sanctity of life, radical egalitarian republicanism grounds its ethical position on a conceptualization of equality, freedom, and solidarity. It reaches the conclusion that force-feeding violates prisoners' ability to exercise their collective freedom.

Force-feeding is also the subject matter of the third chapter, where Yoav Kenny examines the debate on force-feeding hunger-striking Palestinian inmates. He argues that the medical, legal, and ethical discourses influencing the 2015 correction to the Israeli Prison Law authorizing force-feeding of inmates share a blind spot as to the biopolitical aspects of the debate. Specifically, Kenny's study scrutinizes the uses of four key concepts employed by both opponents and proponents of the correction: "hunger strike," "treatment," "force-feeding," and "inmate." Whereas conventional bioethical discourse regards these concepts as neutral and objective, Kenny concentrates on exposing their innate political infrastructure and argues that the legal and bioethical debate over force-feeding continues to rage with such fervor because all of its participants refrain from suggesting clear and explicit definitions for these key concepts, resulting in disregard of their biopolitical implications.

In Chapter 4, Hadas Ziv examines the role of racism and racial discrimination in a series of cases in the Israeli health system. Certainly, there is no policy countenancing overt discrimination in medical care in Israel, but there is also no clear policy opposing the phenomenon of racism in the health system. In fact, argues Ziv, there is no recognition that such phenomena actually occur. Drawing upon the cases of the abductions of Yemenite, Balkan, and Mizrahi children in the 1950s and the subscription of Depo-Provera contraceptives to Ethiopian women in the past two decades, Ziv illustrates how stereotypes and generalizations led the medical establishment to perceive non-Ashkenazi Jews as inferior and incapable of "proper" parenting. The segregation in maternity wards between Jews and non-Jews in several hospitals serves as a third example in Ziv's account of racism in the Israeli health system. According to Ziv, denying the problem of racism contributes to its spread. If continued racism depends on denial, she concludes, fighting it depends on calling it by its name.

Introducing bioethics as inevitably featuring biopolitical practices is also evident in disability critique and activism. In her chapter, Sagit Mor discusses the challenge to clinical bioethics from the perspectives of disability studies and disability rights. Mor offers a "nothing about us without us" approach to bioethics that calls for including disabled people in all levels of decision-making processes regarding issues of disability or touching on the lives of disabled people. In fact, the shift to "a social model of disability" disproves the working assumptions of clinical bioethics: first because of its exclusive reference to the individual, and second because of its opposition to the adoption and the endorsement of an imagined normal state of physical being that implies that any diversion from this state is defined solely in medical terms and is in fact a medical condition. How then can bioethics be disability sensitive? Mor suggests that a "nothing about us without us" approach is already changing Israeli law and policy, although its influence in the Israeli bioethical field is still minor. She argues that the only arena where Israeli bioethical discourse was influenced by the disability critique is the public debate surrounding wrongful life. The reason is the establishing of institutional channels that allow the voices of disabled people to be heard and to make a difference.

The second section concerns familialism and reproduction policies in Israel. Whereas previous studies have already introduced Israel as a repro-tech superpower and have provided several explanations for Israel's leading position in the world in using assisted reproductive technologies, the studies in this collections focus on a social and ethical normative order that stems from a reality where medicalized and technological reproduction is the default mode. They highlight Israeli familialism not only as a social artefact shaped by cultural and political factors, but also as a key institution in Israeli polity and normative order. Thus, this section suggests cases in which Israeli familialism is understood as a prime political factor impacting the regulation of surrogacy, fertility treatments among Palestinian women, home births, newborn screening, and posthumous sperm donation.

In her chapter, Yael Hashiloni-Dolev emphasizes the role of the family as the central reference unit in both policy making and in the practice of reproductive technologies. Drawing upon cases of selective abortions and the status of the embryo, posthumous grandparenthood, and preimplantation genetic diagnosis (PGD) for sibling donors, Hashiloni-Dolev argues that the concept of kinship and family has an impact on the ethics of reproduction on all levels. Further, her analysis suggests that the concept of Israeli kinship and family is rather "clannish" and has not fully adopted individualistic Western ideals in which family members are perceived as separate, autonomous individuals. Hashiloni-Dolev contends that this divergence explains the unique ethical background that induces Israel to be permissive in its reproduction policies.

The dominance of family ideology as a leading factor explaining Israel's normative use of reproduction technologies is also a leading theme in the following two chapters. In their analysis of surrogacy discourse in Israel, Hedva Eyal and Adi Moreno illustrate that familialism is so strong in Israel that the validity and availability of commercial surrogacy is undisputed. Because of this powerful familialism, cross-border surrogacy agents can take advantage of valued ideals of care and the desire to parent in the realm of this highly capitalist market. Interestingly, Israel was the first country to endorse commercial surrogacy twenty years ago, but limited it to heterosexual couples with fertility problems. The authors provide an historical account of the development of cross-border surrogacy by Israelis and the cross-border surrogacy mediation industry. They also discuss the power relations that dominate the emergent triangle of the surrogate mothers, the commissioning parents, and the mediating bodies. According to Eyal and Moreno, surrogacy mediators are a crucial subject for the analysis of these relations of power and for the normalization of reproductive commerce in Israeli society.

Familialism, Jewish history, and the demographic race are preferred explanations for Israel's reproductive policies. However, these explanations actually refer to Jewishness, if not restrict themselves to Ashkenazi Jewishness, and overlook the impact of Israel's reproductive policies on Israeli minorities. Himmat Zu'bi's study is the first to focus on the impact of reproductive policies on Palestinian women in Israel. Drawing upon interviews with Palestinian women who underwent fertility treatment, Zu'bi demonstrates that the difficulties and pain of fertility treatments are shared by Palestinian and Jewish women alike. She further stresses how family pressures to have children are affecting the experience of Palestinian women living in a patriarchal society. Moreover, for Palestinian women, undergoing fertility treatments also means entering what is for them a hostile and alien medical setting, what Zu'bi describes as "an exclusionary and often unfriendly Israeli space and staff." Mastery of the Hebrew language is a necessity. Access to clinics is also a problem. Yet Zu'bi's study reveals that "women were not silent objects in this process and their repertoires of coping strategies were complex and diverse."

The medicalization of fertility is indeed a hallmark of Israeli reproductive policy. Less discussed is the medicalization of birth in Israel. Margherita Brusa and Yechiel Michael Barilan address the history of childbirth in Israel, arguing that childbirth has been medicalized in Israel, parallel to the hospitalization of birth elsewhere in the world. The authors contend that together with the institutionalization of medicalized birth in hospitals and the delegitimization of home births, the effort to establish newborn screening has become a national project. They demonstrate how the principle of "responsible birth" was constructed to be medicalized to the point of promoting a national that which has little to do with the immediate interest of the newborn.

Posthumous assisted reproduction is perhaps the ultimate example of how permissive reproductive policies and norms are in Israel. In their study, Vardit Ravitsky and Ya'arit Bokek-Cohen focus on the cultural, political, and social circumstances that make posthumous assisted reproduction available in Israel. Whereas this reproductive possibility is acceptable in other places if the deceased officially declared a clear and explicit wish, in Israel, such consent can be presumed or inferred. Furthermore, Israeli courts, policymakers, and religious leaders tend to be permissive regarding this practice. Focusing on the penetration of the issue of posthumous assisted reproduction into the lives of combat soldiers, Ravitsky and Bokek-Cohen present the landscape of posthumous reproduction in Israel, which not only entails legal regulation, but is supported by a local setting of historical context, culture, religion, and societal values.

The third section returns to the question of how unique, if at all, is the Israeli case. The concluding five chapters revolve around different aspects of Israeli singularities, asking whether these idiosyncrasies result in Israeli exceptionalism. Aviad E. Raz discusses how the use of genetic services in Israel displays unique features. He points to the use of communal categories such as ethnicity and religion in devising collective genetic profiles as running counter to bioethical policies elsewhere, where the individual is the prime frame of reference in genetic services. However, the Israeli emphasis on collective categories is becoming a model being followed in more and more genetic policies outside the country, rendering the Israeli case not only an outlier, but rather a pioneering model.

The following chapter by Roy Gilbar and Nili Karako-Eyal focuses on the implementation of the Israeli law of euthanasia. The dying patient law has been discussed mainly in terms of the tension between the sanctity of life as a prime ethical value in Judaism and the liberal emphasis on autonomy. In this chapter, the authors test this tension empirically, surveying the actual attitudes and practices of medical professionals dealing with end-of-life decisions in Israel. Their analysis demonstrates that the ethical principles that guided policymakers, such as autonomy and sanctity of life, receive different interpretations in the actual clinical setting. The doctors' own understanding of their role leads them to formulate their own ethical principles regarding the end of life that differ from those of policymakers. The communication modes between the doctor and the patient play a central role in producing alternative principles guiding end-of-life decisions. Gilbar and Karako-Eyal discuss the role patients' relatives play in end-of-life decisions and the ethical viewpoints of the doctors regarding withholding or withdrawing life support treatment and the disclosure of information. Considering the heated debates and controversies among the experts who helped design the dying patient law in Israel, Gilbar and Karako-Eyal's findings present somewhat of a paradox in which the fundamental ethical debates are in reality practically resolved in day-to-day clinical practice in a way that has more to do with contingency than with legal guidelines or clear ethical principles.

A similar paradox is evident in the following chapter concerning the political deal to address the organ shortage in Israel. In their analysis of the history of organ donations and the definition of brain death in Israel, Hagai Boas and Shai J. Lavi show how the singular definition of brain death in Israel developed. Studying the history of the debate over brain death and transplant medicine in Israel, the authors contend that the local bioethical regime of brain death and transplantation diverges significantly from that of brain death controversies in other countries. The authors argue that the debate in Israel was a political one to begin with and its political aspects were never masked by arguments derived from liberal ethics, as occurred in other countries. In Israel, the science of brain death was always seen as a political question.

Does Israel's way of regulating medical technologies result from a singular understanding of ethics? This question guides Michael Weingarten in his historic analysis of the development of clinical ethics in Israel. His analysis suggests that Israeli clinical ethics diverge from Western ethics "first and foremost in the preservation of life and the centrality of family." Scrutinizing ethical stances of Israeli doctors, Weingarten finds a constant tension in Israeli medical ethics between the influence of liberal Western ethics and the pressure of local values that express a different array of value preferences. To a large extent, concludes Weingarten, Israeli medical ethics represent the middle ground between these two poles.

Similar to Weingarten's attempt to find a particular Israeli ethic, Haim Hazan and Raquel Romberg seek to unravel the local bioethical issues surrounding suicide in Israel. They contend that studying suicides outside of their cultural and historical context eliminates their social meaning. Thus, rather than follow the positivistic medicalized approach to suicide prevalent in global suicidology, they focus on the moral judgments and social dramas staged in the public sphere in response to "suicide events." Hazan and Romberg's analysis suggests that local bioethical meanings of suicide, anchored in changing cultural notions of individual and collective shame and shaming, have emerged in the public sphere over the past six decades in Israel, and thereby warrant the author's appraisal of their study concerning "Israeli suicide" rather than "suicides in Israel."

Hazan and Romberg's analysis is the final chapter in this volume and emphasizes our claim that bioethics can and should be studied outside the clinic and that understanding bioethics merely as medical ethics is too narrow a perspective. This line of thought in fact runs through most of the chapters in this volume. This collection offers an analysis of bioethics in Israel that takes into account how norms are translated into local patterns. Interestingly, there is no Hebrew word for bioethics. In fact, the idioms "bio" and "ethics" are alien to the Semitic languages, both Hebrew and Arabic, indicating that bioethics in Israel always involves a work of translation. This linguistic lacuna is more than an etymological curiosity. It is a metaphor for the main puzzle of this volume: what is Israeli bioethics all about? Is Israeli bioethics another case where the particular meets the universal and produces idiosyncrasies, or is the local expression of bioethics a case representing the challenges currently preoccupying bioethical regimes globally? The following chapters will provide answers to these questions by presenting new dimensions of bioethics in Israel.

This collection is the result of an interdisciplinary study group on bioethics in Israel that met once a month at the Edmond J. Safra Center for Ethics at Tel Aviv University. The authors wish to thank the participants of this study group for their efforts and commitment. Many thanks to Prof. Silke Schicktanz from the Department of Medical Ethics and History of Medicine, University Medical Center, Göttingen, Germany and Dr. Anat Rosenthal from the department of health systems management at Ben Gurion University of the Negev for their useful comments on this introduction. Many thanks to Prof. Orly Lobel from the school of law at the University of San Diego for her help and support.

References

Agamben, G. (1998). *Homo Sacer: Sovereign Power and Bare Life* (D. Heller-Boazen, Trans.). Stanford, CA: Stanford University Press.

Altman, A. (1990). *Critical Legal Studies: A Liberal Critique*. Princeton, NJ: Princeton University Press.

Bashford, A. (2014). *Imperial Hygiene: A Critical History of Colonialism, Nationalism and Public Health*. New York: Palgrave Macmillan.

Beagan, B. (2000). Neutralizing Differences: Producing Neutral Doctors for (almost) Neutral Patients, *Social Science and Medicine*, 51, 1253–1265.

Berlinguer, G. (2004). Bioethics, Health and Inequality, *The Lancet*, 364, 1086.

Birenbaum-Carmeli, D. and Carmeli, Y. (2010) (Eds.). *Kin, Gene, Community: Reproductive Technology among Jewish Israelis*. Oxford/New York: Berghahn Books, pp. 153–173.

Bishop, J. and Jotterand, F. (2006). Bioethics as Biopolitics, *Journal of Medicine and Philosophy*, 31, 205–212.

Bowden, P. (1997). *Caring: Gender-Sensitive Ethics*. London: Routledge.

Callahan, D. (2003). Individual Good and Common Good: A Communitarian Approach to Bioethics, *Perspectives in Biology and Medicine*, 46, 496–507.

Cooper, M. (2011). *Life as Surplus: Biotechnology and Capitalism in the Neoliberal Era*. Seattle: University of Washington Press.

Cooter, R. and Pickstone, V. (2003) (Eds.). *Companion to Medicine in the Twentieth Century*. United Kingdom: Taylor & Francis.

Davidovitch, N. and Filc, D. (2006). Reconstructing Data: Evidence-Based Medicine and Evidence-Based Public Health in Context. *Dynamis*, 26, 287–306.

Efrati, I and Lis, Y. (2015, July 30). The Knesset Has Passed the Force Feeding Law. *Haaretz*, p. 1.

Etzioni, A. (2011). Authoritarian vs. Responsive Communitarian Bioethics, *Journal of Medical Ethics*, 37, 17–23.

Evans, J. H. (2002). *Playing God? Human Genetic Engineering and the Rationalization of Public Bioethical Debate*. Chicago: University of Chicago Press.

Filc, D., Davidovich, N., and Gottlieb, N. (2016). A Republican Egalitarian Approach to Bioethics, *International Journal of Health Services*, 46(4): 734–746.

Foucault, M. (2003). *Society Must Be Defended: Lectures at the College de France 1975–1975*. London: Macmillan.

Foucault, M. (2004). *The Birth of Biopolitics*. New York: Picador.

Gilligan, C. (1982). *In a Different Voice*. Cambridge, MA: Harvard University Press.

Hashiloni-Dolev, Y. (2007). *A Life (Un)Worthy of Living: Reproductive Genetics in Israel and Germany*. Secaucus, NJ: Springer.

Held, V. (2006). *The Ethics of Care: Personal, Political and Global*. New York: Oxford University Press.

Huisman, F. and Warner, J. (2006) (Eds.). *Locating Medical History: The Stories and Their Meanings*. Baltimore, MD: Johns Hopkins University Press.

Kahn, S. M. (2000). *Reproducing Jews: A Cultural Account of Assisted Conception in Israel*. Durham, NC: Duke University Press.

Kanaaneh, R. (2002). *Birthing the Nation: Strategies of Palestinian Women in Israel*. Berkeley: University of California Press.

Kasher, A. (2015). The Values of Israeli Bioethics, an Ordered and Complete Picture. In G. Siegal (Ed.), *Blue and White Bioethics: Bioethics and Medical Law in Israel*. Jerusalem: Bialik Publishing House and the Ono Academic College, pp. 36–69 (Hebrew).

Keshet, Y. and Popper-Giveon, A. (2017). Neutrality in Medicine and Health Professionals from Ethnic Minority Groups: The Case of Arab Health Professionals in Israel, *Social Science and Medicine*, 174, 35–42.

Knoppers, B. and Chadwick, R. (2005). Human Genetic Research: Emerging Trends in Ethics, *Nature Reviews Genetics*, 6, 75–81.

Koch, T. (2006). Bioethics as Ideology: Conditional and Unconditional Values, *The Journal of Medicine and Philosophy*, 31, 251–267.

Lavi, S. (2010). The Paradox of Jewish Bioethics in Israel: The Case of Reproductive Technologies. In A. Voigt (Ed.), *Religion in bioethischen Diskursen: Interdisziplinäre, internationale und interreligiöse Perspektiven*. Berlin: De Gruyter, pp. 81–102.

Leach, S., Baldwin-Ragaven, L., and Fitzpatrick, P. (2010). *Feminist Bioethics at the Center, on the Margins*. Baltimore, MD: John Hopkins University Press.

Marx, L. (1994). *Does Technology Drive History? The Dilemma of Technological Determinism*. Cambridge, MA: MIT Press.

McBryde Johnson, H. (2003, Feb. 2). Unspeakable Conversations. *The New York Times Magazine*.

Newell, C. (2006). Disability, Bioethics and Rejected Knowledge, *Journal of Medicine and Philosophy*, 31, 269–283.

Nyrövaara, E. (2011). The Feminist Transformation of Bioethics: An Analysis of Theoretical Perspectives and Practical Applications in Feminist Bioethics. (doctoral thesis), University of Helsinki, Finland.

Porter, D. (1999). *Health, Civilization and the State: A History of Public Health from Ancient to Modern Times*. New York: Routledge.

Prainsack, B. (2015). Israeli Bioethics – A European Perspective. In G. Siegal (Ed.), *Blue and White Bioethics: Bioethics and Medical Law in Israel*. Jerusalem: Bialik Publishing House and the Ono Academic College, pp. 1–28(Hebrew).

Prainsack, B. and Firestine, O. (2006). Science for Survival: Biotechnology Regulation in Israel, *Science and Public Policy*, 33(1): 33–46.

Rajan, K. (2006). *Biocapital: The Constitution of Postgenomic Life*. Durham, NC: Duke University Press.

Reverby, S. (2000). (Ed.). *Tuskegee's Truths: Rethinking the Tuskegee Syphilis Study*. Chapel Hill: University of North Carolina Press.

Reverby, S. and Rosner, D. (2006). "Beyond the Great Doctors" Revisited: A Generation of the "New" Social History of Medicine. In F. Huisman and J. H. Warner (Eds.), *Locating Medical History: The Stories and Their Meaning*. Baltimore, MD, and London: Johns Hopkins University Press, pp. 167–193.

Rimon-Zarfaty, N. (2014). The Influence of New Medical Technologies on Perceptions of the "Fetus" and "Parenthood" among Israeli Parents (PhD dissertation). Ben-Gurion University of the Negev, Israel.

Rose, N. (2007). Molecular Biopolitics, Somatic Ethics and the Spirit of Biocapital, *Social Theory and Health*, 5, 3–29.

Rothman, D. J. (1992). *Strangers at the Bedside: A History of How Law and Bioethics Transformed Medical Decision Making*. New York: Basic Books.

Rubenfeld, S. (2010). (Ed.). *Medicine after the Holocaust: From the Master Race to the Human Genome and Beyond*. Basingstoke: Palgrave Macmillan.

Salter, B. (2007). Bioethics, Politics and the Moral Economy of Human Embryonic Stem Cell Science: The Case of the European Union's Sixth Framework Program, *New Genetics and Society*, 26(3): 269–288.

Schicktanz, S., Schweda, M., and Wynne, B. (2012). The Ethics of "Public Understanding" of Ethics – Why and How Bioethics Expertise Should Include Public and Patients' Voices, *Medicine, Health Care and Philosophy*, 15, 129–139.

Siegal, G. (2015). Introduction. In G. Siegal (Ed.), *Blue and White Bioethics: Bioethics and Medical Law in Israel*. Jerusalem: Bialik Publishing House and the Ono Academic College, pp. 9–15 (Hebrew).

Smith, W. J. (2000). *The Culture of Death: The Assault on Medical Ethics in America*. San Francisco: Encounter Books.

Starr, P. (1982). *The Social Transformation of American Medicine: The Rise of a Sovereign Profession and the Making of a Vast Industry*. New York: Basic Books.
Tong, R. (1998). The Ethics of Care: A Feminist Virtue Ethics of Care for Healthcare Practitioners, *Journal of Medicine and Philosophy* 23, 131–152.
Trotter G. (2006). Bioethics and Deliberative Democracy: Five Warnings from Hobbes, *Journal of Medicine and Philosophy*, 31, 235–250.
Wahrman, M. (2002). *Brave New Judaism: When Science and Scripture Collide*. Hanover, MA: Brandeis University Press.
Wolff, S. (1996). Introduction. In S. Wolff (Ed.), *Feminism and Bioethics: Beyond Reproduction*. Oxford: Oxford University Press, pp. 3–43.

PART I

Bioethics as Biopolitics

1

Securitization of Public Health Preparedness in Israel and Palestine: A Challenge for Public Health Ethics

Nadav Davidovitch and Benjamin Langer

1 INTRODUCTION

In the spring of 2006, when the global outbreak of avian influenza (H5N1) reached first Israel, then the Gaza Strip, and finally Jordan, already in place and ready for response were institutional connections on global, regional, and national scales. At a global scale, Israel, the Palestinian Authority (PA), and Jordan used the World Health Organization's (WHO) 2005 International Health Regulations, even though these regulations were not mandatory for signatory countries until 2007. At the regional scale, the outbreak was controlled by a collaborative effort of the three health ministries, who cooperated through an organization called the Middle Eastern Consortium on Infectious Disease Surveillance (MECIDS). At the national scale, after difficulty experienced by the Israeli Ministry of Agriculture (IMoA) in finding contractors to carry out the culling of infected poultry flocks, the IMoA turned to the Ministry of Defense (IMoD) for assistance.

The response was widely seen as a success story of cross-border cooperation in the face of a tense political situation, perhaps even as an example of how cooperation on "apolitical" issues such as deadly pandemics could lead to more peaceful relations in the region. However, an exploration of how these intersecting global, regional, and national preparedness structures developed also raises questions about what assumptions and values may lie behind seemingly obvious and successful policy decisions. It also demonstrates that principles of public health ethics can be influenced by the social, economic, and cultural contexts in which they are being applied. This chapter explores the development of pandemic preparedness in Israel-Palestine,[1] placing emphasis on Israel-Palestine's unique historical context.

---

[1] *Israel-Palestine* will collectively refer to Israel and the Occupied Palestinian Territories, though since 2006 there have functionally been two Palestinian governments, one in the West Bank and one in Gaza. The authors were able to gain access to material and personnel only from the West Bank, so though there are interactions between the Hamas government in Gaza and both the Palestinian Authority and Israel, *Israel-Palestine* generally refers to Israel and the occupied West Bank.

Introducing these perspectives can help us understand how different framings of a public health problem can have major ethical consequences. In particular, we will discuss what some have called an increasing "securitization" of public health, raising concerns about resource allocation, the role of militaries in public health, and potential trade-offs between equity and expedience. It will be seen here that the Israeli context, in particular what Kimmerling (2001) calls its military-cultural complex, lends itself naturally to securitization processes, while those within the Palestinian context sit less easily with this globalized shift. What are the consequences of this context-specificity for the way we approach public health ethics as a discipline?

Section 2 will briefly discuss the methodology used in this study. Section 3 will explore both the global and regional contexts for the development of pandemic preparedness structures in Israel-Palestine, providing the basis for critical examination. Section 4 will present the results of the interviews and documentary review, paying close attention to the way interviewees use the concepts presented in Section 3 to frame their narratives. Finally, in light of these results, Section 5 will revisit the questions raised in the introduction and reflect on the importance of introducing a public health ethics perspective to enrich current bioethical discourses, especially how it can help encourage the introduction of social, ethical, and political sensitivities to current public health challenges, thus broadening the bioethical discourse.

2 METHODS

Two primary sources were examined: 1) semi-structured interviews with people situated in key decision-making roles in the public health and pandemic preparedness institutions of Israel-Palestine and 2) public documents produced by those same individuals and their organizations on websites, in academic journals, and in the media. The questions were grouped into thematic categories: 1) a narrative of pandemic preparedness in Israel-Palestine; 2) military–civil relations; 3) trade-offs between preparedness and prevention; 4) regional cooperation on pandemics and peacebuilding. Thirteen interviewees participated from the Israeli system of pandemic preparedness: from the Israeli Ministry of Health (IMoH), the IMoA, hospitals, HMOs, the national laboratory system, universities, the medical corps of the Israel Defense Forces (IDF), and the Israeli Home Front Command (HFC). To investigate cooperation between Israelis and Palestinians, the Israeli and the Palestinian point people for MECIDS were interviewed. Seven interviewees participated on the Palestinian side: in a focus group at Birzeit University, from the WHO branch in East Jerusalem, the Palestinian Ministry of Health (PMoH), Al-Quds University, and United Nations Relief and Works Agency for Palestine Refugees in the Near East (UNRWA). Interviewees were chosen using a snowball approach, with each interviewee being asked for advice on further informants. Questions in initial interviews were adjusted for subsequent interviews to better clarify themes. The interviews were transcribed by the authors, and were analyzed for key themes and shared narratives.

3 BACKGROUND

3.1 Extraordinary Threats: Global Public Health Security

The allocation of resources is one of the central aspects of public health ethics, with values such as equity and cost-effectiveness playing key roles, and different potential public health programs competing for limited public resources. Over the past twenty years, the concept of global public health security (GPHS) has become prominent in the international public health conversation,[2] influencing thinking about what is an important concern for global public health, and how best to respond to what is designated a concern. According to Barry Buzan and Lene Hansen (2009), securitization is "the process of presenting an issue in security terms." Inherent in the securitization of a referent object is its elevation from a normal political issue to a radical and perhaps imminent threat to the stability of social, economic, and political life. To understand the thoughts and actions of those who produced the pandemic preparedness structures in Israel-Palestine, it is important to understand how global public health was securitized. Two developments produced this securitization: 1) the emerging infectious diseases (EID) concept; 2) the migration of a preparedness mentality out of security establishments and into public decision making. Here we will address both in turn.

3.1a From Eradication to Emergence: Emerging Infectious Diseases

Entering the 1980s, there were high hopes that humankind was on a linear path toward making infectious diseases a thing of the past. By the 1960s, following the development of tools such as antibiotics, vaccines, and powerful insecticides such as DDT, the term *eradication* had largely replaced *control* when it came to discussing infectious disease (Snowden 2008). In 1969, the U.S. surgeon general claimed that it was "time to close the book on infectious diseases," and by 1979, one of the world's most feared diseases for centuries, smallpox, had been declared eradicated by the WHO (Snowden 2008).

However, following shortly on the heels of the smallpox eradication, HIV/AIDS began to emerge. Throughout the 1980s, more new diseases emerged and old ones thought eradicated showed resurgence, often in more virulent and drug-resistant forms. Science and technology-based developments were thought to be a primary cause: ecological degradation from land-use change, growing inequality due to

---

[2] While we use the term *global public health security*, after the WHO, others have used the terms *global health security* and *health security* in very similar contexts.

economic globalization, and drug and insecticide resistance caused by overuse were all cited as contributing causes (King 2004). This lent a tragic tone to EID discourse – we had been undone by our own successes. A growing sense of the failings of the "eradication" paradigm led to meetings on disease emergence, and eventually to the publication of the 1992 Institute of Medicine report "Emerging Infections." In 1996, thirty-six medical journals in twenty-one countries collaborated to focus issues solely on the topic of EID (King 2004). The EID paradigm had taken root as a new ontology of the global pattern of infectious disease.

3.1b How We Became Unprepared

In the first decade of the twenty-first century, security concerns and global health concerns became increasingly linked. This was in large part a response to the attacks of September 11, 2001, and the 2002 anthrax scare in the United States (RAND 2006). In his 2008 article titled "The Generic Biothreat: Or How We Became Unprepared," Andrew Lakoff explains how "preparedness" expertise and the practices that come with it (predominantly "imaginative enactment" or drills) migrated out of top-secret defense departments to form the rationale for governments to prepare themselves for a "generic biothreat." The idea was a "dual use" preparedness system: at the beginning of the threatening event, the response system cannot discern between a natural and an intentional epidemic, and preparedness for natural events can be enhanced by the involvement of traditional security systems through personnel, budgets, and institutional involvement. A more traditional logic of public health had been *prevention*, focused on minimizing the harm to populations from a set of health risks not likely to disrupt the functioning of governance systems. *Preparedness* thinking, on the other hand, is focused on crisis response, concerning itself with extraordinary or nonconventional biological threats that not only threaten the health of individuals in a population, but also endanger "the critical systems that underpin social and economic life" (Lakoff 2008).

3.2 A Turning Point: The International Health Regulations

Prior to 2005, the International Health Regulations (IHR) covered only cholera, plague, smallpox, and yellow fever (Fidler 2005). Signatory countries had two obligations: 1) reporting any outbreak of those diseases to the international community and 2) ensuring that any response did not cause undue hindrance to international trade and travel. No enforcement mechanisms were available to the WHO to ensure reporting. With the rise of EID and preparedness thinking, a new mechanism was needed to prepare the economically globalized community for a potential global outbreak. While negotiations at the WHO began in 1995, the global SARS outbreak of 2003 significantly sped up the process and pushed the negotiations to completion in 2005 (Fidler 2005).

According to Fidler and Gostin (2006), "the new IHR constitute one of the most radical and far-reaching changes in international law on public health since the beginning of international health co-operation in the mid-nineteenth century." The new IHR expand the scope of the regulations from a handful of diseases to any potential global public health risk, and move from simply calling on countries to report outbreaks to requiring that each country has a pandemic plan in place. In addition, a strong emphasis is placed on surveillance, requiring that each signatory country has the public health and laboratory capacity to ensure adequate disease surveillance and reporting within the country. The new IHR have emerged as the central organizing framework through which global preparedness for pandemics and other global public health events is carried out.

3.3 Ethical Challenges to the Global Public Health Security Approach

GPHS and its components haven't gone unchallenged. Fundamentally, these challenges are ethical questions, touching the fundamentals of public health ethics, for example: how can we balance efficiency with equity and individual rights with the public good, and what institutions are the most appropriate to carry out the public health agenda? There have been two main concerns: 1) It has been charged that by focusing on emergencies, GPHS can produce short-term thinking that sacrifices equity and sustainability in favor of logistics and security. 2) It has also been argued that GPHS, while under the guise of being a purely humanitarian enterprise, is in the service of the political, economic, and security interests of powerful states. These will be addressed in turn.

Many are skeptical of the "dual use" argument, in which preparedness for extraordinary biosecurity threats also bolsters a public health system's traditional functioning. For instance, King (2005) argues that "the institutionalization of biodefense may encourage an exaggerated, open-ended climate of crisis in which ethical deliberations are hurried, obscure, or absent altogether. Such a climate would perpetuate social choices that focus on highly-visible and visceral threats whose actual contribution to the burden of disease is negligible." The fear is that a security framing of global public health may lead to the sacrificing of human rights and global equity to expedience in dealing with global pandemics.

Others question how politically neutral GPHS is. Simon Rushton (2011) argues that "[t]he health security agenda is a significantly skewed one, reflecting the concerns of the most powerful actors in the international system." Nicholas King (2004) contends that while at the beginning of the EID discourse many pushed for reshaping of our political and economic structures in favor of addressing the root causes of EID like inequity and ecological degradation, discussions within governmental bodies shifted to "laboratory investigation and information management. Whether the object was 'global health' or national security, interventions would involve 'passing through' American laboratories, biotechnology firms, pharmaceutical manufacturers, and information science experts." In this argument, the securitization of global public health produces a conceptual narrowing, one that disproportionately serves the interests of more powerful actors.

3.4 States of Emergency: The Case of Israel-Palestine

Sidel and colleagues (2002), speaking of a growing biosecurity institution in the United States, discuss "the risks of commingling public health programs with military, intelligence, and law enforcement programs." This would ring especially strange to a reader from Israel, a nation engaged from its very founding in what is perceived as a "total conflict" with its neighboring nations and its Palestinian population (Kimmerling 2001). The product of this history of militarism in Israel is a heightened security culture, affecting every aspect of Israeli society in what Kimmerling (2001) calls a "military-cultural complex." He suggests that, entering the twenty-first century, this "code of security" was the only remaining cultural characteristic shared between sectors of the diverse Jewish-Israeli population: "Israel has not only faced violent resistance on the part of the hostile local population of the country and other nations of the region, but has also made confrontation with them a source of internal strength for its ... leadership and a tool for material and human resource mobilization." Kimmerling describes his concept of a military-cultural complex as the situation whereby "military and other social problems are so highly intermingled that social and political issues become construed as 'existential security' issues." The military-cultural complex is essentially a securitization engine.

While the Israeli health governance system has been essentially stable since the founding of the Israeli state in 1948, the Palestinian health governance system has been in perpetual flux and fragmentation, emerging as a unified national health system in the West Bank and Gaza only in 1994 following the Oslo Accords and the founding of the PA. The establishment of Israel in the wake of the 1948 Israeli–Arab War saw the destruction of nearly all Palestinian political institutions, leading to the fragmentation of the population under the jurisdiction of different state bodies. In 1967, the West Bank and Gaza Strip were conquered by Israel, and thus the jurisdiction for health services to the occupied population fell to the Civil Administration, the Israeli military government responsible for administering the occupied territories.

Dr. Ephraim Sneh (2002), former head of the Civil Administration from 1985 to 1987, tells of how, from 1967 until his time, an unwritten but well-understood policy of the Civil Administration was essentially to take whatever steps were possible to prevent the establishment of a Palestinian state. This institutional underdevelopment of Palestine led to a dependence on Israel, UNRWA, NGOs, and private health care providers for health services. Sneh describes how, during his term, a reversal happened and the establishment of a Palestinian state became the goal: "In the past we said no, with some exceptions; now, we say yes with some exceptions" (2002). In 1994, control of health services to the occupied territories was passed from the Civil Administration to the PA under the auspices of the Oslo Accords.

In the realm of infectious diseases outbreaks, there has been a relatively large amount of cooperation between the Israeli and Palestinian public health services, expressed in information exchange, laboratory tests conducted unofficially in Israeli laboratories, training of Palestinian personnel, and even round table discussions facilitated by various bodies such as MECIDS. All of this is, however, happening in a very tense social and political context. Just as the conflict and its historical impact shapes the institutional and cultural approaches used by the State of Israel, so does it shape the Palestinians' approach to public health, including preparedness for pandemics. We will see, especially in comparing the two sides, how public health ethics is greatly influenced by contextual factors.

4 RESULTS

4.1 *A History of Pandemic Preparedness in Israel*

"We were dragged into the play afterward. But we were already there!"

– Coordinator of the Epidemic Management Team

How did pandemic preparedness, as a process of *preparedness* as opposed to *prevention*, begin in Israel? The arrangement currently in place in the IMoH was developed in reaction to a West Nile virus (WNV) epidemic in Israel in 2000 (Sagi et al. 2002). Previously, the IMoH had dealt with epidemics, while some "top secret" institutions within the defense establishment had dealt with intentional biological events, and in general these were two different realms and the groups didn't communicate. The steering committee that grew from the 2000 WNV response, though created under the auspices of the IMoH in response to a natural outbreak, was meant to serve in preparing first and foremost for a "biologic warfare event." Further, its work was much accelerated by the events of September 11, 2001, which was seen as a sign of the inevitability of attack (Sagi et al. 2002).

In 1995, the WHO committed itself to overhaul the IHR, and in 1999, it recommended that "all countries establish multidisciplinary National Pandemic Planning Committees (NPPCs), responsible for developing strategies appropriate for their countries in advance of the next pandemic" (1999). While some Israeli officials took notice, according to nearly all interviewees, the impetus that galvanized the Israeli system to develop serious pandemic planning was the 2003 SARS outbreak. In the words of one interviewee, representative of this common feeling, SARS had "a tremendous effect . . . the threat was perceived as real."

The roots of Israeli preparedness for "nonconventional" biological events, however, stretch much farther back than the 1999 WHO recommendations or the 2000 WNV outbreak, back into the Cold War era within Israel's civil defense bodies and the medical corps of the IDF. Preparedness for biological and chemical threats as a subset of general military threats began in the mid-1960s, when Egypt used chemical weapons in the Yemeni civil war. The major step forward in terms of organizational capacity to respond to these threats came in the mid-1980s, when, according to the first coordinator of what became the Epidemic Management Team (EMT), "a group of young physicians in the army, in the medical corps" decided that there was a growing threat of chemical and biological warfare: "we knew that ... we cannot speak openly about those things, and there are very few experts who do deal [with] and understand [these] kind[s] of matters. So we decided for a group of experts that is capable and can open the issues of preparedness of, we called it 'unusual biological events.'"

From the beginning of the EMT, the idea that "there is no great difference between natural biological disasters and artificial, or man-made biological disasters" was present in this group, leading it to be very multidisciplinary, made up of both military and nonmilitary personnel, as well as a wide range of specialties: physicians, epidemiologists, bacteriologists, psychologists, veterinarians, mass media specialists, and others. Though the team was very broad and interdisciplinary, two things were constant: that the coordinator was the head of the biological division of the Chemical, Biological and Radio-Nuclear (CBRN) branch of the medical corps, and that "the head of the team should be ... a general [high-ranking military officer]. ... I mean a general not just because of his military rank ... but somebody who can look broadly on everything."

The focus of the EMT from its founding was conducting drills for specific biological threats, and from those drills producing standard operating procedures for those specific threats. When the EMT was founded, the threat thought to be most imminent was anthrax, and so this was the first drill run and the first set of standard operating procedures established. After the First Gulf War in 1992, the EMT became the "focus of knowledge" for the entire country on these issues, which at this point were still top secret. As the original EMT coordinator said in an interview, "if you were asking me the same questions 20 years ago, you are just falling from another star. No one talked about these things. ... Everything was high confidential, top secret."

In response to the 2000 WNV outbreak, a watershed decision was made within the IDF to transfer the EMT from its institutional home in the CBRN branch of the medical corps to a new home as an independent consulting committee in the IMoH directly under the director-general. Most interviewees discussed this move as a major event in the development of pandemic preparedness, indicating that the EID narrative had become mainstream, as had biological warfare and biological terrorism concerns, and finally that these two threats were seen as different aspects of the same preparedness framework. Many people stated this in one way or another, but none so colorfully and succinctly as the current EMT coordinator: "when you deal with an anthrax epidemic that originates in letters, and in missiles, it's not that different from dealing with an avian influenza that originates in a duck that, you know, poops somewhere when it crosses Israel to Africa."

Finally, the past nearly twelve years, beginning in 2005 but accelerating in 2008, have seen the rise of the Orange Flame Project (OFP), a preparedness initiative focused on nonconventional biological events. Before the OFP, biological threats were identified (anthrax, smallpox, tularemia, etc.) and prepared for individually, mostly within the Ministry of Health and the hospitals. With the OFP, however, the goal was to prepare for a *generic* biological threat, focusing on the first forty-eight hours. The initiative is based on a series of large-scale drills, each focusing on a specific geographic area of Israel, and including all relevant actors in emergency response: police, paramedics, media and communications, public health officials, local government bodies, and the Ministry of the Interior. The result is thousands of people drilling at once and running through the motions of protocols, procedures, and difficult decision making in the field.

4.2 Civil–Military Relations

"No, it's a part of the culture, it's not something that is a directive or a presidential order that comes, it's a matter of culture."

– CHAIR OF THE HOSPITAL SUBCOMMITTEE ON THE IMoH COMMITTEE FOR NONCONVENTIONAL BIOLOGICAL THREATS

When asked what the role of civilian–military cooperation was in preparing for pandemics in Israel, the common answer among Israeli interviewees is epitomized by this response from the original EMT coordinator: "Crucial! Crucial collaborations!" The most obvious and stark evidence of this situation, according to him, is that "In case of a real emergency, who is taking all of the command in Israel? Do you know? In the end if we feel we have a real catastrophe ... we decided that the Ministry of Defense will take all of the command." The current head of public health services insisted on making very clear the distinction between the IMoD and the Israel Defense Forces: "it's not the military, that's not so right, because the Ministry of Defense ... also has the ability to coordinate the other governmental elements, other ministries ... because the Ministry of Defense has more power than the Ministry of Health."

Civil–military collaboration, however, goes much deeper than simple institutional connections and lines of communication between military and civilian bodies. We already saw that the core of knowledge and organization around unusual biological events came from the EMT, which, though technically situated in the IMoH, contains mostly personnel with heavy military backgrounds, and whose coordinator is still centered in the medical corps. There is also another phenomenon occurring in which individual physicians often come through the epidemiology training program in the medical corps and find key positions in the civilian health system. As the head of the Central Virology Laboratory (CVL) said, "people are now having left the army and are embedded in civilian organizations." The consensus was that this was generally a good thing for Israeli public health, as people trained in the army were seen as more "professional" with better logistics training.

However, the concept that in Israel there are "military people" and "nonmilitary people" obscures an even deeper phenomenon, epitomized by the quote opening this section. Put another way by the head of foreign relations for the IMoH, "it's not about they and we, it's about we collectively. And for us it's very, very natural to do it this way. We don't know any other way. . . . Everybody else thinks it's unique. But we think it's natural." The phenomenon being discussed in both of those quotes is the nation-in-arms approach taken to preparedness in Israel, where institutional boundaries between military and civilian break down in practice.

The explanations for this offered by interviewees center on similar ideas: that Israel is a small country with limited resources and under a great deal of external pressure from its geopolitical situation. Within this situation, according to a senior consultant on emergency management for the IMoH, "First of all, Israel has no choice but to be very adept at emergency management because every few years there's either a man-made conflict or a pandemic." The smallness of the community, the sense of urgency, and strong personal connections allow for a kind of intimacy among actors rarely found in such bureaucratic settings. For instance, the current coordinator of the EMT stated about a potential biological event, indicating his cell phone: "if there would be smallpox tomorrow in Israel, everybody [who] needs to take care of it is on this sim card. I know all of them. With my cell phone, I can manage everything."

There was some discussion about whether the prevalence of the military personnel in the civilian public health arena was itself a major factor in the growth of preparedness thinking in Israeli public health. Phrases such as "When you come to the army . . . you sometimes prepare for things that you hope will never happen" were used to describe the impact of military training, and there was a sense that the people who came from the military had a shared perspective and a shared way of thinking. As the coordinator of the IMoH pandemic preparedness committee, himself not a physician, said, "we are coming from the same way of thinking . . . we all think alike, we all perform alike." When asked what was meant exactly by this shared perspective and how it operationally manifested itself, most interviewees had a difficult time identifying its exact constituents or finding examples, although certain words like "professional" and "logistics" came up many times. Perhaps the most concise description came from the original EMT coordinator, when describing why it was that the EMT should be headed by a person of high military rank rather than an infectious disease expert: "An expert [who] understands a bacteria doesn't know what it means to have antibiotic distribution for 2 million people in two days."

4.3 Interacting Policy Frameworks in Pandemic Preparedness

"For the avian flu, for the pandemic, there is no disadvantage [to a culture of preparedness in public health]. ... I'm sure there will be other situations. Nobody's perfect, you see."

– IMoH DIRECTOR OF FOREIGN RELATIONS, ISRAELI IHR AND MECIDS FOCAL POINT

A set of questions that was asked to every Israeli interviewee had to do with their views on the interplay between prevention and preparedness, and what the advantages and disadvantages are of the growth of preparedness mentality in public health. There were generally two ways of thinking about these questions, with most respondents able to express both views in the same interview. They could be called synergistic and competitive. The synergistic perspective saw the resulting development of institutional connections, personal relationships, preparedness plans, and disease surveillance infrastructure as having a positive effect on Israeli public health in general. The competitive perspective suggested a focus on emergencies might take attention and resources away from the kind of everyday public health needs that are known to exist, in a way sacrificing the known for the unknown, prevention for preparedness.

The current IMoH head of public health services, when asked about what factors are taken into consideration when making decisions about resource allocation and how to prepare, spoke first and foremost about scientific evidence, i.e., "if one thing will be effective or not." Second were economic concerns, for instance, "to see if stockpiling a certain amount of antivirals will be cost-effective or cost-saving." Finally, there were ethical concerns, such as "if you can buy only for the high-risk groups ... or if I want to give vaccines only to military personnel or to first responders." Stepping back to ask how this cost-benefit analysis applies to preparedness versus preventive activities, he responded that though there may be some situations in which a trade-off is necessary, "it is not like ... one thing is going up and the other is only going down."

A former IMoH health coordinator for the occupied territories from 1981 to 1993 voiced a middle ground that didn't put too much stock in either major advantage or disadvantage for the overall preventive public health picture: "You know, military guys, they get a kick out of going for a day to talk about what happens in a big disaster. But they know that at the end of the day they're public health people, and they've got to feed the cows and clean the stalls." While this perspective assumes that preparedness for unconventional biological threats will remain such a small part of public health as to not really make much of a dent, the former medical head of the HFC noted the extremely high cost of drills, and that the IMoH "was always fretting about the cost of drills." Also, whether the basic medical infrastructure was adequate as a base for preparedness was called into question by the head of the CVL: "On the other hand if you compare the medical infrastructure, the number of hospitals built ... just now the hospitals, with just a seasonal flu, they are at 150 percent, 200 percent capacity; it was just in the news today. So, this is just for the seasonal flu. If there would be an outbreak, it would be 1,000 percent, something like that."

So how much preparedness is enough? According to the head of the CVL, the fact that the kinds of threats involved are often brand new, and that "we don't know if the big disaster will come," makes this sort of question very difficult to answer: "We are very clever with dealing with the past, but the future, we're not so clever," and therefore if it doesn't come, all the money spent on preparedness can be seen as "money down the drain." The other side of the coin, however, is that if it *does* come and no preparedness measures are in place, the price could be much higher.

So how does one make such decisions? WHO directives, the new IHR, and other countries' pandemic preparedness plans were cited by many of the interviewees as a major force toward pandemic preparedness planning. The head of the CVL said that Israeli pandemic preparedness planning moved very much in synch with global pandemic preparedness thinking.

4.4 Regional Cooperation and the Palestinian System

> "[T]here can be health in our region ... the level of health in our region will be the level of health in the weakest country in the region. This will be the level."
>
> – IMoH DIRECTOR OF FOREIGN RELATIONS, ISRAELI IHR AND MECIDS FOCAL POINT

The sentiment that "diseases know no borders" was expressed by the IMoH head of foreign relations: "birds will fly over our countries. They won't know which country they will fly over ... since the borders are open ... you cannot do it by yourself." As the opening quote to this section suggests, there is a strong sense in which the epidemiological fates of the populations of Israel-Palestine and Jordan are connected, a situation the former IMoH health coordinator for the West Bank and Gaza called "one epidemiological family." The PMoH director of public health also expressed this view: "One of the main issues is we are not really alone in our area."

On its website, MECIDS presents its vision as promoting "long term health, stability and security in the region." MECIDS was founded in 2002, "offering multinational training courses for health workers from Palestine, Israel and Jordan, giving them a chance to meet each other while honing their professional skills and creating a system through which the participating Ministries of Health share information directly." While founded on the initiative of Search for Common Ground, a branch of the NGO Nuclear Threat Initiative, the first aim of MECIDS upon its founding was actually not to do with global pandemics, but to share epidemiologic information on foodborne illness. Around that time, the view of global pandemics in the Israeli establishment did not demonstrate a sense of urgency.

It was only after the SARS event and the threat of H5N1 arose that MECIDS became the major vehicle for harmonizing preparedness plans and sharing information between the Israeli, Palestinian, and Jordanian ministries of health. As the Israeli MECIDS point person said, at first MECIDS was more of a peace-building initiative than a real "health security" initiative: "the idea was to do something together." However, once the H5N1 pandemic began and outbreaks happened in Turkey and Iraq, "the question was whether we are going to do another instrument or rely on this infrastructure; because trust was built around the MECIDS, we decided to do the preparation for avian flu."

The major focus of MECIDS, as the name suggests, is surveillance and the sharing of information. It facilitates personnel, particularly laboratory and epidemiology personnel, to have joint training sessions, and especially for Palestinians and Jordanians to be able to study in Israeli labs and learn diagnostic techniques. The MECIDS site serves as a common store of epidemiological information and statistics shared between health systems to enable the harmonization of not just plans in place in the health system, but the messages going out to the public. Also, outside of the official connections, this consortium provides a venue for the building of informal networks.

Military conflict, however, looms over these interactions. As the IMoH senior consultant on emergency management, who also coordinates some collaborative efforts with Palestinians and Jordanians in emergency medicine, said, "the will is there. The knowledge, and that's important, is certainly there, on all sides," but at the moment the PA is "very cautious about any type of collaboration because it would actually appear to be normalization, and this is not what they want to show to the world." The Israeli MECIDS point person used the phrase "health diplomacy" in describing the politics of organizing something like MECIDS, and offered an example: "You know, politically, it's better if someone from the Palestinian Authority is writing about the collaboration, you see? ... [T]hink about it from the political point of view, from the health diplomacy point of view." This statement brings out the underlying power relations involved in presenting something like MECIDS as a collaborative effort.

In early 2005, the Israeli newspaper *Yedioth Ahronoth* also published two articles on MECIDS, originally published in a short-lived Israeli–Palestinian collaborative health journal called *Bridges*. The Palestinian point person is quoted as saying: "We deal with prevention and control in an atmosphere of mutual concern for the welfare of the public and mutual respect for each other." While the tone set by this statement is decidedly apolitical, and most of the discussion in the Israeli point person's interview is the same, the latter interview ends with: "Dr. Leventhal believes, ironically, that such a global threat may create an opportunity for cooperation and efforts towards peace," suggesting that these apolitical, technical partnerships are seen to have a potential lasting effect on the political situation. The idea seems to be that apolitical areas of cooperation may build enough trust to tackle more politically contentious issues.

4.5 Pandemic Preparedness in Palestine

> "[T]he Palestinian community is actually living in emergency situations on different fronts. The political front, the economic front, the health front, and others."
>
> – PROFESSOR OF PUBLIC HEALTH, AL-QUDS UNIVERSITY

The first time that major central organizing in Palestine was formalized for pandemic preparedness was in response to the 2009 H1N1 influenza outbreak, with the PA releasing its official pandemic preparedness and response plan on December 14, 2009. The PA adopted the 2005 IHR in 2007 when it came into force, and the 2009 plan closely follows the structure of the WHO recommendations. The general feeling about this event and the Palestinian response is essentially that put forward by one Birzeit University public health professor: "the influenza was an international scary kind of thing, and it faded very quickly, and I think the Ministry of Health was very prepared. There were many lectures, and, not only that, but they were attended; every person who was suspected of the flu got medication. But it was overrated by the international community and the thing settled here very quickly like everywhere else."

According to the PMoH head of public health, lectures and exercises were run prior to the outbreak reaching Palestine, with very good cooperation between major stakeholders including UNRWA, the PMoH, and NGOs. UNRWA's director of public health for the West Bank described the method for the exercises that were done jointly between the PMoH, UNRWA, and *juzoor*, a community health NGO. Since in Palestine there is no universal body like a military from which to draw human resources for pandemic response, one question asked to all the Palestinian interviewees was how the system would be managed in a worst-case scenario in which a highly transmissible, highly pathogenic pandemic were to occur. There was no straight answer given to this question. The PMoH head of public health services emphasized that everyone had received education and training on what to do in case of a pandemic emergency, including the school system and the police, and that given a dire scenario they would be able to act accordingly, enforce quarantines, and keep order. The Birzeit University focus group tended to emphasize the role of informal relationships and personal initiative in the kind of disjointed but bureaucratic environment like the PMoH.

As opposed to the H1N1 event, the reference point for a genuine emergency used by all Palestinian interviewees was simply "2002," a time during the Second Intifada when the IDF had re-occupied much of the West Bank and Gaza and many parts of

Palestine were under siege. As noted in the introduction, the Palestinian health governance system is fragmented, and even PMoH functions are largely funded externally by donors. This situation in a way reflects the generally dependent and fragmented nature of Palestinian governance, and has a significant impact on the structure of pandemic planning. The WHO public health coordinator for the West Bank emphasized this fragmentation, and stated that "Concentration of authority is a necessity, since there is much fragmentation between the PA, UNRWA, and many, many NGOs." However, the feeling that a centralized authority to organize the response is a necessity is not uncomplicated or universal. As an Al-Quds University public health professor said: "to be honest, the Palestinian community does not have full faith in institutions in general. So that's why I think ... grassroots organizations and grassroots groups should take the initiative and lead, rather than those professionals, key stakeholders." In fact, the head of public health at Birzeit University made an argument for the continuation of the "fragmented" system, at least until power relations inherent in occupation change: "with our situation as an occupied country we are very lucky to have all these actors in the field of health. ... We can't depend on just one health provider for the time being."

One aspect that came up in many of the interviews with Palestinians was the centrality of instability and war in their experiences, and the tension between these needs and dependence of the system on external funding sources that dictate their own agendas. For instance, one public health professor stated: "We have such an unstable situation that we cannot think of vertical programs relating to global issues. Our primary issue is war. ... The problem is not at the Ministry of Health. The problem the Ministry of Health and other groups face is always how international aid dictates funding." While there is a clear sense of a need for leadership and an acceptance of the PMoH as taking that role, there is also a strong sense that not only *could* the stability of this situation change drastically, it likely *will*. To this can be added uneasiness with the PA in general. As a public health professor said of the PA: "they are not really entrenched. They are looked at as if ... they are not really part of them [the Palestinian people] ... you know cultural language in 1993. They said they [the PA] are coming to us! So, the perception is really that the authority does not necessarily represent them."

The final aspect that was touched on greatly is the dependence Palestinians feel in terms of resources for health goals, especially related to the continued occupation of much of the West Bank and the blockade of Gaza. The WHO head of public health for the West Bank described how in the past ten years it has been relatively easy to get money from the international community for things like disease surveillance for global pandemics or for diseases of global importance like HIV/AIDS. As one member of the focus group put it: "the minute you remove politics and power from a discussion of health, you are making a mistake. And that does not mean that the WHO [is] not doing good deeds. We have superb people here. And they're doing everything they can, but within the constraints of the WHO in Geneva. So it's not about people; it's about policies, and about who sets the world health agenda and for what purpose."

A benefit of having a large civil society presence in the form of NGOs is that "NGOs tend to carry the equity agenda much more than the ministry, so it is an opposing force, a helpful opposing force." The occupation, however, is seen as one of the factors constantly leading to a disempowerment of the Palestinian health system in general, and preparedness in particular, even during relatively nonviolent times. One public health professor stated that "It's not really the restriction of movement because of the checkpoint and the occupation, and restriction of people's movement, but the decisions about the resources themselves.... Israel can prevent things from coming, if they want.... So we feel we are not in control ... of deciding what is best for us."

5 DISCUSSION

As our case study shows, the question of how public health threats are framed has important implications and raises ethical concerns, including the questions of who is going to have a seat at the table, which populations are going to be seen as the relevant "public" for public health interventions, and whether the appropriate approach is prevention or preparedness. Israeli governance, with its military-cultural complex, has a natural tendency toward securitized framings, while Palestinian governance, fragmented, dependent on outside resources and expertise, and perpetually responding to military conflict, may not be able to put equity and human rights first. Due to internal political, historical, and cultural contexts, as well as the influence of global shifts in emphasis, responding to pandemics in Israel-Palestine has shifted toward a GPHS framework. While this framework has occasionally, as in the case of MECIDS, been framed as a means for strengthening peaceful interactions, strengthening institutional collaboration between laboratories is not the same thing as promoting equity and human rights. In fact, by conflating the two, a public health ethics influenced by a GPHS framework may in fact miss the vital importance power relations hold in human security and insecurity.

We should ask ourselves what the cost is of choosing the GPHS framework in the context of the Israeli–Palestinian conflict and how this choice can repress alternatives, especially when considering other public health priorities, including those involving human rights considerations, not necessarily embedded within the "preparedness" agenda. A public health ethics that starts from the political power relations and asks questions that place equity and human rights at the forefront can provide balance to the reactivity of the GPHS approach's focus on catastrophic events. This of course does not mean that preparedness activities are not crucial elements of public health programs, and remaining unprepared for major events can lead to the failure of the critical governance systems necessary to ensure human security and human rights. But, for instance, one could ask why it is easier for a laboratory sample to pass through borders in the region than people, and what the implications are of this for the human security of Palestinians living in unsecure conditions. Bringing ethics to the forefront can ensure that these sorts of questions are not forgotten.

What our case study also shows, however, is that the ethical frameworks chosen by those responsible for governing will be very influenced by local, contextual factors, and that the study of history and culture can help explain why actors behave the way they do. A reflective understanding of why certain questions are being asked versus others, and mechanisms to build alternative approaches based on competing public health ethics frameworks into discussions of public health activities can therefore enrich these discussions and lead to more deliberate actions. It will take a concerted effort to promote a public health approach that asks critical questions about regional power differentials and whether a global agenda is best suited for a local public in a context in which the mentalities of total conflict or dependence on foreign assistance are core assumptions, but the first step in potentially shifting these discussions is the knowledge that one is in fact making an ethical choice in not asking those questions. Even when deciding whether to devote resources toward drills for future extreme or unknown threats or toward traditional public health programs and goals, it will be important to understand the ethical underpinnings of the approach used to decide.

An example of such a reflective approach to applying ethical frameworks to public health work is Dani Filc's 2015 work on promoting a republican egalitarian approach to bioethics. In this work, he poses an alternative perspective linking a republican egalitarian conceptualization of bioethics with a radical egalitarian grounding of the right to health. In our common work both on the right to water in unrecognized Bedouin villages in the Negev and on hunger strikes of Palestinian prisoners, we showed how a radical egalitarian understanding of the right to health and a republican conceptualization of bioethics can be related to public health ethics. Promoting a broad public health ethics framework based in equity and human rights can serve to complement and broaden the scope of traditional bioethics and public health approaches. One might wonder where such an approach might lead when applied to pandemic preparedness in Israel and Palestine, in which both content and context seem to naturally tend toward securitization. There may be questions still unasked that find the light of day when ethical concerns are built into the process.

References

Ajrami, Ashraf. Dec. 27, 2005. Could Bird Flu Promote Peace? Ynet News Online. Accessed Dec. 21, 2010. www.ynetnews.com/articles/1,7340,L-3190741,00.html.

Buzan, Barry and Hansen, Lene. 2009. *The Evolution of International Security Studies*. Chapter 7, page 214. Cambridge University Press.

Fidler, David P. 2005. From International Sanitary Conventions to Global Health Security: The New International Health Regulations. *Chinese Journal of International Law* 4:2, pp. 325–392.

Fidler, David P. and Gostin, Lawrence O. 2006. The New International Health Regulations: An Historic Development for International Law and Public Health. *Journal of Law, Medicine, and Ethics.* **Spring**, pp. 85–94.

Home Front Command. 2010. The Home Front Through Time. Accessed Nov. 1. www.oref.org.il/82-en/PAKAR.aspx.

Jewish Virtual Library. 2010 "Medical Corps." Accessed Sept. 23, 2010. www.jewishvirtuallibrary.org/jsource/Society_&_Culture/medical.html.

Kimmerling, Baruch. 2001. *The Invention and Decline of Israeliness: State, Society, and the Military.* Chapter 7. University of California Press, Los Angeles.

King, Nicholas B. 2004. The Scale Politics of Emerging Diseases. *Osiris* **14**, pp. 62–76.

King, Nicholas B. 2005. The Ethics of Biodefense. *Bioethics* **19**:4, pp. 432–446.

Lakoff, Andrew. 2008. The Generic Biothreat, or, How We Became Unprepared. *Cultural Anthropology* **23**:3, pp. 399–428.

Palestinian Authority Ministry of Health. 2009. Palestinian National Plan for Pandemic Influenza A (H1N1) 2009 Preparedness and Response.

Prince-Gibson, Etta. Dec. 27, 2005. Israel, PA Prepare for Bird Flu. Ynet News Online. Accessed Dec. 21, 2010. www.ynetnews.com/articles/0,7340,L-3191064,00.html.

RAND Corporation. 2006. Infectious Disease and National Security: Strategic Information Needs. Chapter 3, p. 22. Rand Corporation, Santa Monica, CA.

Rushton, Simon. 2001. Global Health Security: Security for Whom? Security from What? *Political Studies* **59**:4, pp. 773–1033. http://onlinelibrary.wiley.com/doi/10.1111/j.1467-9248.2011.00919.x/abstract.

Sagi, R. et al. 2002. Preparedness of the Israeli Health System for a Biologic Warfare Event. *Israeli Medical Association Journal* **4**:, pp. 495–497. www.ncbi.nlm.nih.gov/pubmed/12120458.

Sidel, Victor W., Gould, Robert M., and Cohen, Hillel W. 2002. Bioterrorism Preparedness: Cooptation of Public Health? *Medicine and Global Survival* **7**:2, pp. 82–89.

Sneh, Ephraim. 2002. There Is Another Way: An Attempt to Switch from Occupation to Governance, in *Separate and Cooperate, Cooperate and Separate: The Disengagement of the Palestine Health Care System from Israel and its Emergence as an Independent System*, eds. Barnea, Tamara and Husseini, Rafiq. Praeger Publishing: Westport, CT, pp. 125–34.

Snowden, F. M. 2008. Emerging and Reemerging Diseases: A Historical Perspective. *Immunological Reviews* **225**, pp. 9–26.

Sufian, Sandy. 2002. Arab Healthcare During the British Mandate, 1920–1947, in *Separate and Cooperate, Cooperate and Separate: The Disengagement of the Palestine Health Care System from Israel and Its Emergence as an Independent System*, eds. Barnea, Tamara and Husseini, Rafiq. Praeger Publishing: Westport, CT, pp. 9–30.

World Health Organization. 2007. *A Safer Future: Global Public Health Security in the 21st Century. Message from the Director General*, page vi. WHO Press, Switzerland.

2

Republican Bioethics

Dani Filc

INTRODUCTION

It has become a sort of common knowledge that bioethical thinking in Israel – and bioethical practice in the form of legislation or judiciary decisions – takes place along the liberal/religious communitarian axis. The two poles of this axis are seen either as poles in conflict (Shapira 2014) or as contributing to an original, autochthonous, corpus of bioethics that integrates conflicting values (Sigal 2014). Those who see the two poles as conflicting consider that the main ethical assumptions and rules emerging from both traditions are in opposition: sanctity of life vs. individual autonomy, solidarity and the community's responsibility for each one of its individual members vs. self-definition and freedom of choice (Shapira 2014: 305). Thus, a compromise between the values of the Jewish religious tradition (and other minority groups' religious values) and those that belong to the liberal Occidental culture is necessary (Shapira 2014: 305). Gil Sigal (2014) also registers the tensions between a Jewish religious value system and what he depicts as the Anglo-Saxon one. However, Sigal considers that the tension allows for the emergence of an autochthonous bioethical system (where Jewish values must be more central than the "Anglo-Saxon" ones) that reflects the specificity of the Israeli (understood by Sigal as solely Jewish) community. Prof. Shimon Glick also seeks an original Israeli Jewish alternative to an Occidental bioethical "common sense" in which individual autonomy trumps any other value. He argues for the principle of the infinite value of human life, and for the long-standing Jewish communitarian claim that "[N]o man is an island" and that "[A]n individual's death is not just his or her private and personal affair only, but diminishes the entire community" (2001: 160). Moreover, many of the concrete discussions on bioethical questions in Israel are framed within the liberal/Jewish communitarian polarization, such as questions about the beginning and end of life, reproduction, patients' rights, or force-feeding hunger strikers.

The present chapter puts forward a different approach, and argues that restraining bioethical thinking in Israel to the tension and possible compromises between the liberal and Jewish religious poles is limited both from theoretical and political perspectives. *Theoretically*, the liberal approach is too individualist, has a limited conception of freedom (as noninterference) and of equality (at its best understood as equality of opportunity), and is not enough aware that bioethical decisions are made in contexts of unequal distribution of power and resources. On the other side, in contemporary Israel, the Orthodox Jewish/communitarian approach (such as Sigal's) is exclusionary and self-contradictory. It argues for a bioethical approach embedded in the specificity of the Israeli community, and considers the adoption of liberal/Anglo-Saxon bioethical values by Israeli society as surrendering to foreign values; it does not address the multiethnic and multicultural character of Israel, which is part of its specificity as a community, since Sigal's approach does not take into consideration the values of non-Jewish communities in Israel. Moreover, this approach uncritically accepts, legitimizes, and justifies social hierarchies, structures of domination, and the unequal distribution of resources and power that characterize Israeli society. The dichotomist approach is *politically* limiting, since restricting bioethical thinking to the liberal/Jewish Orthodox discussion does not allow for more radical approaches that challenge structures of domination and inequality. The aim of the present chapter, thus, is to argue for the relevance of a radical egalitarian republican perspective in bioethics, a perspective that not only may potentially solve some of the existing apparently insolvable contradictions between liberalism and Jewish religious communitarianism, but may also make us aware of the different forms and expressions of the unequal distribution of power and resources in Israel (and the Occupied Palestinian Territories, OPT). This, because a radical egalitarian republican perspective does not consider individual agents as isolated individual entities, nor as completely embedded in a caring, non-conflictive community, but as shaped by political institutions, reflecting the way in which power is organized within society. A radical egalitarian conception can contribute to overcome the tension between liberal autonomy and Jewish religious communitarian solidarity, since it does not share the liberal conception of freedom solely as individual autonomy. Egalitarian republicanism understands freedom as embedded in a specific political community, and as the possibility to engage in collective action in order to change unjust distributions of power. Radical egalitarian republicanism sees as central the community as political, active participation in the political community, and equality as equality of participation in the political community. It is true that any community implies taking into account the weight of past history, common culture, and consolidated institutions, and this may reinforce exclusionary trends. However, the emphasis on the political (as different from ethno-cultural or biological) character of the community, and the claim for equal political participation, implies a commitment to an inclusive approach. Egalitarian republicanism can put forward ways by which free and equal political actors may reach agreed conceptions of the common good,[1] agreements able to overcome both the limitations of the individualism that

---

[1] An egalitarian republican understanding of the common good will be discussed later in this chapter.

characterizes the liberal approach, and those of communitarian uncritical identification with hierarchical distributions of power and resources.

Since the term *republicanism* encompasses different meanings, this chapter's next section will make clear the main characteristics of what I call *egalitarian republicanism*. This is particularly important in the Israeli context, since Peled and Shafir's seminal analysis of Israeli citizenship and their criticism of ethno-republicanism resulted in a tendency to conflate between republicanism in general and Israeli ethno-republicanism. In the third section, I will show how the egalitarian republican approach translates into bioethical thinking, and, specifically, what are its possible implications within the Israeli context, by analyzing particular issues involving bioethical decisions.

Wither republicanism? The republican tradition is a heterogeneous one. It is true that there are terms associated with republicanism in all its forms, such as a non-liberal understanding of freedom (whether positive freedom or freedom as non-domination), common good, civic virtue, *vivere civile* (active participation in the life of the polis), corruption, or mixed government (Pocock 1985). However, there are significant differences between authors, and, as Mouritsen claims, "[A]s one looks at the long historical sequence of authors conventionally labelled republican, they are so diverse and conflicting as to make the new republican house appear divided against itself" (2006: 17).

In order to make sense of the diversity, scholars divide republicanism into two main currents: (a) a neo-Aristotelian one that stresses the importance of political participation in self-governed communities, and considers political participation as part of the "good life"; and (b) a civic republican or neo-Roman current that stresses freedom as non-domination (Pettit 2013). For Pettit, domination is the power to potentially arbitrarily interfere with other agents' choices (2013). Since this second current, represented by scholars such as Skinner, Pettit, and Laborde, is more in line with "the anti-perfectionist and pluralist ethos of contemporary liberalism" (Laborde 2008: 2), it has emerged in the past two decades as a political philosophy that can redress some of liberalism's democratic deficits, without abandoning the latter's basic lineaments.

However, this schematic division does not give justice to the richness of republican thinking, nor does it allow for an exhaustive rendering of a radical egalitarian republican perspective. Radical egalitarian republicanism shares with the neo-Aristotelian current the emphasis on the importance of political participation and of freedom as self-government. But it parts with the neo-Aristotelian current since this – following Aristotle himself – usually puts less emphasis on the importance of *equal* political participation, and even supports elitist political institutions.[2]

As for the neo-Roman republican tradition, McCormick forcefully exposes its elitist assumptions concerning the wisdom of the common people, Schwarzmantel

---

[2] See, for example, Hannah Arendt's support of the Senate, a clearly elitist institution.

argues that it seems more in line with the idea of restraining power rather than with the aim of increasing participation and fostering moves toward a deeper democracy, Thompson shows how considering freedom only as non-domination fails to address the different forms of subordination and oppression in contemporary societies, and Schuppert notes that the neo-Roman understanding of freedom as non-domination cannot account for the different forms of structural inequalities, and does not consider material inequalities as problematic (if they do not ground domination) (Schwarzmantel 2006: 142; McCormick 2011; Thompson 2013, 2015; Schuppert 2015).

While I agree with McCormick, Schwarzmantel, Thompson, Schuppert, and Gilabert's criticisms, I do not think that they are relevant for all possible versions of republicanism, but mostly for the neo-Roman version. In my view, we can delineate the main claims and topics of a radical egalitarian version of republicanism, drawing from Greek republicanism, Machiavelli, Rousseau, and the version of republicanism that Fisher (2015) reads within Marxism. This is a version of republicanism that stresses freedom as self-government and equality in political participation and ruling, and that understands the common good as stemming from political conflict.

The starting points of radical egalitarian republicanism are equality and freedom as participation in a self-governed political community. The claim to equality is not based on conceiving of individuals as pre-social and pre-political entities, but on understanding human beings as embedded in a sociopolitical context. Social structures, our being-with-others, are not a follow-up, but rather a precondition of our individual existence. We are politico-social entities because our common and equal vulnerability requires life in common, i.e., political life. Because of our common vulnerability, no man can be an island. Since our political condition is a consequence of our common and equal vulnerability as living beings, political equality, i.e., equal participation in the decisions about the political community, is central to the republican egalitarian perspective. That does not mean that taking part in the political space is mandatory for living a good life, as in Aristotle or Arendt, but that equal participation is the condition for a common good that is truly common, and a condition for individual and collective freedom.

Since human beings are relational beings, politics and civil life are central to our lives and to our humanity. Thus, the radical egalitarian republican conception of freedom is also deeply related to the idea of political participation (Thompson 2013). Liberty is intimately connected to the exercise of political self-government by a collective, meaning that all participate in establishing the common rules and laws (Mouritsen 2006: 17).

For participation to be possible, we need not only to be free of domination, but also free from being structurally put in a position of disadvantage or submitted to "extractive power" (see later in this chapter) by the actions and practices of individuals, groups or institutions (Schuppert 2015: 450). Freedom means independence from social systems organized around oligarchic or elitist interests (Thompson 2013) because in capitalist societies, individuals are embedded in and constituted by social structures that differentially distribute power and resources.

Political equality is both a value in itself and the necessary basis for the following two central characteristics: (a) freedom as self-government, that is, citizens must be free from arbitrary rule by others and must (be able to) participate in the legislation of the laws that oblige them; and (b) the possibility of a politically achieved conception of the common good, that is, a conception of the common good that has been agreed upon through free and equal participation in the public sphere. This common good is not a consensual general will, nor the ideal consensus to which we can arrive by a deliberation that replicates as far as possible the ideal speech situation. The common good is hegemonic in the sense posed by Gramsci, Laclau, and Mouffe. It is the partial stabilization of a specific combination of particular claims that are "universalized" (Laclau 2005). Stabilization is partial because there is no possibility of closure of society, because there is no post-political utopia. Thus, the common good is always contested, and conflict is essential to its constitution.

Based on this understanding of equality and freedom, the main characteristics of a republican egalitarian perspective are political equality in the sense that "[e]veryone ... should have the opportunity to become a citizen, and every citizen should stand on an equal footing, under law," and every person must have the equal possibility to take part in legislating the laws that rule the political community, in the ongoing definition of the common good, and in the actual ruling of the political community. Republicanism requires "steps to be taken to relieve women from subjection to men, workers from subjection to employers, and the members of some racial, ethnic, or cultural groups from subjection to others" (Thompson 2013: 174). Republicanism requires also institutional designs in order to limit elite power to subject the common people (McCormick 2011).

Political equality, that is, the possibility to equally participate in governing the political community, requires – as Rousseau argues – significantly limiting material inequalities. The demands of political equality require active measures to limit material inequality, differentiating – following Rousseau – between "natural inequalities of strength, intelligence, stamina, and the like on the one hand, and artificial inequalities of wealth, social position, status, and power on the other, expressed mainly in private property" (Garrard 2002: 51).

It must be made clear that the republican egalitarian ideas of equality and freedom require not only ex-post correction of material inequalities (through taxation and transfer payments), but ex-ante, through structural and institutional reforms that impede the unequal appropriation of wealth and resources.

Since human beings are sociopolitical beings, embedded in society and belonging to a political community, freedom and equality, though fundamental, are not the only values relevant for radical egalitarian republicanism. Solidarity and the idea of the common good are also important. The idea of solidarity, already in its inception, was different from the idea of fraternity. While the latter, etymologically, implies gendered family links, thus being limited to (male) members and therefore exclusionary, the former emerged as a legal concept open to all members of the legal – political – community.

In Roman law, the concept of *in solidum* meant "an obligation for the whole, joint liability [*Gesamthaftung*], common debt, solidary obligation" (Brunkhorst 2005: 2). Everyone takes responsibility for anyone who cannot pay his debt, in a net of common support where the group is responsible for each individual, and each individual is responsible for everyone else (Brunkhorst 2005). Modern republicanism takes this ancient concept and combines it with the principle of equal participation in ruling the political community. This is a solidarity that stems from the common concern for public matters and equal participation of ordinary citizens in the affairs of the polis, and not only from an abstract legal obligation (Andronache 2006). Solidarity is a reciprocal relation between common fellow citizens, linked by their dual role as legislators and subjects of the law. Solidarity is a guarantee of the equal enjoyment of individual and collective freedom by every member of the political community – and by the political community itself – since in the republican view, following Machiavelli, the individual cannot be free in a subjugated political community. Solidarity stems from and reinforces equal participation of all in the public affairs (Brunkhorst 2005). Republican solidarity means a commitment to fellow members of the political community (Andronache 2006); it stems from the practice of citizenship, understood as an identity that members acquire through political participation, by engaging in "public dialogues and negotiations over how and by whom political power is exercised" (Tully 2000: 215).

In the radical egalitarian conceptualization, solidarity is both open and contestatarian; it is not limited to family bonds or blood relations, nor to being part of an ethnic, cultural, or closed national community. Radical egalitarian republican solidarity does not belong to *Gemeinshaft* but to *Gesellshaft*, expressed as a claim to an equal political community. It is not a link between identical individuals, mutual support based on similarity, but "dialectically combines opposites, contradictions and differences" (Brunkhorst 2005: 4). In fact, solidarity is the emancipatory way by which difference and heterogeneity can "still be held together" (Brunkhorst 2005: 4). While fraternity is pre-political, republican solidarity is always already political, stemming from (and allowing claims for) equal political participation in legislating and ruling. Insofar as each human being is *zoon politikon* – a political being – solidarity is open, realized in a concrete and a universal political community.

The idea of the common good is central to the republican tradition. For classical republicanism, one of the meanings of civic virtue is for the individual to put the community's interests above his own (Honohan and Jennings 2006: 12).

While liberals consider that a substantive common good implies some degree of coercion, and is opposed to pluralism, for republicans, the fact that we are political beings embedded in a society requires a certain view of a common good, "in the sense of an indivisible good, which a social perspective necessarily offers us, since it sees men as realizing their potential only in a certain common structure" (Taylor 1985: 298). This common good is not only different from particular interests, but – as Rousseau claimed for the general will – neither is it the aggregate of the partial interests and identities of each and every member of the political community (Schwarzmantel 2006). Moreover, the common good is not only an agreement on some common procedures, but has a more substantive content (Schwarzmantel 2006).

Since in contemporary societies, individuals are characterized by multiple subject positions, and the ways in which the multiple subject positions are organized into social groups are always political, the common good is not self-evident or unanimous. There is no straightforward or non-conflictive expression of the people's will. Does this conclusion bring us back to the liberal opposition to any form of substantial common good? I don't think so. In fact, in every society, there is a more-than-procedural common good, even though it not always (or almost never) works for the many. This common good is a central element of hegemony, understood in the Gramscian sense. It usually represents the interests of the dominant group, but becomes consensual by also taking into account, at least partially, the interests of different subordinated groups. As part of a hegemonic project, the common good cannot really be Rousseau's general will, but is much more than the aggregate of individual interests, or the sole reflection of the interests of the few. Moreover, as part of a hegemonic project, the common good is never final, but is always contested, always the result of social conflict. Radical egalitarian republicanism is aware that the common good arises from social conflict, and is always contested. Thus, radical egalitarian republicanism aims to maximize the equal possibility of each and every one to participate in the configuration of that common good and to democratize the constitution of the common good. Radical egalitarian republicanism aims to democratize the delimitation of the practical norms that characterize the common good, to broaden public goods so as to maximize equal distribution of wealth and income, and to limit as much as possible the identitarian meaning of the common good, in order to leave open access to membership in the polity and access to co-participate in the definition and attainment of the common good.

In combining a conceptualization of liberty as self-government (individual and collective), equality, solidarity, and an understanding of the common good as always contested – thus open, political, embedded in a political and not ethno-cultural or biological community – in viewing participatory democracy as the practice that connects those different elements, radical egalitarian republicanism offers an alternative to the elitist characteristics of classic and neo-Roman republicanism. Moreover, this current of republican thought offers an alternative to the liberal/communitarian binary opposition.

Radical egalitarian republicanism provides a perspective that contributes to overcome the current polarization between secular liberal and religious communitarian approaches to bioethical questions in Israel, since it shares elements of both traditions. As liberalism, on one hand, egalitarian republicanism stresses the importance of freedom and equality as universal. On the other hand, it shares with communitarianism the view that no man is an island, considering individuals as embedded in their societies, and individual agency as shaped by social institutions. However, radical egalitarian republicanism presents advantages over both approaches. As explained previously, it offers a broader understanding of liberty and equality than liberalism. By emphasizing equality of participation in the ruling of the political community, it develops a more complex and deeper conceptualization of liberty than the liberal understanding of freedom as noninterference. It offers a much broader conceptualization of equality than the liberal one, a conceptualization of equality grounded on our common vulnerability, and extending from the legal field to the political and the social ones, since the unequal distribution of wealth increases vulnerability and makes equal political participation in ruling impossible (Thompson 2013).

Though radical egalitarian republicanism stresses that individuals are always embedded in and shaped by social institutions, it has as its only criterion to inclusion the capacity for political participation stemming from our common, universal vulnerability. While it could seem paradoxical to ground political participation on our common vulnerability, since the latter is sometimes associated with passivity, I do not think this is the case. First, vulnerability is also associated with resilience, and resilience implies an active attitude. But second, and more important for our current discussion, vulnerability means that we are not self-sufficient. We live in society because we are vulnerable and in need of others,[3] and because we live in society we are political beings.

Since our vulnerability is common and universal, membership in a political community should transcend particular group identities and is open to political decisions, thus always open to change (Schwarzmantel 2006). Moreover, for radical republican egalitarianism, the common good is not "natural," eternal, pre-constituted, or responding to the ethno-cultural characteristics of a determinate group, but hegemonic, thus always partial and contested. This version of republicanism, thus, is not vulnerable to the critic of perfectionism (see, for example, Lovett and Whitfield 2016). While, as opposed to liberalism, it is aware that public institutions and policies always encourage a certain conception of the good, egalitarian republicanism considers any conception of the good not as objectively better, but as the result of political, i.e., hegemonic struggles stemming from conflict in a public sphere that allows interaction between different groups (Schwarzmantel 2006). Since, as Laclau and Mouffe argue, there is no definitive closure of the social, there is no last and objective conception of the good. However, insofar as political participation is

---

[3] Our common vulnerability is what grounds an ethics of care, an ethics of being there for the other.

increasingly equal, the hegemonic common good is increasingly democratic, and will tend to represent the interests and aims of the many, and not of the few. Politics is – and will be – always conflictive; interests are not only individual but collective, thus increasing democratization does not mean that we will achieve a non-conflictive common good (as Rousseau's general will), or that by increasing democratic participation the common good will be nothing more than a simple aggregation of individual conceptions of the good. But insofar as power and resources will be more equally distributed and insofar as political participation will be increasingly equal, the hegemonic constitution of the common good will be more in tune with the interests and aims of broader sectors of the political community.

Finally, a last advantage of egalitarian republicanism, and especially important in terms of an Israeli bioethics, is that it extends the idea of freedom in such a way that it not only addresses the actions of agents, but also the ways in which social institutions and unequal distribution of resources and power result in violations of freedom (Thompson 2013), and extends the idea of equality to include political participation in ruling and the required equality in the distribution of resources and power.

In sum, radical egalitarian republicanism proposes a conceptualization of freedom, equality, solidarity, and the common good that can ground the development of a critical approach to bioethics.

RADICAL EGALITARIAN REPUBLICAN BIOETHICS

Having developed historically from medical ethics, the dominant liberal conception of bioethics focuses mainly on the individual and on health care. A focus on the individual, a lack of criticism of the context in which choices are made, and an absence of consideration of the institutional basis that unequally distributes power and resources still characterize dominant bioethical thinking, especially in the United States. So much so, that even liberal philosophers like Norman Daniels have criticized the individualistic myopia of mainstream bioethical thinking, which does not examine "the broader institutional settings and policies that mediate population health."[4] On the other hand, at least in the Israeli context, communitarian approaches function as ways of justifying existing structures and institutions that exclude, exploit, and discriminate Palestinians in the OPT, Israeli Palestinians, and Jewish groups such as Mizrahim or Ethiopian Jews.

In order to show the contribution of a radical egalitarian approach to bioethics, and to exemplify its differences from both the liberal and the communitarian approaches, I will provide a definition of the right to health grounded in the

---

[4] European bioethicists have explored alternative paths to the liberal individualist one. Holm argues for a strong beneficence principle. More in line with the ideas explored in the present chapter, Hayri puts forward the idea of solidarity and the fact that individuals are always socially embedded. However, while mentioning Aristotle and Marx, he does not present the concept of solidarity as part of a more general alternative to the liberal worldview.

egalitarian republican approach, and then focus on two topics that are part of the Israeli bioethical discussion: force-feeding and the development of forms of private/public mix, i.e., ways of organizing and financing health care that combine the public and the private sector.

How can we define the right to health in a way coherent with the egalitarian republican conceptualization of freedom, equality, solidarity, and the common good? The liberal conceptualization of the right to health focuses on the individual and stresses mainly personal choice. In its most limited version, the right to health is understood as the right to body integrity and to "a universal right to pursue one's health and wellbeing, including a right to access health care markets" (Moskop 1983: 220). In its more egalitarian version, it grounds the right to health care on the principle of equality of opportunity (Daniels 1985), but still within the framework of ontological and methodological individualism that characterizes liberal thinking (Filc 2007). In line with the egalitarian republican approach elaborated earlier, I propose to understand the right to health as meaning that every person has a claim to the amount of goods and services – including health care – needed to ensure a level of health equal to that of any other person, when inter-individual differences in health are the product of social organization or can be reduced by treatment, and every person has a claim to equal health care for equal needs in those cases in which inter-individual differences in health result from natural (i.e., biological) variations, or from personal choices when those choices are not determined by the unequal distribution of resources and power.[5] This definition is grounded on the broad egalitarian republican understanding of equality, approaches health as a requisite for achieving republican freedom, and requires republican civic (and not communitarian ethno-cultural) solidarity. Moreover, the radical egalitarian health rights approach stresses the importance of social structures and the need for a different institutional framework, one that will make a universal right to health possible. This approach to the right to health also emphasizes the centrality of politics in building adequate institutions, and in modifying those social structures that cause inequalities in health.

A republican egalitarian definition of the right to health guides us in approaching specific bioethical issues. As mentioned previously, I will analyze two issues relevant to bioethical thinking in Israel, in order to exemplify the egalitarian republican approach. The World Medical Association's stand on force-feeding, a stand defended by the Israeli Medical Association (IMA) in its opposition to the law passed by the Knesset allowing for force-feeding hunger strikers, is grounded on the liberal worldview. For the liberal approach, since the patient's autonomy and freedom of choice overcome any other consideration, force-feeding is considered totally unethical, and physicians should not be part of attempts to force-feed prisoners in any circumstance. The communitarian-religious position has been exposed by

---

[5] See Whitehead (1992) for a clarifying classification of the causes of disparities in health.

Professor Shimon Glick several years ago, in the public discussion that followed the hunger strike of the followers of Rabbi Uzzi Meshulam. As against the liberal view that personal autonomy and freedom of choice trump any other consideration, Glick argued for the sanctity of life as a central value, and for the idea that, since no man is an island, the death of a human being is not only his/her personal affair, but involves his/her family, friends, colleagues, and the community as a whole (1997). Gil Sigal (2015) exposed the communitarian and anti-universal view in defense of the law that allows force-feeding and in opposition to the IMA's position:

> There are no absolute values in ethics. . . . The Israeli ethical thinking has the right to autonomy[;] we are not an American or European colony. [Israeli ethical thinking] is a cultural, social, legal and ethical product with a particular and clear voice. When we look at the world we see four principles: patient's autonomy, non-maleficence, the beneficence principle and equity among patients. This is the Anglo-American thinking, and it lacks two other principles: the sanctity of life and solidarity. While the hunger striker claims respect for his right to autonomy, this right is in opposition with the sanctity of life principle. The Israeli law gives precedence to the right to life in extreme cases. Those which oppose the law deny the right to an original and specific Israeli ethics, and subordinate themselves to foreign medical ethicists.

The egalitarian republican view is different from both the liberal and the communitarian ones. An egalitarian republican approach denies that it is ethical to force-feed hunger-striking prisoners appealing to an "autochthonous," community-specific bioethics, where the values of the Jewish community are imposed on Palestinian hunger strikers. Thus, the republican egalitarian approach shares with the liberal stand its opposition to force-feeding (especially in the case of Palestinian hunger strikers), and shares the opposition to a law whose aim was to diminish Palestinian prisoners' ability to oppose administrative detentions through hunger strikes. However, an egalitarian republican approach to bioethics does not ground its position on the supremacy of absolute individual autonomy and freedom of choice, but on its conceptualization of equality, freedom, and solidarity.

As we saw in the previous section, for egalitarian republicanism, relations between individuals are rooted in society and shaped by the way power is organized within each society. Autonomy, in the republican tradition, is not the individual freedom of choice, the choice of the individual consumer whose wants are always sovereign. Autonomy is citizen participation in self-government, which implies also the balance between individuals' desires and interests, and the common good. This balance is always political in that it is negotiated among all the members of the political community. Moreover, from an egalitarian republican perspective, the principle of autonomy has no lexical priority over other bioethical principles such as non-maleficence, beneficence, justice, or solidarity. The relations and specific order of priorities between the different principles result from negotiation in conditions of equal political participation. For example, the principle of beneficence (as well as the principle of non-maleficence) should not be understood either in its original and paternalistic version (where the physician or the researcher knows and decides on behalf of the patient what works for his/her benefit), nor in an individualistic consumer version (where the "client" decides what he or she considers of benefit). The principle of beneficence should be understood as a decision grounded in the negotiated, collective framing of a common good.

Privileging individual choice over any other value originates in the liberal idea of freedom as noninterference. For egalitarian republicanism, though, freedom implies not only non-domination, but also collective action aimed at modifying unequal and unjust concentrations of power in order to allow self-government and political equality. The egalitarian republican approach opposes force-feeding because it understands it as a violation of prisoners' aspiration to republican freedom, within a structural colonial situation in which Palestinians as a collective are denied republican freedom and equality. In this view, thus, there is a difference between force-feeding political hunger strikers, whose decision is an expression of their – republican – freedom stemming from an opposition to a situation of oppression, and force-feeding people suffering from severe eating disorders, where the medical decision must take into account the principles of solidarity and the sanctity of life. The liberal stand, for which individual autonomy and freedom of choice trump any other considerations, finds difficulties in discerning between both circumstances.

A second example of the contribution of an egalitarian republican approach to bioethics is the case of the development of forms of public-private mix in the Israeli health care system. Different forms of public-private partnerships have been implemented worldwide in order to design, finance, build, and maintain hospitals and other health care infrastructures, and even in some cases to provide services (Acerete et al. 2011; Barlow et al. 2013). In Israel, the public-private mix takes forms that blur the boundaries between the public and private services. The main forms are the selling of private insurance schemes by the public sick funds and the provision of private services by public hospitals. The public sick funds sell private insurance schemes that include duplicate and supplementary components: financing of privately performed surgical procedures covered by the public insurance (allowing the choice of surgeon and skipping the queue), and provision of diagnostic procedures and treatments not included in the public health basket. Public hospitals provide private services not included in the public health basket (such as periodic check-ups or certain diagnostic procedures), or provide a private alternative for surgical procedures covered by the public insurance, allowing choice of surgeon and shorter waiting times (called Sharap). In this case, paradoxically, the liberal and communitarian religious views coincide in supporting the development of options such as Sharap, or broadening the private insurance sold by the public sick funds, for example, by including in those insurance schemes oncologic life-prolonging drugs that are not covered by the public health basket. Liberals justify their support of these developments by appealing to freedom of choice. This is exemplified by the patients' rights law, which demands that physicians present patients with all therapeutic options, even those not included in the public health basket, in order for patients to be able to exercise an informed choice.[6] Communitarians, such as the current minister of health (a member of an ultra-Orthodox religious party), support inclusion of life-prolonging drugs in the private insurance schemes, since they consider the latter as forms of intragroup solidarity, grounded on the values of specific communities within Israeli society. On the contrary, an egalitarian republican approach is against the inclusion of life-prolonging drugs in those insurance schemes, since it violates the definition of the right to health outlined previously in this chapter. As against the communitarian position, egalitarian republicanism argues that the inclusion of life-prolonging drugs in the sick-funds insurance schemes is grounded on an exclusionary understanding of solidarity and not one that involves the whole political community, and – by excluding some 20 percent of the population of access to those drugs – damages their possibility to be healthy enough in order to enjoy republican freedom and access to equal political participation. As against the liberal claim, the egalitarian republican approach argues that, in this case, solidarity and an inclusive conception of the common good trump individual autonomy and freedom of choice.

The discussion of these two examples shows that an egalitarian republican approach to bioethics contributes an alternative to the traditional liberal/communitarian polarization. This approach is especially relevant to address bioethical questions in Israeli society, first, because it can critically address the structural inequalities that characterize the Israeli society; and, second, because it may free bioethical thinking in Israel from a certain stalemate stemming from the tension between the liberal and the communitarian/religious views.

References

Acerete, B., Stafford, A., and Stapleton, P., 2011, Spanish Healthcare Public Private Partnerships: The "Alzira Model," *Critical Perspectives on Accounting* 22: 533–549.

---

[6] The liberal egalitarian stand is more complex. Some liberal egalitarians – such as Dworkin – would also support the inclusion of life-prolonging drugs in the sick-funds insurance schemes. You could even claim that this solution is in line with Rawls's second principle, since it could be claimed that it is a form of inequality that improves the situation of the worst off (at least when compared with a situation in which those drugs are accessible only privately or through insurance schemes sold by private insurance companies). However, liberal egalitarians could argue against the inclusion of life-prolonging drugs in the private schemes, based on thinkers such as Anderson and Iris Marion Young or the capabilities approach.

Andronache, L., 2006, Contemporary Republican Theories, in Honohan, I. and Jennings, J. (eds.) *Republicanism in Theory and Practice*, London: Routledge. 109–121.

Barlow, J., Roehrich, J., and Wright, S., 2013, Europe Sees Mixed Results from Public-Private Partnerships for Building and Managing Health Care Facilities and Services, *Health Affairs* 32: 146–154.

Brunkhorst, H., 2005, *Solidarity: From Civic Friendship to a Global Legal Community*, Cambridge, MA: MIT Press.

Daniels, N., 1985, *Just Health Care*, Cambridge: Cambridge University Press.

Filc, D., 2007, The Liberal Grounding of the Right to Health Care: An Egalitarian Critique, *Theoria* 112: 51–72.

Fisher, N., 2015, *Marxist Ethics within Western Political Theory: A Dialogue with Republicanism, Communitarianism and Liberalism*, New York: Palgrave MacMillan.

Garrard, G., 2002, *Rousseau's Counter-Enlightenment: A Republican Critique of the Philosophes*, Albany: State University of New York Press.

Gilabert, P., 2015, Solidarity, Equality and Freedom in Pettit's Republicanism, *Critical Review of International Social and Political Philosophy* 18: 644–651.

Glick, S., 1997, Unlimited Human Autonomy: A Cultural Bias?, *New England Journal of Medicine* 336: 954–956.

2001, *Who Decides? The Patient, the Physician or the Rabbi?* Presented as the Second Annual Jakobovitz Memorial Lecture, November 2001, London.

Honohan, I. and Jennings, J., 2006, Introduction, in Honohan, I. and Jennings, J. (eds.) *Republicanism in Theory and Practice*, London: Routledge. 1–14.

Laborde, C., 2008, *Critical Republicanism*, Oxford: Oxford University Press.

Laclau, E., 2005, *On Populist Reason*, London: Verso.

Laclau, E. and Mouffe, C., 1985, *Hegemony and Socialist Strategy*, London: Verso.

Lovett, F. and Whitfield, G., 2016, Republicanism, Perfectionism, and Neutrality, *The Journal of Political Philosophy* 4: 120–134.

Lukacs, G., 1975, *The Young Hegel*, New York: Rodney Livingston.

McCormick, J., 2011, *Machiavellian Democracy*, Cambridge: Cambridge University Press.

Moskop, J., 1983, Rawlsian Justice and a Human Right to Health Care, *Journal of Medicine and Philosophy* 8: 329–338.

Mouritsen, P., 2006, Four Models of Republican Liberty and Self Government, in Honohan, I. and Jennings, J. (eds.) *Republicanism in Theory and Practice*, London: Routledge. 17–37.

Pettit, P., 2013, Two Republican Traditions, in Neiberger, A. and Schink, P. (eds.) *Republican Democracy, Liberty, Law and Politics*, Edinburgh: Edinburgh University Press. 169–204.

Pocock, J., 1985, Virtues, Rights and Manners: A Model for Historians of Political Thought, in Pocock J. (ed.) *Virtue, Commerce and History: Essays on Political Thought and History, Chiefly in the Eighteenth Century*, Cambridge: Cambridge University Press. 37–50.

Schuppert, F., 2015, Non-domination, Non-alienation and Social Equality: Towards a Republican Understanding of Equality, *Critical Review of International Social and Political Philosophy* 18: 440–455.

Schwarzmantel J., 2006, Republican Theory and Democratic Transformation, in Honohan, I. and Jennings, J. (eds.) *Republicanism in Theory and Practice*, London: Routledge. 140–153.

Shapira, A., 2014, The Dying Patient in Israel between Halachic-Religious and Liberal-Occidental Norms: A Due "Blue and White" Ethics?, in Sigal G. (ed.), *Blue and White Bio-ethics: Bio-ethics and Medical Law in Israel*, Jerusalem: Ono Academic College (Hebrew). 304–315.

Sigal, G., 2014, "Blue and White" Bio-ethics: Bio-ethics and Medical Law in Israel, in Sigal G. (ed.), *Blue and White Bio-ethics: Bio-ethics and Medical Law in Israel*, Jerusalem: Ono Academic College (Hebrew). 15–35.

    2015, "The Discussion Is Not about Force-Feeding but about Saving Lives." *Haaretz*. August 11. www.haaretz.co.il/news/health/.premium-1.2704870.

Taylor, C., 1985, *Philosophy and the Human Sciences*, Cambridge: Cambridge University Press.

Thompson, M., 2013, Reconstructing Republican Freedom: A Critique of the Neo-republican Concept of Freedom as Non-domination, *Philosophy and Social Criticism* 39: 277–298.

    2015, The Two Faces of Domination in Republican Political Theory, *European Journal of Political Theory* 0: 1–21.

Tully, J., 2000, The Challenge of Reimagining Citizenship and Belonging in Multicultural and Multinational Societies, in McKinnon, C. and Hampsher-Monk, I. (eds.) *Demands of Citizenship*, London: Continuum.

Whitehead M., 1992, The Concepts and Principles of Equity and Health, *International Journal of Health Services* 22: 429–445.

3

Force and Feeding: From Bioethics to Biopolitics in Recent Israeli Legislation about Force-Feeding Hunger-Striking Inmates

Yoav Kenny

1 INTRODUCTION

On July 30, 2015, the Israeli Knesset passed a correction to the existing 1971 Prison Law (henceforth: "the Correction"). The Correction qualified the district court to authorize forced feeding of hunger-striking inmates in Israeli prisons when their health or lives could be in danger. The Correction was the final chapter of an extensive and complicated legal and political process, which had begun in response to long hunger strikes by Palestinian security prisoners and administrative detainees in 2012.

Long before its passage, the Correction had already been the object of numerous legal, medical, ethical, and political debates. It prompted strong responses from various statutory entities and local and international NGOs and led to heated debates among Israel's academia, media, and general public. Even after the Correction was passed, the problems and tensions surrounding it persisted. Thus, when army lawyers were faced with two exceptionally long hunger strikes of Palestinian administrative detainees in late 2015, they did not appeal to the district court as provided for in the Correction, and instead negotiated pleas and deals. Even when the detainees' lawyers appealed to the Israeli Supreme Court, the state did not raise or discuss the Correction and instead proposed ad hoc compromises to address the cases (Supreme Court rulings 5575/15; 5580/15;452/16). In September 2016, these various ad hoc solutions were consolidated and systematized when the Israeli Supreme Court rejected all the appeals seeking cancelation of the Correction. The Supreme Court accepted the state's position that the Correction was a constitutional and proportionate addition to the earlier legislation. The court ruled that the Correction impinged on the rights and dignity of inmates only to the extent

---

This is a revised and updated version of an earlier text that appeared in Hebrew in *Law, Society and Culture* [special issue on Law and Food, Yofi Tirosh and Aeyal Gross (eds.)], Tel Aviv University, 2017. I thank the editors of the Hebrew journal, the editors of this volume, Marianne Constable, Olivia Custer, Itamar Mann, and an anonymous reader for their useful and helpful comments.

necessary to fulfill both what the court referred to as "the dominant purpose" of guarding the life of a person in the custody of the state and "the secondary purpose" of homeland security and public order (Supreme Court rulings 5304/15; 5441/15; 5994/15).

While the debate surrounding the Correction is complicated and multifaceted, its crux has remained the same since its inception and did not change even after the Supreme Court issued its ruling.[1] On the general liberal level, the Correction presents a dilemma between the obligation of the state to ensure the basic nutrition of its population and the "right to starve" of the autonomous individual.[2] In the current Israeli context, this dilemma translates into a number of basic arguments.[3] According to the state, while hunger striking is in itself a legitimate act of protest emanating from the right to free speech and is therefore defended by Israeli law, when the hunger strike endangers the life and health of an inmate, the state must force-feed him or her. The state's responsibility has two major justifications. First, unlike free citizens, inmates' lives, health, and well-being are the direct responsibility of the state. Section 11 of the Israeli Prison Law and section 322 of the Israeli Penal Code state that inmates, who cannot supply their basic needs on their own, are "under the legal guardianship of the head warden." Second, hunger-striking inmates are acting in a wider public context of protest or political resistance. Deterioration in their health, let alone their death, could lead to "large-scale disruptions of order, or violent outbreaks, in solidarity with the striker and his cause," which the state must try to avoid as part of its responsibility for public safety and security (Bill, 772).[4]

In contrast, those who criticize the Correction claim that forcefully feeding a person who freely and consciously chooses to go on a hunger strike is wrong under any circumstances. These critics contend that force-feeding impairs both the basic right to autonomy and the fundamental principle of informed consent in medical ethics prohibiting any medical treatment for which the patient has not given free and conscious consent. Accordingly, the most persistent and resolute criticism of the Correction came from the Israeli Medical Association (IMA). Moreover, nearly all those opposing the Correction refer to the prohibition of force-feeding in the Tokyo and Malta Declarations of the World Medical

---

[1] For example, following the rejection of the Israeli Medical Association's appeal, its chairperson declared that, despite the ruling, he could not imagine a physician who would perform this "violent act which may cause great medical damage." Physicians for Human Rights, whose Supreme Court appeal was also rejected, released a statement that "the Supreme Court trumped medical ethics and enabled a damaging law which should have never been legislated" (Khoury, Polver, and Efrati 2016).
[2] English law, for example, discusses "the right to starve" explicitly and often favorably in relation to hunger strikes (Brockman 1999: 454).
[3] This summary is based on: the bill for the Correction (Bill, 870 [June 9, 2014], 762–776; hereafter: "the Bill"); the Supreme Court appeals mentioned in note 1 of this chapter; and the following documents [all in Hebrew]: Karmon et al. 2013; Nizri 2013; Wygoda 2013; Israeli Medical Association 2014b; Kremnitzer et al. 2014; National Bioethics Council 2014.
[4] This position was demonstrated when the military was ordered to deploy "iron dome" missile batteries in response to hunger striker Muhammad Alaan's going into a coma (Cohen and Efrati 2015).

Association (WMA).[5] A related critique argues that the Correction does not improve or add to the bioethical practices of the existing Israeli Patient's Rights Law (1996). Section 27 of this law applies it to prisons. Section 15(2) of it details strict conditions, including the approval of a designated ethics committee, for any medical treatment given to a patient against his or her will. According to those opposing the Correction, these legal requirements render force-feeding unnecessary and prove that, despite its medical and bioethical jargon, the Correction's main purpose is to prevent political and public gain from hunger-striking inmates. Indeed, the Correction is regarded as supplying legal grounds for "regulating a medical issue ... by security officials ... [who] are driven by political dictates." Thus, while force-feeding is unquestionably related to medical and bioethical issues, the Correction is accused of being "essentially political," since "such a specific law, which only addresses hunger-striking inmates, is suspect of political bias" (Kremnitzer et al. 2014; Karmon et al. 2013; National Bioethics Council 2014).

The crux of the debate is evidently not a static issue reflecting a stable dilemma. Rather, the debate is composed of a dynamic intersection of four distinct axes: medical-bioethical; correctional-punitive; juridical-legal; and political-security. The significance of each axis and its reciprocal influence on other axes determines its importance or weight in the debate. The following will not map out these intersections, nor endorse any one of them or the position it represents. Rather, this study will focus on the concepts employed by all the participants in the debate, explicitly or implicitly, thus constituting and stabilizing the shared plane of these discursive axes. By exposing the problems and tensions that arise when similar and even identical uses of the same concepts yield contradictory legal positions, this study will demonstrate how the ostensibly legal discussion about medical issues is, in fact, a political debate about fundamental questions of power and control. Rather than analyzing the issue of force-feeding hunger-striking inmates using bioethics, which applies the discourse of rights and autonomy to moral debates about medical processes, this study posits that the issue should be examined through the prism of Foucauldian biopolitics. This approach examines the disciplinary ends of incarceration against the backdrop of a wider conception of political power as a decentralized structure of control, domination, and supervision, the objects of which are the bodies, lives, and deaths of the governed population (Foucault 1978, 2007). This

---

[5] Section 6 of the WMA Declaration of Tokyo – Guidelines for Physicians Concerning Torture and Other Cruel, Inhuman or Degrading Treatment or Punishment in Relation to Detention and Imprisonment states that "[w]here a prisoner refuses nourishment and is considered by the physician as capable of forming an unimpaired and rational judgment concerning the consequences of such a voluntary refusal of nourishment, he or she shall not be fed artificially." www.wma.net/en/30publica tions/10policies/c18. Sections 11 and 13 of the WMA Declaration of Malta on Hunger Strikers state that "[i]t is ethical to allow a determined hunger striker to die in dignity rather than submit that person to repeated interventions against his or her will," and that "[f]orcible feeding is never ethically acceptable." www.wma.net/en/30publications/10policies/h31.

particular focus will question the dichotomous structure that led the current form of the debate to an impasse and will shed new light on the arguments surrounding the debate by suggesting an alternative conceptual groundwork better suited to their political foundations.

2 TREATING HUNGER-STRIKING INMATES WITH FORCE-FEEDING: FOUR CONCEPTUAL OBSTACLES

In the opening glossary of the Correction, as is often the case, its operational rationale is already implied. By choosing to define "ethics committee," "Patient's Rights Law," "medical treatment," "caretaker," "medical institution," "physician," and "hunger strike" the lawmakers present their intention that the Correction applies only to bioethical standards for legal interference with medical practices. However, a closer look at four concepts that appear in this glossary in various forms and that frame the Correction and the broader debate reveals a different explanation.

The first concept is "hunger strike," which is the only concept that the Correction defines independently and not according to an existing glossary in a previous law. The second concept is "treatment," which is in fact a "specter-concept," as it is part of the Correction through its exclusion, having originally been part of the bill as distinct from "medical treatment," but was removed from the final version. The third concept is "force-feeding," which, despite its obvious importance and relevance, is devoid of any mention in the Correction. The fourth concept is "inmate," which is not defined in the Correction, but rather in the Prison Law it amends, thus applying to the Correction as well. While the Correction uses these four concepts in complementary and mutually influential ways, examining each of them separately reveals unique components in the structuring of the debate about the legal, ethical, and political status of the Correction.

2.1 *Hunger Strike*

With regard to the problem of hunger striking, which force-feeding aims to solve, both sides of the debate uncritically accept the definition of the Correction, which describes a hunger strike as "a willful abstinence from food or drink, including partially, in order to protest or to gain a specific goal." This definition offers a procedural widening and an essential narrowing of an earlier Israeli Prison Service (IPS) definition, according to which an inmate is hunger striking only when "without due justification [he] does not eat at least four consecutive meals even if he is drinking water." An inmate who "eats part of the meal (including liquids other than water) will not be considered as hunger striking" (IPS Order 04.16.00, sec. 4). The IPS definition is more quantitatively accurate than the Correction's definition, as it distinguishes short or partial forgoing of nutrition from ongoing self-starvation, which jeopardizes health and can lead to death. However, the IPS definition ignores the protest element involved in hunger striking and nullifies the political aspects inmates ascribe to it. Rather, the IPS formulation represents a formal institutional definition expressing the functional need to decide whether an inmate has transgressed prison rules, specifically section 56(8) of the Prison Law, which prohibits any refusal to eat prison meals.

According to the explanations section of the Correction bill, the need to update this technical and quantitative definition of the IPS arose from the position that "the essential test to carrying out the court's authority [to allow force-feeding] ... is contingent upon the subjective medical condition of the striker ... and not upon the nature and characteristics of the strike" (Bill, 769). Given the natural physical differences among inmates, the shift from an objective calculation of the number of meals to a "subjective medical condition" seems appropriate. However, despite its move to medical subjectivity, the Correction does not alter the way in which the objective and quantitative rationale of prison rules enables judicial intervention in the treatment of hunger-striking inmates. This tension not only demonstrates a more fundamental position implicit in the medical and bioethical wording of the Correction, but it also exposes two contradictions in its definition of hunger strikes.

First, it is precisely the insistence on subjective medical conditions that exposes the Correction to criticism for being political and security-oriented rather than humanitarian and health-oriented. Section 19.14(4) of the Correction lists the medical issues the court should consider when deciding on force-feeding hunger-striking inmates: physical and mental condition, medical history, relevance of alternative treatments, etc. However, security and public order considerations are also noticeably important imperatives, as the following section states that "the court shall consider fear for human lives or ... national security." The separation of the two sections suggests that the lives the Correction seeks to save are not those of hunger-striking inmates, but those of citizens who might get hurt in the event that hunger strikers died, followed by ensuing violence and a deterioration in security.[6]

Second, although the Correction emphasizes the specific legal category of hunger-striking inmates, its broad definition of "hunger strike" actually applies to all intentional and purposeful fasting, inside or outside prison. The bill for the Correction referred to the wardens' responsibility for the lives and health of inmates both to explain "the more complex situation" of hunger-striking inmates and to rationalize denying inmates the legitimate right to engage in a hunger strike. This latter right is normally part of the "constitutional defense" that Israeli law provides as

---

[6] The problematic nature of this separation is evident in paragraph 144 of the Supreme Court ruling 5304/15, which stresses that section 19.14(5) should be used "scarcely and in exceptional cases, given an appropriate infrastructure of evidence." Moreover, although Supreme Court Justice Mazoz joined his fellow judges in rejecting the appeal, in section 22 of his closing remarks, he claimed that the state "will be wise to reconsider the cancelation of section 19.14(5)," which he labeled "the security section," since "the fundamental goals of the [new] law seem to be achieved [even without this section] ... and ... its existence raises suspicions and arguments."

an element of "the right to free speech" (Bill, 762). However, if the wardens' responsibility is the only criterion for distinguishing a hunger-striking inmate from others engaging in cases of conscious and purposeful self-starvation, then two difficulties arise immediately:

(A) It becomes practically impossible to justify any force-feeding that exceeds the basic nutritional needs required to treat the medical condition of the hunger striker. As scholars from the Israel Democracy Institute have stated, infringing on the autonomy of an inmate defies the long-established principle that incarceration must not affect any right other than that of freedom of movement. Therefore, as long as the refusal to eat or drink is voluntary and conscious, force-feeding is not part of the duty to care for an inmate (Kremnitzer et al. 2014; par. 4–5). Despite attempts to present the need to care for inmates as the rationale for violating this basic principle of inmates' rights, the formulations and definitions of the Correction indicate that the real reason for doing so is "public safety" and "national security." Ironically, since the relevant sections of the Prison Law do not mention this justification, the implicit political purpose of the Correction is exposed precisely by these formulations and definitions.

(B) The declared care-taking and health-oriented agenda of the definition of "hunger strike" presented in the Correction is actually redundant. Assuming that the purpose of the Correction is to care for inmates and that hunger striking is understood as any refusal to eat or drink, then it is unclear why an additional judicial procedure is necessary, in light of the Patient's Rights Law. Section 14 (2) of this law allows physicians to carry out medical practices and authorizes ethics committees to approve nonconsensual and forced treatment, with section 27 explicitly mentioning its applicability to inmates. Beyond the political security reasons for this apparently superfluous judicial intervention, this unnecessary legal duplication also affects the way in which prisons understand their duty to care for inmates. For example, in the current Israeli legal situation, where formal and quantitative conceptualization of hunger strikes ignores political motivations and contexts, it is unclear how prisons should treat an anorexic inmate whose refusal to eat has become life threatening. This problem is even more severe when the inmate in question is a security prisoner or an administrative detainee. While the medical process itself would be similar in cases of both hunger strikers and anorexics, unlike anorexic patients, hunger-striking inmates do not suffer from psychological pathologies.[7] Should an ethics committee be formed, as provided for in the Patient's Rights Law, or should the warden appeal to the court according to the Correction?

---

[7] Clearly, hunger strikes can cause unstable and even pathological mental states, but those are outcomes of a conscious, rational decision to go on hunger strike and not reasons for such a decision. For a further discussion on the relation between hunger strikes and anorexia in the present Israeli context, see Goldin 2014.

2.2 Treatment

Another concept whose definition in the Correction further complicates the debate is "treatment," which plays an important role in the Correction precisely because it was removed from it. The originally proposed bill for the Correction defined treatment as "giving food or liquids, also artificially, or any other medical treatment" (Bill, 769). This definition clearly differs from the position of the IMA, whose official guidelines to physicians do not regard providing food to a hunger-striking inmate as "treating an ailment," but rather as meeting a "basic need of life" (IMA 2014b: 4). The justification for judicial intervention and correctional action with medical and care-oriented arguments reappears in the Correction bill, but in stark contrast to how the permutations of the definitions of "hunger strike" evolved. Whereas "hunger strike" was problematic because of vague and too general formulations, "treatment" is problematic because its overly specific definition reveals once more how the arguments for judicial intervention in what is supposed to be a professional medical procedure are in fact neither humanitarian nor medical. Consequently, the bill for the Correction distinguished between "treatment" and "medical treatment":

> Medical treatment for hunger strikers may include a wide variety of treatments – starting with measuring physiological values, intravenous therapy, with or without various additives (vitamins, minerals, sugar etc.), all the way to inserting a nasogastric or orogastric feeding tube to the patient's stomach or total parenteral nutrition (TPN). The distinction between different types of treatment, their meanings and implications, including in the aspect of the patient's dignity – is carried out as part of the court's considerations ... and based on medical evaluation. (Bill, 769)

Despite this medical evaluation, and as has already been mentioned, transferring the authority to decide on treatment types and the responsibility for the patient's dignity from professional medical venues to the court is a major object of criticism regarding the Correction. Indeed, not only are the medical and humanitarian declarations of the Correction already covered by the Patient's Rights Law, the Correction also justifies medical intervention by relying on political and security reasons that are not directly related to the issue. Finally, the Correction makes the court the setting for professional medical procedures and practices that would be better made outside of it.

While "giving food" was not included in the Correction's final definition of "treatment," the initial intention to frame it with medical and humanitarian arguments indicates that the rationale of the Correction implicitly acknowledges the theoretical difficulties and the practical problems of using such arguments to try to justify force-feeding inmates. This specific attempt failed and the medical discussion of force-feeding was removed from the Correction, but the history of its place in the bill is sufficient to reveal the political security agenda behind the original distinction between "treatment" and "medical treatment." Just as occurred with "hunger strike," the implicit nature of this agenda is evident with the problematic modification of the terms "treatment" and "medical treatment." It not only blurs conceptual boundaries, making it difficult to understand the Correction, but also nullifies the sought-after differentiation between the Correction and the Patient's Rights Law, thus failing to offer an answer to those claiming that the Correction is both political and unnecessary.

2.3 Force-Feeding

The exclusion of nutrition from the definition of "treatment" not only causes medical care-oriented and political security-oriented arguments to interweave in ways that contradict the declared intention of the Correction. It also makes it more difficult to understand the problematic treatment in question: namely, the use of force to artificially feed hunger-striking inmates. Indeed, as long as "giving food and liquids" is not mentioned in section 19.16(4) of the Correction, which allows prison guards to use "reasonable force" to "enable treatment," this section and the Correction in general remain vague at best. Moreover, even without this exclusion of nutrition, the Correction is equally vague in other contexts. For example, it uses different terms to refer to the force-feeding of hunger-striking inmates. "Compulsory medical treatment" is mentioned as what the ethics committees, covered by the Patient's Rights Law, can authorize. "Forced-feeding" is the term used in the survey of the legal status in other countries. Additionally, "giving nourishment compulsively" and "giving nourishment forcefully" are described as those medical practices that the WMA Malta Declaration has forbidden (Bill, 764–766).[8] Consequently, those opposing the Correction also use disordered terminology. While the title of the report of the National Bioethics Council uses "compulsory feeding," the report itself refers to both "coerced treatment" and "coerced feeding" and the Israel Democracy Institute mentions both "giving treatment forcefully" and "forced-feeding" (National Bioethics Council 2014; Kremnitzer et al. 2014; par 1–3).

Therefore, any intervention in the debate about feeding hunger-striking inmates must make a distinction among "force," "coercion," and "compulsion." Given the daily reality of the rules and practices of incarceration, the use of "coercion" and "compulsion" seems obvious in the context of the far-reaching ramifications of the artificial feeding of inmates against their will. In other words, and as the Correction bill rightly emphasized, a main component of personal autonomy that is denied to inmates is control over their food: what, how much, where, when, and with whom they eat. While the circumstances of their feeding are a direct outcome of the loss of freedom of movement inherent in incarceration, they do not violate the minimal

---

[8] Note that some of these terms are inadequate translations from Hebrew. The source of these inadequacies is the way in which Hebrew distinguishes between "food" (*okhel*) and "nourishment" (*mazon*, from the same lexical root as *tzuna* [nutrition]), thus making "feeding" (*hazana*, as opposed to *ha'akhala*) closer to nourishment than to food both etymologically and essentially.

personal autonomy of inmates that prisons must protect. Insofar as coercion means causing someone to do something against his or her will, any type of eating while incarcerated is to some degree coerced. Therefore, the use of the term "coercion" in the context of feeding hunger-striking inmates against their will not only misleadingly presents this practice as respectful of the human autonomy of inmates, it also conceals the corporal violence involved in this practice.

This can also be inferred from the shift from the use of "compulsory eating" and "coerced feeding," which were sometimes used in public debates over hunger-striking suffragettes in the early 1900s in Britain, to "force-feeding" or "forced feeding," which dominate contemporary cases all over the world (Thompson et al. 1909; Grant 2011).[9] Furthermore, in the Malta and Tokyo Declarations of the WMA, the application of physical force transforms artificial feeding from a legitimate medical treatment to unethical cruel punishment. Indeed, precisely because "hunger strike" is so broadly defined in the Correction and "giving food" is understood in the bill as "medical treatment," it is especially important to emphasize the forceful element in artificially feeding an inmate against his or her will, regardless of the specifics of the inmate's refusal to eat. In sum, in the absence of a perfect lexical solution, "force-feeding" seems to be the most suitable term for expressing the myriad of meanings and conceptual assumptions that are referred to in the current debate.

2.4 Inmate

Underlying all of the aforementioned conceptual considerations is the first line of the first section of the Prison Law, which defines an "inmate" as "anyone who is in the legal custody of a prison." Initially, this definition seems to work both for supporters of the Correction, who claim that incarceration in and of itself, and not any of its particular circumstances, requires a specific legal solution for hunger-striking inmates, and for its critics, according to whom focusing on incarceration as such is essentially political. Nevertheless, both sides implicitly agree that defining the subject of incarceration as an "inmate" is not sufficiently accurate. The Correction bill and the documents written by its opponents emphasize the fact that the hunger strikes that prompted the debate were undertaken by either security prisoners or administrative detainees. The first group, security prisoners, is not defined in any law, but is only categorized in administrative and operational terms in procedure 04.05.00 of the IPS. The latter group, administrative detainees, is notoriously at the center of a long and intense legal and ethical debate as to whether the incarceration of its members is indeed "legal custody" (Feurstein 2009).

The resulting intersection of politics, national security, and incarceration is clear. However, contrary to what could be inferred from how the Correction uses the

---

[9] For a rare contemporary exception, see Reyes 2007.

political public struggle surrounding hunger-striking inmates to present force-feeding as necessary for "public safety and security," to date, none of the relevant hunger-striking inmates in Israel has protested directly against the political situation. Nor have any of them demonstrated active participation in the public debate, let alone the armed conflict, between Israel and the Palestinians. Undoubtedly, these hunger-striking inmates are part of the conflict, either as convicted or suspected members of violent Palestinian organizations, or as victims of violence on the part of the Israeli military and police. However, in the specific context of this study, their lack of political engagement is irrelevant because their hunger strikes are not meant to protest the occupation of the West Bank, the blockade of Gaza, or even Israel or Zionism in general. Rather, they are undertaken to protest specific conditions of incarceration: for security prisoners, these include solitary confinement, revoked visiting rights, and cancelation of permissions to study; for administrative detainees, their protests are against the actual situation of being detained without a trial, or an indictment.[10]

Certainly, criminal prisoners also go on hunger strikes and these strikes also raise questions about the security and political contexts of the conditions of imprisonment and of the operational rationale of the punitive system in its entirety (Guenther 2015). However, since the legality of incarceration of criminal prisoners is not contested and the use of sanctions within the prison is not disputed, the Patient's Rights Law is clearly sufficient for ordering any type of treatment for those types of prisoners engaging in hunger strikes. In contrast, the force-feeding of hunger-striking inmates is considered through the political public-security prism in the Correction. There, it is incumbent on both sides of the debate to strive for more accurate terminology. Such terminology should acknowledge that virtually all hunger-striking inmates in Israel are either Palestinian security prisoners or Palestinian administrative detainees, two populations created and defined by legal and correctional mechanisms whose raison d'être has much more to do with national security and politics than with the rule of law and the criminal code.[11] In this sense, the current debate challenges the Correction as well as a previous court ruling that maintained that "the hunger strike cannot be a factor in the decision on the lawfulness of an administrative detention in itself" (Supreme Court Ruling, 3267/12). This ruling

---

[10] A recent example is the case of Bilal Kayed, who was put in administrative detention immediately after being released from fourteen years in prison as a security prisoner, and started a hunger strike in response (Khoury 2016).
Obviously, this does not mean that on a more general and abstract level such protests against conditions of imprisonment and administrative detention are not part of the broader Palestinian struggle against the Israeli occupation (Nashef 2011; Rosenfeld 2011).

[11] Two recent exceptions are Meir Ettinger and Evyatar Slonim, Jewish citizens who were put in administrative detention after being suspected of terrorist attacks against Palestinians and went on hunger strikes. While their political objectives were obviously different than those of Palestinian detainees, the formal rationale of their hunger strikes was similar to those discussed earlier in this chapter and the objects of their protests were specific incarceration conditions and not general political purposes (Bob, 2016).

highlights the conceptual difficulties inherent in the Correction, arising from how it uses the terms "hunger strike," "treatment," and "force-feeding." Indeed, the real critique of the Correction should not concentrate on its being political and distinguishing between inmates and free citizens, but rather on the fact that this binary distinction *is not political enough* and should be refined by focusing on security prisoners and administrative detainees.[12]

The next section will explain why Foucauldian biopolitics may enable a more accurate political conceptualization of hunger-striking inmates that does not overlook the legal and ethical links between hunger strikes and administrative detention. Foucault's biopolitical thought will help politicize the discussion in order to accommodate a more substantial critique and address the conceptual problems presented earlier in this chapter. Because Foucault's theory recognizes security and discipline as integral elements of the political construction of power, it succeeds in presenting an alternative paradigm to the rights- and autonomy-oriented legal discourse currently dominating the debate.

3 DISCIPLINE, PUNISH, AND FEED: THE BIOPOLITICS OF INCARCERATION, HUNGER, AND FEEDING

In 1971, Michel Foucault and others founded the Prison Information Group (Group d'information sur les prisons [GIP]) in response to a series of hunger strikes of political prisoners in French prisons (Miller 2000: 187–188). The manifesto Foucault read at the founding event begins as follows:

> None of us is sure to escape prison.... We are kept under "close observation" [*garde à vue*].... They tell us that prisons are over-populated. But what if it was the population that was being over-imprisoned? Little information is published on prisons. It is one of the hidden regions of our social system, one of the dark zones of our life....
>
> We propose to make known what the prison is: who goes there, how and why they go there, what happens there, and what the life of the prisoners is, and that, equally, of the surveillance personnel; what the buildings, the food, and hygiene are like; how the internal regulations, medical control, and the workshops function; how one gets out and what it is to be, in our society, one of those who came out. (Foucault et al. 1971)

The conceptual relevance to the current debate about the Correction is clear: Foucault mentions food as a key element in the life of inmates. He exposes the

---

[12] Indeed, the Israeli Supreme Court stated that "although this issue was not raised here explicitly, it cannot be ignored that many of the instances of the question of treating a hunger-striking inmate come about in relation to administrative detainees." The preventive nature of administrative detention raises "additional difficulties" beyond the legal difficulties having to do with sentenced prisoners, since it underlines "the question of the security risk that the detainee might pose" (Supreme Court Ruling 5304/15; sec. 140).

political essence of the medical-correctional interface by mentioning "medical control" directly after "internal regulations" and he discusses "close observation," whose French origin, *garde à vue*, not only alludes to the well-known Foucauldian links between visibility and discipline, but is also the phrase used to describe the then common French practice of administratively detaining political activists (Macey 1993; 515 n. 1). In order to demonstrate how these initial allusions can be developed into a Foucauldian understanding of force-feeding hunger-striking inmates, his work must first be placed in a broader context.

The preliminary ideas and the terminology presented in the GIP manifesto were of great importance to the development of Foucault's thought in those years (Monod 1997; Hoffman 2013: ch. 2; Koopman 2015). This process reached its famous peak with the publications of *Discipline and Punish: The Birth of the Prison* (1975) and *The History of Sexuality I: The Will to Know* (1976), as well as the lecture series "Society Must Be Defended" (1975–1976). The central theoretical and conceptual achievement of these works was an original political genealogy of power (*pouvoir*). This genealogy exposed the ways in which power operated in institutional sites of professional and scientific knowledge, which until then were considered apolitical, and charted the fundamental reciprocity between governance and these sites of knowledge/power. Foucault focused on the shift from the classic political paradigm of direct and absolute sovereign control to the modern political paradigm of decentralized governance that controls the daily lives of citizens through institutions, such as barracks, clinics, mental asylums, schools, prisons, factories, etc., and through the discourses, knowledge, and practices these institutions produce as exclusively "scientific" and "official."

According to Foucault, this paradigm shift is encapsulated in the two complementing ways through which "power gave itself the function of administering life" (1978: 138). The first focuses on the physical functions of the individual living body, which is perceived "as a machine" and therefore is trained, controlled, and shaped through "*anatomo-politics*" in order to yield optimal results in relation to the political and economic goals of society; this is discipline. The second views the individual as a concrete yet unspecified exemplar of the entire population and therefore focuses on controlling, monitoring, and regulating the biological processes that are common to all living members of the population as such; this is biopolitics (Foucault 1978: 139). Foucault claims that the use of techniques and mechanisms that both optimize and maximize discipline through the "subjection of bodies" and optimize and maximize biopolitics by regulating the population started "an era of 'bio-power,'" in which the knowledge/power pairing caused human life itself to be the subject of political technologies (Foucault 1978: 139).

Since the combination of subjected living bodies and a controlled population is inherent to incarceration, the prison forms the emblematic knowledge/power site and embodies the intersection of sovereign, disciplinary, and biopolitical aspects of power better than any other state institution:

> [P]rison is the only place where power is manifested in its naked state, in its most excessive form, and where it is justified as moral force. ... [In prison], for once, power doesn't hide or mask itself; it reveals itself as tyranny pursued into the tiniest details; it is cynical and at the same time pure and entirely "justified," because its practice can be totally formulated within the framework of morality. (Foucault and Deleuze 1977: 210)

It is already apparent how this conclusion can be applied to how the political powers in Israel tried to use the Correction to the Prison Law as a bioethical justification of force-feeding hunger-striking inmates. However, in order to understand fully the biopolitical nature of this practice, it should be examined against the backdrop of Foucault's claim that modern political power cannot be evaluated only through the legal prism of rights and laws. This prism, Foucault claims, impairs our ability to understand the political essence of power that constitutes and shapes the relations between the individual and the state, where sovereignty is just one of the political forces affecting human lives (1977: 141, 215; 2003).

As mentioned previously, supporters of the Correction try to justify it by citing the duty of the state to provide and care for inmates, who are one of the population groups who cannot do so themselves. Foucault points out that the state first took this duty upon itself in disciplinary institutions with punitive objectives and particularly in prisons. The state fed inmates as part of its responsibility for their lives, but at the same time, by controlling and regulating quantities and ingredients, it also used nutrition as a means of discipline (Johnston 1985; Vernon 2007: 159).[13] Bearing in mind that hunger-striking political prisoners inspired Foucault's thinking on the biopolitical construction of knowledge/power institutions, it can now be understood that hunger strikes are acts of political protest whose essence is a refusal to accept the combination of sovereign, disciplinary, and biopolitical power that the state, quite literally, wishes to shove down the throats of those under its rule.

This refusal demonstrates Foucault's claim that "there is no binary and all-encompassing opposition between rulers and ruled at the root of power relations," since, among other things, "[w]here there is power there is resistance ... [which] is never in a position of exteriority in relation to power" (1978: 94–95). In other words, the practices and technologies that constitute and uphold biopower facilitate the actions of both the governing regime and those who resist it (Foucault 2001: 346; Thompson 2003). In the present context, this means that a refusal to be fed by the state is an expression of power precisely because it exposes the way in which, through feeding, the state establishes punishment and welfare as two sides of the same (bio) political coin (Vernon 2007: 275). Consequently, this also demonstrates why supposedly medical-humanitarian arguments cannot help but express the political and ideological interests of the government.

---

[13] For a recent legal and political analysis of the issue in the Israeli-Palestinian context, see Gross and Feldman 2015.

While the defiant character of hunger strikes and their biopolitical foundations were absent from the Israeli debate about force-feeding, in recent decades, these issues played important roles in critical discussions of other instances of this practice. For example, the hunger strikes of the suffragettes were regarded as early feminist manifestations of the use of the body as a means of "[mobilizing] bare life for emancipatory struggle" (Ziarek 2008: 98–99).[14] Similarly, hunger strikes of Irish republicans in the 1980s, along with "dirty protests" (smearing feces on cell walls) and self-immolation, were discussed as modes of protest that used the "political fetishization of the body." They demonstrate how the body, being the last "site of power," facilitates violent oppression practices culminating in force-feeding, and also enables "redirection and reversal" of power, which concludes with the "hunger strike unto death" (Feldman 1991: 144, 163, 178). In addition, the hunger strikes of political prisoners in Turkey in 2000 were placed in the wider global context of "the weaponization of life" by terrorists and activists alike (Bargu 2014: intro., 140, 158). Finally, a biopolitical reading of the American "global war on terror" presented the "indefinite detentions" of inmates in Guantanamo both as a reason for their hunger strikes and as a necessary legal condition for the government's power to force-feed them (Butler 2006: ch. 3, 157 n. 10).

While this short and partial survey cannot fully explore the complexities and particularities of the specific hunger strikes examined, it does demonstrate that the theoretical and conceptual infrastructure Foucault provided paves the way for a biopolitical reconceptualization of the Israeli debate on force-feeding hunger-striking inmates, particularly in relation to security prisoners and administrative detainees. Accordingly, the current discussion will conclude by outlining how biopolitical conceptualization could overcome the existing conceptual obstacles and promote a better understanding of the current Israeli iteration of the debate surrounding force-feeding hunger-striking inmates.

4 CONCLUSION: TOWARD A BIOPOLITICAL CONCEPTUALIZATION OF FORCE-FEEDING HUNGER-STRIKING INMATES

At this point it should be clear that, to a large extent, the legal and bioethical debate over new Israeli legislation regarding force-feeding of hunger-striking prisoners persists with such fervor because of ambiguous conceptual assumptions. Both supporters of the Correction and its critics refrain from suggesting clear and explicit definitions of hunger strikes, treatment, force-feeding, and administrative detainees and security prisoners, who should be but are not differentiated from sentenced inmates. This prevents both sides from formulating clear bioethical positions that could direct the actions of correctional, legal, and medical practitioners in relevant

---

[14] The biopolitical conceptualization of the term "bare life" Ziarek uses here originates from the work of Giorgio Agamben (Agamben 1998).

situations. The biopolitical essence of institutionalized state feeding examined in this study identifies this conceptual inadequacy and the debate it engenders at the intersection of *feeding*, as an act of state power that simultaneously aims at both punishment and welfare; *the living body*, as the material site in and through which this act unfolds; and *life*, including its end in death, as an object of biopolitical power's control and surveillance. This understanding calls for a new delineation of the conceptual boundaries of the debate.

First, because the state is directly responsible for feeding only those who reside in its institutions of welfare or discipline, there is no need to discuss anyone outside these institutions as "hunger striking." It can certainly be argued that insofar as the state is committed to the welfare of its population, it should assume a responsibility to ensure "nutritional security" to everyone. However, while free citizens can fulfill their nutritional potential by themselves, inmates, soldiers, hospital patients, pupils, and anyone living in a state institution cannot and it becomes the direct obligation of the state to feed them. Accordingly, deliberate fasting that takes place outside of state institutions is in fact self-starvation of an autonomous individual deciding on the times, quantities, and ingredients of his or her feeding, including abstinence from it, even when it leads to death (O'Keeffe 1984).[15] When an individual is confined to a state-controlled institution, such decisions about sustaining or jeopardizing life are not his or hers to make. A confined individual does not stop eating and starve, but actually refuses nutrition provided by the state; namely, the individual is hunger striking. Therefore, there must be a differentiation between this biopolitical practice of protest and resistance and a free individual's decision to engage in abstinence and possibly suicide. This distinction is explicitly expressed in the declarations of hunger strikers who claim that they do not want to die but are willing to die in the struggle to make their lives worth living; specifically, free from unjust manifestations of disciplinary power (Efrati 2015).

In addition, and contrary to the broad definition of hunger strike used by the Correction and despite the need to care for the well-being of inmates, as long as abstinence from food is partial and does not risk the fasting inmate, it does not amount to hunger striking and does not evoke any need for intervention, either medical or forceful. Nonetheless, this does not mean the quantitative objective definition of IPS procedure 04.16.00 should be accepted. Indeed, precisely because the relevant focus is the survival of the particular living body of the hunger-striking inmate, the discussion should not be objective and legal, but rather subjective and political.

Given this corporal particularity, and because, regarding feeding, disciplinary punishment and welfare appear to be two sides of the same biopolitical coin, a second conclusion is that any attempt to offer a sharp distinction between medical,

---

[15] For a bioethical discussion of suicide in Israel, see Hazan and Romberg's contribution in Chapter 15 of this volume.

humanitarian, correctional, and security-oriented objectives of treating a living body through force-feeding by a state power is bound to fail. These objectives, the discursive fields they generate, and the points where they intersect should all be taken into consideration when trying to determine the legitimacy of the force with which hunger-striking inmates are fed.

Consequently, in a fundamental biopolitical sense, the concept of force-feeding only applies to cases where the living body of an inmate exists in conditions where it is not explicitly illegal to expose it to direct force. In present-day Israeli prisons, such conditions are reached when the body in question belongs to a security prisoner or political prisoner, who may be subject to corporal sanctions that are prohibited with criminal prisoners, and even more so when the body belongs to an administrative detainee, whose entire incarcerated existence is neither defined nor temporally limited by any clear verdict or legislation. It is only these cases that are relevant for any discussion on force-feeding, because in all other cases of abstinence from food by inmates, the Patient's Rights Law and the ethics committees it establishes provide sufficient answers to any questions about forceful corporal interventions. As the Correction demonstrates in its essentially crude attempt to solve a political wrong by granting unusual judicial authority, when life and body are subject to disciplinary and normalizing force in the context of political/security imprisonment or administrative detention, this manifestation of force cannot be fully explained through normative bioethical and legal rationalizations. It therefore necessitates directly addressing its political essence.

Those opposing the Correction demand a political commitment that does not hide behind bioethical legislation. The argument presented in this chapter appears to favor the position of those opponents of the Correction. However, their position is wrong both in promoting equal treatment of inmates and free citizens and in adhering to the popular conception of the hunger-striking inmate as the weakest political agent whose body and life are at the mercy of the sovereign. The biopolitical conceptualization of the living body as the battleground of political power rejects this conception and views the hunger-striking inmate as an active and potent agent. This occurs by applying the somatic emphasis of biopolitics to the refusal to eat. Resisting the material conditions necessary for life and bodily existence thus becomes a way to demand improvements to the conditions in which the inmate's living body is incarcerated and to claim what is needed in order to return to the realm of life that is protected, even under incarceration, by such bioethical norms as the ones ensured by the Patient's Rights Law.

Furthermore, understanding the administrative detainee as the archetypical figure in the context of this analysis is clearer when examining the detainee in relation to his or her dying body and impending death. The end of life is the horizon of bodily existence that enables the combination of biopolitical power and sovereign power to operate on the subject's life through the implicit and deferred threat of death. Since the temporality of the life of the administrative detainee is the potentially unlimited time of what Butler called "indefinite detention," biopolitical control over the detainee's body and life is maximal. The detainee's life and body are suspended in a way that gives any personal embodiment of the sovereign government, from the prison guard to the prime minister, the prerogative to subject the detainee to direct bare force. In contrast, when an administrative detainee goes on a hunger strike, he or she compels the state and all representatives of disciplinary power to address his or her condition and demands according to a new strict timetable. This new timetable no longer adheres to the artificial, linear, and objective schedule of legal procedures that the sovereign can defer or hasten at will, but rather is dictated by the subjective biological time that is literally embodied in the detainee's dying body. Thus, precisely because the administrative detainee is subjected to the strongest and most explicit form of the sovereign government's disciplinary power, he or she succeeds in protesting and resisting this power on the practical level by hunger striking. This also exposes the political nature of force-feeding, as well as its essential unjustifiability on the theoretical level according to bioethical and medical arguments.

Clearly, these inferences and the biopolitical conceptualizations on which they draw cannot provide solutions to all the questions and problems involved with the attempt to create a constant normative paradigm regarding force-feeding hunger-striking inmates in Israeli prisons, nor will they result in a revision of the relevant definitions in the Prison Law and in its Correction. This study has explored and examined the theoretical difficulties, political agendas, and conceptual gaps involved in trying to create a legal discourse of rights and autonomy about this purportedly bioethical dilemma. Its conclusions suggest that examining this dilemma through a biopolitical lens might extricate the debate from its current impasse and allow it to address the genuine legal, ethical, and political complexities involved in the force-feeding of hunger-striking inmates.

References
Israeli Supreme Court Rulings

3267/12 Khlakhala vs. IDF Commander in Judea and Samaria
5304/15 Israel Medical Association et al. vs. Israeli Knesset et al.
5441/15 Mizan (organization for human rights) et al. vs. Israeli Knesset et al.
5575;5580/15 Mohammad Allaan vs. Israeli Security Service et al.
5994/15 Physicians for Human Rights et al. vs. the State of Israel
452 /16 Mohammad al-Qiq vs. IDF Commander in Judea and Samaria et al.

Newspaper Articles

Bob, Yonah J. Second Jewish Detainee Joins Hunger Strike. *Jerusalem Post*, January 26, 2016.

Cohen, Gili and Efrati, Ido. Iron Dome Batteries Deployed in Ashdod and Beer Sheba Out of Fear of Escalation Should the Hunger Striker Die. *Haaretz*, August 20, 2015.

Efrati, Ido. The Dilemma of Mohammed Allaan's Physicians: What to Do When the Patient Wants to Live but Is Willing to Die. *Haaretz*, August 15, 2015.

Khoury, Jackie. Slated for Release from Israeli Jail after 14 Years, Palestinian Gets Six More Months Without Trial. *Haaretz*, June 15, 2016.

Khoury, Jackie, Polver, Sharon, and Efrati, Ido. The Supreme Court Authorized Force-Feeding of Hunger-Striking Security Prisoners. *Haaretz*, September 11, 2016.

Documents, Reports, Letters, and Evaluation Papers (Hebrew)

Feurstein, Ophir. *Without Trial: Administrative Detention of Palestinian by Israel and the Law Regarding the Incarceration of Illegal Combatants*. Jerusalem: B'Tzelem and the Center for the Defence of the Individual, 2009.

Israeli Medical Association. Position Paper about the Correction to the Prison Law Regarding Force-Feeding, June 2014a.

Israeli Medical Association. Guide to Physicians Treating Hunger Striking Prisoners/Detainees, June 2014b.

Karmon, Garciela et al. Letter from Physicians for Human Rights to the Israeli Attorney General, July 15, 2013.

Kremnitzer, Mordechai et al. Draft of the Correction to the Israeli Prison Law 2014: An Evaluation Submitted by Members of the Israel Democracy Institute to the Ministerial Committee on Lawmaking, May 15, 2014.

National Bioethics Council. A Response to the Intention to Correct the Prison Law in Regards to Force-Feeding Hunger-Striking Inmates, April 6, 2014.

Nizri, Raz. Reply to Garciela Carmon et al. Letter from the Deputy Attorney General, September 2, 2013.

Wygoda, Michael. Force-Feeding a Hunger-Striking Inmate. Evaluation Paper. Department of Jewish Law in the Israel Ministry of Justice, April 28, 2013.

Academic Works

Agamben, Giorgio. *Homo Sacer: Sovereign Power and Bare Life* (Heller-Roazen, D., trans.). Stanford, CA: Stanford University Press, 1998.

Bargu, Banu. *Starve and Immolate: The Politics of Human Weapons*. New York: Columbia University Press, 2014.

Brockman, Bea. Food Refusal in Prisoners: A Communication or a Method of Self-Killing? The Role of the Psychiatrist and Resulting Ethical Challenges, *Journal of Medical Ethics* 25 (1999).

Butler, Judith. *Precarious Life: The Powers of Mourning and Violence*. London: Verso, 2006.

Feldman, Allen. *Formations of Violence: The Narrative of the Body and Political Terror in Northern Ireland*. Chicago: University of Chicago Press, 1991.

Foucault, Michel. *Discipline and Punish: The Birth of the Prison* (Sheridan, A., trans.). New York: Vintage, 1977.

The History of Sexuality Vol. 1 (Hurley, R., trans.). New York: Pantheon Books, 1978.

The Subject and Power, in *Essential Works of Foucault (1954–1984): Vol. 3: Power* (Hurley, R. et al., trans). New York: New Press, 2001.

Society Must Be Defended (Macey, D., trans.). New York: Picador, 2003.

Security Territory Population: Lectures at the College de France 1977–1978 (Burchell, G., trans.). New York: Picador, 2007.

Foucault, Michel and Deleuze, Gilles. Intellectuals and Power, in *Language, Counter-Memory, Practice*. Ithaca, NY: Cornell University Press, 1977.

Foucault, Michel et al. Création d'une groupe d'information sur les prisons. *Esprit* (Mars. 1971), pp. 531–532 (Elden, S., trans.) at: progressivegeographies.com/2013/08/02/manifesto-of-the-groupe-dinformation-sur-les-pri sons-a-full-translation.

Goldin, Sigal. Is Anorexia a Hunger Strike? Sociological Notes on Self-Starvation and Force Feeding of Eating Disorders Patients. Edmond J. Safra Center conf. Dec. 2014 (in Hebrew).

Grant, Kevin. British Suffragettes and the Russian Method of Hunger Strike, *Comparative Studies in Society and History*, 53.1 (2011), 113–143.

Gross, Aeyal and Feldman, Tamar. "We Didn't Want to Hear the Word Calories": Rethinking Food Security, Food Power, and Food Sovereignty – Lessons from the Gaza Closure, *Berkeley Journal of International Law* 33.2 (2015), 379–441.

Guenther, Lisa. Political Action at the End of the World: Hannah Arendt and the California Prison Hunger Strikes, *Canadian Journal of Human Rights* 4.1 (2015), 33–56.

Hoffman, Marcelo. *Foucault and Power: The Influence of Political Engagement on Theories of Power*. London: Bloomsbury, 2013.

Johnston, Valerie. *Diets in Workhouses and Prisons*. New York: Garland, 1985.

Koopman, Colin. Conduct and Power: Foucault's Methodological Expansions in 1971, in *Active Intolerance: Michel Foucault, the Prisons Information Group, and the Future of Abolition*. Zurn, Perry and Zilts, Andrew (eds.). London: Palgrave Macmillan, 2015.

Macey, David. *The Lives of Michel Foucault*. London: Random House, 1993.

Miller, James. *The Passion of Michel Foucault*. Cambridge, MA: Harvard University Press, 2000.

Monod, Jean-Claude. *Foucault et la police des conduits*. Paris: Michalon, 1997.

Nashef, Esmail. Towards a Materialist Reading of Political Imprisonment in Palestine, in *Threat: Palestinian Political Prisoners in Israel*. Baker, Abeer and Matar, Anat (eds.). London: Pluto, 2011, 25–36.

O'Keeffe, Terence. Suicide and Self-Starvation, *Philosophy* 59.229 (1984), 349–363.

Reyes, Hernan. Force-Feeding and Coercion: No Physician Complicity, *American Medical Association Journal of Ethics* 9.10 (2007), 703–708.

Rosenfeld, Maya. 2011. The Centrality of the Prisoners' Movement to the Palestinian Struggle against the Israeli Occupation: A Historical Perspective, in *Threat: Palestinian Political Prisoners in Israel*, 3–24.

Thompson, Edward et al. Fasting Prisoners and Compulsory Feeding, *The British Medical Journal* 2.2546 (1909), 1191–1193.
Thompson, Kevin. Forms of Resistance: Foucault on Tactical Reversal and Self-Formation, *Continental Philosophy Review* 36:2 (2003), 11–38.
Vernon, James. *Hunger: A Modern History*. Cambridge, MA: Harvard University Press, 2007.
Ziarek, Ewa P. Bare Life on Strike: Notes on the Biopolitics of Race and Gender, *South Atlantic Quarterly* 107.1 (2008), 89–105.

4

A Cognitive Dissonant Health System: Can We Combat Racism without Admitting It Exists?

Hadas Ziv

In the course of my work with Physicians for Human Rights-Israel (PHRI), I have heard from individuals of the pain and anger they carry as a result of their encounters with the medical community. In many accounts, it was clear that this harmful conduct was based on a stereotyped perception held by the medical community as to their culture. Indeed, affairs that I thought mainly of a historical interest showed themselves relevant to the lives of the second and third generations of those communities who were injured by the medical community. Moreover, even if some communities are no longer seen in a stereotyped manner as they were absorbed into the consensus, others new and old are still the victims of racist and paternalistic attitudes. I base my chapter on my meetings with victims of such conduct because it is to them that I owe my better understanding of current power relationships and racism in Israel today and their connections to its early years' racism toward new immigrants, especially those arriving from Middle Eastern countries. I focus my chapter on the special role the medical community and institutions take in the "nation-building" project where their attitudes toward the inclusion or exclusion of different communities were manifested.

To discuss this phenomenon, I will describe several well-known affairs in the relationships between the medical community and new immigrants to Israel, mainly from Asia and Africa, and Palestinian citizens of Israel: the involvement of medical personnel in the abduction of Yemenite, Mizrahi, and Balkan children; the subscription of Depo-Provera contraceptives to Ethiopian women; and the segregation of women in maternity wards according to their ethnicity.

I will present factors that caused harm to the community while examining whether the situation was a unique momentary failure or rather a systemic and structural one. An examination of the medical teams' conduct both in real time and later (sometimes decades later) will enable the identification of the exclusion mechanisms and barriers that impact the various communities in Israel.

The medical establishment usually denies the dimension of racism or claims that the cases in question are individual and self-contained. However, a historic review of the attitude of the health care system toward disempowered populations shows that not only are expressions of racism not limited to individual health care workers, but systemic expressions recur again and again in the history of medicine in Israel as in other countries' past or present.[1]

Why Racism: There is more emphasis in research, but also in our daily work, on socioeconomic status "as an underlying factor in the pervasive disparities in health observed for racial/ethnic minority populations."[2] However, as Shavers rightly states, "little information or consideration seems to be given to the social history and prevailing social climate that contribute to racial/ethnic socioeconomic disparities namely, the role of racism/racial discrimination." Thus, we often overlook the effect racism had and has in creating these disparities in the first place, by discriminating against minorities in education, housing, and employment, and influencing the way they are treated by the legal and medical systems.[3] These socioeconomic disparities and political conditions produce and racialize inequalities in health in the first place[4] and must be addressed if we wish to close those gaps.

Racism in the Medical Community: When talking about racism in the medical community, a lot of attention was put into the scientific discourse, enabled by medicine and its interest in genetics. Indeed, much was written of the history of doctors and their part in eugenic projects. Past traumas led to new codes of ethics restoring the image of the medical profession. Less attention was given to the self-image of the medical community as a hurdle in combating racism, to the fact that racism persists in the health system exactly because it is *the* space, *the professional community* that vows to carry the values of humanism and equality. Though it sounds self-contradictory, I claim that because the medical community stresses its ethic mission and ethos, because it was educated to believe that it is above or beyond social conflicts, it finds it harder to admit that it is part of and thus similar to the structures of any given society. The leadership of the medical community backs its denial of racism by saying that there is no policy that supports it. What I will try to show is that there is a conduct and atmosphere that allows racism in the health system, and that there is certainly no policy to truly fight it. Directors of hospitals boast of the wonderful relationship among their staff members of different ethnic origins – but are oblivious to the fact that the existing power relationships are based on the silence of the minority, that what they hold as "consensus" as a given "fact" is to others a question. This "chosen

---

[1] See, for example, Shvarts, Shifra, Davidovitch, Nadav, Seidelman, Rhona, and Goldberg, Avishai, "Medical Selection and the Debate over Mass Immigration in the New State of Israel (1948–1951)," *CBMH/BCHM* 22.1 (2005), pp. 5–34. They clearly say that a large number of historical works indicates how thin the line can be between scientific and objective criteria and unfounded prejudices and racism.
[2] Shavers, Vickie L. and Shavers, Brenda S., "Racism and Health Inequity among Americans," *Journal of the National Medical Association*, 98.3 (2006).
[3] Ibid.
[4] Metzl, Jonathan M. and Hansen, Helena, "Structural Competency: Theorizing a New Medical Engagement with Stigma and Inequality," *Social Science & Medicine*, 103 (2014), pp. 126–133.

ignorance," almost a value in their eyes, is part of what enables the institutional racism, as I will describe later, and is a major obstacle to change both past failures and current misconduct.

As I hope to make clear in this discussion, the affairs I am to describe manifest institutional racism of a health system that accepts the racist assumptions held by the general society. Since such claims are met with denial, let me explain what I mean by racism, and why I insist on using it to describe the conduct of the medical community in those affairs I discuss.

I wish to emphasize that I do not describe here manifestations of racism by individual medical personnel – although those are certainly there – but rather the institutional racism, "the collective failure of an organization to provide an appropriate and professional service to people because of their color, culture, or ethnic group."[5] Of course the more individuals identify with racist positions and attitudes the more it will be difficult to struggle against, but it is the institutional racism that allows and legitimizes the individual one, and it is the institutional racism that silences – softly or aggressively – any claims against it.

Also, denial of racism in the affairs I discuss is based on the claim that those affairs cannot be held as racist because there was no claim of genetic superiority but a cultural one. But, as powerfully argued, racism inscribes itself in practices, in discourses, and in representations. And if so, acts are more important than the doctrine behind them.[6] It is thus that we must ask if indeed we should "attach so much importance to justifications which continue to retain the same structure (that of denial of rights) while moving from the language of religion into that of science, or from the language of biology into the discourses of culture or history, when in practice these justifications simply lead to the same old acts."[7]

While racism in our society is discussed openly,[8] racism in the health system is much more evasive. This is first and foremost because the medical community refuses to admit its institutional existence, wishing to keep its positive – or at least neutral – image as an island of sanity in a troubled society. As I will show later in the discussion on segregation in maternity wards, even when admitting that there is a separation according to ethnic origin, the leadership of the medical community insists on presenting it in terms of "cultural sensitivity" or "responsiveness to customers'/patients' requests." But this is already a step forward, as at least there was some agreement as to the fact of segregation. Usually, the medical community is caught in what one may term as a cognitive dissonance. Its members know racism is unacceptable, and so when faced with complaints, they tend to deny them altogether. As

---

[5] Bhugra, Dinesh and Ayonrinde, Oyedeji, "Racism, Racial Life Events and Mental Ill Health," *Advances in Psychiatric Treatment*, 7 (2001), pp. 343–349.
[6] Balibar, Etienne, "Is There 'Neo-racism?'" *Race, Nation, Class: Ambiguous Identities* (Etienne & Wallerstein), Verso 1991, p. 17.
[7] Ibid., p. 18.
[8] See, for example, www.fightracism.org/Article.asp?aid=203, for racist talk by public figures, and for racism in social media http://www.fightracism.org/Article.asp?aid=393 (Hebrew).

a result, racism is almost not discussed. It is exactly this dismissal, this unwillingness to discuss it, that enables racism to persist, "because beliefs and attitudes that are not blatantly racist but result in racist behavior or outcomes are often not perceived to be racist," because "racism thrives on denial."[9]

Allowing our health system to avoid discussing its racism enables racism's horrendous implications to go on – blaming the victims for their poor health results, scientifically justifying the system's conduct using professional discourse that deliberately excludes patients and dismisses their claims, and not changing the way we educate our future medical personnel or ensuring their diversity. The following discussion will describe the way institutional racism operates, and how denial and silencing not only allow its operation, but exacerbates its horrendous implications.

BETWEEN THE ABDUCTION OF YEMENITE, MIZRAHI, AND BALKAN CHILDREN AND THE SUBSCRIPTION OF DEPO-PROVERA CONTRACEPTIVES TO ETHIOPIAN WOMEN

In Israel's first years, several severe affairs occurred in which the medical community was involved that left residues of mistrust and pain among the injured communities. Perhaps the most famous of these is the affair of **the Abduction of Yemenite, Mizrahi, and Balkan children.** Between the years 1948 and 1954, more than 50,000 Jews immigrated to Israel from Yemen and were sent to transit camps. Numerous testimonies have accumulated from those years about the abduction of infants and babies from the community, with one out of every eight Yemenite babies[10] being taken away from their parents without the parents knowing what happened to them. The parents were told their children had died, but in many cases, the children were given up for adoption or transferred to institutions. The health care system and arguments based on medical principles played a key role in the abductions.

While writing this chapter, I called Amram – an NGO of Mizrahi (Middle Eastern Jews) activists collecting testimonies[11] from parents of abducted children and advocating for official recognition of the affair. I asked Amram's representative how many of the testimonies they have collected speak about the involvement of health personnel. She did not even hesitate before she answered, "all of them." From the testimonies collected, one can discern a pattern: the young parents were asked to

---

[9] Shavers and Shavers, "Racism and Health Inequity among Americans," p. 387.
[10] Sangero, Boaz, "Where There Is No Suspicion There Is No Real Investigation: The Report of the Committee of Inquiry into the Disappearance of the Children of Jewish Yemenite Immigrants to Israel in 1948–1954" (Hebrew), *Theory and Criticism*, 2002, available only in Hebrew. Abstract: http://theory-and-criticism.vanleer.org.il/En/Where+There+Is+No+Suspicion+There+Is+No+Real+Investigation+The+Report+of+the+Committee+of+Inquiry+into+the+Disappearance+of+the+Children+of+Jewish+Yemenite+Immigrants+to+Israel+in+1948-1954_h_hd_308_22.aspx.
[11] www.edut-amram.org/.

move their children from the tents of the absorption camps to the children's homes, the reason being that the camps were dangerous to the children's health. Sometimes they were told they must be moved to hospitals far from the camps. In many cases, nurses and doctors told them that the babies they visited and who had looked vivid and healthy had died during the night. They were not allowed to see the bodies or to know where the graves were. In several cases, babies were returned following a strong protest by the parents.

At the official commission of inquiry, several nurses and social workers testified that they transferred healthy children in ambulances from the children's homes to hospitals. In a nurse's testimony on the children's home in the transit camp of Ein Shemer,[12] the abduction of children is associated with a visit of a mission from abroad:

> A foreign group, speaking English or French, stayed at Ein Shemer for about two weeks, during which many children disappeared. Almost every day one or two children disappeared. The children were usually healthy. . . . When I finished my shift they were healthy, when I came back the next day children were missing from their beds. . . . I asked the next day why the children were not in their beds and I was told the children had developed a fever and been transferred to Rambam Hospital in Haifa. And anyone who went to Haifa never came back.[13]

A rare voice of protest is found in a letter from Dr. Lichtig, then the head of the Department of Hospitals in the Ministry of Health, to the governmental hospitals in Haifa, Pardes Katz, Sarafand, and Dajani, dated April 21, 1950. Its subject is "returning six children received from the camps":

> There have been cases that children left the hospitals without being returned to their parents. There were apparently quick-moving people who were interested in adopting children. The "bereaved" parents looked for their children and they were gone. There is no need to explain and emphasize that we must make every effort to prevent the recurrence of such cases. . . . The camp administration will be responsible for the return of the children to their parents since it is also responsible for sending them to the hospital.[14]

Yet such documents and many other testimonies were not enough to lead to an earnest investigation. The painful affair came up again when the parents received mobilization orders for their children (calls for mandatory military service), the very children the state had claimed died years ago. The various commissions that were set up in the wake of public pressure all acted in service of the state's attempt to present

---

[12] Ein Shemer is a *kibbutz* in the north of Israel.
[13] Zayed, Shoshi, *The Child Is Gone: The Yemenite Children Affair*. Jerusalem: Gefen, 2001 (Hebrew).
[14] Hatuka, Shlomi, "The Tragedy of the Lost Yemenite Children: In the Footsteps of the Adoptees," *Haokets* (2014). www.haokets.org/2013/10/04/%D7%A4%D7%A8%D7%A9%D7%AA-%D7%99%D7%9C%D7%93%D7%99-%D7%AA%D7%99%D7%9E%D7%9F-%D7%9E%D7%A1%D7%A2-%D7%91%D7%A2%D7%A7%D7%91%D7%95%D7%AA-%D7%94%D7%98%D7%A8%D7%92%D7%93%D7%99%D7%94-%D7%A9%D7%9C-%D7%94%D7%9E/.

the affair as one to which no factual basis had been found, and that was not the result of a systemic failure. "An analysis of the report indicates that the commission's attitude toward the severe acts of commission and omission, some of them enumerated in its pages, is forgiving in the extreme. Thus, for example, even the destruction of archives under its very nose, while the commission was at work in recent years, does not set off an alarm for its members and does not give rise to discussion of suspicion."[15] Different testimonies support this assertion and show how the commission never bothered to find those witnesses that a journalist with fewer resources talked to.[16]

Several factors stand out in this affair:

- **The medical community's conduct was governed by a stereotyped perception as to the ability of Mizrahi/Yemenite parents to raise and educate their children and of the nature and quality of their parenthood.** Indeed, such attitude was quite prevalent in the medical community toward different communities. In Israel, Dr. Joseph Meir,[17] a pivotal figure in shaping Israel's public health policy, promoted the ideas of eugenics. At the beginning of the 1950s, he published an article in which he harshly criticized the reproduction prize of 100 lirot[18] that David Ben-Gurion promised to every mother who gave birth to ten children: "we have no interest in the 10th child or even in the seventh in poor families from the East. ... In today's reality we should pray frequently for a second child in a family that is a part of the intelligentsia. The poor classes of the population must not be instructed to have many children, but rather restricted."[19] Dr. Sheba,[20] another prominent medical figure in those years, also reverenced due to his past military position, asserted that "the children live in families with no understanding as to the

---

[15] Sangero, "Where There Is No Suspicion There Is No Real Investigation."
[16] For example, in Tzipi Talmor's documentary *One Way Road* (1993), a woman describes how her baby was taken forcefully from her by a nurse she recognized by name. When the nurse is approached by Talmor in her documentary, she refuses to even answer. In another article, a testimony is brought about of a woman who was told her daughter had died when she came to take her from Rambam Hospital, but when, together with a Yemenite nurse, she went up to the department, she found her (see Mashiah, Yigal, "The Disappearance of Yemenite Children: An Organized Scam or Criminal Negligence?" *Haaretz*, September 5, 1997 (Hebrew). www.haaretz.co.il/yemenite-children/1.2919123).
[17] Dr. Joseph Meir was the director of the Clalit Health Maintenance Organization from 1928 until the establishment of the State of Israel, and the director general of the Ministry of Health from 1949 to 1950.
[18] Israel's currency at the time.
[19] Traubmann, Tamara, "Do Not Have Children if They Won't Be Healthy," *Haaretz*, June 11, 2004. www.haaretz.com/do-not-have-children-if-they-won-t-be-healthy-1.124913.
[20] Sheba commanded the medical corps of Israel's army (IDF) from 1948 to 1950, and then served as the director general of the Ministry of Health until 1953. He later became the director of the Tel HaShomer Hospital, later named in his honor.

care of a child, and there are no chances in the near future for any improvement through guiding these simple people."[21]
- **Complete denial – by the legal, political, and medical leaderships of the complaints of abduction – insinuated that victims' claims are irrational.** Both in real time and for decades later, victims were met with a legal and medical systems that did not seriously look into the complaints, did not earnestly investigate it, or as Prof. Boaz Sangero stated: "when there is no suspicion there is no genuine investigation."[22]
- **Compounded with the trust of the new immigrants in the state, this denial in turn resulted in victims' guilt feelings** – Why didn't we insist and fight back? Why did we trust the medical system? – resulting in shame and silence. This silence is now broken by the third generation of those families.[23]

The recurrent pattern of paternalistic and racist conduct by the medical community toward specific ethnic communities proves that the lessons/morals were not learned. Decades later, the same factors play a role in what is known as **the Depo-Provera affair.** The affair, named after the contraceptive, reveals that racism or treatment "tailored" to a particular community continues to exist, based on a distorted social perception implemented in medical practice. Note that Depo-Provera[24] is an approved contraceptive. However, it is not commonly used and is not offered to most patients. Therefore, the thrust of the following criticism is over the way it was presented and given to Ethiopian women.

The affair was first exposed in 2008 in an article in the *Yedioth Ahronoth* daily newspaper[25] describing a policy of extensive prescription of Depo-Provera for Ethiopian women in several locations. Following the report, a study was conducted by Hedva Eyal[26] for the Isha L'Isha, a feminist organization, and was later described in a report by investigative journalist Gal Gabbay.[27] These and other sources paint a picture of sweeping use of this contraceptive for Ethiopian women in such a way that did not allow them to make an informed choice out of the variety of contraceptives available in Israel. The report showed that after coming to Israel, there was a steep decline in their birthrate. For instance, among fifty-seven Ethiopian families living

---

[21] Sheba, meeting of the Public Council for Immigration (Aliyah) Issues, Jerusalem, July 10, 1952.
[22] Sangero, "Where There Is No Suspicion There Is No Real Investigation."
[23] Shame is a recurrent theme in many testimonies. See www.edut-amram.org/testimonies/toval-madmon/ (Hebrew).
[24] Depo-Provera is an approved contraceptive. However, its consumers' leaflet says that the contraceptive is for use "when there is a medical indication for contraception and other contraceptives cannot be used for that purpose." Retrieved February 20, 2016 from www.old.health.gov.il/units/pharmacy/trufot/alonim/Depo-Provera_sus_for_inj_PL_Heb_1439973347725.pdf.
[25] Abba, Dani A., "Neighborhoods Without Babies," *Yedioth Ahronoth*, January 6, 2008 (Hebrew).
[26] Eyal, Hedva, *Depo Provera: A Contraceptive Method Given via Injection – A Report on its Prescription Policy among Women of the Ethiopian Community in Israel*, 2009, Isha L'Isha and Kvinna till Kvinna.
[27] Gabbay, Gal, *Vacum*, December 6, 2012, Educational TV (Hebrew).

in the Pardes Katz neighborhood of Bnei Brak, there was only one birth in three years.

Just like in the abduction of Yemenite children, similar factors were at work here:

- **The medical community's conduct manifested a stereotyped attitude about Ethiopian parents and their ability to raise, provide for, and educate their children.** This was manifested by doctors' choice to prescribe Depo-Provera for Ethiopian women in absorption centers in a sweeping manner. It is also quite clear from their professional union's reaction following the protest:

> "Women [of] Ethiopian origin have a higher tendency to use Depo-Provera, as this is the prevalent contraceptive in the country of origin. It should be noted – in relation to the prevalent contraceptives in Israel, that the IUD (Intrauterine Device) is hardly known in Ethiopia, and few are the women [who] use the pills there. In any case, Depo-Provera is anyway a contraceptive safer to health than the pill."

This statement makes one wonder why – if it is indeed so safe and recommended – none of my friends have ever heard of it, or been offered it. It also stands in contradiction to the consumers' leaflet recommending its usage when "other contraceptives cannot be used."

- **The medical community's demonstrated prejudice as to Ethiopian women and their ability to make an informed and independent choice as to the contraceptives they use, or to follow the pills' regime.**

ESCORT:	Do a lot of women come here to get it?
CLALIT EMPLOYEE:	Uh-huh.
ESCORT:	Yes? Ethiopian women or ... only Ethiopian women?
CLALIT EMPLOYEE:	(nods) Some, but mainly Ethiopian women, because they forget, and they don't know, and the explanations are difficult for them. So it's best that they get one shot every three months. And for three months they are calm, and so are we, supposedly, because actually they don't understand anything.[28]

Although the employee is not of the medical profession, she does describe the reality of what happens in that clinic, and reflects the general attitude maybe more honestly than if one would have asked the doctor himself.

- **Denial**: Again, the complaints of a tailored treatment were met with complete denial by most of the medical community (exceptions will be presented later in this chapter). Following several MKs' request, the state

[28] Recorded with a candid camera and shown on TV: www.youtube.com/watch?v=pSOolTmYpc (Hebrew only).

comptroller decided to investigate the affair. Although unable to receive information from the American Jewish Joint Distribution official involved in the family-planning program in Ethiopia, and although he did not meet any of the women who testified to receiving the Depo-Provera, he still exempted the system from having such a "policy" – and thus from any responsibility.[29]

MECHANISMS OF DENIAL AND DISMISSAL AND THE NATURE OF KNOWING

When met with the communities' complaint or worries, the medical community reacts with a mixture of denials, using professional discourse that derides the claims, and even attacks those who protest. Its perception and ethos of its profession as nondiscriminatory, committed to social justice,[30] scientific, and humanistic makes it almost incapable of listening to such accusations. I will detail some of these attempted discussions so I can later explore what actions are recommended if we wish to change this power balance for the benefit of both patients and healers.

When addressed with a request by Amram and PHRI for a meeting to discuss the abduction of Yemenite children, the nurses' ethics chamber responded by passing the focus from a moral and ethical discussion to a legal one, from one that focuses on the medical community to one that should take place in the legal field:

> I would state that the issue is painful and sensitive, but we have no ability to examine it. We know that the issue was discussed and testimonies collected. If you have any reservations as to the treatment of the issue, it is only appropriate that you will appeal to the suitable courts.

This response serves to highlight that – according to their opinion – there is no special role for the nurses in this affair, or in the much-needed process for recognition and healing. To stress this even further, and even fend off responsibility, the "we have no knowledge" claim comes next:

> As to the involvement of nursing personnel, no testimonies to such involvement were brought to us.

---

[29] The report is not available publicly, but some of it was given to journalists. See Yaron, Lee, "No Evidence That Ethiopian-Israeli Were Forced to Take Birth-Control Shot, Comptroller Says," *Haaretz*, January 20, 2016. www.haaretz.com/israel-news/.premium-1.698394.

[30] Brennan, Troy and others (Members of the Medical Professionalism Project: ABIM Foundation), "Medical Professionalism in the New Millennium: A Physician Charter," *Annals of Internal Medicine*, 136.3 (2002).

Lingering on the past for one sentence, the letter immediately comes back to the present, as if telling us that history belongs to the past, and their (and maybe ours?) focus should lie with the present and future:

> Furthermore, today there is much more awareness of the issue among professionals. Any action related to child adoption or to taking them out of their families is made according to the law, and is characterized by high sensitivity and professionalism.[31]

This for me symbolizes a reluctance to deal with the past and dwarfing it with a supposedly spotless present. Indeed, there was a lot of progress in the legal situation concerning the decision to take children out of their homes, but, even if the present was perfect (and it isn't), one would expect from those whose profession is to heal an understanding that a first necessary step for healing is recognition.

The Israeli Medical Association did not respond to the request for months (for its late response, see later in this chapter). Yet the former chairperson of the ethics committee was interviewed on the issue on Reshet Bet (Israel Public Radio).[32] I wish to explore this interview in some detail as an example of dismissal in the guise of acceptance.

The medical community enjoys a prestige of professionalism, holding knowledge that nonprofessionals cannot have access to. In the interview, the speaker plays with this notion, and takes for granted that his professional authority will serve him, and his point of view, even on matters he knows nothing about. And yet when he wishes to undermine the facts presented to him, he meticulously sheds this authority and states he does not have the required knowledge to assert what the truth is.

The speaker begins by admitting he is not in possession of the required knowledge:

> Of course **I don't have any knowledge** of what really happened. It goes back to my early childhood.

Indeed, how can he be expected to have a clear position in a reality **he** perceives of competing opinions?

> I don't know what **really** happened. On the one hand there are very harsh accusations, on the other very sweeping denials.

However, the speaker's claim for knowledge changes when it comes "home" to the medical community. It is now that knowledge does exist (even if of poor nature by his own claim):

---

[31] The original letter (in Hebrew) is at PHRI, January 28, 2016.
[32] www.iba.org.il/bet/?entity=1166974&type=1, June 25, 2016 (Hebrew).

> **I do know** from what I learnt in retrospect and remember vaguely from my years as a child in Haifa, that the State in those years was a State in formation, the *balagan* [mess] – if I am allowed to use this term – … was very big. So I wish to believe – maybe naively – that there was no order, a mess. Whether there was an orderly plan, a real calculated move, initiated, clear and intentional of abducting children, this is a thing the mind cannot bear. (my emphases)

Suddenly childhood is not used to claim no possibility of having knowledge, but is recollected, somewhat nostalgically, to serve as a claim for being there, for having the permission to claim somehow "knowing."

But the claim for his knowledge is not enough to undermine the accusations against the medical community. What is "known" by others is put into question. And so, in a sentence supporting the call for making the protocols public, a doubt is already inscrted as to the existence of such materials:

> IMA should demand the State to expose the protocols [of the investigation committee HZ] **if they really exist**. If there are investigative materials on this issue.

Using the conditional "if," the speaker puts in doubt the very existence of materials, of protocols, thus undermining what is common knowledge. The IMA official and his late response[33] is not so far off from the spirit of this interview. For months, the IMA kept silent; only when the opening of the protocols became a public issue was the IMA finally ready to answer. "It seems that there is no point in having the meeting until the full documents are revealed." This puts the affair – and the IMA's responsibility to make amends as the leadership of the doctors' community – in question. As if without the exposure of all the documents there is nothing to talk about. While I do not underestimate the importance of the documents at all, I do not believe that they hold all the facts. As mentioned before, some of the archives of hospitals were burnt during the first commission of inquiry, whether accidently or intentionally. We also know that all registration and formal documents are held by the same institutions that were involved in the wrongdoing, so it is problematic to condition the meeting on their exposure. Worse, it insinuates that only these official records have access to the "truth," thus not giving respect – or lending an ear – to the testimonies of the victims.

Moreover, the letter goes on to reject the request for a meeting by refuting there is indeed interest in the injured community:

> The Abducted "Yemenite Children" are expected to be today of 60–70 years old. And as far as we know there were no appeals made by these adult men to find their biological parents or to perform genetic exams with the purpose of exposing their roots. When new data will be brought on the issue we shall be happy to meet.

---

[33] Received in PHRI offices on July 18, 2016.

By claiming a lack of interest from the abducted children, the IMA puts in doubt the affair itself and the authenticity of Amram as representing the injured community. This attitude is not due to fear of confronting the establishment, as the IMA did confront it on different matters at the same period,[34] but rather of a concordance with the establishment's views. The scope of this chapter cannot explore the extent to which doctors specifically identify themselves with the image of the nation and how it leads them to reject any claims against it especially if it has to do with its first years – an era tended to be looked at nostalgically.

In regards to the Depo-Provera affair, the response of the medical community was diverse. Certain doctors did state that prescribing this contraceptive was not a common method, although it was legitimate. However, the heads of the system at the time it was first published refused to acknowledge there was a problem of sweeping administration of Depo-Provera to Ethiopian women, and argued that the decision responded to the Ethiopian women's cultural characteristics. The exception was the response received from Prof. Roni Gamzu – the director general of the Ministry of Health and himself a gynecologist (January 20, 2013) – to a letter sent by the coalition of organizations (January 10, 2013) on the use of Depo-Provera.

In his response, the director general refrained from addressing the investigation's findings, but did explicitly order to uphold the ethical guidelines that should have been a clear consensus for the entire medical community: to put an emphasis on giving a woman sufficient and adequate information so she can make an informed consent. However, even though the response was worded carefully, it was enough, along with Health Minister Yael German's support for establishing a parliamentary commission of investigation,[35] to draw the ire of senior members of the medical community. For example, in an especially strong letter protesting the director general's memo and the idea of an investigation, Prof. Daniel Seidman, president of the Israeli Society of Contraception and Sexual Health, and Prof. Moshe Ben-Ami, chairman of the Israeli Society of Obstetrics and Gynecology, asserted that this was unfounded libel.

> Israel's enemies are already hurling heavy accusations at the State of Israel and its doctors as a result of this libel, one that brings to mind dark times in history when Jewish doctors in Europe were subjected to similarly false accusations. The day is not far when Israeli doctors will be afraid to travel abroad lest they be charged with deliberately harming women as a result of an official racist policy by the State of Israel.[36]

Strangely enough, while denying such a policy existed, a professional explanation to this exact policy is given: (1) Depo-Provera is what Ethiopian women tend to use in their country of origin, where there is almost no knowledge of intrauterine device

---

[34] At that time, the IMA was involved in a struggle against a forced-feeding law that the government was supporting.
[35] Knesset Labor, Welfare and Health Committee Meeting, July 10, 2013; see knesset.gov.il/protocols/data/rtf/avoda/2013-07-10.rtf (Hebrew).
[36] Letter from July 14, 2013, available at doctorsonly.co.il/2013/07/61418/ (Hebrew).

(IUD) birth control; (2) it is safer than the pill; and (3) the decrease recorded in birthrate cannot be attributed to the Depo-Provera, but to demographic changes due to immigration. Even more worrying is their objection to the Ministry of Health directive not to give the Depo-Provera automatically to Ethiopian women – something that should be ethically clear to any doctor. Interestingly, following the general director's directive, a decrease of 40 percent in the usage of Depo-Provera was recorded. This in itself supports the claims that when given a choice, the women do not use Depo-Provera. But for the signatories of this letter, who seem to distrust the women's ability to use other contraceptives, it is nothing less than a nightmare of future unwanted pregnancies.

It is worth emphasizing that this letter again uses a mixture of right and wrong so as to block any possible recognition of wrongdoing. Indeed, the reader of this letter can find some truths in it; so is the fact that Depo-Provera is a cheap contraceptive, and so is the claim that Ethiopian women from low socioeconomic status cannot afford some of the other more expensive contraceptives because those are not in the basic basket of services. But all of those are smoke in the eyes of the reader, hiding the simple truth: many simply were not given the chance to make an informed, independent decision.

One should also note the use of nationalist arguments in the letter, turning the violators into victims, and not just any victims, but those of racist blood libels in Jewish history. The signatories to the letter view doctors as synonymous with the nation; therefore, anyone attacking the first necessarily attacks the second. Using nationalistic arguments, whether of security or Israel's image in the world, in the automatic rejection of the charges coming from within the injured community is not unusual. Indeed, it is many times a useful and extremely powerful instrument for hiding information and silencing dissent. This silencing and attempts to quell the complaints of the injured communities leaves the wounds open:

> The rift between the Ministry of Health and members of the community is ongoing. ... The trust is almost irreparable for the simple reason that, if we look at the blood donation affair, and then move 10 years forward from the time [the] first affair came to light in 1996, and then we see in 2006 the second affair, and now the Depo-Provera and the State of Israel, then there is no doubt at all. ... The story cannot be covered by a committee like this. It has to be in a very serious committee.[37]

IF RACISM DEPENDS ON DENIAL, FIGHTING IT DEPENDS ON CALLING IT BY ITS NAME

I wish to conclude with a current struggle PHRI is involved in: segregation in maternity wards. I will use it to examine whether we are improving in the struggle against racism in our health system. By examining the tactics used by the different

[37] MK Pnina Tamano-Shata, Knesset Labor, Welfare and Health Committee Meeting, 2013 (Hebrew).

actors participating, I will try to indicate which tools could be effective in such a struggle.

Persistent reports in the media, followed by a PHRI independent investigation, showed that some maternity wards have an unofficial policy of separating women according to their ethnic origin. Unlike the two previous affairs discussed, where the medical community could manipulatively claim – at least as its starting position – there is not enough evidence (in the Yemenite, Mizrahi, and Balkan children affair due to time passed, in the Depo-Provera affair due to not being able to find the directive, the "smoking gun"), in this affair, denial was almost impossible due to real-time exposures in the media using recorded phone calls and blogs of women consulting which hospitals show "consideration" to requests for separation. But, maybe more significant to our discussion, those interested in denial – and they have tried it – were faced with nurses and doctors from within the system supporting these allegations.

Nevertheless, denial was again the first tactic to be used by the system, giving more weight to the refutations made by directors of hospitals rather than to testimonies recounted by nurses and gynecologists. And so, in response to PHRI complaints, the IMA chairperson answered:[38] "from an inquiry I held with the committee of the union of hospital directors, I found that there is no policy of ethnic segregation in maternity wards in hospitals of Israel." However, assuring us that there is no policy as such, does not lead to the conclusion that in practice there is indeed no separation. Moreover, the IMA did not hold an independent examination as to these complaints and accepted the words of the directors at face value. But apart from fact that the IMA was contented with this shallow examination, and with the lip service to its commitment to "values of equality in the health system," the writer contradicts himself by saying that he learned that "assigning women to the rooms is done according to their medical condition, *while showing consideration to their preferences* as far as can be done" (my emphasis). Needless to say, those preferences to which consideration is shown are sometimes racist in character.

Two weeks later, PHRI received another letter, this time by the chairperson of the ethics committee at the IMA.[39] This one uses a different tactic of denial, arguing that they have no knowledge of such practice, and pays the same lip service to the values of equality.

In addition to the correspondence, a meeting was held between the IMA and PHRI and was attended by the IMA chairperson and ethics committee chairperson, and three women representatives from PHRI – a doctor, a midwife, and myself. In the face of testimonies from the doctor and the midwife that such a practice exists, the chairperson of the ethics committee phoned a director of a hospital in Jerusalem who refuted the allegations. The conclusion was that if

---

[38] IMA chairperson's letter to PHRI, April 24, 2013.
[39] IMA chairperson of ethics committee letter to PHRI, May 8, 2013.

there is an argument on the facts – whether there is or is not a practice of segregation – they cannot do anything. This goes in line with their inconclusive written responses to our appeals. For sure, the IMA could have chosen an alternative way, doing a more in-depth check, and taking upon itself to work against racism in our health system. For example, in changing the way doctors are educated, to include in their curriculum awareness of the social and economic conditions that work to the disadvantage of minorities, and the way this is reproduced within the medical system itself. They could think less of closing ranks around their members and engage in a discussion with civil society to advance equality. They could be far more outspoken against institutional racism, as they were in other struggles of ethics such as against forced feeding.

And yet, although there is still a long way to go in this struggle, we are, relatively speaking, on better grounds in this case (comparing with the two previous ones) due to two factors:

a) **It is out in the public:** Women who support and ask for segregation are open about it; they use social media to ask and report which hospitals are more favorable to their "requests" to be in a room without Arabs. These demands are openly discussed in the public media and receive support from the openly racist MK Smutrich and his defenders[40] and are thus not contested so much on the factual basis, at least not in the public discussion. Indeed, it is easier to discuss racism and the struggle against it when it is not guised in the pretense of cultural sensitivity as some in the medical community tried to do. Interestingly, the public nature of the discussion reveals its bottom-up racism – patients' requests for segregation are met with a system that enables the practice. This is different from the two other affairs characterized by top-down racism of a system that initiated the "tailored" treatment.

b) **Testimonies from within the medical community:** Nurses and doctors themselves testified that such a practice does exist. Attempts by others from within the system to deny it are easily invalidated even in their own accounts as I shall demonstrate.

It is worth exploring the public debate in the Knesset committee[41] to see how the ethos of the medical system is being contested with its reality.

First, let me explore a quite remarkable testimony by a young doctor, Dr. Lina Kassem:

---

[40] MK Smutrich and his wife claimed that, given the sanctity of birth, it is only natural to want to be served by a Jewish midwife, and to wish not to be next to our enemies. See, for example, Rosen, Yisrael, "A Public Defense of MK Betzalel Smutrich and the Maternity Wards," Zomet Institute website. www.zomet.org.il/eng/?CategoryID=160&ArticleID=9171.

[41] Knesset Committee on the Status of Women and Gender Equality, Segregation in Maternity Wards in Hospitals, April 13, 2016. https://oknesset.org/committee/meeting/12249/ (Hebrew only).

> I started my way as an intern in women's health. ... I wish to reflect [on] what happens in Shaarei Zedek Hospital. ... I was also in Mt. Scopus in my internship where there is clear segregation in the maternity ward, the rooms of the Arabs are not mixed with [the] rooms of Jews. The midwife calls the nurse in the ward after the birth, and tells her I refer you [to] a "speaker" [not a Hebrew speaker] which is a code = at least in Mt. Scopus. ... for an Arab. ... It is true that the policy of the hospital is not supportive of racism, and I did not personally encounter racism, but the general atmosphere among midwives and nurses in the wards is blatantly racist especially in Shaarei Zedek. I invite you to spend a night in the labor rooms and listen to the talks. They do not call a woman by her name at all, they call her: the Ethiopian, the Arab, the Russian – this is the general atmosphere. An Arab woman [who] comes from East Jerusalem to give birth in Shaarei Zedek is [met] with [an attitude characterized by] many stereotypes and [by] prejudice. They assign them to the rooms at the end of the corridor, ... I wish to share with you an experience: a midwife brings a new Arab baby to the babies' room, and the nurses tell her: what, you brought another terrorist?

Although Dr. Kassem says that there is no policy of segregation, I believe her testimony does not contradict my insistence on structural racism. This is because structural racism does not need a public or a written policy. In many respects, it even operates better without it. Its existence in the gray zone allows for its denial, and so it is harder to pinpoint and uproot. The answer of Prof. HaLevi, the director of the hospital mentioned earlier, demonstrates this:

> [I]f the honorable doctor, in her short internship in Shaarei Zedek, would have come to my office and [said]: "this is what I heard from a staff member," not only ... would [we] not allow it to pass, I [would] have reacted severely up to dismissing this person.

The account of Dr. Kassem is extremely personal and honest. She comes across as a full persona – a woman, a doctor, an Israeli citizen, a Palestinian – and she recounts her experience as a young intern, as a woman in a maternity ward, in a very open way. However, this exposure enables her rebuke by her senior using his seniority and adopting a male chauvinistic discourse. This response is completely oblivious (whether aware or unaware) to the power gap between a young intern and a director of hospital, let alone that she is an Israeli-Palestinian and he belongs to the ruling Jewish majority. And so, while there is no policy as such, there is a structure that enables this chosen oblivion to racism, thus allowing it to persist.

The director of Shaarei Zedek is not alone. The support that the practice of segregation receives from senior health professionals is remarkable. Also striking is its tension with the claim for "neutrality" and equal care, in the spirit of the old "separate but equal" doctrine now seeing a revival in the "new right" in Europe.

The testimony of Prof. Hochner Drorith, the director of Mount Scopus Hospital, exposes the importance the ethos of equality in her professional world has for her, conceiving the world of medicine as an island of sanity in a troubled society:

> I work[ed] for more than 30 years in Hadassa Mt. Scopus, which is definitely a place where there is a lot of contact between Jews and Arabs. We have Arabs in our staff, and for me **everyone is equal** – clear cut, no question about it. I always think that we are fortunate in **our profession to maybe really be what we call a bridge for peace**. (my emphasis)

Again, like HaLevi, Prof. Hochner is unaware of the possibility that this concept of a bridge for peace might not be as solid as she imagines, that maybe it is made possible only because the Arab members accept, or do not protest publicly, the so-called status quo established and defined by the Jewish majority.

This lack of awareness allows Prof. Hochner to justify her support for the practice of separation, explaining that it is not racism since the minority itself requests separation:

> I did not think that the [media exposure of segregation in maternity wards] is good. . . . I thought it is jumping on the wrong issue. I don't think that when **we decide to respond positively to requests** – and I want you to know that there are Arab women after birth who request not to be with Jews, they request it clear cut, and even when there are terrible situations, they say: we are afraid.

Accepting this as a justification for segregation is a mirror reflection of the realities in our society that lives and accepts segregation in many other realms of our lives. To present a policy of segregation in terms of a positive response – consideration – to patients' wishes undermines the ethos she insists on, of medicine as a bridge to peace.

Indeed, as she goes on with her attempt to explain why separation is not racist, medicine is exposed as it truly is – another space where society is cracking at the seams:

> Listen, we live in a very problematic political reality, we have problems in [the] relationship of Jews and Arabs. **We as medical professionals give a completely equal care to Jews and Arabs – clear cut**. Especially in maternity, where it is not really medical care, but more [a] hostel for a woman after giving birth, we make an effort to respond positively to requests. (my emphasis)

To support her claim that segregation is not racist, she uses other separations such as between ultra-Orthodox and secular women, where it is clearly not a race issue.[42] She then goes on to claim that "it is clear you cannot say this is

---

[42] Again, one may argue whether a hospital should bow to cultural/religious segregation, but this is out of the scope of this chapter.

discrimination, and separation is a very relative definition." Striking is her insistence that the fact that "No Arab woman will be put in the corridor just because the only vacant bed is next to a Jewish woman – clear cut, I take on it full responsibility," as if the fact that segregation has a limit (lying in the corridor) is enough of a defense against claims of racism. When addressed with the question of whether this is a policy, she explains that even when someone asks not to be near an Ethiopian woman, they will respond positively. Again, the mere fact that she knew to choose an Ethiopian as her example in the Jewish community shows that she does in fact recognize the racism prevalent in Israeli society. After all, she did not use as an example somebody asking not to be near a white/Western Jew, because this is unthinkable in the current power relationship.

Similarly, insisting that this conduct is not racist, Prof. Jonathan HaLevi repeats the image of hospitals as an island, but the reality that comes up is one that contradicts his intention:

> I will try to prove to you that [the hospitals] are really an **island** of complete absence of racism, an island – so **if there is something in Israeli society that promotes peace it is the hospitals**. (my emphasis)

He then explains that they have a very small number of Arab women in maternity wards:

> Naturally, yesterday in ward A there were two Arabs, both in the same room, and twenty other rooms of Jews. No one asked, but if you go in, you will see that ultra-Orthodox tend to be together, secular women tend to be together. It works out. They tend to be together, really because of the visits [of families] not because of requests.

He neglects to explain how this tendency is brought into action, how they end up in the same room. When faced with the question of how this tendency of being together is manifested (Do they decide? Do you put them there?), he answers:

> They come on a stretcher from the labor room to the nurse desk at the maternity ward, and the nurse asks them, sometimes yes, and sometimes she herself says. Do you prefer to stay in a specific room? And sometimes she does not even ask, not asking and not being asked.

Prof. HaLevi describes a situation in which women and nurses alike accept the reality of separation to such a degree that it does not even need to be spoken. Indeed, HaLevi calls it "a natural tendency" when he, like Prof. Hochner, expresses his support for the practice, by taking it from ethnic separation to one that is cultural:

Naturally when on the same stretcher a secular woman arrives with tattoos and a nose ring, the nurse will not put her with Faiga Hinda [a typical name of an ultra-Orthodox woman] in the same room. Is this discrimination? This is the natural tendency.

As Prof. HaLevi continues his exposition, we discover that he is not only speaking from the patients' perspective. Suddenly even this proclaimed island of sanity is not that ideal and tensions in the medical staff itself come to the fore: "People, this is what happens. We have 120 maternity nurses, only one Arab, not a popular profession." Again, he is oblivious to the fact that a few kilometers from his hospital within the same city of Jerusalem operates the Red Crescent maternity hospital, to mention one, where enough Arab maternity nurses work. So, if it is not the unpopularity of the profession, can it then be something in the Shaarei Zedek maternity wards that deters Arabs?

No human is an island, and doctors and nurses are human: As I hope is made clear from this discussion of the conduct of the medical community in the three affairs and from their reactions to the complaints, we do have a problem of institutional racism. But it is clear that before tackling racism, we must cope with its denial. In order for this to happen, physicians especially need to acknowledge that they have benefited from our society's institutional racism. As Jones[43] rightly says, racism is a system "that structures opportunity and assigns value based on phenotype, the way people look, [and] unfairly disadvantages some individuals and communities." But while maybe this is easier to acknowledge, I believe that doctors, like many elites, tend to ignore the other side of the equation – that "at the same time that the system is unfairly disadvantaging some individuals and communities, it is also unfairly advantaging other individuals and communities." To acknowledge themselves as unfairly advantaged means to crack their belief that what they hold, their professional prestige, their accomplishments and respect, are not – or at least not solely – due to their superiority in brains and efforts, but due to their opening position, their privileges.

The medical community is not alone in its enjoyment of privileges. Patients from privileged communities enjoy this same system. In places where money joins racism, such as in maternity wards where the woman has a choice of where to go (and with her, the payment and profit to the hospital), hospitals will find racism harder to fight. The struggle against racism in our health system is therefore not separate from the struggle against classism or from the struggle against racism in all other institutions in our society. But to say this does not exempt the health system from holding its own brave and honest struggle against its own racism, because maybe it is not an island of sanity, but it <u>can be a safe haven and a compass to society if it takes its own ethical values seriously.</u>

---

[43] Jones, Camara P., "Confronting Institutionalized Racism," *Phylon* 50.1/2 (2002), p. 8.

References

Abba, Dani, A., Neighborhoods Without Babies, *Yedioth Ahronoth*, January 6, 2008 (Hebrew).

Balibar, Etienne, Is There "Neo-racism?" *Race, Nation, Class: Ambiguous Identities* (Etienne & Wallerstein), Verso 1991.

Bhugra, Dinesh and Ayonrinde, Oyedeji, Racism, Racial Life Events and Mental Ill Health, *Advances in Psychiatric Treatment*, 7 (2001), pp. 343–349.

Brennan, Troy and others (Members of the Medical Professionalism Project: ABIM Foundation), Medical Professionalism in the New Millennium: A Physician Charter, *Annals of Internal Medicine*, 136.3 (2002).

Eyal, Hedva, *Depo Provera: A Contraceptive Method Given via Injection – A Report on Its Prescription Policy among Women of the Ethiopian Community in Israel*, 2009, Isha L'Isha and Kvinna till Kvinna.

Gabbay, Gal, *Vacum*, December 6, 2012, Educational TV (Hebrew).

Hatuka, Shlomi, The Tragedy of the Lost Yemenite Children: In the Footsteps of the Adoptees, *Haokets* (2014).

Jones, Camara P., Confronting Institutionalized Racism, *Phylon* 50.1/2 (2002), pp. 7–22.

Knesset, Labor, Welfare and Health Committee Meeting, July 10, 2013 (Hebrew).

Knesset Committee on the Status of Women and Gender Equality, Segregation in Maternity Wards in Hospitals, April 13, 2016 (Hebrew).

Mashiah, Yigal, The Disappearance of Yemenite Children: An Organized Scam or Criminal Negligence? *Haaretz*, September 5, 1997 (Hebrew).

Metzl, Jonathan, M. and Hansen, Helena, Structural Competency: Theorizing a New Medical Engagement with Stigma and Inequality, *Social Science & Medicine*, 103 (2014), pp. 126–133.

Rosen, Yisrael, A Public Defense of MK Betzalel Smutrich and the Maternity Wards, Zomet Institute Website.

Sangero, Boaz, Where There Is No Suspicion There Is No Real Investigation: The Report of the Committee of Inquiry into the Disappearance of the Children of Jewish Yemenite Immigrants to Israel in 1948–1954, *Theory and Criticism*, 2002 (Hebrew).

Shavers, Vickie L. and Shavers, Brenda S., Racism and Health Inequity among Americans, *Journal of the National Medical Association*, 98.3 (2006)

Shvarts Shifra, Davidovitch Nadav, Seidelman, Rhona, and Goldberg Avishai, Medical Selection and the Debate over Mass Immigration in the New State of Israel (1948–1951), *CBMH/BCHM* 22.1 (2005) pp. 5–34.

Talmor, Tzipi, *One Way Road* (1993).

Traubmann, Tamara, Do Not Have Children if They Won't Be Healthy, *Haaretz*, June 11, 2004.

Yaron, Lee, No Evidence That Ethiopian-Israeli Women Were Forced to Take Birth-Control Shot, Comptroller Says, *Haaretz*, January 20, 2016.

Zayed, Shoshi, *The Child Is Gone: The Yemenite Children Affair*. Jerusalem: Gefen, 2001 (Hebrew).

Primary Sources

The Coalition Against Racism in Israel http://www.fightracism.org/en/.
Amram's Testimonies Project www.edut-amram.org/ (Hebrew only).
Consumers Leaflet for Depo-Provera: www.old.health.gov.il/units/pharmacy/trufot/alonim/Depo-Provera_sus_for_inj_PL_Heb_1439973347725.pdf.

5

Nothing about Us without Us: A Disability Challenge to Bioethics

Sagit Mor

A INTRODUCTION

Disability theory and disability activism pose a fundamental challenge to bioethics. The rise of disability critique and activism has demonstrated that seemingly self-evident assumptions about disability have always been a silent yet salient feature of bioethics theory and practice in questions relating to life and death, sickness and health, provision of health care services, allocations of resources, and more (Asch 2001). Bioethics and disability have a shared history and common concerns with regard to the authority and the structure of medical knowledge (Amundson and Tresky 2008). However, bioethics has historically endorsed an individual-medical approach to disability that values and prioritizes medical-professional knowledge, but devalues and marginalizes disabled people's knowledge and experiences (Asch 2001). Even progressive accounts of bioethics tend to adopt an individual-medical approach to disability that views life with a disability as a life of lesser value and a burden on the family and society (Amundson and Tresky 2008). Under this view, disabled people are perceived as incompetent to make decisions for themselves and incapable of participation in public deliberation processes.

In response, the disability challenge to bioethics involves not only a new understanding of disability, but also a new place for disabled people in society and in bioethics – as active participants in decision-making processes (Rinck and Calkins 1996; Asch 2001; Dhanda 2006). This new place for disabled people is encapsulated in the disability rights movement's slogan: *nothing about us without us* (Charlton 1998). This slogan became internationally renowned and widely used by disabled activists around the globe as it captures the essence of the disability struggle: to be part of society and to take an active role in individual and collective decision-making processes in all aspects of life. However, its meaning as a framework of analysis was not clarified so far.

This chapter introduces a reading of this slogan as a call for individual and collective voice and representation in decision-making processes in general, and particularly in decisions of a bioethical nature. It suggests that a *nothing about us without us* approach entails both an individual dimension that concerns personal decisions regarding one's own life, and a collective dimension that concerns the involvement of disabled people as a group in all levels of public deliberation, including policymaking, legislative processes, public committees, and statutory committees. This chapter also calls to create formal channels that institutionalize the incorporation of disabled people's voices and perspectives into public deliberation processes. The latter is illustrated through a close look at the Israeli Disability Rights Commission's role in promoting disability rights, and particularly its involvement in the recent developments concerning wrongful life claims in Israel.

As this chapter shows, the inclusion of disabled people's voices and perspectives has both procedural and substantive implications as it eventually changes both the process and the outcome. Meaningful involvement and representation of disabled people in policy design has the potential of undermining deeply rooted underlying assumptions about disabled people and transforming the meaning of disability in medical settings and wherever medical knowledge is utilized and prioritized.

B THE DISABILITY CRITIQUE OF BIOETHICS

The disability critique of bioethics is part of a larger endeavor to transform prevalent understandings of disability and to reimagine a new place for disabled people in society. Disability studies scholars and activists seek to move away from an understanding of disability as an individual tragedy and a medical pathology toward a new view of disability as a contextual, relational, and interactive phenomenon that is shaped by social, political, cultural, historical, and economic forces (Oliver 1990; Linton 1998; Shakespeare 2006). A central pillar of a disability studies analysis is the critique of the dominance of the medical approach to disability (Wendell 1996; Imrie 1997; Swain and French 2000). In response, disability activists and scholars offered an alternative view of disability as a social construction and a human variation, and of disabled people as a minority group deserving of civil rights (Shapiro 1994; Scotch 1986). This vision pertains not only to traditional domains of medicine and health, but to any realm of life where medical knowledge and expertise have become authoritative, including schooling, housing, employment, social benefits and allowances, legal capacity, and more (Imrie 1997; Linton 1998). In fact, when it comes to disability, no sphere of life is free of the medical discourse and its underlying assumptions about disability as abnormality, deviance, and pathology (Brisenden 1986).

The disability critique of bioethics is fundamental, as it challenges the field's core assumptions, deliberation methodologies, frames of reference, and modes of operation. Most classical issues in bioethics have either an explicit or implicit disability component (Asch 2001). Beginning- and end-of-life decisions, the regulation of reproductive technologies, and the provision of and access to health care services are enormously impacted by stated and unstated social understandings and cultural assumptions about disability and disabled people (Kuczewski 2001). Such topics include prenatal testing, selection against (and for) disability in IVF and PGD treatments, forced sterilization of women with disabilities, physician-assisted suicide, selection criteria for lifesaving treatments, organ donation priority lists, enhancement technologies, and more. Each technological innovation poses new opportunities and new challenges. However, until recently, such issues were not perceived as disability-related matters because disability in itself was not understood as a social or an analytical prism of analysis (Asch 2001).

The disability critique demands from bioethics consistent resistance to the medicalization of disability and a persistent effort to insert disabled people's voices and perspectives into decision-making processes and to reconceptualize those issues as matters of civil and human rights. The slogan *nothing about us without us* represents this call for meaningful participation in all spheres of life, and, as I suggest, can serve as a framework of analysis for a bioethics mode of operation.

1 The Medicalization of Disability

Arguing against the medicalization of disability may sound like an oxymoron since the dominant understanding of disability is mediated through the lens of medical knowledge. The opposite of disabled, many people would say, is "healthy" or "normal," suggesting that disability is an inherent state of sickness, a medical condition, an abnormality, and a deviance from charts of standard human development (Davis 1995; Amundson 2000). This medical view of disability rests on the pathologization of disability that occurred with the scientific and the industrial revolutions and was shaped by the ideas of the eugenics movement and social Darwinism (Foucault 1973, 1990; Davis 1995, 2013). Today, old eugenics is considered immoral and illegitimate. However, new technologies and practices present continuing challenges in the form of new eugenics, one that is less direct and coercive but still characterized by a strong state-supported social pressure against disability (Shakespeare 2006). This is true for Israeli public discourse as well as for Israeli bioethical discourse, which only rarely confront their own assumptions about disability and hardly ever demonstrate a social, contextual, non-tragic view of disability.

The rise of modern bioethics was a response to the atrocities of Nazi eugenics and to medical treatments and experiments that were forcefully conducted on human beings (Rothman 1991; Stevens 2014). It was part of a broader process of growing suspicion, skepticism, and resistance to the authority of the individual physician and the medical establishment. This larger process included the emergence of the patients' rights movement, the expansion of medical malpractice claims, the changing patterns of doctor–patient relationships, and changes in medical sociology and anthropology. These parallel trends enriched bioethical discussions, but also challenged bioethics core assumptions, as the feminist critique of medicine and health care demonstrates (Norsigian 2011).

While disability was always in the backdrop of these discussions, it took time until it occupied a central role. The disability critique rests on two general components: the moral dimension, which concerns the value of life with a disability and the value of disabled people as human beings and political subjects; and the misinformation dimension, which involves the inadequate and inaccurate basis of knowledge about the lived experience with disability (Parens and Asch 1999). In *Disability, Bioethics, and Human Rights*, Asch provides a comprehensive review of the various fields where disability and bioethics intersect and interact. Asch rightly stresses that disability critique and bioethics share "a commitment to patient autonomy, skepticism about professional power and paternalism and championing of consumer protection" (2001: 299). However, bioethics, which "insists that individuals should be able to determine the situations under which they find life intolerable" (p. 299), has never listened to disabled people's experiences and voices. Even when bioethics opened up to feminist and racial critiques, disability remained the ultimate "abnormalcy" that does not fit the liberal ideal of autonomous individual (Davis 2013).

In Israel, the disability perspective is still absent from bioethical discussions. There is, indeed, a growing body of literature examining the understanding of disability in Zionism and in early Israel. Such scholarship shows that the impact of eugenic theory on Zionism was complex. On one hand, it infused anti-Semitic stereotypes of Jews as inherently inferior and an obstacle to a better race and a better society. At the same time, it prompted prominent Zionist thinkers who advocated the bodily transformation of the Jewish people as individuals and as a collective from weak, sick, and "parasitic" old Jews to a strong, healthy, and productive Jewry of Muscles (Weiss 2002; Mor 2006). Recent studies explore the particular manifestations of the medical approach to disability on Israeli early social and welfare policies (Mor 2007; Admon-Rick 2013; Holler 2014).

Although Israel was slower to respond to the global trends that gave rise to bioethics, eventually a local profession and local institutions emerged that developed and implemented a local version of bioethics and local forms of resistance to the primacy of medical authority and the medical establishment (Shalev 2003). One recent important strand of criticism concerns the field of reproductive technologies, which interrogates the implications of Israel as a pro-natal society (Portugese 1998), as well as the social pressure toward the production of "healthy" or "perfect" children (Remmnick 2006; Hashiloni-Dolev 2007). While these studies do question the legitimacy of preventing the birth of disabled children, they usually do not incorporate a disability critique that focuses on social disablement and the cultural construction of disability.

So far, the only arena of traditional bioethics where a disability perspective has been seriously considered in Israel is wrongful life (Hammer 2012; Karako-Ayal 2013; Mor 2014). As I later show, the insertion of this perspective was made possible through the involvement of the Disability Rights Commission in the process. In other arenas, even in closely related fields, such as prenatal testing and abortion policy, the disability perspective is largely absent.

2 Nothing about Us without Us

The disability movement, in academia and on the ground, attempted to transform the power relations that render disabled people powerless, marginal, excluded, abused, and silenced. It exposed the biases and shortcoming of the medical discourse, and offered an alternative understanding of disability. This alternative does not perceive the individual as the source of the problem, but rather focuses on person–environment interaction that results in social disablement (Oliver 1990; Goodley 2010); it focuses on cultural assumptions, social practices, and institutional structures that prevent disabled people from full and equal participation (Linton 1998). Under this view, disability is a social construction rather than a fixed trait, a human variation rather than a medical pathology, and disabled people are a minority group whose members share similar forms and patterns of exclusion, oppression, and discrimination.

This paradigm shift was a product of a transformative process in which disabled people started speaking for themselves and resisting the oppressive mechanisms that silenced them (Shapiro 1994; Charlton 1998). Following the lead of former civil rights and liberation movements, they translated their individual experiences into collective claims and their collective claims into political actions. Notable early speakers were disabled activists and scholars who were able to transcend social and environmental barriers and access higher education. In the words of Ed Roberts, a prominent leader of the U.S. and the global disability movements: "if we have learned one thing from the civil rights movement in the U.S., it's that when others speak for you, you lose" (Charlton 1998: 3). The phrase *nothing about us without us* was officially introduced by James Charlton, a disabled activist, scholar, and lawyer who traveled around the globe and met disabled activists (1998). As Charlton explains, "The slogan's power derives from its location of the source of many types of (disability) oppression and its simultaneous opposition to such oppression in the context of control and voice" (p. 3).

Consequently, one of the primary goals of the disability movement was to insert a rights-oriented approach to disability that puts the person, as a full human being, a legal subject, and a rights-holder, at the center. The global turn to disability rights had two major phases. The first rights-based frame was the *civil rights* approach as introduced by the Americans with Disabilities Act (ADA, 1990), which became a global model of disability rights. It focused on access, antidiscrimination, and reasonable accommodations, and aimed to replace the welfare discourse that preceded it (Heyer 2015). The second framework of disability rights claims was the *human rights* approach, which officially took hold in 2006 with the adoption of the international Convention on the Rights of Persons with Disabilities (CRPD). The Convention's human rights approach included both social and civil rights and imposed affirmative duties on the state to protect, promote, and realize the rights of disabled people in all sphere and aspects of life, including specific sections concerning work and employment, health, education, family, housing, legal capacity, and more (Kanter 2006; Heyer 2015). The UN drafting process was celebrated as a participatory process in which disabled people took part both as states' formal delegates and as independent civil society representatives (Kanter 2006; Sabatello and Schulze 2013). Although both frameworks of disability rights were led and developed by an alliance of disabled and nondisabled persons, they would not have begun and evolved as they did without the activism and input of disabled people.

The disability rights perspective with its emphasis on participation in decision-making processes arrived in Israel in the 1990s. In 1998, Israel adopted its own Equal Rights for Persons with Disability Law (ERPDL), a local version of a civil rights legislation that utilizes an antidiscrimination approach while remaining committed to social services as an important component of disability rights (Ziv 1999). In 2006, Israel signed the CRPD, and in 2012, it ratified the Convention with a formal commitment to make necessary changes in domestic legislation. The ERPDL presented several developments with regard to voice, participation, and self-determination of disabled people. On an individual level, the law stated: "a person with a disability has the right to make decisions that pertain to her/his life according to her/his wishes and preferences," but added that this right shall be exercised in conformity with any existing law (ERPDL § 4). While this section provides that disabled people have the right to make decisions, it still upholds existing legislation, meaning primarily the Legal Capacity and Guardianship Law. On a collective level, the ERPDL established the Disability Rights Commission and an advisory committee next to the Commission the majority of which members would be disabled persons. It also mandated consultation with the Commission and with disability organizations in legislative and regulatory processes. With the ratification of the CRPD, Israel's commitment to disability rights became stronger on both levels. With regard to individual decision-making, Israel committed to change its legal capacity law in light of Article 12, and indeed did so in 2016. With regard to collective representation, the CRPD explicitly required states' parties to "consult with and actively involve" disabled people "in the development and implementation of legislation and policies" (Article 4(3)). Moreover, the very adoption and ratification processes made the Disability Rights Commission a central player in the field and a source of pride for the Israeli government in the international arena.

The development of a disability rights language created a bridge and a workable language to incorporate disability-based claims into bioethics. Yet the disability challenge to bioethics is deeper than that. On the substantive level, incorporating a disability perspective would require bioethics to transform its own underlying set of values from classical liberalism that emphasizes autonomy and rationality to a more socially responsive approach that emphasizes difference, solidarity, and interconnectedness (Asch 2001; Scully 2008). On a more procedural, yet still fundamental level, a *nothing about us without us* perspective requires not only to incorporate disability-based language, claims, and values, but to actually facilitate a way for disabled people to take meaningful part in decision-making processes. The rest of this analysis will focus on the procedural level while demonstrating the close connection between the two.

C INDIVIDUAL VOICE IN DECISIONS CONCERNING ONE'S OWN LIFE

I suggest that incorporating and implementing a *nothing about us without us* perspective involves two separate, yet closely related levels of discussion. The first is an individual level, which emphasizes the place of the individual in *personal decision making* pertaining to one's own life. The second is a collective level, which concerns the involvement of the group as a whole at all levels of *policymaking or public deliberation*. I will start with the first.

On an individual level, it is undeniable that disabled people in Israel and abroad were historically denied the freedom to choose and make decisions for themselves, or to take active part in decisions concerning their own individual lives. The following discussion suggests three levels of analysis that demonstrate the scope and complexity of that denial of voice and choice: denial of legal capacity, lack of voice and access to administrative proceedings, and limited range of options available. All these dimensions together have prevented disabled people from being the authors of their own lives and in control of their destiny.

1 Legal Capacity and Informed Consent

For disability rights advocates, legal capacity laws demonstrate the ultimate denial of disabled people's rights. Many disabled people have been historically denied legal status through legal capacity and guardianship laws that declared them incompetent to take any legal action, to manage their financial resources, or to control their daily lives and their own bodies (Dhanda 2006; Tolub and Kanter 2014; Flynn 2016). Moreover, they did not take part in the very process that announced them legally incapable and their interests or preferences were not represented in such proceedings (Tolub and Kanter 2014; Tolub 2015). Such denial of legal subjectivity usually relies on a narrow medical assessment without considering other, more enabling, or least restrictive, options (Dhanda 2006; Tolub and Kanter 2014). Recently, such options began to emerge with the introduction of disability rights and the search for creative alternatives.

The CRPD responded to that reality with Article 12, which concerns equal protection before the law. Article 12 mandates that "persons with disabilities have the right to recognition everywhere as persons before the law"; that they should "enjoy legal capacity on an equal basis with others in all aspects of life"; and that state parties should provide access to the support they may require in exercising their legal capacity. Moreover, "measures relating to the exercise of legal capacity respect the rights, will and preferences of the person, are free of conflict of interest and undue influence, are proportional and tailored to the person's circumstances, apply for the shortest time possible and are subject to regular review by a competent, independent and impartial authority or judicial body."

As mentioned earlier, when Israel ratified the CRPD, it was clear that its legal capacity rules and practices must change to conform to the new regime of disability human rights. Eventually, in 2016, the law was amended[1] and included two novel mechanisms: supported decision making and enduring power of attorney. The first aims to replace the old role of a guardian with a new function of a decision-making supporter who assists the person with obtaining and understanding information and with executing his or her decisions (§ 67B).[2] The second provides an option of leaving instructions while still having full legal capacity for the time of diminishing mental capacity (Chapter 2A).[3] The new law determines the principle of the least restrictive alternative (§ 33A) and puts limits and restrictions if a guardian is appointed concerning the appointment process and the guardian's powers (§ 33A).

Unfortunately, the new law does not establish an unequivocal duty to hear the person at any legal proceedings concerning his or her life. Nevertheless, it sets some rules with regard to the person's standing, including a duty to hear the person when choosing a guardian; placing the person's wishes as a guiding principle in a guardian's discretion; and a partial right for legal representation in some instances, including the very decision to appoint a guardian.

This change has further implications for bioethics and the medical profession. First, it affects the practice of welfare and health professionals. Until today, legal capacity decisions relied on medical assessments produced by medical experts or health-related professionals (Dhanda 2006; Salzman 2011; Tolub and Kanter 2014). Now their role is changing: they should be more aware of the limits of their knowledge, insert new principles into their individual practice, and work toward enabling instead of disabling legal capacity (Dhanda 2006).

Second, and more specifically to the medical context, disabled people were often declared incompetent to provide informed consent, opening the gate for forced treatment without sufficient explanation or preparation (Salzman 2011). Traditionally, when a guardian was appointed, s/he was legally authorized to make any decision in the name of the person, including medical treatments and other bodily issues (Salzman 2011; Tolub and Kanter 2014). According to the new

---

[1] For an overview of the law, see http://bizchut.org.il/en/576. For partial official translation of the law, see http://bizchut.org.il/en/wp-content/uploads/2016/04/new-Israeli-law-on-supported-decision-making.docx.
[2] This part of the law will become effective in two years.
[3] This part of the law will become effective in one year.

amendment, if a court of law eventually appoints a guardian, the judicial decision should specifically define the scope of matters it covers, including specific attention to medical matters (33A(d)).

The new law also addresses situations of conflicting views in medical and other body-related matters. Thus, when a person and a guardian disagree on such matters, the dispute will be brought before an ethics committee or a court of law (67F(4)), which may consider appointing independent legal representation to the person (§ 68A). When an enduring power of attorney is granted, the person's will triumphs (§ 32F(c)(2) & 32I(e)(2)). In contrast, when a decision-making supporter is appointed (§ 67B), such conflict cannot arise because s/he cannot make any decision in the person's name, but rather should help them reach their own decision.

2 Voice and Access to Administrative Proceedings

While guardianships laws are the most radical form of denying one's capacity for personal decision making, there are other, less direct forms of restrictions and barriers that impact one's ability to choose. Disabled people were historically excluded from decisions concerning all other aspects of their lives, including education, housing, and employment. Because disabled people are widely perceived as lacking the autonomy and rationality to make their own decisions (Nussbaum 2006), their wishes, preferences, opinions, experience, and situated knowledge are discredited and treated as unreliable, unfounded, and unnecessary (Linton 1998). Furthermore, these proceedings are often inaccessible in terms of physical access, modes of communication, and transmission of information. Because disabled people were historically excluded from these processes, their absence has been routinized and neutralized, and consequently legitimized. Instead, these decisions were usually made by teams of experts, mostly from the welfare and health professions. The person's medical diagnosis was central to that decision and medical assessments had a crucial role in determining one's "placement." These professional decisions were made without seriously considering the person's preferences, often assuming the person was incapable of making a right choice or understanding the situation.

One example could be the Israeli law concerning housing for persons with developmental disabilities that is governed by the Welfare (Treatment of Retarded Persons) Law (1969). The law was amended in 2000, but still determines that an administrative "diagnosis committee" will determine the person's most suitable living arrangement (§ 7A). The committee is comprised of a social worker, a psychologist, an educator, a psychiatrist, and a physician; no housing expert, accommodations expert, or disability rights advocate. Although the committee is instructed to hear the person's preferences, the weight of these preferences in the decision-making process is unclear. Moreover, in reality, the committee tends to hear the "person in charge" of the "retarded person," in the law's phrasing, and not the person himself or herself. In contrast, Article 19 to the CRPD declares that "all persons with disabilities have the equal right to live in the community, with choices equal to others" and "the opportunity to choose their place of residence and where and with whom they live." The latter is important: the choice of place includes a choice of location and companionship. Under this scheme, the role of experts is to assist disabled people to make their choices a reality and to provide the necessary conditions for that.

In addition, lack of physical access prevents disabled people from participating in these very processes. Inaccessible court systems, inaccessible administrative tribunals, and most ironically inaccessible disability determination hearings prevent disabled people from fully participating in processes that determine their own benefits, services, and rights (Blanck, Wilichowski, and Schmeling 2003; Mor 2016). In 2006, the Israel Equal Rights for Persons with Disabilities Law was amended and a comprehensive accessibility chapter was added. The law requires that public facilities and services will be accessible, including the legal system and governmental facilities, such as health, education, and welfare services.[4] In 2013, new accessibility regulations were issued concerning virtually all types of legal, semi-legal, or administrative proceedings. The regulations cover all courts of law, administrative courts, disciplinary or ethics committees established by law, any agency with a semi-legal authority, and any governmental agency that has the power to determine one's medical condition or eligibility to social services (§ 42).[5] The ERPDL and the regulations address a wide range of needs that acknowledges the plurality of disability: physical access for persons with mobility and other impairments; Braille, large print, and accessible forms and Web-based information for persons with visual impairments; sign language, voice-enhancing technologies, and other forms of communication technologies for persons with hearing impairments; assistive technologies and simple language techniques for persons with speech and cognitive disabilities, accommodated procedures, instructions, and guidelines, and more (ERPDL, § 19A).

3 Limited Range of Options

Finally, the limited range of options available to disabled people negatively affects their ability to make personal choices. Until recently, the only options available were paternalistic, segregated, isolating, and of lesser quality. Special education, institutional housing, or sheltered employment are often the only available options for people with all types of disabilities, especially those who do not have the means to pay for private access or better services. Furthermore, even when more options seem

---

[4] See the ERPDL, First and Second Supplements.
[5] Regulations Regarding Equal Rights for Persons with Disability (Access to Service Accommodations), 2013, Supplement, First and Second Supplement.

to be open and available, they are often practically unavailable due to lack of access and accommodations.

Again, the CRPD provides an alternative vision for all spheres of life. For example, in the realm of education, Article 24 stipulates that disabled students should have access to "an inclusive, quality and free primary education and secondary education on an equal basis with others," including "reasonable accommodation of the individual's requirements," and "receive the support required, within the general education system, to facilitate their effective education." In Israel, until the Special Education Law (1988) was enacted, there was no state-run schooling system for children with disabilities despite existing education laws that required free mandatory schooling for all. The 1988 law attempted to change that reality but eventually prioritized segregated schooling over inclusion. That was the background to the Israeli Supreme Court precedential decision in *Yated v. Ministry of Education* (2000). In *Yated*, a group of parents to children with disabilities challenged the existing law that provided educational services and support only to those children who studied in the special education system. Ironically, those who were mainstreamed into the "regular" system were not eligible for any support. The result, they argued, was discriminatory against students with disabilities in general, but particularly against children of lower socioeconomic backgrounds who could not afford to pay privately for accommodations, services, and support and therefore remained in the "special" system. Following the *Yated* decision, the Knesset amended the Special Education Law, explicitly dictating that students in inclusive education are eligible to all the special services that they need and that the law provides (§ 20B).[6] Still, a general right to inclusive education is insufficient. Lack of access and additional institutional and structural barriers may prevent those students from making the choice they should have been able to make. Thus, children with physical or sensual disability who are otherwise eligible to study in the "general" education system are still encountering grave obstacles in the education system because of lack of access to buildings and facilities, absence of sign language services, or inaccessible reading materials.

Similarly, in the realm of housing, institutional living arrangements are often the only option available for disabled people. If only large institutions and group homes are available, then disabled people are denied the option of living independently in the community. Moreover, in absence of community-based services, disabled people cannot make the choice of living independently (Kanter 2012). Another example would be sheltered employment that usually constitutes an exception to labor and employment laws, exempting employers from minimum wage standards, and providing no social benefits and limited legal protection from arbitrariness and exploitation (World Report on Disability 2011: ch. 8). In the realm of health, lack of access

---

[6] Implementation of this law is more complex, but what I would like to show is that the guiding principles have changed.

to healthcare services infringes the person's right to health, limits choice of healthcare services, and leads to lower standard of care (World Health Organization 2011: ch. 3).

For all these reasons, an abstract right to make choices is crucial but insufficient. Making facilities and services attainable to disabled people requires the removal of social, environment, and structural barriers of various types. Learning about these barriers is achieved only by enhancing the meaningful and active participation of disabled people in personal and collective decision-making processes, and by genuinely listening to disabled people's voices and experience.

The *nothing about us without us* approach challenges this reality and manifests a call to allow the effective and meaningful participation of disabled people in processes that concern their lives and to open up the options available to disabled people so they can actually develop and pursue their own choices and have control over their lives. The CRPD provides an illuminating comprehensive alternative vision that brings awareness to the many choices that are denied to disabled people, even today, and demonstrate how a progressive understanding of education, housing, employment, health care services, and so forth can enhance disabled people's choices and put them on an equal level with others.

The disability challenge to bioethics is therefore to actively search for disabled people's voices, to amplify them, and to give them priority in any decision-making processes in which a health professional is involved. It is also to make decision-making processes more accessible, and to search for alternatives that enhance one's capabilities and liberty (Kuczewski 2001).

D COLLECTIVE VOICE IN PUBLIC DELIBERATION PROCESSES

The second level of analysis that I offer concerns the collective dimension of disabled people's voices and experience. Disabled people, as a group, were historically excluded from public deliberation processes on all levels: legislative processes, regulatory debates, policymaking, public committees, statutory committees, and so forth. The claim for collective voice or group representation pertains to any of these sites. The need for a disability perspective is of particular importance in bioethics and other medical and social welfare–related issues because of their relevance to disabled people's actual lives and their role in shaping the sociocultural meaning of disability. Inserting a disability perspective into these processes aims to change both the process and the outcome of public deliberation. It is relevant both to the stage when general rules and policies are determined and to the stage when they are implemented in individual cases by public agencies. For example, the incorporation of disabled people's voices is important both when designing new legal capacity rules and when deciding a particular case, in which a specific individual is facing a limitation on his or her decision-making capability. The following discussion will focus on two aspects of the demand for a "collective voice" in decision-making processes: identifying and representing a collective voice and identifying a topic as a disability matter that requires the input of a disability perspective. I leave aside questions concerning the definition of what is disability or who is a disabled person.

1 "Without Us": Physical and Intellectual Presence

The importance of group representation in public deliberation processes is clear and widely agreed upon, but the ways to achieve it are complex and highly contested. One of the most challenging tasks is identifying and representing the collective voice of any disadvantaged group. In the context of disability, this task has several distinctive aspects.

The absence of disabled or other minority voices can take various forms. Mari Matsuda, a critical race theory scholar, suggested to always ask "Who is not in this room and why are they not here?"; while addressing such presence both "literally and intellectually" (1989: 4). With regard to *literal presence*, the question is whether disabled people were physically part of the discussion. Clearly, it is often the case that when a certain policy was discussed, there was not even one disabled person "in the room." When it comes to bioethics or social welfare, the discussion is usually dominated by experts and professionals and the barriers for disabled people's participation are even higher. At the same time, it is hard to assume from the seeming absence of disabled people that they were not there because many disabilities are invisible. Moreover, persons with invisible disabilities may in fact prefer to remain "closeted" to avoid revealing or discussing their disabilities (Samuels 2003).

In terms of *intellectual presence*, the question is whether a disability perspective was part of the discussion. Having a disabled person in the room does not guarantee that the interests, rights, needs, or concerns of disabled people were sufficiently addressed. It is possible, for instance, that the disabled person in the room was not involved in disability activism or committed to disability as a public agenda, either because he or she was not educated about disability rights, or since he or she was not identifying with it as a worthy cause. He or she could also feel uncomfortable to bring a disability perspective to the table. That means that an apparent physical presence of a disabled person in the room is insufficient to guarantee that a disability-conscious discussion took place. Assessing the intellectual presence requires therefore close attention to the content of the discussion: the arguments that were made, the level of commitment to a disability rights perspective, the representation of a plurality of voices from the disability community, and the impact that such voices and concerns had in the deliberation process and on the outcome.

The next set of questions concerns *the diversity of disability*. The disability group is extremely diverse. It comprises numerous conditions, impairments, and illnesses of various types and levels with different manifestations and various, sometimes contradictory needs, and with varying cultural meanings attached to them. In addition, disabled people are located in a variety of social positions and trajectories, including gender, race, ethnicity, LGBT, age, class, and so forth. They are also divided by inner categorizations that are dictated by the circumstances of their injury, or by internal debates about the best solution for a given issue. Awareness of the diversity of disability is key to ensure the inclusion of a plurality of voices of disabled people. This plurality of experiences, backgrounds, and opinions and of the multiple marginalities that disabled people may experience complicates all aspects of collective representation in public deliberation processes. A single "token" disability representative is clearly insufficient.

An effective response to these concerns is the insertion of structural mechanisms, such as consultation procedures or formal representation in public deliberation procedures. The ERPDL, for instance, created two mechanisms that aim to address this difficulty in legislative and regulatory processes: it requires consultation with the Disability Rights Commission and with disability rights organizations.

As disability becomes an established social category and disabled people turn into a "recognized" social minority with an agenda and pride, the need for a disability perspective extends to other contexts and calls to consider the expansion of these mechanisms to additional realms of public policy. The following section addresses this question.

2 "About Us": Disability Matters

So when does disability matter in public policy? Attending to the physical and intellectual presence of a plurality of disabled people's voices in public deliberation processes is necessary both when the topic specifically concerns disabled people and when the topic is a general one. Historically, disabled people were excluded from public deliberation processes even when the topic under discussion was a disability-related matter. Indeed, in many instances, the issue was not framed as a disability issue. But even when framed as such, the participation of disabled people in policy design was not considered or discussed. Clearly, in an era when disabled persons, as individuals, were considered unfit to make decisions about their own lives, their participation in public deliberations was even more inconceivable. Only recent disability activism and scholarship were able to frame these issues as disability matters that are dominated by a medical-individual approach.

Today, with the rise of disability rights and activism, disabled people's voices and experiences are increasingly taken into account, particularly in typical disability rights issues, such as access and discrimination. However, when the issue is more remote or less clearly framed as a disability rights matter, particularly when it is perceived as a matter of professional expertise, persons with disabilities' views and experiential knowledge are not incorporated in the deliberative process. This is the case in issues relating to social policy, such as education, housing, and disability allowances, and in matters of health and bioethics, such as psychiatric treatment, access to health care services, wrongful life claims, prenatal screenings, abortion policy, PGD, or end-of-life decisions. Yet the broader meaning of nothing *about us without us* concerns any field of law and public policy, including those with no apparent disability angle. In fact, every matter of public deliberation is a field where disability matters. This is because all general laws and policies apply to all members of society, including disabled people, who are too part of the general public.

What is needed is a built-in commitment to a disability perspective. Today, attention to the voices and perspectives of disabled people is often "accidental" or voluntary, resulting from a local initiative or civil society pressure, not from structured participatory mechanisms. I suggest that formal rules about the incorporation of disabled people's perspectives in decision-making processes have the potential of changing the landscape of public deliberation. The following will focus on the Disability Rights Commission, a mechanism that demonstrates the potential impact of adopting a *nothing about us without us* approach in disability law and policy in Israel.

E INSTITUTIONALIZING VOICE: THE ISRAELI DISABILITY RIGHTS COMMISSION

The Disability Rights Commission is one example of a possible built-in mechanism that brings the voices of disabled people into public deliberation and policy design, including bioethical discussions. The Disability Rights Commission was formed by the ERPDL in 1998. A close look at the legislation reveals a dual role for the Commission: promoting disability rights and bringing a disability perspective into future legislative, regulatory, and other processes. In order to achieve these goals, the Commission was granted an official role in regulatory processes through statutory consultation and advisory mechanisms. Still a challenge was to make sure that the Commission actually represents the worldviews, the needs, and the experiences of disabled people. The legislation did not go as far as requiring that the Commissioner or the Commission's staff will be persons with disabilities, but it did establish an advisory committee to the Commission comprised of professionals, legal experts, individuals with disabilities, and representative disability organizations that at least half of its members should be persons with disabilities. This very structure is an example of a formal mechanism that promotes the systematic insertion of disabled people's voices and of a disability agenda into public deliberation processes. It also allows the incorporation of diverse experiences and voices of disabled people. Moreover, the ERPDL mandates consultation with disability organizations in regulatory processes, in addition to the Commission, thereby broadening the channels of disability-based perspectives.

With time, the Disability Rights Commission gained credibility and earned its status as an important agency with expertise in disability rights. It became regularly involved in an increasing amount of legislative, regulatory, and other policy-making processes, including topics not under mandatory consultation. One major avenue of action in recent years has been the advancing of the accessibility regulations following the Accessibility Chapter in the ERPDL, including the regulations concerning access to administrative proceedings and disability determination processes that I mentioned earlier. Another primary task has been the adoption and implementation of the CRPD. As part of these efforts, the Commission took an active role in promoting the changes to the Legal Capacity and Guardianship Law. In both instances, the initiative came first from Bizchut, the leading disability rights organization in Israel, who was the first to promote these issues (i.e., legal capacity and access), and was supported and advanced by many other disability advocacy groups and organizations. Still, the Commission became an important actor at the Ministry of Justice in these legislative efforts, particularly toward and following the ratification of the CRPD.

Most interesting for bioethics was the role the Disability Rights Commission played in the public deliberation concerning the future of wrongful life claims in Israel. Wrongful life claims concern the birth of a disabled person whose life could have been prevented through prenatal screening technologies. In these claims, the claimant argues that s/he would rather not be born than living with the disability s/he has. These are highly contested claims from philosophical, logical, legal, and ethical perspectives (Hensel 2005; Perry 2008). From a disability perspective, this is an extreme example of an explicit assertion that life with a disability is not worth living (Hensel 2005; Mor 2014).

Wrongful life claims were first allowed to Israeli courts in 1986 (*Zeitsov*). With time, they became more prevalent and more complex from legal, medical, and social aspects (Karako Ayal 2013; Mor 2014). In 2012, the Supreme Court of Israel announced, in a precedential decision in the *Hammer* case, that wrongful life claims are no longer accepted in Israeli courts.[7] Instead, the Court allowed wrongful birth claims, in which the parents claim against the lost opportunity to terminate the pregnancy. The *Hammer* decision was greatly impacted by the Report of the Public Committee on the Matter of "Wrongful Life-Giving" (2012), which recommended abolishing wrongful life and establishing instead a new form of disability allowance for newborns with disabilities, while still allowing wrongful birth claims in courts.

The involvement and contribution of the Disability Rights Commission to these developments is illuminating yet still untold. First, the Commission led to the very establishment of the Public Committee by questioning and resisting the State Civil Litigation Department's position, which supported wrongful life but sought to limit its scope. This conflict of views led the attorney general to decide that the issue is too complex and that a public committee is needed. It also led the minister of justice to appoint Commissioner Ahiya Kamara, a disabled person and a long-time disability advocate, to the Public Committee. The Commission also urged the involvement

---

[7] In the years that followed, the Supreme Court extended the opportunity to submit wrongful life claims because of complexities concerning limitation.

and the hearing of additional disabled people and organizations in the process, which resulted in the nomination of Mordechai Virshubski, a prominent long-time disabled advocate, to the committee and the hearing of several disability activists, advocates, and scholars. All have emphasized the negative impact of wrongful life claims on the social construction of disability and the need for extensive financial support for disabled people because of the extra costs of disability.

Second, the inclusion of a disability perspective has changed the language and the rhetoric of the Public Committee Report and the eventual *Hammer* decision. Both documents turned from the offensive language of "defect" (*mum*) to the more modern, respectful, rights-based terms "disability" (Report of the Public Committee on the Matter of "Wrongful Life-Giving" 2012: 3, note 2). In addition, both documents have emphasized the ERPDL as an important milestone in the social understanding of disability, acknowledged the social construction of disability, and addressed the inherent tension between wrongful life claims and disability rights. Finally, the involvement of the Commission has influenced the outcome of the Report and the Supreme Court decision. After consulting the Advisory Committee, the Commission advanced the administrative-social path of new disability allowances to newborns with disabilities that the Committee adopted, but was willing to compromise and support the parallel wrongful birth claims that prevailed in *Hammer*.

While the end result of upholding wrongful birth claims is not free of criticism (Mor 2014), the very process demonstrates how institutional channels can make disability participation possible and even meaningful.

F CONCLUSION

To conclude this chapter, *nothing about us without us* is a challenging idea to disability policy in any realm, including bioethics. It resists the medicalization of disability, it contests the authority of medical and expert knowledge in individual and collective decision-making processes, and it suggests or demands an alternative based on first-person experiential knowledge and on a vision of rights, equality, dignity, self-determination, and group representation.

Furthermore, the disability critique of bioethics exposes the potential scope of bioethics itself as a framework of analysis as it extends to any field that relies on medical knowledge and expertise. If bioethics is about the ethics of medical decision making, then it applies to any arena in which medical knowledge, medical practice, or the medical profession are playing a primary role in decision-making processes. In the context of disability, it means almost any sphere of life.

Throughout this chapter, I addressed recent legal developments of increasing participation of disabled people in decision-making processes in formerly predominantly medicalized spheres of Israeli law. Among them are the newly amended Israeli Legal Capacity and Guardianship Law, the accessibility regulations concerning access to disability determinations processes, reforms in education and independent living, and the changes in wrongful life claims. These examples illustrate the implications of adopting and implementing a *nothing about us without us* approach. Each development illustrates different aspects of individual and collective voice and participation and raises questions about the connections between the two levels of analysis. The cases manifest a move away from traditional bioethical discussions to more distant realms in which the dominance of a medical approach to disability is less apparent. All cases demonstrate how meaningful involvement and representation of disabled people in lawmaking and policy design have the potential to change not only the process, but also the outcome of public deliberation in bioethics and beyond.

References

Admon-Rick, Gaby. Impaired Encoding: Calculating, Ordering, and the "Disability Percentages" Classification System. *Science, Technology & Human Values* (2013): 0162243913508326.

Americans with Disabilities Act, 1990, Pub. L. No. 101–336, 104 Stat. 327–33 (codified at 42 U.S.C. §§ 12101–13 (1990)).

Amundson, Ron. Against Normal Function. *Studies in History and Philosophy of Science Part C: Studies in History and Philosophy of Biological and Biomedical Sciences* 31.1 (2000): 33–53.

Amundson, Ron and Shari Tresky. Bioethics and Disability Rights: Conflicting Values and Perspectives. *Journal of Bioethical Inquiry* 5.2–3 (2008): 111–123.

Asch, Adrienne. Disability, Bioethics and Human Rights. *Handbook of Disability Studies* 307 (2001).

Blanck, Peter, Ann Wilichowski, and James Schmeling. Disability Civil Rights Law and Policy: Accessible Courtroom Technology. *Wm. & Mary Bill Rts. J.* 12 (2003): 825.

Brisenden, Simon. Independent Living and the Medical Model of Disability. *Disability, Handicap & Society* 1.2 (1986): 173–178.

Charlton, James I. *Nothing about Us without Us: Disability Oppression and Empowerment*. University of California Press, 1998.

Davis, Lennard J. *Enforcing Normalcy: Disability, Deafness, and the Body*. Verso, 1995.

Davis, Lennard J. *The End of Normal*. University of Michigan Press, 2013.

Dhanda, Amita. Legal Capacity in the Disability Rights Convention: Stranglehold of the Past or Lodestar for the Future. *Syracuse J. Int'l L. & Com.* 34 (2006): 429.

Equal Rights for People with Disabilities Law, 5758–1998, S.H. 152(Hebrew).

Flynn, Eilionóir. *Disabled Justice?: Access to Justice and the UN Convention on the Rights of Persons with Disabilities*. Routledge, 2016.

Foucault, Michel. *The Birth of the Clinique. An Archeology of Medical Perception*. Pantheon, 1973.

Foucault, Michel. *The History of Sexuality: An Introduction, Volume I*. Trans. Robert Hurley. Vintage, 1990.

Goodley, Dan. *Disability Studies: An Interdisciplinary Introduction*. Sage, 2010.
Hammer et al. v. Prof. Amit et al., C.A. 1326/07 (2012) (Hebrew).
Hashiloni-Dolev, Yael. *A Life (Un)Worthy of Living: Reproductive Genetics in Israel and Germany*. Vol. 34. Springer Science & Business Media, 2007.
Hensel, Wendy F. Disabling Impact of Wrongful Birth and Wrongful Life Actions. *Harvard Civil Rights-Civil Liberties Law Review* 40: 141–195 (2005).
Heyer, Katharina. *Rights Enabled: The Disability Revolution, from the US, to Germany and Japan, to the United Nations*. University of Michigan Press, 2015.
Holler, Roni. Disability and Employment Policy in the Israeli Welfare State: Between Exclusion and Inclusion. *Disability & Society* 29.9 (2014): 1369–1382.
Imrie, Rob. Rethinking the Relationships between Disability, Rehabilitation, and Society. *Disability and Rehabilitation* 19.7 (1997): 263–271.
Kanter, Arlene S. Promise and Challenge of the United Nations Convention on the Rights of Persons with Disabilities. *Syracuse J. Int'l L. & Com.* 34 (2006): 287.
Kanter, Arlene S. There's No Place Like Home: The Right to Live in the Community for People with Disabilities, under International Law and the Domestic Laws of the United States and Israel. *Israel Law Review* 45.02 (2012): 181–233.
Karako-Eyal, Nili. A Critical Disability Theory Analysis of Wrongful Life/Birth Actions in Israel. *International Journal of Private Law* 6.3 (2013): 289–302.
Kuczewski, Mark G. Disability: An Agenda for Bioethics. *American Journal of Bioethics* 1.3 (2001): 36–44.
Linton, Simi. *Claiming Disability: Knowledge and Identity*. New York University Press, 1998.
Matsuda, Mari J. Pragmatism Modified and the False Consciousness Problem. *S. Cal. L. Rev.* 63 (1989): 1763.
Mor, Sagit. Between Charity, Welfare, and Warfare: A Disability Legal Studies Analysis of Privilege and Neglect in Israeli Disability Policy. *Yale JL & Human.* 18 (2006): 63.
Mor, Sagit. "Tell My Sister to Come and Get Me Out of Here": A Reading of Ableism and Orientalism in Israel's Immigration Policy (The First Decade). *Disability Studies Quarterly* 27.4 (2007).
Mor, Sagit. The Dialectics of Wrongful Life and Wrongful Birth Claims in Israel: A Disability Critique. *Studies in Law, Politics, and Society* 63 (2014): 113–146.
Mor, Sagit. The Right to Access and Access to Justice – A Disability Perspective. *Hukim – Journal on Legislation* 8, 15–83 (2016) (Hebrew).
Norsigian, Judy. *Our Bodies, Ourselves*. Simon and Schuster, 2011.
Nussbaum, Martha C. *Frontiers of Justice: Disability, Nationality, Species Membership*. Harvard University Press, 2006.
Oliver, Michael. *The Politics of Disablement: A Sociological Approach*. London, 1990.
Parens, Erik and Adrienne Asch. The Disability Rights Critique of Prenatal Genetic Testing (Special Supplement). *Hastings Center Report* 29.5 (1999): S1–S22.
Perry, Ronen. It's a Wonderful Life. *Cornell L.Rev.* 93 (2008): 329–399.
Portugese, Jacqueline. *Fertility Policy in Israel: The Politics of Religion, Gender, and Nation*. Greenwood Publishing Group, 1998.

Remennick, Larissa. The Quest for the Perfect Baby: Why Do Israeli Women Seek Prenatal Genetic Testing? *Sociology of Health & Illness* 28.1 (2006): 21–53.

Report of the Public Committee on the Matter of "Wrongful Life-Giving" (2012, March). Jerusalem (Hebrew). http://index.justice.gov.il/Pubilcations/News/Documents/doc.doc.

Rinck, Christine and Carl F. Calkins. Challenges across the Life Span for Persons with Disabilities. *Bioethics Forum* 12.3 (1996): 37–46.

Rothman, David J. *Strangers at the Bedside: A History of How Law and Bioethics Transformed Medical Decision Making.* Basic Books, 1991.

Sabatello, Maya and Marianne Schulze, eds. *Human Rights and Disability Advocacy.* University of Pennsylvania Press, 2013.

Salzman, Leslie. Guardianship for Persons with Mental Illness – A Legal and Appropriate Alternative? *Saint Louis University Journal of Health Law & Policy* 4 (2011).

Samuels, Ellen Jean. My Body, My Closet: Invisible Disability and the Limits of Coming-Out Discourse. *GLQ: A Journal of Lesbian and Gay Studies* 9.1 (2003): 233–255.

Scotch, Richard K. *From Good Will to Civil Rights.* Temple University Press, 1986.

Scully, Jackie Leach. *Disability Bioethics: Moral Bodies, Moral Difference.* Rowman & Littlefield, 2008.

Shakespeare, Tom. *Disability Rights and Wrongs.* Routledge, 2006.

Shalev, Carmel. *Health, Law, and Human Rights.* Tel Aviv University Press, 2003 (Hebrew).

Shapiro, Joseph P. *No Pity: People with Disabilities Forging a New Civil Rights Movement.* Three Rivers Press, 1994.

Stevens, M. L. T. The History of Bioethics: Its Rise and Significance. Reference Module in Biomedical Sciences (2014) www.sciencedirect.com/science/article/pii/B9780128012383001756.

Swain, John and Sally French. Towards an Affirmation Model of Disability. *Disability & Society* 15.4 (2000): 569–582.

Tolub, Yotam. *A Bizchut Report: Alternatives to Guardianship in Financial Affairs.* 2015.

Tolub, Yotam and Kanter Arlene. Whose Life Is It Anyway?: The Challenge to Autonomy on Legal Capacity of People with Disabilities. *Tel Aviv U. J. L. & Soc. Change* 6 (2014): 45–65 (Hebrew).

Weiss, Meira. *The Chosen Body: The Politics of the Body in Israeli Society.* Stanford University Press. 2002.

Wendell, Susan. *The Rejected Body: Feminist Philosophical Reflections on Disability.* Psychology Press, 1996.

World Health Organization. *World Report on Disability.* 2011.

Zeitsov v. Katz, CA 512/81 [1986] IsrSC 40(2) 85 (Hebrew).

Ziv, Neta. Disability Law in Israel and the United States – A Comparative Perspective. *Israel Yearbook on Human Rights*, (1999): 171–202.

Zola, Ervin Kenneth. Medicine as an Institution of Social Control. *Ekistics* 41.245, HEALTH (April 1976): 210–214.

PART II

Familialism and Reproduction

6

The Effect of Jewish-Israeli Family Ideology on Policy Regarding Reproductive Technologies

Yael Hashiloni-Dolev

INTRODUCTION

It has often been argued that Israelis "do" bioethics – be it genetic engineering of crops, stem cell research, or embryo selection – "the Israeli way" (Prainsack and Firestine 2006). The Israeli approach differs from that of other nations, especially when contrasted with the dominant Western-Christian bioethical discourse with which Israeli bioethics constantly negotiates and compares itself. This chapter will focus on a specific bioethical field, that of assisted reproductive technology (ART), in which Israel is seen as uniquely permissive and groundbreaking in comparison with most other advanced liberal societies. There have been numerous efforts to explain this peculiarity (Birenbaum-Carmeli 2010; Ivry 2009; Kahn 2000; Lavi 2010; Prainsack and Firestine 2006; Weiss 2002). Complementing them, this chapter focuses on the perspective of the family, arguing that Jewish-Israeli family ideology plays a crucial role in shaping Israeli policy, and that this viewpoint, which has been somewhat neglected in previous research, offers an important contribution to the discussion.

I will first present how kinship has generally been studied in relation to ART, and locate this chapter within this theoretical framework. I will then briefly portray Jewish-Israeli family norms and myths regarding family life, arguing that these depictions, whether real or ideally imagined, contribute to Israeli policy regarding various new reproductive technologies. Drawing on my own research as well as secondary literature, my three case studies will be: (a) selective abortions and the status of the embryo/fetus; (b) posthumous reproduction, focusing in particular on the subject of posthumous grandparents; and (c) preimplantation genetic diagnosis (PGD) for the purpose of creating sibling donors. Hence I will first examine commitments and obligations across two to three generations, and then between siblings of the same cohort.

Since much of my previous research has focused on Israel and Germany, this chapter will be somewhat biased toward comparisons with German family ideology. I am not suggesting, however, that the German approach in particular is representative of a general Western family ideology. Obviously, many differences can be found among advanced liberal societies themselves. Rather, the level of analysis offered here is meant to outline the broad differences between Jewish-Israeli family ideology and other Western ideologies, of which the German one will be used as a primary example, highlighting at the same time its own singularity (Raz and Schiktanz 2016).

As a political entity, Israel perceives itself – and much of its elite aspires to be – a modern, liberal, democratic state; yet it displays many traditional, non-Western features, most notably its very high fertility rate (compared to all other liberal democracies), low divorce rate, and familialism (Fogiel-Bijaoui 2002).

My central argument is that despite its modern appeal, the Jewish-Israeli family is rather "clannish," and has not fully adopted individualistic Western ideals in which family members are perceived as separate, autonomous individuals. Instead, the members of the Israeli-Jewish family are perceived as indivisible and mutually obligated, from womb (fetuses) to tomb (posthumous continuation of the bloodline). My specific thesis is that it is this attitude toward the family that contributes to the "permissiveness" of the Israeli reproductive approach. My more general thesis is that family ideology is a major factor affecting bioethical reasoning, much like philosophical heritage, religious tradition, or political legacy.

ART AND KINSHIP STUDIES

Early research on kinship and ART questioned the technology's implications for definitions of relatedness. Since kinship is principally defined as the ties established through reproduction, many studies were concerned with the new family relationships that could be formed via these innovative technologies (Franklin 1997; Levine 2008). Their primary questions were: What makes us related? What makes a family in contemporary times, or more specifically, who is "the" parent? How many parents/mothers can one have (an egg donor, a gestational surrogate mother, or the nurturing parents)? Is the family a matter of choice, contract, or blood/genes?

Further, early writing on assisted reproduction emphasized its challenge to traditional concepts of family and kinship, stressing its subversive potential. This trend has been reversed in the more recent literature, however, which argues that current family models shaped by ART are based equally on conventional and radical paradigms (Levine 2008). Generalizing broadly, Levine (2008) states that two strands of writing on the kinship implications of ART can be discerned: one argues that new reproductive technologies have changed our understanding of kinship (Dolgin 2000; Edwards 2000; Franklin 1995), and the other views these technologies as grounded on traditional ideas of blood ties and genetics (Inhorn 2003; Modell 1989; Teman 2003). Yet early writers such as Strathern already suggested that ART may enable "both *more* tradition and *more* modernity at the same time" (1996: 45).

This chapter joins the school of thought that argues that the innovative and liberal utilization of ART actually builds on traditional ideals of family structure, adding a special emphasis on individuality versus "togetherness." Writing about family law, Dolgin (2000) contends that its focus has shifted from the vision of families as holistic, hierarchical social units that both encompass and supersede the identities of individual members to the rights and duties of adult family members toward one another as autonomous individuals. Reproductive technologies and the confusion they have engendered about biological parentage have, according to Dolgin (2000), encouraged – or perhaps compelled – courts to view families, and even the parent–child relationship, as an association of autonomous individuals linked together by choice and design. But this is not the end of the story. The genetic revolution, which spawned the genetic family, has once again eroded the focus on individual family members. Whereas in the modern family, the unit of value is the individual, Dolgin argues that the unit of value in the genetic family is once again the whole *and* its parts.

While I would not suggest that the Israeli family has sidestepped this process of modernization/individualization, or the coexistence of modern and genetic families, I will argue that, in terms of societal norms, it is more close-knit than the typical or ideal Western family. At the same time, innovations in the field of ART, and their manifestation in Israeli society, have brought to the fore tensions around the individual within the family, obligations between different family members (between generations and across siblings), and boundaries between the nuclear and extended family. In contrast to Western bioethics, which is dominated by the concept of individual autonomy, my claim is that Israeli bioethics is characterized by a less individualistic cultural understanding regarding family members, affecting bioethical reasoning as well as personal and policy decisions in the field of ART.

JEWISH-ISRAELI FAMILY IDEOLOGY

Despite Israel's sizeable non-Jewish, mostly Arab population (about 20 percent of the country's total), my focus here will be on the Jewish family, since policymaking in Israel is strongly influenced by the majority state culture. Let me clarify from the outset that I am not positing that a unique Jewish family – or more specifically a Jewish-Israeli family – actually exists. Echoing Bourdieu, I view the family as "a fiction, a social artefact, an illusion in the most ordinary sense of the word, but a 'well-founded illusion,' because, being produced and reproduced with the guarantee of the state, it receives from the state at every moment the means to exist and persist" (Bourdieu 1996: 25). Nonetheless, the Jewish family is a highly diverse artefact, taking many forms in different homes. Obviously, Jews both inside and outside Israel have not escaped the trends affecting families in the West such as late marriage or no marriage at all; high divorce rates; single-parent families; and "new" families of all types. As a sociologist, both the demographic facts of the Jewish-Israeli family (for example, divorce and fertility rates) and the myths and stereotypes informing its ideology are significant for my analysis.

Since most contemporary Jews live either in Israel or in the United States, let us begin with a brief review of early studies of the American Jewish family. In 1966, Balswick argued that American Jewish families were somewhat more cohesive than other American families. His observation was based on Jewish tradition, in which various religious holidays serve to bring the family together, and in which the home is regarded as the basic religious institution. In this family, individuals are taught that they can maximize their personal growth and achieve their highest fulfillment solely in marriage and the continuation of the extended family. Ever since, the Jewish family in the United States has been largely spared negative stereotyping in the social science literature, and has usually been described in positive terms as closely knit, and as a social institution that assists its sons' and daughters' social mobility and maintains strong bonds (Hyman 1986). However, as early as 1983, Cherlin and Celebuski demonstrated that the differences between Catholic, Protestant, and Jewish families are more modest than scholarly and popular writing might lead us to believe. Overall, regarding the American Jewish family of the 1970s, they concluded that the differences between Jewish and non-Jewish families, except in the domain of childrearing, where Jews seemed to be following a strategy suited to enhancing their children's social, economic, and intellectual achievements, were in fact quite minor.

Popular culture has taken a more complex view of the Jewish family. On one hand, representations of the warmth and stability of the premodern Jewish family are often idealized. This romantic image of an affectionate, united, supportive family is also echoed in the present. On the other hand, this loving family is also described as an emotionally intense group of individuals smothered by their Jewish mothers and the family circle, which is simultaneously supportive, embracing, and suffocating (Hyman 1986). The best-known example of this is the stereotype of the Jewish mother, who is depicted as closely enmeshed with her children's lives, extremely ambitious, manipulative, self-centered, and domineering (Rothbell 1986), or, in the language of this chapter, as not allowing her children their individuality or separateness.

In Israel, scholars of the Jewish-Israeli family have insisted that it is indeed unique. Fogiel-Bijaoui (2002) describes Israeli society as the most familialistic of the postindustrial societies since, comparatively, Israelis tend to marry in large numbers, divorce infrequently, and produce many children, despite the process of individualization that Israeli society is undergoing and its affinity with Western culture. What can account for this exceptionality? Following a revolutionary period in which the early Zionist settlers rejected the family and experimented with alternative family structures on the *kibbutz* (Beit-Hallahmi 1981), the situation has turned around, making Israel extremely family-oriented. This characteristic has been attributed to several features of Israeli society, among them its constant state of conflict, history, religious heritage, and demographic composition (Shamgar-Handelman and Bar-Yosef 1991). The Jewish religion, in contrast to the Christian ethos, has no religious saints or figures who practice celibacy such as the Virgin Mary, Jesus, or priests and nuns whose major loyalty is to God and the Church. The Jewish family does not compete with religious institutions. Rather, the Jewish home is where much of Jewish ritual is practiced, and the nuclear family is defined as the building block of the community. Likewise, centuries of living in hostile societies led to a strengthening of family ties and obligations. The Jews' status as a people of persecuted strangers enhanced the need for strong group solidarity and trust in order to survive and flourish. Jewish genocide, especially during the Holocaust, also supported the yearning for lost family ties and a collective heritage. In Israel, other factors have been added to the mix: being a community of immigrants commonly reinforces family ties and the need for family support. Repeated wars and fears of extinction also translate into pro-natalism and strengthening of the family. Additionally, large portions of the Jewish-Israeli community arrived from the Middle East, where the family has undergone less transformation than in much of the Western world (Shamgar-Handelman and Bar-Yosef 1991).

My argument is that Jewish-Israeli families are obviously not different from their counterparts around the world in defining a family as a system of mutual love and caring; however, awareness of the difficulty of achieving this ideal, or of the inner tensions between individuals within a family, varies widely among cultures. Israeli familialism tends to overlook the fact that while families are ideally a safe haven protecting their members from a cruel world, they are also quite often a conflicted social group where different members hold diverse interests and where violence and abuse are not a rarity. Ackelsberg (1995), writing of the Jewish ethical precept of *shalom bayit* (peace in the home), explains that it expresses the belief that the whole family is more than the sum of its individual parts. The concept rests on the ideal of a unified and peaceful family whose members work in cooperation and agreement about their goals, and it assumes the presence of harmony and fairness. But when those characteristics are absent, pressure to conform to *shalom bayit* expectations can mask oppression, mostly of women and children (Ackelsberg 1995).

Israel combines the symbolic repertoires of traditional societies with the technological resources of medically advanced societies (Gooldin 2007). I will strive to demonstrate how these repertoires affect the utilization of technology, specifically, what they enable and what they suppress. My claim is that what the Israeli family is – or ought to be – is not a stable concept; rather, it is a constantly shifting notion, changing along with the new technologies while mutually constituting one other. Likewise, as the following analysis will show, the ideal of the family is defined in diverse ways to justify various medical procedures and new family formations.

THE SECOND GENERATION: THE CHILD-TO-BE

Numerous studies (Birenbaum-Carmeli 2010; Hashiloni-Dolev 2007; Ivry 2009; Kahn 2000; Weiss 2002) have shown that Israeli women and the Israeli legal, religious, and medical establishments are exceptionally supportive of prenatal diagnosis and its outcome: selective abortions based on the health of the unborn child. Compared to most other medically advanced nations, Israel seems to have embraced the practice of prenatal diagnosis (PND), premarital genetic testing, and selective abortions to a far greater extent (Raz 2010; Remennick 2006; Sher et al. 2003). Opposition to PND, which is prevalent in the Western world, is commonly grounded in arguments having to do with the protection of the embryo/fetus and a general opposition to abortion (Heyd 1989; Kaczor 2005; Kaplan and Tong 1996; Krones et al. 2006); medicalization and "genitalization" of reproduction (Conrad 1999; Lippman 1992; Nye 2003; Sawicki 1999); devaluation of the life of the disabled through the practice of eugenics (Duster 2003; Parens and Asch 2000; Wertz 1998); and the creation of "designer babies," depriving children of their right to come into this world unselected by their parents (Habermas 2003).

Such opposition is largely lacking in Israeli public discourse. This has been explained by many different factors, among them strong pro-natalism; depictions of the Ashkenazi gene pool (of Jews originating from Eastern Europe) as especially problematic, leading to genetic anxiety (Birenbaum-Carmeli 2004; Davis et al. 2010); intolerance toward disability, and a pro-eugenics public (Weiss 2002); attitudes of professionals (Hashiloni-Dolev 2007) and even leaders of disabled advocacy groups (Raz 2004); and fear of the burden of care for a disabled child at a time when the welfare system is shrinking (Remennick 2006).

All these factors have certainly played a part in shaping prenatal care in Israel. However, for the purpose of this chapter, I will focus on the child-to-be, demonstrating that one of the reasons enabling – and more so, supporting – its selection is the view of the child not as an autonomous being, but as part of its mother during pregnancy and, subsequently, as part of its family.

Since treatment and cure lag behind the ability to discover abnormal conditions during pregnancy, PND currently goes hand in hand with selective abortions. However, in sharp contrast to the American or German political history of abortions, legal termination of pregnancy has remained largely peripheral to Israeli public debate (Morag-Levine 1994). Israeli abortion policy does not touch on the potential conflict between the interests of mothers and those of fetuses, as protection of the fetus is virtually a nonissue (Gross 1999). Indeed, Israeli law offers no rationale for its regulation of abortion, referring neither to the status and rights of the fetus nor to those of the pregnant woman. Thus the Israeli fetus has no legal standing and is not recognized as an autonomous being. This understanding of the (non-)status of the fetus, as reflected in Israeli abortion law and public debate, very much echoes Jewish doctrine. In the eyes of ancient Jewish law, the fetus is deemed an organic part of its mother rather than an independent entity, and hence has no legal rights (Jakobovits 1967). Abortion is not regarded as murder, though it may amount to killing. The difference between the two lies in the circumstances: killing of an "aggressor" – even an "innocent" one – is allowed in self-defense, and a fetus may be so regarded when the mother's health is at risk. The woman's own health thus overrides the theoretical interests of the fetus (Feldman 1986). So although Judaism strongly supports the sanctity of life, there are nonetheless circumstances in which abortion is permitted, since a fetus – and even more so an embryo or pre-embryo – is not considered alive or a separate entity.

In recent years, a new voice against abortion has emerged in Israel in the form of Efrat-C.R.I.B. (Committee for the Rescue of Israel's Babies), led by a religious physician. However, Efrat focuses on helping financially distressed pregnant women, and does not oppose selective abortions per se. On its website, it clearly distances itself from prolife opinions; rather, it is dedicated to bringing more Jewish babies into the world, in cases where abortion is being contemplated due to financial need and/or lack of social support (www.efrat.org.il/english/).

Likewise, note that many Orthodox Jewish women both in Israel and the United States test for "genetic compatibility" with their future partner prior to marriage (Raz and Vizner 2008), but are usually reluctant to perform prenatal diagnosis and selective abortions. Michael Barilan (2005) claims that this reluctance is not indicative of Jewish law, but rather of the tensions between the law and the ethos of the law, inasmuch as abortions are not strongly condemned by Jewish law itself.

Coming back to the comparison with non-Jewish culture, Jewish doctrine is far more flexible concerning abortions than, for instance, Catholic doctrine, which views ensoulment as taking place at the moment of conception; the fetus is therefore a separate "life," and the taking of that life impinges upon the salvation of its soul after death (Jakobovits 1967). A conflict thus occurs between the pregnant mother and what is seen as an autonomous life growing within her. The Catholic understanding of the independent moral status of the embryo from the moment of fertilization has had a very strong effect on the moral discussion regarding abortions as well as reproductive technologies in Western societies.

In a study comparing Israeli and German perceptions of the moral standing of the fetus, Hashiloni-Dolev and Weiner demonstrated that despite their similar level of medical expertise, German and Israeli genetic counselors view the fetus within different ethical frameworks. German counselors perceive the fetus as an autonomous being and debate the particular biological stages through which this autonomy is acquired, while Israeli counselors do not consider the moral status of the fetus independent of its relations with its family. Hence Israeli counselors deploy a "relational ethic," in contrast to their German counterparts, who posit a "biological ethic" (Hashiloni-Dolev and Weiner 2008).

Accordingly, German counselors reproduce the model of fetal developmental stages (in itself a construction), which dovetails with perceptions of the fetus as a "life" and thus a bearer of independent rights that are understood to contradict those of the mother. By contrast, Israeli counselors reject biological ethics, leading to a perception of the fetus defined primarily by its enmeshment with others.

In her seminal work on prenatal diagnosis, Rayna Rapp (1999) studied the attitudes of women from different ethnic backgrounds toward selective abortions. When faced with difficult moral decisions regarding the health of their future child, upper-middle-class white women struggled over whether it was selfish of them to screen for potential problems. They were plagued by feelings of guilt emanating from the need to strike a balance between personal self-fulfillment and its dark side, namely, self-centeredness and, correspondingly, being a "bad mother." On the other hand, multiethnic working-class women and Latin American women struggling to acclimate in the United States, when forced to decide whether to accept a child with special needs, questioned the impact of raising such a child on the entire family.

The difference between the groups was obviously partly economic, as a child with special needs would cause less "damage" to the more affluent family. Nonetheless, the contrast also attests to how family members think of each other, suggesting that the more Westernized see them as individuals in conflict, each wanting to reach self-fulfillment, whereas the non-Western and the poor take a more holistic view of the family unit. Regarding Jewish American women, Rapp describes them as especially enthusiastic regarding PND and its outcomes, attributing this to their high degree of trust in science and medicine. I would like to suggest that their attitude might also be indicative of their family ideology, which tends toward the more traditional side of the continuum despite their social class (typically upper-middle).

In view of this, my argument is that the notion of what constitutes good and responsible motherhood/parenthood during pregnancy is related to broader family ideology. Israeli social norms equate "good mothering" in pregnancy with taking "genetic responsibility" for future offspring and the entire family (Remennick 2006; Rimon-Zarfaty 2014), since fetuses are seen first and foremost as part of their mothers and hence subordinate to them. Children in Israeli-Jewish society are seen similarly as parts of the family group and its joint interests, and not as separate beings with individual rights. Likewise, future children are rarely described in Israeli culture as "gifts" that should be accepted "as is" in order to maintain and display the receiver's morality, in contrast to the common Western "gift" metaphor in the discussion of reprogenetics (Sandel 2007; Scully et al. 2006). It follows that the selection of future children in keeping with their family's interests, especially the wish not to be burdened with extra care as well as the "right" to have a healthy child, are not morally condemned in Israel. Rather, it is regarded positively, as fully congruent with responsible and good parenthood, since children are "naturally" expected to fulfill the needs and even desires of their family.

This understanding stands in stark contrast to the Habermasian critique, which has strongly influenced German ethical discourse in this area (Habermas 2003; Krones and Richter 2004). Habermas denounces parents who would become the designers of their future children, as doing so, in his view, transgresses the legitimate boundaries between children and their parents, and deprives children of the potential for the fully ethical existence of their (autonomous) self, in addition to violating the natural relationship between generations.

THE THIRD GENERATION: THE POSTHUMOUS GRANDCHILD

Posthumous reproduction (PHR) after the death of a genetic father, mother, or even both parents has become a possibility since sperm, eggs, and pre-embryos can be cryopreserved, and, in the case of sperm and eggs, retrieved post mortem. Breaching the barriers between life and death (yet allowing a significant gap in time between death and reproduction) holds great promise for a certain form of eternal life, but at the same time generates uneasiness, as it is sometimes associated with necrophilia, incest, or Frankenstein-type scenarios (Kroløkke and Adrian 2013). Accordingly, the regulation of PHR – usually involving cases of a genetically dead father, which are far more common and technically less complicated – varies internationally. Some countries, such as Germany, Sweden, Italy, France, Canada (except for British Columbia), Hungary, Slovenia, Norway, Malaysia, and Taiwan, are restrictive, while others, such as England, Belgium, Australia, and some U.S. states, allow the procedure only if the deceased had clearly stated his wishes prior to death (Ahluwalia and Arora 2011). Israel is known for its particularly permissive regulations in this respect. In 2003, the Israeli attorney general (IAG) issued regulations allowing PHR for deceased men. The regulations outlined a two-step procedure (Landau 2004): retrieval of sperm from a dying or deceased man at the request of his female partner, whether married or not; and court authorization to use the sperm, determined on a case-by-case basis, taking into consideration the deceased man's dignity and presumed wishes. Nine years later, the Mor-Yosef National Committee (2012), which was appointed to propose recommendations for unified legislation regarding assisted reproduction in Israel, recommended that PHR be permitted in cases of deceased women as well. Its recommendations were not implemented, and no existing law covers this situation.

What makes Israel exceptional in regard to PHR is twofold. First, the IAG regulations (2003) are based on the assumption of "presumed wish," namely, that a man who lived in a loving relationship with a woman would wish to have her carry his child after his death (Ravitsky 2004). Under this assumption, there is no need for the deceased man to have provided his explicit consent for posthumous reproduction prior to death. This stands in contrast to professional guidelines or laws elsewhere (American Society for Reproductive Medicine – Ethics Committee 2013; Bahadur 2002; Pennings et al. 2006 Tremellen and Savulescu 2015), which repeatedly demand explicit (and not presumed) consent. Such consent is required in order to protect the man's autonomy, assuming that not all men wish to become posthumous fathers, or maybe even fathers at all, and that the loved ones left behind may not be able to truly represent the wishes of the deceased. But Israeli exceptionalism does not end here.

A second, related procedure – posthumous grandparenthood – has, to the best of my knowledge, been permitted and performed to date only in Israel. However, there are some as yet unresolved cases in other countries as well, for example, the United Kingdom (Fearon 2016). According to European and American professional guidelines, parents of the deceased (or other family members, with the exception of the partner) have no ethical claim to the gametes of the deceased (ASRM 2013; Pennings et al. 2006). In Israel as well (according to the IAG regulations of 2003), parents have no legal standing regarding the sperm of their deceased sons; nonetheless, more than ten requests had been submitted to Israeli family courts as of 2013 – and probably more in subsequent years – by parents seeking permission to use their deceased sons' sperm to create genetic grandchildren (Rimon-Greenspan and Ravitsky 2013). These cases were each based on a contract between the potential grandparents and a single woman who did not know their son but wished to use his sperm to become the mother of their future grandchild; the women made the plea to the courts and committed to raising the child in question. In many of these instances, the courts gave their permission for the use of the sperm, and children were born.

In keeping with this trend, New Family (an Israeli family rights advocacy organization supporting all types of families, including those created by PHR) reported on its website in 2014 that the new IAG had approved a legal plea for posthumous grandparenthood, in contrast to his predecessor, though no formal document has been issued on the subject (Cohen 2013). Additionally, in late 2014, parents of a young deceased man, together with a woman who wished to be impregnated with their son's sperm, were given court permission to use the sperm, with no need to testify about the wishes of the dead, which were unknown (Cohen-Friedman 2014). In his opinion to the court on this matter, the then-IAG repeated the rationale of the original guidelines, which stated that having children is an intimate decision of the mating partners, but then opened the door to exceptional cases to be evaluated by the courts, and thus, to PHR (*M.P. v. Israeli Ministry of Health*, 2014). In September 2016, for the first time, a family court in Israel approved the use by parents of their son's sperm, a donated egg, and a gestational surrogate to produce a child that they plan to raise without the involvement of the biological mother(s) (*Shahar v. Israeli Attorney General*, 2016).

In the United States, parents of the deceased enter the policy debate about PHR mainly via the potential conflict between them and an intimate partner, as they can try to block the partner's request for the retrieval or use of gametes (Hans and Frey 2013). Similar cases have also occurred in Israel, mostly reflecting fights over inheritance. Yet the most recent Israeli legal disputes in this area have yielded contradictory findings. In 2013, the parents of a dead man sued his widow who remarried and decided not to have children from their son's cryopreserved sperm. The parents demanded permission to use their son's sperm with a single woman who had not known their son while alive, but the widow objected to their claim and prevented them from obtaining the sperm. The family court ruled in the parents' favor and against their daughter-in-law. The widowed daughter-in-law did not give up, and appealed to the district court. Her chief argument was that her late husband would not have wished to have children posthumously with another woman. In 2015, the district court rejected the widow's appeal and ruled once more in favor of the parents (*Jane Doe v. Central District Attorney's Office*, 2015). This case finally reached the Israeli Supreme Court of Justice, where at the end of 2016, former court decisions had been turned over, supporting this time the widow's position (*John Doe v. IGA and Sheba Hospital*, Supreme Court of Justice, Jerusalem 2016). In a different case, in early 2016, the family court in Jerusalem ruled in favor of parents who asked to use their dead son's sperm despite his widow's objections, respecting their wish to continue their family, which had no other offspring (*John Doe v. Jerusalem District Attorney's Office*, 2016). However, after the very recent Supreme Court verdict, this tendency is arrested.

In justifying the original IAG policy, and later court decisions that opened the door to posthumous reproduction even wider (not only to partners of the deceased, but also to their parents and single women not known to the deceased), very definite assumptions were made about the presumed wishes of the young men in addition to family relations and obligations. The attorney general justified his position from 2003 by referring to the biblical practice of levirate marriage according to which, when a man dies childless, his brother is obliged to marry his widow, and their first child is to carry on the name of the deceased and be his heir (Israel Attorney General 2003). The traditional justification for this abandoned practice has to do with inheritance laws as well as with the continuity of the family line in the case of a man who dies childless. Leaving the world without offspring was a concern among ancient Israelites and seems to still guide contemporary policy, which promotes the desire for genetic continuity and for existence after death by leaving offspring. Other arguments supportive of the "presumed wish" legal solution raise patriarchal and pro-natalist evolutionary or instinct-based justifications, assuming that all men, dead or alive, are interested in the spread and continuation of their sperm and that all couples wish to procreate (Hashiloni-Dolev and Triger 2016; Landau 1999; Shalev 2002).

It is not only the supreme importance attached to the continuation of the bloodline that is exceptional in the Jewish-Israeli case, but also the way that different family members are positioned vis-à vis this normative ideal. My claim is that while in less familialistic cultures, procreation is looked upon as an intimate matter between the potential mating partners, in Israeli Jewish society, young couples' reproductive plans are considered a matter of concern to the extended family. Adult children are expected to grant grandchildren to their parents (Donath 2011); similarly, in Palestinian society, the boundaries between the family of origin and the newly established family are rather vague (Zu'bi, Chapter 8 in this volume). Parents and their adult children are not perceived as separate, even once the children have grown up and can form their own discrete families.

Likewise, intergenerational conflicts are downplayed in the Israeli Jewish imagination, since the generations are not considered separate. This viewpoint makes it possible for organizations such as New Family to claim that the Israeli state must respect parents' desire to pay tribute to their deceased sons by allowing them to create the next generation, as they are trusted to be the best representatives of their sons' intentions (Sherwood 2011). It also allows the family courts to argue that, in certain cases, parents are the ones best positioned to know and express their sons' "true wishes" and that this solution is a "harmonious coming together of the interests of all parties involved" (Rimon-Greenspan and Ravitsky 2013: 1).

In one of the cases between a bereaved widow and parents who wished to become grandparents against the wishes of their widowed daughter-in-law, the courts made great efforts to prove that this would have been the choice of the deceased. The evidence supporting this presumed intention was very problematic: testimonies of women who had had brief love affairs with him while he was alive, and love letters he had written to his wife, which were interpreted quite controversially (Hashiloni-Dolev and Triger 2016). The district court concluded its arguments with the statement that due to the Decalogue commandment to honor one's parents, and since the deceased and his wife had respected and consulted his parents on various matters, the court assumed that, had the deceased known that his parents were of the opinion that he would have wanted to have children posthumously with a woman he had not met while alive, he would have respected their understanding of his presumed wishes. As we can see, it was virtually impossible in this case to disentangle the desires of the living parents from those of their late son, while the widow was not trusted to represent the presumed wishes of her dead husband. Although this case had a different ending, due to the Supreme Court's decision to turn over all lower courts' decisions regarding this dispute, it still proves my claim that the borders between generations are vague and contested.

As will be shown in the next case study as well, members of the Jewish Israeli family are seen primarily as relatives, not as individuals. As such, they are expected to fulfill the needs or desires of the family, while the group itself is imagined to be harmonious and conflict-free (Hashiloni-Dolev, Hacker, and Boas 2014). What the foregoing cases demonstrate is that parents of deceased young men were and still are (if no widow fights against them) permitted by Israeli courts to be extremely active in pursuing grandparenthood, overlooking the ethical question of the autonomy of the deceased by presuming to know their wishes. This is easily justified, since the parents' wishes and interests are believed to correspond with those of their sons. Yet this case study of posthumous grandparenthood also shows that, not surprisingly, conflicts do take place within families. It thus becomes unclear what constitutes a family, and which version of it the state supports – that of the married couple or the parents and children – and how death affects all of these.

The contradictions between different court decisions made in recent conflicts, where the wishes of the parents (and thus of the original genetic family) initially prevailed over the wishes of the surviving partner of the new nuclear/chosen family, and then later on were disapproved by the Supreme Court, demonstrate current tensions between the original and chosen families. Yet it appears that some type of "right to posthumous grandparenthood," even if limited, is emerging in Israeli courts.

THE NEXT/SAME GENERATION: THE SIBLING DONOR

Preimplantation genetic diagnosis (PGD) is an early form of prenatal diagnosis, performed mainly to detect genetic defects in pre-embryos, which are then not implanted in a woman's body. Less commonly, PGD is done in order to select a sibling donor who will serve as a cord blood or bone marrow donor to an existing affected child. In our earlier studies (Hashiloni-Dolev and Shkedi 2007, 2010), Shiri Shkedi and I looked at the regulation of PGD for purposes of sibling donation in Israel, England, and Germany. Our findings revealed that this groundbreaking technology was approved with no genuine opposition in Israel, limited but later widely permitted in England, and banned in Germany. Subsequently, in 2011, PGD became permitted in Germany under certain circumstances, namely, if there is reason to believe that the child-to-be carries a high risk of serious hereditary disease, or in order to establish whether the embryo is seriously damaged and thus very likely to result in miscarriage or stillbirth (Braun 2016). Despite these changes, PGD for purposes of sibling donation remains restricted in Germany as of this writing.

Analyzing the different policy trajectories in these three societies in the early 2000s, we demonstrated that in contrast to Germany and England – where, despite all their differences, the social category at the heart of the debate was the individual child – in Israel, the welfare of the entire family was the primary preoccupation. Both Germany and England made the future sibling donor the focus of their concern, emphasizing the potential medical and/or psychological risks (in England), or risks to its freedom and autonomy (in Germany), whereas the Israeli discussion centered on the welfare of the entire (present and future) family.

Looking more specifically at the Israeli and German cases (Hashiloni-Dolev and Shkedi 2007), we argued that while family ties in both Israel and Germany are certainly highly valued, and much thought is given to the appropriate relationships between parents and children, the family ethic that characterizes these two societies is dissimilar. Analyzing the arguments used by the opponents of PGD in Germany, we demonstrated that they rested on a threefold view of family relationships: an idealistic view, which demands unconditional love and acceptance between family members (even before birth); a view of family members as predominantly individuals holding autonomous rights, and not as members of a unified body with similar interests; and a view of the family as a potentially highly exploitative social group. Consequently, we argued that because family relationships are so complex and have the potential for both endless love and extreme exploitation, reproduction in Germany is left to the rule of nature. In Israel, on the other hand, it is considered far more legitimate for parents to "design" or select their children as an expression of their parental love, caring, and responsibility toward the future child and its entire family. This view is consistent with the perception of children not only as individual subjects, but as members of a unified body consisting of different members whose interests are imagined to be aligned. Consequently, PGD for the purpose of sibling donation is viewed in Israel as a lifesaving blessing that serves all family members rather than as a medical procedure creating family conflicts.

This Israeli emphasis on the well-being of the entire family is coupled with a disregard for the potential risks to either the future child or its mother, who is expected to take upon herself a complex medical treatment. Conversely, highlighting the rights of the sibling donor in Germany coincides with less attention being given to the welfare of the parents or the existing sick child.

Raz and colleagues (2016) studied popular (as opposed to policymakers') views of sibling donation achieved through PGD in Germany and Israel. The study compared the reception and interpretations in both societies of the novel/film *My Sister's Keeper*, which portrays a family where one daughter is the sibling donor of her sick sister. Raz and colleagues revealed that in both countries, most commentaries presented positions similar to the one articulated by policymakers. While in Germany, most film reviewers argued against sibling donation, referring to the instrumentalization of the donor and depicting her as "raw material" or "spare parts," the majority of Israeli commentators expressed positive views of the procedure for its lifesaving potential. Additionally, the decoding of commentaries to the film supported the hypothesis of different family ethics, compounded in Germany by such concerns as loss of dignity, instrumentalization, the killing of discarded pre-embryos, and prenatal screening for disabilities. In Israel, some minor positions were critical of the view of the family as a unified body of members with similar interests, and questioned the axiom of saving life at all costs.

SUMMARY

Despite a common technological background, there is great diversity regarding the regulation and use of new reproductive technologies around the world. In this chapter, I have demonstrated how Israeli society localizes challenges posed by ART in the context of its family ideology. My thesis is that, in addition to other theories that have aimed to explain Israeli exceptionalism in this area, another important factor is the study of how the individual and the family are viewed in Israeli Jewish culture, and consequently, how ART is regulated by the state and its policies.

I suggest that observing the fields of prenatal diagnosis, posthumous reproduction (including posthumous grandparenthood), and preimplantation genetic diagnosis for sibling donation in Israel yields an additional perspective, which is centered on the belief systems regarding family ties and obligations that underlie Israel's reproductive policies. My argument is that the Israeli family has not fully experienced the process of modernization and individualization, since it is ideologically more closely knit than the typical/ideal Western family. In all three case studies, I have shown that the fetus, the sibling donor, and the deceased sperm donor are enmeshed with their families in such a way that they are expected to fulfill the wishes or interests of the families, and that their possible individual interests are overlooked. The imagined will of the not-yet-born, or the already-dead, is understood as matching current family wishes and needs; thus obligations between generations and siblings outweigh individual interests as well as the wishes of married/chosen partners. This reduced emphasis on individual autonomy lies at the heart of Israel's comparatively permissive reproductive policies, which embody a mixture of tradition and modernity. Yet Israeli modernism is ultimately not identical to that of Western liberal societies due to the country's particular family ideology. Bioethical reasoning in Israel and elsewhere should therefore be understood in light of the family ideology that shapes its assumptions, no less than its philosophical heritage, religious traditions, and political legacy.

References

Ackelsberg, M. A. (1995). Jewish Family Ethics in a Post-halachic Age. In E. N. Dorff and L. E. Newman (Eds.), *Contemporary Jewish Ethics and Morality: A Reader* (pp. 3–315). New York and Oxford: Oxford University Press.

Ahluwalia, U. and Arora, M. (2011). Posthumous Reproduction and Its Legal Perspective. *International Journal of Infertility and Fetal Medicine*, 2(1), 914. doi:10.5005/jp-journals-10016-1010.

American Society for Reproductive Medicine – Ethics Committee. (2013). Posthumous Collection and Use of Reproductive Tissue: A Committee Opinion. *Fertility & Sterility*, 99, 1842–1845.

Bahadur, G. (2002). Death and Conception. *Human Reproduction*, 17(10), 2769–2775.

Balswick, J. (1966). Are American-Jewish Families Closely Knit? A Review of the Literature. *Jewish Social Studies*, 28(3), 159–167.

Barilan, M. Y. (2005). "Biomedical Ethics and Halakha" and "Abortion." In J. Neusner et al. (Eds.), *The Encyclopedia of Judaism*, second ed. Leiden: Brill.

Beit-Hallahmi, B. (1981). The Kibbutz Family: Revival or Survival. *Journal of Family Issues*, 2(3), 259.

Birenbaum-Carmeli, D. (2004). Prevalence of Jews as Subjects in Genetic Research: Figures, Explanation, and Potential Implications. *American Journal of Medical Genetics*, 130A(1), 76–83.

Birenbaum-Carmeli, D. and Carmeli, Y. (2010). (Eds.). *Kin, Gene, Community: Reproductive Technology among Jewish Israelis*. Oxford and New York: Berghahn Books.

Bourdieu, P. (1996). On the Family as a Realized Category. *Theory, Culture & Society*, 13, 19–26.

Braun, K. (2016). "From Ethical Exceptionalism to Ethical Exceptions: The Rule and Exception Model and the Changing Meaning of Ethics in German Bioregulation." *Developing World Bioethics*.

Cherlin, A. and Celebuski, C. (1983). Are Jewish Families Different? Some Evidence from the General Social Survey. *Journal of Marriage and Family*, 45(4), 903–910.

Cohen, D. (2013). AG Approves Parents' Use of Dead Son's Sperm. *New Family*. Retrieved from www.newfamily.org.il/en/4989/ag-approves-parents-use-of-dead-sons-sperm-3 (Hebrew).

Cohen-Friedman, N. (2014, December 16). Tomer Passed Away, and a Woman He Did Not Know Will Become the Mother of His Child. *Ynet*. Retrieved from www.ynet.co.il/articles/0,7340,L-4603097,00.html (Hebrew).

Conrad, P. (1999). A Mirage of Genes. *Sociology of Health & Illness*, 21(2), 228–241.

Davis, D. S., Gerson, N., Ponsaran, R., and Siminoff, L. A. (2010). Ashkenazi Jews: Overburdened and Overexposed? *New Genetics and Society*, 29(3), 241–260.

Dolgin, J. L. (2000). Choice, Tradition, and the New Genetics: The Fragmentation of the Ideology of Family. *Conn Law Rev.*, 32(2), 523–566.

Donath, O. (2011). *Making a Choice: Being Child-Free in Israel*. Tel Aviv: Miskal-Yedioth Ahronoth Books (Hebrew).

Duster, T. ([1990] 2003). *Backdoor to Eugenics*. New York: Routledge.

Edwards, J. 2000. *Born and Bred: Idioms of Kinship and New Technologies in England*. Oxford: Oxford University Press.

Fearon, K. (2016, July 11). A Victory for Consent – But What About the Welfare of the Child? *Bionews*. Retrieved from www.bionews.org.uk/page_670138.asp.

Feldman, D. M. (1986). *Health and Medicine in Jewish Tradition*. New York: Crossroad.

Fogiel-Bijaoui, S. (2002). Familism, Postmodernity and the State: The Case of Israel. *The Journal of Israeli History*, 21(1–2), 38–62.

Franklin, S. (1997). *Embodied Progress: A Cultural Account of Assisted Conception*. London: Routledge.

Franklin, S. (1995). Postmodern Procreation: A Cultural Account of Assisted Reproduction. In F. D. Ginsburg and R. Rapp (Eds.), *Conceiving the New World Order: The Global Politics of Reproduction* (pp. 323–345). Berkeley: University of California Press.

Gooldin, S. (2007). Technologies of Happiness: Fertility Management in a Pro-natal Context. In Y. Shenhav and Y. Yossi (Eds.), *Citizenship Gaps: Migration, Fertility, and Identity* (pp. 265–302). Jerusalem: Van Leer/Hakibbutz Hameuchad (Hebrew).

Gross, M. L. (1999). After Feticide: Coping with Late-Term Abortion in Israel, Western Europe, and the United States. *Cambridge Quarterly of Healthcare Ethics*, 8(04), 449–462.

Habermas, J. (2003). *The Future of Human Nature*. Cambridge: Polity Press.

Hans, J. D. and Frey, L. M. (2013). American Attitudes in Context: Posthumous Use of Cryopreserved Gametes. *Journal of Clinical Research & Bioethics*, S1–006. doi:10.4172/2155-9627.S1-006.

Hashiloni-Dolev, Y. (2007). *A Life (Un)Worthy of Living: Reproductive Genetics in Israel and Germany*. International Library of Ethics, Law and the New Medicine, 34. Dordrecht: Springer.

Hashiloni-Dolev, Y., Hacker, D., and Boas, H. (2014). The Will of the Deceased: Three Israeli Case Studies. *Israeli Sociology*, 16(1) (Hebrew).

Hashiloni-Dolev, Y. and Shkedi, S. (2007). On New Reproductive Technologies and Family Ethics: Preimplantation Genetic Diagnosis (PGD) for Sibling Donors (SD) in Israel and Germany. *Social Science and Medicine*, 65(10), 2081–2092.

Hashiloni-Dolev, Y. and Shkedi, S. (2010). The Regulation of Preimplantation Genetic Diagnosis (PGD) for Sibling Donors in Israel, Germany and England: Balancing Potential Benefits and Risks. In D. Birenbaum-Carmeli and Y. Carmeli (Eds.), *Kin, Gene, Community: Reproductive Technology among Jewish Israelis* (pp. 61–83). Oxford/New-York: Berghahn Books.

Hashiloni-Dolev, Y. and Triger, Z. (2016). Between the deceased's wish and the wishes of his surviving relatives: Posthumous children, patriarchy, pronatalism, and the myth of continuity of the seed. *Tel-Aviv University Law Review*, 39(3), 661–706 (Hebrew).

Hashiloni-Dolev, Y. and Weiner, N. (2008). New reproductive technologies, genetic counselling and the standing of the fetus: Views from Germany and Israel. *Sociology of Health & Illness*, 30(7), 1055–1069.

Heyd, D. (1989). *Ethics and Medicine*. Tel Aviv, Israel: The Broadcast University, Ministry of Defense Publishing (Hebrew).

Hyman, P. E. (1986). Introduction: Perspectives on the Evolving Jewish Family. In S. M. Cohen and P. E. Hyman (Eds.), *The Jewish Family: Myths and Reality* (pp. 3–29). New York & London: Holmes & Meyer.

Inhorn, M. C. (2003). *Local Babies, Global Science: Gender, Religion, and In Vitro Fertilization in Egypt*. New York: Routledge.

Israel Attorney General. (2003). Retrieving Sperm Post-Mortem and its Use. Retrieved from www.justice.gov.il/NR/rdonlyres/2DCE0B40-B4D6-441F-A792-342A33982AD6/0/12202.pdf (Hebrew).

Ivry, T. (2009). *Embodying Culture: Pregnancy in Japan and Israel*. New Brunswick, NJ: Rutgers University Press.

Jakobovits, I. (1967). *Jewish Medical Ethics: A Comparative and Historical Study of the Jewish Religious Attitude to Medicine and its Practice*. New York: Bloch.

Jane Doe v. Central District Prosecutor's Office, Family Court (Petah Tikva) 31344-09-13, Nevo Legal Database (March 18, 2015) (Hebrew).

John Doe v. Jerusalem District Prosecutor's Office, Family Court (Jerusalem) 27169-11-13 (not published) (Hebrew).

Kaczor, C. R. (2005). *The Edge of Life: Human Dignity and Contemporary Bioethics*. Dordrecht, Netherlands: Springer.

Kahn, S. M. (2000). *Reproducing Jews: A Cultural Account of Assisted Conception in Israel*. Durham, NC: Duke University Press.

Kaplan, L. J. and Tong, R. (1996). *Controlling our Reproductive Destiny: A Technological and Philosophical Perspective*. Cambridge, MA: MIT Press.

Kroløkke, C. H. and Adrian, S. W. (2013). Sperm on Ice: Fatherhood and Life after Death. *Australian Feminist Studies*, 28, 263–278.

Krones, T. and Richter, G. (2004). Preimplantation Genetic Diagnosis: European Perspectives and the German Situation. *Journal of Medicine and Philosophy*, 29, 623–640.

Krones, T., Schlüter, E., Neuwohner, E., El Ansari, S., Wissner, T., and Richter, G. (2006). What Is the Preimplantation Embryo? *Social Science & Medicine*, 63 (1), 1–20.

Landau, R. (1999). Planned Orphanhood. *Social Science and Medicine*, 49, 185–196.

Landau, R. (2004). Posthumous Sperm Retrieval for the Purpose of Later Insemination or IVF in Israel: An Ethical and Psychosocial Critique. *Human Reproduction*, 19, 1952–1956.

Lavi, S. (2013, April). *The Mourning After: Posthumous Sperm Retrieval and the New Laws of Mourning*. Presented as part of the LJST Law & Mourning Lecture Series, Amherst College.

Lavi, S. (2010). The Paradox of Jewish Bioethics in Israel: The Case of Reproductive Technologies. In A. Voigt (Ed.), *Religion in bioethischen Diskursen: Interdisziplinäre, internationale und interreligiöse Perspektiven* (pp. 81–102). Berlin: De Gruyter.

Levine, N. E. (2008). Alternative Kinship, Marriage, and Reproduction. *Annual Review of Anthropology*, 37, 375–389.

Levine, N. M. (1994). Abortion in Israel: Community, Rights, and the Context of Compromise. *Law & Social Inquiry*, 19(2), 313–336.

Lippman, A. (1992). Led (Astray) by Genetic Maps: The Cartography of the Human Genome and Health Care. *Social Science & Medicine*, 35(12), 1469–1476.

Modell, J. (1989). Last Chance Babies: Interpretations of Parenthood in an In Vitro Fertilization Program. *Medical Anthropology Quarterly*, 3(2), 124–138.

Mor-Yosef National Committee. (2012). Recommendations of the Public Commission Regarding Examination of Legislative Regulation: Theme of Fertility and Birth in Israel. Retrieved from www.health.gov.il/publications files/bap2012.pdf (Hebrew).

Morag-Levine, N. (1994). Abortion in Israel: Community, Rights and the Context of Compromise. *Law and Social Inquiry*, 19(2), 313–335.

M. P. v. *Israel Ministry of Health*, Family Court (Jerusalem) 28130-07-14, Nevo Legal Database (Nov. 17, 2014) (Hebrew).

Nye, R. A. (2003). The Evolution of the Concept of Medicalization in the Late Twentieth Century. *Journal of the History of the Behavioral Sciences*, 39(2), 115–129.

Parens, E. and Asch, A. (Eds.). (2000). *Prenatal Testing and Disability Rights*. Washington, DC: Georgetown University Press.

Pennings, G., de Wert, G., Shenfield, F., Cohen, J., Devroey, P., and Tarlatzis, B. (2006). ESHRE Task Force on Ethics and Law 11: Posthumous Assisted Reproduction. *Human Reproduction*, 21, 3050–3053.

Prainsack, B. and Firestine, O. (2006). "Science for Survival": Biotechnology Regulation in Israel. *Science and Public Policy*, 33(1), 33–46.

Rapp, R. (1999). *Testing Women, Testing the Fetus: The Social Impact of Amniocentesis in America* (pp. 118–128). New York and London: Routledge.

Ravitsky, V. (2004). Posthumous Reproduction Guidelines in Israel. *The Hastings Center Report*, 34(2), 6–7.

Raz, A. E. (2010). *Community Genetics and Genetic Alliances: Eugenics, Carrier Testing, and Networks of Risk*. New York: Routledge.

Raz, A. E. (2004). Important to Test, Important to Support: Attitudes toward Disability Rights and Prenatal Diagnosis among Leaders of Support Groups for Genetic Disorders in Israel. *Social Science & Medicine*, 59(9), 1857–1866.

Raz, A. E. and Schicktanz, S. (2016). *Comparative Empirical Bioethics: Dilemmas of Genetic Testing and Euthanasia in Israel and Germany*. Springer, 2016.

Raz, A. E., Schues, C., Wilhelm, N., and Rehmann-Sutter, C. (2016). Saving or Subordinating Life? Popular Views in Israel and Germany of Donor Siblings Created through PGD. *Journal of Medical Humanities*, 37(1), 1–17. doi:10.1007/s10912-016-9388-2.

Raz, A. E. and Vizner, Y. (2008). Carrier Matching and Collective Socialization in Community Genetics: Dor Yeshorim and the Reinforcement of Stigma. *Social Science & Medicine*, 67(9), 1361–1369.

Remennick, L. (2006). The Quest for the Perfect Baby: Why Do Israeli Women Seek Prenatal Genetic Testing? *Sociology of Health & Illness*, 28(1), 21–53.

Rimon-Greenspan, H. and Ravitsky, V. (2013). New Frontiers in Posthumous Reproduction. *BioNews*. Retrieved from www.bionews.org.uk/page_313451.asp?hlight=Ravitsky.

Rimon-Zarfaty, N. (2014). The Influence of New Medical Technologies on Perceptions of the "Fetus" and "Parenthood" among Israeli Parents (Doctoral dissertation). Ben-Gurion University of the Negev (Hebrew).

Rothbell, G. (1986). The Jewish Mother: Social Construction of a Popular Image. In S. M. Cohen and P. E. Hyman (Eds.), *The Jewish Family: Myths and Reality*. New York and London: Holmes & Meyer.

Sandel, M. (2007). *The Case Against Perfection*. Cambridge. MA: Harvard University Press.

Sawicki, J. (1999). Disciplining Mothers: Feminism and the New Reproductive Technologies. In J. Price and M. Shildrick (Eds.), *Feminist Theory and the Body: A Reader* (pp.190–202). Edinburgh: Edinburgh University Press.

Scully, J. L., Shakespeare, T., and Banks, S. (2006). Gift not Commodity? Lay People Deliberating Social Sex Selection. *Sociology of Health & Illness*, 28(6), 749–767.

Shahar et al. v. Israeli Attorney General, Family Court (Petah Tikva) 16699-06-13 (Sept. 28, 2016) (Hebrew).

Shalev, C. (2002). Posthumous Insemination: May He Rest in Peace. *Medical Law*, 27, 96–99 (Hebrew).

Shamgar-Handelman, L. and Bar-Yosef, R. (1991). *Families in Israel*. Jerusalem: Academon. Introduction (Hebrew).

Sher, C., Romano-Zelekha, O., Green, M. S., and Shohat, T. (2003). Factors Affecting Performance of Prenatal Genetic Testing by Israeli Jewish Women. *American Journal of Medical Genetics*, 120A(3), 418–422.

Sherwood, H. (2011). Israeli Couple Seek Right to Use Dead Son's Sperm. *The Guardian*. Retrieved from www.theguardian.com/world/2011/feb/08/israeli-parents-dead-son-sperm.

Strathern, M. (1996). Enabling Identity? Biology, Choice and the New Reproductive Technologies. In S. Hall and P. Du Gay (Eds.), *Questions of Cultural Identity* (pp. 7–51). London: Sage.

Teman, E. (2003). The Medicalization of "Nature" in the "Artificial Body": Surrogate Motherhood in Israel. *Medical Anthropology Quarterly*, 17(1), 78–98.

Tremellen, K., Savulescu, J., 2015. A Discussion Supporting Presumed Consent for Posthumous Sperm Procurement and Conception. *Reprod Biomed Online* 30, 6–13.

Weiss, M. (2002). *The Chosen Body: The Politics of the Body in Israeli Society*. Stanford, CA: Stanford University Press.

Wertz, D. C. (1998). Eugenics Is Alive and Well: A Survey of Genetic Professionals around the World. *Science in Context*, 11(3–4), 493–510.

7

"Quiet, Dependent, Nice, and Loyal": Surrogacy Agencies' Discourse of International Surrogacy

Hedva Eyal and Adi Moreno

INTRODUCTION

In 2014, Peter Andrews and Fiona Woods published a book that celebrated thirty-six global entrepreneurs who "transform human societies" and make the world a better place (2014). The authors chose the protagonists for their book according to the challenges the human race is facing at the moment: climate change, the economic crisis, finding a cure for the AIDS epidemic, and more. On their list, alongside known figures such as Oprah Winfrey, Mark Zuckerberg, and Ingvar Kampard (the founder of IKEA furniture and design superstores), they placed one Israeli, Doron Mamet, who is the founder of the Tammuz international surrogacy agency. Mamet is a known figure in the Israeli public, who has reached international acclaim as the protagonist of the *Google Baby* 2010 Emmy award winner documentary. In response to his inclusion in the book, Mamet stated that:

> Neither us, nor the surrogates chose to be in this situation. We, intended parents, would have liked to be able to carry the pregnancy on our own, and the surrogates would have been happy to be in a better financial situation. . . . However, given the state of affairs, both sides are happy there is a solution. Any attempt, in the name of ethics, to prevent our right to parenthood and the surrogate's right to improve her situation is tainted by severe ethical fault. (Mako, December 9, 2013)

Israel is widely acknowledged for its pro-natal values (Birenbaum-Carmeli and Carmeli 2010; Donat 2007; Fogiel-Bijaoui 1999; Gooldin 2008; Nahman 2006) and for its leadership position in the global reproductive industry (Mashiach et al. 2010). The fact that an Israeli surrogacy broker was chosen as one of thirty-six leading entrepreneurs around the globe, and the way he chose to frame his message, raises awareness of the manner in which commercial surrogacy is incorporated within the contemporary neoliberal global economy as a site for the rearticulation of social norms as well as for profit extraction. This is true especially in a state such as Israel where families and childrearing bear great social significance.

Surrogacy, and assisted reproductive technologies more broadly, have transformed in the recent three decades from a contested challenge against the "facts of life" to welcomed enablers of new families, relationships, and new understandings of the natural itself (Franklin 2013; Hudson et al. 2011; Inhorn and Patrizio 2012). Sarah Franklin (2013) demonstrated that ARTs create more than children – they create new relationships and relationship kinds that were not available before. In the crossroad of commerce and intimate ethical challenges, women's bodies and fertility capacities become the raw materials that the industry operates upon, as well as potential assets for the women who participate in it.

Cross-border reproductive care (CBRC) is a global medical-technological market that is broadly driven by a mixture of for-profit interests and intimate imaginations and aspirations (Laufer-Ukeles 2013; Rudrappa and Collins 2015). As an intimate market, CBRC operates simultaneously as a vehicle of greater social possibilities, by widening access to reproductive services beyond the limitations of nation-states or conservative societies, while also being a vehicle of greater subjugation of bodies and body parts in the realms of global capitalism. Under the auspice of intimate industry, a surrogacy businessman such as Mamet can be seen as a social entrepreneur and as initiating social change, especially in the context of same-sex families, who, in Israel, cannot access the services he offers within the state's borders.

In her recent book on commercial surrogacy in India, Sharmila Rudrappa (2015) addresses commissioning parents and surrogates as "moral pioneers," who, like in Rayna Rapp's (1999) analysis, need to find their own moral path through the novel technologies that enable new forms of family creation. In their attempts, they base their ethics on already existing "local and ongoing gender, generation, class/caste relations, and religious regulation" (Rapp 2011: 73). That is, the moral decisions that take part in ARTs are congruent with the larger picture of neoliberal moral economies, in which the social order has disseminated and disintegrated into a plethora of institutions and interactions (Rose 2001). Yet there are significant sites for the articulation of reproductive norms, the reproductive clinic, for instance, which was vastly documented as a site for the neutralization, normalization, and routinization of assisted reproduction (Thompson 2005). In this chapter, we focus on another site that is not sufficiently investigated in the reproductive literature: the surrogacy agency.

CBRC has become a booming, multimillion-dollar industry involving the movement of customers across political, social, and religious borders (Inhorn and Patrizio 2012). While nation-states employ varying degrees of regulations and prohibitions of these practices, within state borders and overseas, the patchy regulatory framework encourages rather than limits the rise of CBRC and the mediators who direct and navigate the flow of customers, service providers, and materials toward less-prohibitive locales (Inhorn and Patrizio 2012). This aspect of the industry, and especially the operation of CBRC brokers (also referred to as "agencies" or "intermediaries"), is the aim of our analysis.

Israel offers an intriguing case study for the development of CBRC. On one hand, Israel was the first state to legalize commercial surrogacy, and it offers a unique model of state regulation and validation of each surrogacy contract. On the other hand, the current legislation limits the identity of commissioning parents (who can only be heterosexual couples, with medical reasons to approach surrogacy) while leaving overseas surrogacy outside of the current legislation (Samama 2011; Teman 2010). This mixture of endorsement of commercial surrogacy alongside prohibition for singles and gay couples encouraged the creation of a cross-border market, which is largely mediated by Israeli agents who create contacts oversees and aid Israeli commissioning parents in accessing surrogacy and egg donation services. At the time of our research, we identified eleven such agencies offering a variety of surrogacy locations, contracts, and standards.

Despite the steep rise and breadth of research into CBRC practices, and especially the rich data gathered by growing numbers of ethnographers, bioethicists, and health researchers (see review of literature by Hudson et al. 2011), there is still a lack of empirical data pertaining to the market in CBRC and in cross-border surrogacy. These data are lacking in terms of understanding the full scope of the market, which is currently only based on assumptions and self-reporting by a few of the states involved (Ferraretti et al. 2010), and there is very little data and analysis of the operation of CBRC brokers (Inhorn and Patrizio 2012). We address this lacunae by setting cross-border surrogacy at the center of our analysis, evaluating the discourse these brokers use in marketing surrogacy practices to potential clientele. By reviewing the site of the surrogacy agency, we address these questions: What are the social and ethical grounds on which surrogacy contracts with non-Israeli surrogates are based? What are the mental frames that legitimate this trade and what regulatory mechanisms are set in place in such surrogacy processes? We do not address the relations between the reproductive parties here (namely, commissioning parents and surrogates), but rather focus solely on the intermediaries. However, our findings correspond with work already being done regarding surrogacy relations in India and elsewhere (Pande 2010; Rudrappa 2015; Sama 2012; Samama 2012).

We base our analysis on the discourse that agencies use to describe surrogates and surrogacy on their marketing websites. The research data are drawn from the websites of all agencies and organizations in Israel who marketed cross-border surrogacy at the time of our research, between the end of 2013 and the end of 2014, and analyzed as a form of qualitative text (Bryman 2012; Denzin and Lincoln 2000; Markham 2004). The texts were taken as a discourse, i.e., as practices that constitute a body of knowledge and as a means of imparting meaning to reality through words and images (Fairclough 2010). The narratives that rise from the websites illustrate how they determine women's rights, health, and choices and set the path to ethical deliberations and financial outcomes. In our analysis, we show the implied meanings within the discursive practices of surrogacy agents, the hidden contradictions, as well as use the gathered information regarding surrogacy practices as a baseline for comparison with the marketing promises. This mode of analysis provides further understanding of the intricate operation of the global commerce in reproductive care.

PIONEERING COMMERCIAL SURROGACY: THE CASE OF ISRAEL

It is widely established that Israeli society demonstrates pro-natalist values, and that as a state, Israel has become a leader in the practice and development of assisted reproductive technologies (Birenbaum-Carmeli and Carmeli 2010; Donat 2007; Fogiel-Bijaoui 1999; Kahn 2000; Mashiach et al. 2010). Having children is considered a necessary facet of adult living by a vast majority of the Israeli public (Carmeli and Birenbaum-Carmeli 2010; Donat 2007; Fogiel-Bijaoui 1999; Mor-Yosef et al. 2012). Driven by the Jewish religious commandment of *Pru U'rvu* (be fruitful and multiply), by the state's racial ideology encouraging Jewish reproduction as part of the "demographic race" (Berkovitch 1997; Nahman 2013), and by Holocaust memories on one hand and neoliberal ideologies of self-fulfillment on the other, having children is largely perceived as a basic human right (Birenbaum-Carmeli and Carmeli 2010; Gooldin 2008; Lustenberger 2014; Nahman 2013), one that should be supported by generous state funding (Gooldin 2008).[1]

Reproductive technologies in Israel are widely disseminated, both in practice, as a result of generous public funding (Birenbaum-Carmeli 2007; Gooldin 2008; Hashiloni-Dolev 2006), and discursively, with a plethora of media accounts of families who successfully accessed various reproductive technologies, typically presented as a form of triumphant struggle. The social importance of family making and the breadth of assisted technology usage has made surrogacy a normative family structure in Israel, especially among members of the male gay community (Moreno 2016a). We do not see Israel as standing out in this respect in the contemporary developed world, but rather as an intensified case study that may shed light on processes that occur in other societies. Particularly, Israel's developed reproductive bureaucracy offers robust data gathering of all surrogacy cases conducted in Israel and by Israeli citizens overseas. These uniquely rich data, when accompanied by the state's relatively small size, enabled us to conduct exhaustive research of the cross-border reproductive commerce.

Israel's Embryo Carrying Agreements Act (1996) was the first legislation worldwide that specifically approved and regulated surrogacy contracts. In contradiction with most surrogacy legislation worldwide, the Israeli legislation permits payment to the surrogate while discouraging noncommercial surrogacy. The legislation sets limitations on the practice of surrogacy, such as that the commissioning parents are required to provide medical documentation regarding the women's condition, and that the commissioning parents must be a heterosexual couple, but it does not limit the involvement of for-profit organizations in marketing and mediating in surrogacy agreements. This lacunae in regulation is pertinent to agencies operating in the local market and to agencies who propose surrogacy services overseas. However, the surrogacy

---

[1] The importance of childrearing in Israeli society was also reiterated by several Israeli Supreme Court rulings: 2266/99, 2401/95, 2458/01, quoted by Mor Yosef et al. 2012: 5–6.

contracts themselves are regulated within Israel, and operate with no regulatory oversight when performed outside of the state borders, which, as we discuss further, enables the CBRC agencies to offer lower rates and shorter durations for the surrogacy processes they arrange (Lipkin and Samama 2010: 281).

The limitations in the Israeli surrogacy act and the relatively high cost of surrogacy procedures within Israel drove the creation of the market for cross-border surrogacy services. Official numbers, which exist since 2005, show a steep rise in surrogacy usage around 2010, whereas since 2011, the number of overseas surrogacy births exceeds the number of local ones (Moreno 2016a). The reasons to access this market are varied, and do not solely derive from the current Israeli heteronormative legislation (Teman 2010). For some parents, particularly gay couples and single women, overseas surrogacy was the only permitted surrogacy route; while for others, lower costs, less bureaucracy, and the benefits of geographical distance from the surrogate women and egg donors were the main causes to choose CBRC. Figure 7.1 describes surrogacy usage by Israeli citizens within and outside the state's border.

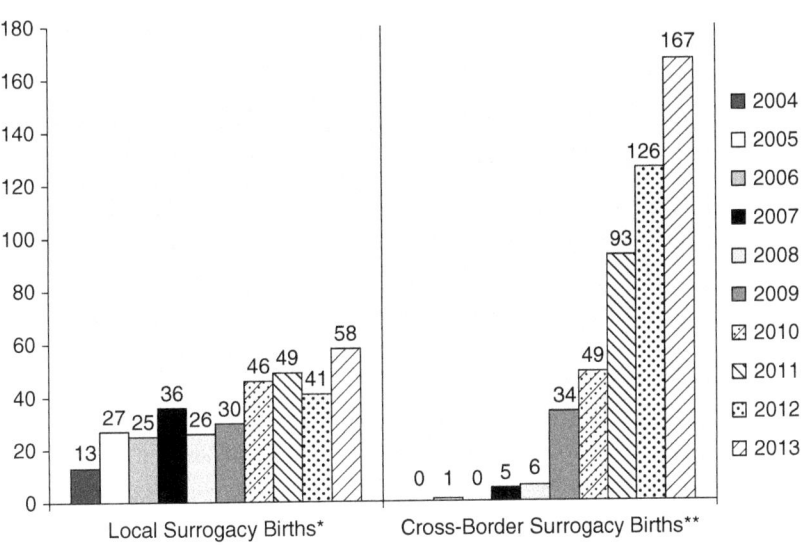

FIGURE 7.1 Local and cross-border surrogacy usage among Israeli citizens[2]
*Local surrogacy births include only births of heterosexual commissioning parents.
** Cross-border surrogacy births comprise all registered surrogacy births involving Israeli citizens; these include heterosexual couples, gay couples, and single men and women.

---

[2] Table copied from Moreno 2016a; Figure Sources: 1996–2011: www.knesset.gov.il/mmm/data/pdf/mo3065.pdf,
2012: www.haaretz.co.il/news/education/.premium-1.2055593,
2013: www.haaretz.co.il/news/education/.premium-1.2258545. For exact numbers see also table G.2 in Appendix G.

The rise in surrogacy births was accompanied by a lively public debate regarding surrogacy usage. For the most part, media coverage and political responses to surrogacy were positive, as medically assisted reproduction is considered legitimate in Israeli public opinion, including the religious and conservative sectors (Kahn 2000; Nahman 2013), and as childbirth is considered an ultimate life goal, even in the case of non-normative families such as same-sex couples. At the same time, there was a response by feminist action groups who were wary of the potential harm to women who take part in these processes, especially in the context of cross-border surrogacy. The feminist critique was voiced in national newspaper op-eds, TV talk shows, and parliamentary discussions and fed into the deliberations into amending Israel's surrogacy legislation (Mor-Yosef et al. 2012).

This is the context in which Israeli surrogacy brokers operate – on one hand, pro-natal values and support for medical interventions; on the other hand, feminist voices that raise concerns regarding exploitation and harm and an ongoing debate regarding reproductive choice and reproductive rights. Within this site, a discourse regarding surrogacy broadly and specific surrogacy practices develops, and determines the material conditions of surrogacy processes performed by Israeli citizens, in Israel and elsewhere.

UNDERSTANDING ISRAEL'S ONLINE REPRODUCTIVE MARKETING

According to our online survey, in 2013, eleven cross-border surrogacy agencies were operating in Israel. These agencies offered surrogacy arrangements in various geographical locations, such as India, Ukraine, Georgia, Thailand, Nepal, and the United States. The agencies' websites offer very detailed information, which includes the medical-legal procedure, the benefits of conducting surrogacy in the target state, an approximate cost for the surrogacy processes that they offer, and the agencies' core ideology or marketing message.

Many of these websites offer a grand narrative on the circumstances that led to the opening of the agency. This often includes a personal experience with surrogacy by the founders that led them to feel a calling into this occupation. One surrogacy center, "Baby Bloom," was founded after an Israeli gay couple had a baby girl through surrogacy in the United States. As a result of "[t]his personal experience and the various ambiguities in the [surrogacy] field [one of the parents] decided to initiate a complete solution, financially affordable and leading professionally." Another agency, Time4Child, was set up in Thailand by an "[Israeli] couple who lives in this country and examined the subject personally." They also stated that they started the company with the desire to simplify the process and make it more accessible: "it is important that every men [sic] who wishes to bring a child into the world will be able to do it regardless of his sexual orientation or marital status." In a similar manner, other agencies used phrases such as: "we wholeheartedly believe that our task is to help you bring new life into the world" (New Life Agency); "we chose surrogacy services as our calling and mission" (Manor Medic); "The primordial aspiration for parenthood ... " (Path to Parenthood).

The language used portrays a combination of personal narratives and appeal to altruistic notions as a marketing aid. Phrases such as "mission," "new life," and "belief," which are borrowed from social arenas of altruism and solidarity, are brought into the commercial field as legitimizers of the trade, and therefore as means to increase profits by increasing the agencies' appeal for potential customers.

It is worth noting here that we provide an analysis of the marketing language that is addressed at potential commissioning parents. We do not discuss in this chapter the dialog (if such exists) between commissioning parents and surrogates directly – but focus our attention on the interaction between the agencies and their customers, and the terms of the surrogacy contracts as they appear in the marketing websites.

We analyze cross-border surrogacy marketing discourse according to four categories: 1. the framing of the surrogacy procedure broadly, including the manner in which surrogates are portrayed in this process; 2. the relationship between commissioning parents and surrogates; 3. control over the surrogate during the process; and 4. the depiction of the medical procedures. Through these lenses, we encompass the complete stages of surrogacy – from choosing to enter into surrogacy agreements until after childbirth – and address the different aspects of the surrogacy process: social, legal, and medical.

How Surrogacy Agencies Frame Cross-Border Surrogacy

The manner in which surrogacy agencies describe the practice of surrogacy, and especially the manner in which the surrogates are described, creates a discursive framework that governs surrogacy relations and ultimately affects the material practices that come out of these discourses. The choice of words, such as "donors," "gifts," "gratitude," and "compensation" on one hand, or "rent," "commodity," and "payment" on the other therefore bears crucial importance to understanding commercial surrogacy in its full complexity. As can be seen in the works of various reproduction researchers (Dempsey 2012; Nahman 2013; Nordqvist 2011; Pande 2011; Rudrappa 2015), gift and altruism terms are common across different sections of the reproductive industry – including both gamete donors and surrogates. We focus our attention on surrogacy since it always entails a biological relationship – at least between the fetus and the surrogate, and often entails desires for prolonged social relationships – between children, surrogates, and commissioning parents. The language that frames this relationship has bearing upon the actual relations that will be formed during and after the process (Moreno 2016b).

Despite references to altruism and gift giving, financial costs are crucial for most cross-border surrogacy services. According to most of the agencies' websites, a significant advantage of cross-border surrogacy is its lower cost compared with surrogacy in Israel (this was true at the time of our research to all surrogacy destinations other than the United States). Alongside the cost, the agencies stressed that cross-border surrogacy arrangements entail much simpler and more flexible bureaucracy. Here are some of their descriptions:

> Immediate surrogacy procedure, without delays and committees. (Manor Medic)

> Flexibility – if there is no feasibility or no interest to use the commissioning mother's eggs, then it is possible to receive egg donation [sic], in Israel there is no such possibility. The bureaucracy is simpler and there is no need to receive any committee's approval. (New Family)

> Upon recommendation of the fertility clinic, it is possible to change surrogates in cases that the pregnancy failed, with no added cost. In Israel commissioning parents are permitted to receive six treatment rounds and eighteen months of commitment to one surrogate only. In cases that the parents wish to change surrogates [in Israel] they are expected to compensate the surrogate and wait for a long time until the approval of a new surrogate. (Right to Parenthood)

Israeli bureaucracy, which is determined by the Embryo Carrying Agreements Act (1996), mandates that surrogacy contracts will be approved by a statutory committee and will include reciprocal commitment between the commissioning parents and the surrogate. This contractual reciprocal commitment is described here as a redundant burden that adds hurdles in the path of commissioning parents. In a cross-border setting, the marketing language makes clear, lack of regulations offers shortcuts to parenthood. The implied meaning is that by choosing to carry out surrogacy in a state with fewer regulatory bodies, commissioning parents increase the efficiency of the process, as time equals money.

The Israeli bureaucracy was put in place in order to protect the surrogate. For instance, commissioning parents have to carry on with the same surrogate even when one or more embryo attempts failed. It is therefore clear that the lack of regulation, while benefiting the commissioning parents, harms the surrogate's rights as she is "replaced," that is, fired, with no monetary compensation (and hence, with no extra cost to commissioning parents). Unlike some European countries, Israel as a state refrains from attempting to stop its citizens from accessing surrogacy in such locations and only verifies that the surrogacy contracts were signed according to local law, and that the surrogate waived her parental rights without coercion.

Cross-border surrogacy is therefore framed as less effort, quicker, and promising better results for less pay to the commissioning parents. This is achieved through passing on the risks to the surrogate herself, who bears both the physical risks of pregnancy and the financial risk of contractual failure in case of miscarriage or failed embryo transfer.

The agencies' websites enables assessing how the different mediators treat the surrogates they employ. One agency (Manor Medic) displays a list of criteria for favoring their services over surrogacy within Israel. These include:

TABLE 7.1 *State Comparison*

Subject	Georgia	Israel
Approval Committee	Immediate, without delay	Half a year
Surrogates' Availability	Immediate	6–12 months
Changing Surrogates	After 3–4 cycles the surrogate is replaced immediately[3]	Impossible
The Surrogates	Are gentle, quiet, dependent, nice and loyal!	Most of them [the surrogates] are problematic and extrovert

(Manor Medic)

According to this agency's text, a desired surrogate is a submissive and dependent woman, one who could be exchanged immediately and without any hurdles. The comparison that was brought forth between Israeli women and Georgian women demonstrates also how these women's racialization is used as means of advertising usage of their body, while using colonial-like assumptions about Georgian women's submissiveness and availability for usage by the agency's customers. Similar language for the description of Eastern European women as submissive appears also by egg commerce vendors, or on different surrogacy sites. Ran Reznik, a leading Israeli medical journalist, writes:

> "These women are not sad, they are submissive," says Dr. Geva in an attempt to explain the situation of the poverty-stricken women, who were forced to undergo medical procedures bearing potential risks, in order to support their children in a state with a majority of poor residents (average salary in the Ukraine is 210–350 euros per month). (*Israel Ha'yom*, June 10, 2011)

The agencies boast of the wide variety of women who wish to work as surrogates. For instance: "In Ukraine there is a large repository of fit and healthy surrogates, and therefore the wait time is very short" (Right to Parenthood). Another agency claims that Thailand welcomes the growth of surrogacy processes in its country (Manor Medic). This claim was presented while Thailand and Israel were negotiating the closure of Thai surrogacy for Israeli commissioning parents, and this option has been barred since.[4] The allegedly high number of women who wish to become surrogates turns them into an abundant commodity, ready for consumption and distribution and thus boosting the alleged proficiency of the surrogacy agency.

[3] This text has recently changed and currently (2016) proposes replacing the surrogate after one or two failed embryo transfers.
[4] Israeli Foreign Office, Surrogacy Processes in Thailand – Travel Warning, December 24, 2013, http://mfa.gov.il/MFAHEB/ConsularService/TravelAdvisory/Pages/Thailand_241213.aspx (Hebrew).
  Zezna, J. "No Surrogate's Signatures Received," *Israel Today*, January 21, 2014, www.israelhayom.co.il/article/151393 (Hebrew).

According to Margaret Radin (1996), an issue that arises from commodification of the human body and human intimacy is the manner in which commodification reduces persons into an item that is exchangeable (with money and other goods) and fungible (with other human bodies). The surrogacy agencies' discourse shows quite literally how the surrogates become depersonalized and fungible, defined only by the outcomes of the reproductive process that occurs in their bodies.

The appearance of commercial surrogacy industry raised many concerns among feminists and critical authors (Franklin 2013). They saw surrogacy as an opening of additional commodification and subjugation of the female body to patriarchal science and the market (Arditti et al. 1984; Corea 1986; Raymond 1998; Rothman 1984). In this respect, the agencies' discourse fulfills these dystopian depictions of surrogacy outcomes.

Additional agencies that specialized in surrogacy in India (Tammuz and Path to Parenthood) offered on their websites the surrogates' motivation to choose surrogacy, asserting that: "The surrogates' motivation is financial mainly. This process enables them to secure their families and children's future" (Tammuz). Surrogacy, according to this, is a means of economic survival for potential surrogates. This is implied in the text ("secure their families and children's future"), but the actual economic background that the surrogates come from, and its meaning for their choice in surrogacy, remains outside the discussion. In many cases, these claim appear without specifying the actual pay the surrogate will receive, which often is not as high as the agencies intend to portray on their websites.[5]

The financial agreement with the surrogate is also mentioned as a preliminary response to potential customers' concerns. Thus, the website raises the question: "how can we ensure that the surrogate hands over the baby after s/he is born?" and answers: "the surrogate participates in this process for monetary compensation **only**, the last payment to the surrogate mother is transferred to her only after registering the child as Israeli and receiving travel document for him" (Path to Parenthood, emphasis added).

Israeli agencies are not different from surrogacy brokers in other emerging surrogacy markets. For instance, Rudrappa and Collins (2015) show how Indian surrogacy agencies construct a monolithic imagery of Indian women as third-world women in need of rescue by the wage they receive through the fertility industry. They conclude:

> The very structural factors that make working-class Indian women particularly suited for surrogacy also allow for the circulation of reproductive imaginaries of benevolence and rescue from poverty. This reproductive imaginary is a myth. (p. 956)

---

[5] Such examples appear on the pay table provided by Time4Child and Viva Surrogacy.

These descriptions clearly state that poverty and the attempt to improve living conditions are driving women's motivations to participate in the complex and risk-bearing process of gestational surrogacy. However, these descriptions are presented here as a form of safety net for the commissioning parents, guaranteeing that their financial need will ensure prompt delivery of the child. This discourse constructs a dichotomy between the financial aspect and a potential emotional and intimate aspect that may develop between the surrogate and the child she is gestating, in strict opposition with findings from various ethnographies studies that stress that surrogates perform a labor that is at once commercial and deeply intimate and emotional (Laufer-Ukeles 2013). It is also worth noting that the same transaction – the surrogacy agreement – is depicted as intimate and altruistic, and as commercial and with controllable outcomes, without accounting for the apparent contradictions between the two.

Commissioning parents, as well as the surrogacy agencies, are not accountable for the surrogate women's poverty and financial hardship. However, we do see a link between the economic context and the surrogates' limited negotiation in regards to the terms and securities of the surrogacy arrangements, and the manner in which their poverty becomes guarantor to the fulfillment of the contract.

Relationships between the Commissioning Parents and the Surrogate

Research suggests that relationships with the commissioning parents might have a significant impact on the surrogate's satisfaction with the surrogacy process (Samama 2012; Teman 2010). These studies show that respectful relationships, when accompanied by displays of gratitude from the commissioning parents to the surrogate, engender a positive and empowering surrogacy experience and can enable forming long-term relationships based on reciprocity and mutual care. However, in the case of cross-border surrogacy, the agencies' websites show that the possibility of direct relationships between the surrogates and the commissioning parents is very limited in most surrogacy locations, and largely dependent on the commissioning parents' intent:

> In Ukraine the commissioning parents maintain the right to choose whether to have contact with the surrogate or not. They do not have to be exposed to all the pressures that may arise throughout the surrogacy process. (Right to Parenthood)

> The intensity of the relationship is mainly dependent upon the [desire of the] intended father. Some parents prefer not to become "attached" to the surrogate and therefore wish to not have contact with her while others wish to experience the pregnancy with the surrogate and choose to become involved. (Path to Parenthood)

Relationships, which are the core of kinship, are depicted here as troublesome – involving pressure, undesired attachment. On the other hand, they can offer an experience, which in marketing language is often synonym with fun and pleasure.

As can be seen from the quotes, the control over the relationship with the surrogate is placed in the hands of the commissioning parents – if they wish, they can be in contact with the surrogate and if not, they will have no contact with her during the pregnancy. In the second quote, only the desire of the commissioning father is expressed, which suggests the existence of a gendered hierarchy in the commissioning family, and not just toward the surrogate. Moreover, the contact with the surrogate is not maintained in order to create an intimate family relationship with her, but rather as closeness to a bodily yet detached experience – the experience of the pregnancy. This pregnancy is removed from the surrogate's personality, history, feelings, and desires and becomes a purely impersonal experience that the commissioning father can "share." In both quotes, there is no place for the surrogate's desires, whether she wishes to have some contact with the commissioning parents, or whether she would prefer to refrain from such contact.

The manner in which surrogacy agents direct their clients to refrain from direct contact with the surrogates is also mentioned by Triger (2015), in his analysis of his experience as an Israeli commissioning father in India. According to Triger, the local Indian agency even attempted to monitor the gratitude payments that parents wished to give the surrogate after the contract reached a happy ending, and the parents needed to use cunning in order to pass envelopes of money directly to the surrogate, without the agents' taking over this money or requesting a large percentage of it for themselves.

Apart from the parents' and brokers' control over the relationship with the surrogate during surrogacy pregnancy, many agencies stated that medical and psychological evaluations will also be used as selection criteria of the surrogates, and the surrogates only:

> The surrogates [are] all Thai who live in Bangkok and nearby suburbs. They all undergo meticulous medical examinations and psychological evaluations before starting the process. The surrogates have children of their own and intact pregnancy past. Also [sic] the surrogates are chosen according to a profile which is sent to the intended parents with general and medical features. (Time4Child)

> We will send you complete details of the candidate of your choice. The detail that we provide is personal detail of the candidate [and medical] family history.... Our fertility doctor can recommend the best donor based on [her] antral follicle count. (New Life)

These websites make clear that the commissioning parents receive detailed, intimate information regarding the surrogate's physical and mental capabilities, but remain silent regarding any detail that is given by the commissioning parents and provided to the surrogate. Apart from the U.S. surrogacy procedures, in most commercial surrogacy locations, the commissioning parents choose the surrogate without any choice on the surrogate's side, and often even without providing her with information regarding the parents' identity. This sets surrogacy as a very biased commercial transaction – the money holder has control over available choices during the process, whereas the surrogate is presented as a resource that is available in abundance and therefore has limited negotiation power. The intermediary, the agencies themselves, lean in favor of their paying customers instead of providing mediation services for both sides, and effectively set the terms that make money into the determining factor.

Surveillance and Control

As pregnancy becomes a market commodity, the processes of impregnation and gestation require greater control in order to provide assurance for consumers and for mediators. The agencies' websites reported that during the surrogacy process, the surrogates are under strict surveillance, which may include moving into designated housing governed by the agency during the surrogacy pregnancy. The demand that the surrogate will leave her home and family for the nine months of the pregnancy may have various reasons, such as easing her workload during the pregnancy and providing support and care. But from reading through the agencies' websites, only one reason is presented – control:

> Our surrogates live with their children in housing provided by the company in the vicinity of a private hospital and with complete oversight of the medical team, a house manager and a cleaner that care for their [the surrogates] proper conduct during treatments and pregnancy. (Parenthood Center)

> During the pregnancy the surrogates move into apartments that are rented for them in the vicinity of the clinic. They visit the clinic regularly. The pregnancy is monitored in full by the medical center that we work with.
> During the pregnancy the surrogates undergo all standard pregnancy tests and in additional frequent periodical blood tests which ascertain their overall health condition. (Tammuz)

> In most cases the surrogate and her children move into special housing. All her exits outside the housing area are accompanied by a female staff member ... [our] liaison staff monitors the surrogate's behavior during the pregnancy and make sure that she is protecting the pregnancy and follows the doctors' instructions. (Path to Parenthood)

The surrogates' stay in the housing facilities run by the local agencies is therefore meant to make them available for constant surveillance, ensuring their discipline in carrying out the doctors' orders and their everyday behaviors. The outcome is that their bodily autonomy is expropriated by the surrogacy agency and the surrogacy contract. In moving into the surrogates' hostel, they become subjected to the control of the house manager, nurses, and doctors; that in some cases even limits their ability to exit the house unaccompanied. This is presented by the agencies as legitimate means to secure their investment, that is, the pregnancy process that was paid for by the commissioning parents. The surrogate's body becomes, at least during these surrogacy pregnancies, a product that is owned or leased by the surrogacy agency, clinic, and commissioning parents. Through her body, the surrogate herself is subjugated to the commercial process, a mere object in the Kantian sense.

The Medical Procedure and Surrogates' Bodily Autonomy

The operation of medical professionals and medical procedures cannot be seen as neutral and health-oriented. As Nikolas Rose (2001) discussed in the case of genetic counseling, the site of the surrogacy agency becomes a site of the enactment of biopolitics, of making "life and death" decisions quite literally, as in the case of potential newborn children. Professional knowledges become main justificatory means for political and ethical dilemmas that arise throughout surrogacy fertilization and gestation. As mentioned previously, most agencies state that their surrogates undergo various tests before and during the surrogacy pregnancy. The criteria to enter into surrogacy agreement require that the surrogate will be a mother to at least one child and provide detailed information about her medical history and past pregnancies.[6] In addition, the majority of the agencies also state that the surrogate is fully committed to the process and grants her permission in advance for any potential medical process that may be required in order to reach the goal of a healthy child. Here are a few examples:

> The surrogate agrees to undergo as many cycles as may be required. However, it is the prerogative of the intended parents to replace her already after the first [failed] cycle. (Path to Parenthood)

> They all go through meticulous medical and psychological tests before starting the process. (Time4Child)

It is clear from these quotes that the aim of the medical treatment is to ensure fertility and childbirth. We acknowledge that medical care and supervision is necessary during the surrogacy pregnancy. However, the agencies' discourse shows bluntly the lack of attention to potential harm to the surrogates' health, and to any medical care in cases of failed pregnancy or medical harms that may occur *after* the surrogacy pregnancy has already terminated. These medical risks may include sexually transmitted diseases, infections, increased risk of ovarian cancer, and more, and they are regarded as standard risks of the treatments that accompany gestational surrogacy[7] yet disregarded when surrogacy agents publicize their commodities.

---

[6] These criteria appears as universal, across various geographical locations.
[7] M. Gugucheva, *Surrogacy in America*, CRG report.22 (2010); F. E. van Leeuwen et al., "Risk of Borderline and Invasive Ovarian Tumors after Ovarian Stimulation in In Vitro Fertilization for a Large Dutch Cohort," *Hum. Reprod.* 26(12), 3456 (2011); Surrogacy in Israel: Status Report 2010 and

We have treated surrogacy as a site of intimate commerce. But these quotes highlight another important aspect of commercial gestational surrogacy – the role that doctors and medical personnel play in this bio-economic trade, in turning pregnancy into a controllable, and therefore sellable product. The presence of doctors allegedly ensures the procedure's safety and success. Surrogacy becomes another step in the medicalization of pregnancy, a social process that transformed a unique female capacity into a site for the operation of (male) science (Corea 1986; Rich 1976). In the process, women's control over their bodies, especially when the pregnancy has become a commodity or form of labor, becomes marginalized and subjected to economic trade. As arises from the agencies' testimonies, surrogates often do not receive compensation for failures during the pregnancy process, and can be made redundant if the customers or the mediators wish. The surrogates are not protected by labor laws in this respect, or by human rights paradigms that should have protected their bodily autonomy and integrity.

CONCLUSIONS

The Israeli cross-border surrogacy market offers a unique perspective into the operation of the global surrogacy trade. On one hand, the state regulates the local surrogacy market and restricts access to it, while on the other hand, extraterritorial practices stay outside of the regulatory means, thus encouraging the growth of a market for cross-border reproductive care. Under these conditions, and taking into account Israel's pro-natalist culture and support for biomedicine, the CBRC market is highly visible and respected, which makes it easier to access and monitor.

Surrogacy contracts operate as a mixture of market economy and social relations. They form, effectively, markets of intimacy (Laufer-Ukeles 2013; Radin 1996). Surrogacy intermediaries (known as surrogacy brokers or agencies) play a crucial role in the development of surrogacy practices, sites, and cross-border alliances. Yet the place of these brokers is grossly under-researched and often marginalized in existing literature (Inhorn and Patrizio 2012). We addressed this lacunae by analyzing the publicity discourse of eleven Israeli cross-border surrogacy agencies, describing the manner in which these agencies construct surrogacy practices, the surrogates they employ, and the imagined relationships between reproductive collaborators.

Surrogacy brokers' discourse is paradoxical. On one hand, it is based in social values: reproductive rights, care for suffering others, the alleviation of childlessness, freedom of choice, and women's control over their own bodies and the reciprocity of altruism and care between commissioning parents and surrogates. In utilizing this discourse, the brokers show flexibility in incorporating much of the second-wave feminist critique toward surrogacy. On the other hand, these social values pave the

Proposals for Legislative Amendment, Nuphar Lipkin and Etti Samama, Isha L'Isha – Haifa Feminist Center. 2010.

path for a commercial business, involving the marketing and employment of women from other, often poorer geographical locations. These processes involve various marketing techniques and contract requirements. Intimate social gestures, which signify human relationships and desire for children and family making, are priced and marketed by the economy industry for the benefit of intermediaries and service providers.

Framing surrogacy as a noble act that the surrogates perform for the commissioning parents and for their own children places additional stigma on surrogates who bargain for greater pay and aligns the customers' expectations with the industry interests of reducing costs (Pande 2010). Thus, while the surrogacy agreement is depicted as altruistic and the payment as a form of gratitude, surrogates are effectively stripped of labor rights and protections, and especially of protections against wrongful termination and employment without compensation (Majumdar 2014; Pande 2011; Raymond 1990). The terms of the business arrangement are expressed in a manner that maximizes profit, extends the market, and keeps costs as low as possible, often by externalizing risk onto the surrogate (and her body). Free choice and consent are assessed as they would be in any other economic field, regardless of the actual nature of the product, which involves human relationships, bodies, and emotions.

The agencies construct surrogacy, and through it the surrogates, as a product. They describe the Global South's surrogates as passive and submissive, as well as exchangeable and immediately available, subject to the commissioning parents' needs. Crucial choices regarding the surrogacy pregnancy, such as the level of relationship between surrogates and commissioning parents or the medical procedures that will be carried out in the surrogates' bodies are in the hands of the commissioning parents, mediated by the surrogacy professionals – agents and doctors. The analysis of the agencies' websites shows clearly that in most cases, the surrogates' decisions and desires are deemed insignificant.

Research has found that women become surrogates as a result of financial necessity (Parry 2015; Rudrappa 2015; Samama 2012). In the context of their material realities, they are making a choice, but the marketing language that is used in order to promote surrogacy obfuscates the fact that this choice was made within limited life options. Similarly to other aspects of childbirth and the human body, choice has become a legitimizing strategy for the surrogacy business. Still, the surrogates' choice is bound to the *entry* into the reproductive industry, and is stripped away from surrogates *throughout* the duration of the surrogacy pregnancy. We found that the discourse regarding choice was limited to the sections encouraging parents to enter into surrogacy agreements, while at the same time much effort was spent on ensuring control over the pregnancy, that is, control over the surrogate during the pregnancy, thus limiting her choices and her bodily autonomy in this process. We believe that maintaining the surrogates' choice and autonomy throughout the surrogacy arrangement is a mandatory requirement, albeit not the only requirement, for a possibility of ethical surrogacy practices.

The analysis presented here demonstrated how commercial surrogacy practices operate against a backdrop of extreme inequality between surrogates and the commissioning parents. None of the agencies we surveyed proposed mediation services that see the sides as equal in their status and bargaining power. The opposite is true – the basis of the agencies' operation, as brought through their marketing information, is to adapt to a standard of business transactions favoring low costs, which means low payments to surrogates and egg providers who become the raw materials for the industry to operate upon. Through the process, the risks of the business, from the possibility of loss of pregnancy to bodily harm and even loss of lives, are passed to the surrogates and egg donors, mostly poor women from countries with diminished labor protections to begin with.

While sweatshops in the Global South are known for subjugating the human body and effort for the needs of global capitalism, in commercial surrogacy, women who gestate for money do not only use their bodies as sources of income, but also cope with emotional and psychic hardships (Hochschild 2011; Samama 2012) and are expected by the industry to become detached from the children they carry (Pande 2010). Surrogates' material realities show patterns that are common to many women around the globe: their financial possibilities are limited and their personal choices are confined to gendered social norms that expect women to show devotion and self-sacrifice as women and mothers.

Another aspect that is part and parcel of the discourse regarding commercial surrogacy's legitimacy is the commissioning parents' choices themselves. Contrary to common sense, the terminology regarding approaching surrogacy as a consumer often depicts commissioning parents as choice-less, or as martyrs on a relentless path to the desired parenthood, a final recourse in the way of couples who are desperate to have a child. It seems that similarly to Franke's (2001) suggestion, once technological possibility for reproduction becomes widely available, a social norm arises that enforces its use. In reality, commissioning parents choose not only to take part in the surrogacy industry, they also choose where to conduct their surrogacy arrangements, under which terms, and through which agency. They also make countless choices throughout surrogacy pregnancies, regarding the medical procedures conducted, the level of pay to the surrogate and other persons employed in the process, the kind of relationships they wish to generate with other reproductive collaborators and how to incorporate them (or not) in the process of making these decisions. Although commissioning parents did not create the cross-border reproductive industry, they are fueling it in their choices and preferences for low costs and added flexibility. It is important to note, however, that the commissioning parents' choice is also often bound as a choice to enter the arrangements, while during the surrogacy process itself their ability to affect the process is mediated by the deals available in the reproductive market. The appearance of medical-legal-commercial technology thus becomes a site for the production of moral scripts that eventually become new social norms.

References

Andrews, P. and Wood, F., 2014. *Uberpreneurs: How to Create Innovative Global Businesses and Transform Human Societies*. New York: Palgrave Macmillan.

Arditti, R., Klein, R. D., and Minden, S., 1984. *Test Tube Women: What Future for Motherhood?* London: Pandora Press.

Berkovitch, N., 1997. Motherhood as a National Mission: The Construction of Womanhood in the Legal Discourse in Israel. *Women's Studies International Forum*, 20(5/6), pp. 605–619.

Birenbaum-Carmeli, D., 2007. Contested Surrogacy and the Gender Order: An Israeli Case Study. *Journal of Middle East Women's Studies*, 3(3), pp. 21–44.

Birenbaum-Carmeli, D. and Carmeli, Y. S., 2010. Introduction. In Y. S. Carmeli and D. Birenbaum-Carmeli, eds. *Kin, Gene, Community: Reproductive Technologies among Jewish Israelis*. Oxford: Berghahn Books, p. 372.

Bryman, A., 2012. *Social Research Methods*. Oxford: Oxford University Press.

Carmeli, Y. S. and Birenbaum-Carmeli, D., 2010. *Kin, Gene, Community: Reproductive Technologies among Jewish Israelis* Y. S. Carmeli and D. Birenbaum-Carmeli, eds., Oxford: Berghahn Books.

Corea, G., 1986. *The Mother Machine: Reproductive Technologies from Artificial Insemination to Artificial Wombs*. London: The Women's Press.

Dempsey, D., 2012. More Like a Donor or More Like a Father? Gay Men's Concepts of Relatedness to Children. *Sexualities*, 15(2), pp. 156–174.

Denzin, N. K. and Lincoln, Y. s, 2000. *The Handbook of Qualitative Research*, second ed. N. K. Denzin and Y. s Lincoln, eds., Thousand Oaks, CA: Sage Publications.

Donat, O., 2007. *Fractured Pro-natalism*. Tel-Aviv University (Hebrew).

Fairclough, N., 2010. *Critical Discourse Analysis: The Critical Study of Language*, second ed., New York: Routledge.

Ferraretti, A. P. et al., 2010. Cross-Border Reproductive Care: A Phenomenon Expressing the Controversial Aspects of Reproductive Technologies. *Reproductive BioMedicine Online*, 20(2), pp. 261–266.

Fogiel-Bijaoui, S., 1999. *Families in Israel: Between Familism and Postmodernism*. Tel-Aviv: Hakibbutz Hameuchad.

Franke, K. M., 2001. Theorizing Yes: An Essay on Feminism, Law, and Desire. *Columbia Law Review*, 101(1), pp. 181–208.

Franklin, S., 2013. *Biological Relatives: IVF, Stem Cells, and the Future of Kinship*, Durham, NC, and London: Duke University Press.

Gooldin, S., 2008. Technologies of Happiness: Fertility Management in a Pro-natal Context. In Y. Yona and A. Kemp, eds. *Citizenship Gaps: Migration, Fertility and Identity in Israel*. Jerusalem: The Van Leer Institute, pp. 167–206.

Hashiloni-Dolev, Y., 2006. Between Mothers, Fetuses and Society: Reproductive Genetics in the Israeli-Jewish Context. *Nashim: A Journal of Jewish Women's Studies & Gender Issues*, 12, pp. 129–150.

Hochschild, A. R., 2011. Emotional Life on the Market Frontier. *Annual Review of Sociology*, 37(1), pp. 21–33.

Hudson, N. et al., 2011. Cross-Border Reproductive Care: A Review of the Literature. *Reproductive Biomedicine Online*, 22, pp. 673–685.

Inhorn, M. C. and Patrizio, P., 2012. The Global Landscape of Cross-Border Reproductive Care: Twenty Key Findings for the New Millennium. *Current Opinion in Obstetrics & Gynecology*, 24(3), pp. 158–163.

Kahn, S. M., 2000. *Reproducing Jews: A Cultural Account of Assisted Conception in Israel*. Durham, NC, and London: Duke University Press.

Laufer-Ukeles, P., 2013. Mothering for Money: Regulating Commercial Intimacy. *Indiana Law Journal*, 88(4).

Lipkin, N. and Samama, E., 2010. *Surrogacy in Israel – Status Report 2010 and Proposals for Legislative Amendment*. Haifa.

Lustenberger, S., 2014. Questions of Belonging: Same-Sex Parenthood and Judaism in Transformation. *Sexualities*, 17(5–6), pp. 529–545.

Majumdar, A., 2014. Nurturing an Alien Pregnancy: Surrogate Mothers, Intended Parents and Disembodied Relationships. *Indian Journal of Gender Studies*, 21(2), pp. 199–224.

Markham, A., 2004. Internet Communication as a Tool for Qualitative Research. In C. Seale et al., eds. *Qualitative Research: Theory, Method and Practice*. London: Sage Publications, pp. 358–74.

Mashiach, S. et al., 2010. The Contribution of Israeli Researchers to Reproductive Medicine: Fertility Experts' Perspective. In Y. S. Carmeli and D. Birenbaum-Carmeli, eds. *Kin, Gene, Community*. Oxford: Berghahn Books, pp. 51–60.

Mor-Yosef, S. et al., 2012. *Recommendations of the Public Committee for the Regularization of Fertility and Reproduction in Israel*. Jerusalem.

Moreno, A., 2016a. *Crossing Borders: Remaking Gay Fatherhood in the Global Market*. University of Manchester.

Moreno, A., 2016b. Families on the Market Front. In *Intimate Economies: Bodies, Emotions and Sexualities on the Global Market*. New York: Palgrave Macmillan.

Nahman, M. R., 2006. Materializing Israeliness: Difference and Mixture in Transnational Ova Donation. *Science as Culture*, 15(3), pp. 199–213.

Nahman, M. R., 2013. *Extractions: An Ethnography of Reproductive Tourism*. New York: Palgrave Macmillan.

Nordqvist, P., 2011. "Dealing with Sperm": Comparing Lesbians' Clinical and Non-Clinical Donor Conception Processes. *Sociology of Health & Illness*, 33(1), pp. 114–129.

Pande, A., 2010. Commercial Surrogacy in India: Manufacturing a Perfect Mother-Worker. *Signs: Journal of Women in Culture and Society*, 35(4), pp. 969–992.

Pande, A., 2011. Transnational Commercial Surrogacy in India: Gifts for Global Sisters? *Reproductive Biomedicine Online*, 23(5), pp. 618–625.

Parry, B., 2015. Narratives of Neoliberalism: "Clinical Labour" in Context. *Medical Humanities*, 41, pp. 31–37.
Radin, M. J., 1996. *Contested Commodities: The Trouble with Trade in Sex, Children, Body Parts, and Other Things.* Cambridge: Cambridge University Press.
Rapp, R., 2011. Reproductive Entanglements: Body, State, and Culture in the Dys/Regulation of Child-Bearing. *Social Research*, 78(3), pp. 693–718.
Rapp, R., 1999. *Testing Women, Testing the Fetus: The Social Impact of Amniocentesis in America.* New York and London: Routledge.
Raymond, J. G., 1990. Reproductive Gifts and Gift Giving: The Altruistic Woman. *The Hastings Center Report*, 20(6), pp. 7–11.
Raymond, J. G., 1998. *Women as Wombs: Reproductive Technologies and the Battle over Women's Freedom.* Melbourne: Spinifex Press.
Rich, A., 1976. *Of Woman Born: Motherhood as Institution and Experience.* New York: Norton.
Rose, N., 2001. The Politics of Life Itself. *Theory, Culture & Society*, 18(6), pp. 1–30.
Rothman, B. K., 1984. The Meaning of Choice in Reproductive Technology. In R. Arditti, R. Duelli Klein, and S. Minden, eds. *Test-Tube Women: What Future for Motherhood?* London: Pandora, pp. 22–33.
Rudrappa, S., 2015. *Discounted Life: The Price of Global Surrogacy in India.* New York: New York University Press.
Rudrappa, S. and Collins, C., 2015. Altruistic Agencies and Compassionate Consumers: Moral Framing of Transnational Surrogacy. *Gender & Society*, 29(6), pp. 937–959.
Sama, R. G. for W. and H., 2012. *Birthing a Market: A Study on Commercial Surrogacy.* New Delhi.
Samama, E., 2011. From Baby M to Google Baby. 15 Years to the Israeli Surrogacy Law. In *15 Years to Israeli Surrogacy Law.* Tel-Aviv: Tel-Aviv University.
Samama, E., 2012. *A Womb for Rent: "Within Me, but Not Mine." The Surrogacy Law in Israel: Vision, Policy and Reality.* Ben-Gurion University of the Negev.
Teman, E., 2010. The Last Outpost of the Nuclear Family: A Cultural Critique of Israeli Surrogacy Law. In Y. S. Carmeli and D. Birenbaum-Carmeli, eds. *Kin, Gene, Community.* Oxford: Berghahn Books.
Thompson, C. 2005. *Making Parents: The Ontological Choreography of Reproductive Technologies. Inside Technology.* Cambridge, MA: MIT Press.
Triger, Z., 2015. A Different Journey: Experiences of Israeli Surrogacy Parents in India. *Theory and Criticism*, 44, pp. 177–202 (Hebrew).

Appendix

SURROGACY AGENCIES

Baby Bloom: www.babybloom.co.il/
Center for Parenthood through Surrogacy: www.pundekauthodo.co.il
Demona Surrogacy Kazakhstan: http://pundekaut-surrogate.com/he/procedure.html

Manor Medic: www.manormedic.co.il/
New Family: www.newfamily.org.il/legal-info/parenthood-articles
New Life (Israel): http://newlifeisrael.co.il/
Path to Parenthood, the agency for international surrogacy: www.globalsurrogacy.org/he/surrogacy-he.html
The Right to Parenthood: www.pundekaut.org/
Tammuz Surrogacy: www.tammuz.com/main.php
Time4Child Thailand Surrogacy: www.time4child.com/
Viva Surrogacy: www.vivasurrogacy.com/default.asp?id=10012

8

Palestinian Fertility in the Israeli Sphere: Palestinian Women in Israel Undergoing IVF Treatments

Himmat Zu'bi

INTRODUCTION

Palestinian women in Israel confront oppression and marginalization distinct from both Palestinian men and Israeli women.[1] The state's institutional oppression, and its exclusion of the Palestinian "citizen/stranger" (Robinson 2013) is compounded by social conservatism. Exploring reproductive fertility treatments and reproductive politics reveals unique perspectives on this web of social expectations, national imperatives, and colonial exclusion.

New technologies of reproduction, developed in the last decades of the twentieth century and in the early twenty-first century, aim to provide solutions for women and couples suffering from fertility problems. Many women begin fertility treatments with the emotional, social, and mental burdens of infertility. In a broader social milieu that places a national and familial premium on reproduction, these burdens are compounded (Inhorn 1996, 2003). The treatment itself is invasive and medicalizes women's bodies, their hormonal make-up, and their monthly cycles (Callan and Hennessey 1988; Boivin and Takekman 1996; Hammarberg, Astbury, and Baker 2001).

Research on in vitro fertilization (IVF) both in Israel and far beyond has recently accelerated (Remennick 2000; Birenbaum-Carmeli 2003, 2004; Haelyon 2004, 2007; Hashiloni-Dolev 2004; Gooldin 2008, 2013). These studies mostly focus on the effects of reproductive technologies on Israeli women. What these technologies mean for Palestinian women, who are excluded from the state's self-definition while having a contingent access to its health system, remain unstudied.

Palestinian women's bodies and their reproduction are central pillars of the settler colonial state's attempts to control and eliminate the internal other (Shalhoub-Kevorkian, Ihmoud, and Dahir-Nashif 2014). Palestinian citizens in Israel are the descendants of the 150,000 people who remained on the land of Palestine that would come to be called Israel. These people were separated from the 700,000 to 900,000 Palestinians who fled or were expelled in 1948 as a result of the *Nakba* (catastrophe)

---

[1] The term "Israeli" is used here to denote Jewish-Israeli women.

of 1948 (Khalidi 1992). In many ways, they are the living reminder of Israel's always-already other, Palestine. They would live under military rule until 1966, and since then navigate the blurry and ambiguous lines of being estranged people residing on their own land. These Palestinians are often referred to as "Israeli-Arabs" or the "Palestinian minority." Both terms are outcomes of a colonial epistemology. Palestinians in Israel are not a minority; they did not land in Israel, it landed on them. On some basic levels, Palestinians can never be full and equal citizens in a state that self-denies as Jewish. Palestinians in Israel now number more than 20 percent of the Israeli population. They pose as much of a challenge to Israel's self-proclaimed status as both Jewish and democratic, as does the now fifty years of occupation of the West Bank and Gaza.

Palestinian women in Israel have privileged access to a health care system that their compatriots in the West Bank and Gaza are not afforded. Given the specificities of the "citizen stranger," how do women navigate these technological opportunities and interventions in and through their bodies? What does the national and social experience of an "inferior citizenship" entail? (Rouhana 1997; Jamal 2007) What do these interventions entail, what do they make possible, and what compromises do they require?

At the heart of this study, the paradoxical condition of conditional access is the National Health Insurance Law, issued in 1995 and descended from early Zionist sick funds with clear nationalist goals. Around 1912, Jewish laborers founded mutual aid sick funds to provide services for Zionist workers. In 1920, the various labor unions united to form the General Federation of Hebrew Workers (the Histadrut) and developed cooperative institutions, among them a common Histadrut sick fund. It was in 1959, eleven years after the establishment of Israel, that the Histadrut decided to allow Arabs to become full members. The Mapai Party, which controlled the Histadrut sick fund, used the opening of its clinics as a reward for Arab electoral support, and thus many communities remained without clinics. Although many Palestinians have in fact become Histadrut members, this didn't secure them services comparable to those enjoyed by Jews. The 1995 law of universal health coverage did not include provisions for "corrective measures," and the gap between Palestinians and Jews continued to exist (Kanaaneh 2002). In exploring Palestinian women's engagements with fertility treatments, this study reveals new ways of understandings state, citizenship, and belonging that are both social and familial.

Indeed, a Palestinian woman's uterus is not a neutral space for neither Israeli state officials or Israeli public rhetoric. Whereas an Israeli woman's uterus is a source of rejuvenation, rebirth, and reproduction of the national body, the Palestinian woman's uterus is a source of danger. Her very body has the potential to reproduce the "fifth pillar" of her national and communal affiliations. Across national lines, both Palestinian and Israeli, the demographic imperative instrumentalizes the woman's uterus as an vehicle of triumph and defeat.

This study is based on fifteen interviews that took place in 2010 and 2011.[2] All the women were between the ages of twenty-three and thirty-six. All the women were married. The large majority – twelve of the fifteen – were married between the ages of eighteen and twenty-four. One was married at the age of sixteen, two were married at the age of thirty plus. With the exception of one woman who completed ten years of education, all of the interviewees had attained a high school diploma. Five women were homemakers, eight were educators, one was both a teacher and an optician, and one was a therapist. While all of the interviewees were attempting to achieve their first pregnancy, the causes of their infertility differed or remained undiagnosed,[3] as did the temporality of their treatments and the number of IVF cycles they had undergone.

THE MEANING OF THE CHILD

The results of this study reveal that Palestinian women holding Israeli citizenship undergoing fertility treatment in Israel share similar experiences with women around the world: their experiences have much in common with those of women across the Arab world, as well as with those of Israeli women. Nonetheless, the complexity of their lives, their social and national status, has contributed additional dimensions that make the experiences of Palestinian women in Israel different and unique.

Scholarship has long shown that despite ongoing transformations of family structures in the Arab and Muslim world (Zaatari 2003; Enloe 2004), patriarchal norms continue

---

[2] I employed three primary strategies to enlist interviewees for the study:

   A. Personal contact with patients and women in my own community: I approached women whom I knew were undergoing fertility treatment. I also contacted other women in my community who were not undergoing fertility treatments, explained the purpose of my research, and requested that they contact other women they know who were undergoing treatments. I asked for the patients' contact information only after they had agreed in principle to talk with me, without committing to participating in the study. I identified and enlisted four women using this strategy.
   B. Snowball sampling: I asked the women I was interviewing for help in identifying additional women. They were generally very responsive. This strategy helped me identify seven additional women.
   C. Contact with a specialist doctor (prior to contacting a doctor specializing in fertility, I tried approaching a number of fertility clinics, but the response was poor and clinic managers were not helpful): My personal acquaintance with a doctor specializing in fertility was extremely helpful. It was through this doctor that I found four additional patients. I stressed to the interviewees enlisted through this doctor the confidentiality of their interviews and that the doctor would not have access to any of them. The purpose of this clarification was to ensure they felt free to talk about their experiences in the therapeutic sphere, including their treatment by the doctor and other members of his medical staff.

[3] A medical reason for infertility was not diagnosed for seven of the interviewees. Four reported that the infertility was related to their husbands and in one case to both sides of the couple. In the three remaining cases, the causes of infertility were related to the woman interviewee.

to shape social, familial, and gender relations in Arab and Muslim countries and well beyond (Barakat 1993, 2000; Joseph 1993a, 1993b, 2000; Inhorn 2003, 2006).

The present study confirms some of these findings. Palestinian women in Israel also ascribe great importance to children and view motherhood as a central value in their lives. There was little difference between the interviewees with regards to this question, and I found no correlation between level of education or occupation and attitudes toward motherhood.

Jamal has two degrees from one of the most prestigious universities in Israel and works full time as a counselor and teacher: "Children are happiness. What is the point of marriage without children? If you have a child, you feel that there's meaning to your life, and your status in the family becomes higher."

Nihal has been working full time as a medical assistant for the past nine years and held a senior position in a private company at the time of the interview. She agrees: "Children are the meaning of marriage. What is the point of marriage without children?"

Like women in other parts of the Arab world (Moghadam 1993; Inhorn 1996), Palestinian women in Israel perceive children to be what bestows value on married women and provides stability to the marriage. This perception is shared by all interviewees, regardless of their social status, education, or occupation.

Mariam views children as a crucial element in strengthening her position in her husband's family: "If you have no children, you have no support. My family got all anxious because I didn't get pregnant, and they started putting pressure on me. What are you waiting for? Why aren't you doing anything about it? A child is a woman's support. Even if you don't agree with them, they begin to affect you."

Most of the women interviewed shared this experience. Children, according to the study's results, provide women with a sense of stability in their marital life. For Nadira, they guarantee the success of her marriage: "Listen, his parents weren't that happy about his choice. They wanted him to marry someone from the family, but he insisted. I have to have a child; he will be my guarantee to hold on to the marriage."

QUESTIONING "FREE WILL"

The national identity and citizenship of Palestinians in Israel are an additional significant component of the experiences of women undergoing fertility treatments. Israel, where these Palestinian women live, is defined in research literature as a pro-natal state and this has an impact on Palestinian women, as this study shows.

Israel encourages procreation as a result of two influences that define motherhood as an ultimate value: first, tradition, that is, Jewish religious-halachic traditions; and, second, Israeli-Zionist heritage. These two forces are political ideologies that identify normative Israeli femininity with fertility and procreation (Amir and Benjamin 1997;

Berkovitch 1997; Remennick 2000, 2008; Birenbaum-Carmeli 2003, 2004; Shalev and Goldin 2006; Inhorn and Birenbaum-Carmeli 2008; Birenbaum-Carmeli and Dirnfeld 2008).

This message has become entrenched in Jewish thought over the generations and finds expression in Zionist ideology, which holds that the Jewish people need a Jewish home, and the Jewish home requires a Jewish people. This unique combination of Jewish religious traditions, demographic competition with the Arabs, and the fear of death in battle, as well as the moral commitment of the State of Israel to make up for the Jews slaughtered in the Holocaust (Gooldin 2013), has driven a relatively high birthrate among Jewish Israelis (Remennick 2000).

Pro-natal policy in Israel has been expressed in a variety of ways,[4] and it is evident in the fact that Israel has the greatest proportional number of public clinics devoted to IVF (Shalev 1998; Kahn 2000; Haelyon 2006). The National Health Insurance Law stipulates that the state funds all types of new fertility treatments, including artificial insemination, egg donations, and IVF. This policy enjoyed the support of politicians, doctors, health agents, and the media, and was internalized by women (Birenbaum-Carmeli and Dirnfeld 2008: 184).

Israeli scholars note that medicalization and expert discourse about women's bodies and reproductive systems, as well as discourse about "natural" and "unnatural" pregnancy, have affected Israeli women's perceptions of the "normal" female body and the way the reproductive system should function (Haelyon 2004: 104).

Palestinian women in Israel are exposed to the same hegemonic discourses of Israeli society, and as such, they too appear to undergo a process described by Haelyon as "internal colonization," in which women internalize categories about the pathological weakness of women's reproductive systems in the case of infertility (2004: 104).

Most of the women interviewed for this study, even prior to medical diagnosis, assumed that it was their bodies that were responsible for the failure to conceive. And this assumption of responsibility led to feelings of guilt. As a result of this internal colonization, and by cause of the ready availability of fertility treatments in Israel, the women saw doctors in order to diagnose the problem and solve it.

Most of the interviewees – eleven out of the fifteen – who wanted, planned, or dreamed of having children immediately after marriage consulted doctors during their first year of marriage. Four of them even went to see a doctor just months after their wedding and withheld the fact that they had been married for less than a year. They did this knowing that medical intervention is undertaken only after a year of sexual intercourse without using prophylactics.

---

[4] These ways include an initiative for maternity benefits given to Jewish women through the Jewish Agency, a ban on contraception up until the 1950s, a ban on abortions until 1976, and a special grant for a tenth child (Yuval Davis 1996; Kanaaneh 2002). This policy also found expression in the establishment of the Center for Demography in 1968, which defined its mission as implementing a fertility policy aiming to create an environment conducive to fertility and to bring about a rise in fertility necessary for the Jewish people (Inhorn and Birenbaum-Carmeli 2008: 183).

Shuruk, like the other interviewees, had internalized the importance of medical guidelines: "I heard that the doctor will not consider treatment unless it's been a year since the wedding." This information was gleaned from their surroundings, even before going to see a doctor, as exemplified by Shuruk's words, "I heard." This phenomenon is testimony to the effects of medical discourse on social discourse and social perceptions of women's bodies.

In addition to the role of medical discourse in the process of internal colonization, social forces and discourses (Foucault 1980) common in Palestinian society reinforce the message, as demonstrated by women seeking treatment less than a year after marriage and hiding that fact.

Mayson recounts that she got married and wanted to have children immediately. There were strong expectations, particularly from her husband's family. The feeling of "failure" to fulfill these social and familial expectation led her to seek medical help. These social expectations regarding a woman's body and duties are clearly expressed by Mayson:

> I wanted children right after the wedding. Everyone expected it from me: My parents expected it, but especially his parents. I didn't work and I was at home all the time. I felt the pressure and expectations all the time. I lived the expectations and disappointments each month, as I got my period.

Although the women used language that indicates free will, such as Mayson's "I wanted children," or Nuhad's "I didn't get pregnant even though I wanted to," it is impossible to overlook the unique experience of Palestinian women in Israel. Their reality is shaped by a range of discourses: social discourses rooted in conservative and Arab pro-natalism, and the nationalist and medical discourses prevalent in Israel encouraging procreation and families, even if not aimed at Palestinian women (perhaps even the opposite). Regardless, these discourses shape the women's internalization of their role as women, as well as the roles of their bodies and reproductive systems in fulfilling this role.

The importance of children in the lives of Palestinian women, together with the social, institutional, medical, and national forces shaping women's perceptions of their bodies on one hand, and their social role on the other, calls the issue of "free will" into question. A deeper exploration in the case of some of the interviewees, those who declared that they did not plan to have children immediately after their wedding, supports this suspicion.

One woman, Areej, said that she and her husband had agreed to postpone children for a few years, but succumbed to pressure in the end: "It was agreed between us; I wouldn't get pregnant right after the wedding. We planned a few years of freedom. But that changed quickly. It was very difficult for both of us to resist the pressures: 'So, you're not pregnant?' 'What, no news?' 'What are you waiting for?' 'What are you missing?' And even more annoying questions like: 'I know a good doctor. Do you want me to get you his number?'" Clearly, the challenges Palestinian women face prior to entering therapeutic space are primarily the result of numerous social, political, and medical discourses, and their role in constructing women's social and cultural roles.

CHALLENGES IN THE THERAPEUTIC SPACE

Navigating Medical Authority

Palestinian women's experiences in the therapeutic space are wrought with challenges, usually not much different from the experiences of other women undergoing fertility treatments (Remennick 2000; Benjamin and Haelyon 2002; Inhorn 2002). My interviewees were just as mired in emotional and physical struggles as appears in the scholarship more broadly.

Most of the women interviewed in this project accepted new reproductive technologies as the means of treating their problem. Social voices defined a "normal" woman's body as one that becomes pregnant, and the role of a married woman as motherhood. This medicalization and disciplining of the body leads women to turn to medical diagnosis and dismiss other solutions and interventions, such as adoption or choosing to be childless. For many of my interviewees, infertility was deeply linked to feelings of guilt and unworthiness.

For these women, their emotional struggles stemming from infertility and from subsequent social pressure trumped their desire to acquire information on the interventions in and medicalization of their bodies. With the exception of three, none of the women used medical terminology when describing the causes of their infertility or the medical processes they underwent. Nuhad, who had prior experience with the health care system, was one of the few able to name her medical condition and clearly identify her treatments: "After, I went for tests, without anyone's knowledge. And I already knew that I had a problem called PCOS[5] in English, a condition where the woman has accelerated activity in her ovaries. The ovaries produce a large number of eggs, but these eggs don't develop to the state where they can be fertilized." She proceeded to describe her treatment: "In the second cycle, they extracted thirty ova, but were only able to fertilize one, which they put back.... I knew this wasn't good, that the odds would be smaller. I went to the nurse and told her that this doesn't make sense and tried to find out why this was happening.... I keep track of the implantation, watching how they put the fertilized egg back into the uterus."

The other interviewees, even those whose infertility had been diagnosed, did not engage in medical terms for their conditions or the procedures they underwent.

---

[5] Polycystic ovarian syndrome is a condition in which a woman's levels of the sex hormones estrogen and progesterone are out of balance. This leads to the growth of ovarian cysts (www.healthline.com/health/polycystic-ovary-disease).

Most could not name the drugs they were taking as part of the process. Their narrative of the treatment was usually disorganized and lacked chronological cohesion. As the interviewer, I found it difficult at times to keep track of the medical processes they underwent, since they kept breaking off to talk about their emotional experiences.

Despite their divestment from the medical terms and processes, all of the interviewees paid close attention to their treatment instructions and carefully followed them. For most of the women, the therapeutic space was a means to an end, treated instrumentally in order to achieve their goals. Their treatment instructions were more important than the diagnosis, the name or side effects of the medication, and the type of treatment plan. Taniya put it as follows: "I went into treatment with one goal: the child. I trust the doctor. The treatment is important in order to realize that goal."

The social forces that value procreation, combined with Israeli reproductive policies and the limitation of alternative nonmedical solutions such as adoption, exacerbate the process of "internal colonization" and lead women to accept treatment unquestioningly and increase their commitment to the process (Inhorn and Birenbaum-Carmeli 2008: 189). This appears to be the reason women ascribed such importance to their instructions as soon as they began the process and took care to follow them closely.

Nuhad, for example, described her relationship to the doctor's instructions: "I trusted the doctors and followed their orders. They know more than anyone else. After all, I got a child from the treatment, didn't I?" Even in cases where the interviewees felt that something was wrong, they trusted the doctor and his team to identify the problem on their own. They did not report it to the doctors. Nihal, for example, recounted: "I was careful and took the medications exactly as the doctor wrote down in the plan. I felt terrible, but I would still go for all the tests: blood, ultrasound, follow-ups with the doctor and everything. ... You could tell I wasn't feeling well. They didn't notice at the hospital. I didn't go to work; I couldn't. ... I didn't feel well. And one day I just couldn't take it and I went to the hospital, where they found out that my whole body was full of water. I was in mortal danger."

In summary, most of the women relied primarily, and often exclusively, on the information they received from the medical team. Only three women searched for additional information and attempted to find ways to deal with the challenges posed by the professional terminology they encountered. Mayson, with a high school education, recounts: "I [tried] to read the brochure for the medication before I [took] it. I also tried to find information on the Internet. I didn't always understand what was written there because it was in Hebrew, but also because it used professional terminology that I didn't always understand."

Abir, who has a university education, explained the difficulties in finding information about her treatment: "Look, it's lucky my husband's father is a doctor. We're lucky, otherwise, even with all the education he and I have, we wouldn't have understood it on our own: not the test results and not to know how and where to look for more information. The problem isn't with the searching. We know how to look, but you need to know you can trust the information you find, and to understand it too."

Bodily Feminine Self-Image

This study similarly found that Palestinian women appear to have suppressed their pain and avoided complaining. Benjamin and Haelyon believe that it is the very act of suppressing of the pain involved in IVF treatments that is the reason why women do not share their pain (2002: 673). Nadira described this suppression of physical pain: "No one understands what you're going through, except perhaps women undergoing fertility treatments. The doctors don't give you room to complain. The rest of the staff also gives the impression that they are fed up with hearing about the pain. So you learn to keep it to yourself."

The treatments also had implications for the interviewees' bodily feminine self-image. Most reported gaining weight. They differed in the degree to which they came to terms with these changes. Areej, for example, found the weight gain tolerable: "I am constantly watching [my weight], because I always gain weight during treatment . . . does it bother me? Sure it bothers me, but I am willing to pay the price in order to achieve the goal – pregnancy. Afterwards, when I get what I want, I'll lose weight." Nihal, in contrast, was less accepting of the same changes: "I got really fat during treatment. My stomach grew and I looked like I was pregnant. I was embarrassed to leave the house."

Like a Car in a Garage

The interviewees faced many emotional challenges in the therapeutic space, and these appear to take precedence over the physical difficulties in their interviews. Clearly, these difficulties are not unique to Palestinian women, and the results of this portion of the study are similar to those from other studies in other parts of the world, though particularly so in pro-natal patriarchal societies.

Most women reported strong emotions when entering the therapeutic space. Some reported feeling like lab rats (Greil 2002). Ruba was bitter about the belated discovery of a barrier in her womb after four years of treatment: "What did they do for four years? We could have saved a lot of time. I felt as if those entire four years they were just trying and didn't really know how to treat me; as if he [the doctor] was experimenting at my expense."

Many of the women shared the challenging experience of feeling invisible in the therapeutic space. Clearly this feeling of invisibility is stronger among women treated in public hospitals as compared to women treated in private ones. Inas explained: "When you are treated by a team, rather than a private doctor, X is like Y is like Z. Everyone gets the same treatment. It's not like being in private care, under the treatment and monitoring of one doctor."

The feeling that one's body is objectified under treatment and transformed into a machine (Inhorn 1994, 1996; Greil 2002) was mentioned in many of the interviews. Shuruk suggested: "It was terribly difficult; a different doctor each time. Sometimes I would say to the people around me: I feel like a car ... it [the treatment] makes you feel like you're in a garage."

All the interviewees discussed the difficulty of the intimate exposure entailed in the treatment. They felt as if they were losing control of their bodies, were humiliated, and experienced loss of privacy and dignity (Greil 2002). Rim, for example, said of being exposed during tests: "I barely get undressed in front of my husband. To get undressed and spread my legs in front of everyone was the most difficult and humiliating moment in the whole treatment."

Interviewees experienced emotional cycles in the process of their medical treatment. Each reported mood shifts, beginning with optimism, excitement, and expectation, followed by fears and ending with disappointment (Remennick 2000). The women's sense of responsibility increased during the waiting period. They felt the prospect of conception depended entirely on them. Inas describes the waiting period after implantation: "During the waiting period after implantation every movement counts, you aren't allowed to lift heavy things, you can't do this and you can't do that. . . . I have to be careful and pay attention to every movement."

And after the waiting period ends with failure, deep disappointment and a sense of personal failure were ubiquitous. As Mariam puts it: "As difficult as the process was, the extraction and the implantation and all that, the most difficult thing was receiving the negative result. I would be emotionally devastated. I would cry for a week and do nothing. Just ask, 'Why? Why is this happening?' The doctors say everything is fine, so why didn't it work?"

This sense of responsibility for the treatment's outcome and the feeling of disappointment are exacerbated by social expectations and feelings that this is everyone's child. The very public nature of infertility and its transformation from a private issue to a public one (Remennick 2000; Van Balen and Inhorn 2002) increases these pressures, and subsequently the women's sense of responsibility. Mariam recounts: "During the waiting period, after the implantation, everyone comes by every day. And when it doesn't work, you feel that this is it, no one asks. I say, 'What? I was important up until now, and now I'm not?' Sometimes I think to myself that all they are interested in is the child, and that I don't matter."

Even if the treatment strongly affects their quality of life, it would appear that social and political forces are extremely powerful in the case of Palestinian women. None of the women I interviewed considered quitting treatments, and not one of them sought a way out of the process (Benjamin and Haelyon 2002). They wanted a child at any cost to their own physical and emotional well-being.

Palestinian Fertility in Israeli Space

Although fertility and reproduction in Israel have been studied extensively, most studies have ignored the unique effects of Israel's reproductive policies on Palestinian women. Alternatively, policy analysis has focused on the demographic struggle between Jews and Palestinians, and the decline in Palestinian fertility rates in its turn is explained within a framework of modernization. Palestinian women's perceptions and experiences are overlooked.

One exception was Birenbaum-Carmeli's study of fertility policy in Israel (Birenbaum-Carmeli 2003; Inhorn and Birenbaum-Carmeli 2008),[6] which claims that in cases of both ultra-Orthodox and Muslim women in Israel, childbearing is a source of considerable social prestige, and not necessarily adverse for the women (Birenbaum-Carmeli 2003: 111).

Sigal Cooldin[7] argues that liberal framing of IVF in Israel generates a potential for alliances between traditionally rival sectors and blurs dichotomous rivalries between Jews and Arabs (Gooldin 2013). Jaqueline Portugese focuses on successive Israeli governments' fertility policies with regards to Palestinian citizens, revealing fundamental differences between the state's policies toward its Arab citizens and its Jewish ones.[8]

This scholarship has contributed to our broader understanding of these intimate struggles that span the public and the private. However, the figure of the woman herself and her perceptions of her body, herself, and her interaction with the medical established remain largely unaddressed.

Rhoda Kanaaneh's study of Israel's selective birth policy (2002) is a noteworthy exception. She explores Palestinian women's perceptions of Israel's fertility policy (Kanaaneh, 2002).[9] Kannaneh claims that the politicization of medicine in general, and of reproduction in particular, combined with a demographic struggle between Jews and Arabs, compounds the difficulties Arabs experience in the healthcare

---

[6] Birenbaum-Carmeli analyzes the effects of Israeli fertility policy on Palestinian women in comparison to other groups in Israeli society. She argues that Palestinian women are subject to the rules and regulations of these technologies, similar to Israeli women, but that there a number of distinctions related to cultural differences and the complex relationship between the two groups (Birenbaum-Carmeli 2003: 109).

[7] Gooldin's study is based on an analysis of Israeli public dispute, parliamentary discussions, and media coverage and an online forum of IVF consumers (both in Hebrew).

[8] She asserts that the state strives to reduce differences in fertility rates between the two groups by reducing birthrates among Arabs, mostly indirectly, in order to avoid appearing undemocratic in the eyes of the world (Portugese 1998: 165).

[9] Kanaaneh argues that the state expended much indirect effort to reduce the high birthrates among Arabs through Jewish-Zionist nongovernmental organizations. The most obvious example of these efforts, alongside the Law of Return (1950), is the abolishment of the grant for a tenth child, ten years after the program was established, when it became clear that most of the women applying for the grant were Arab. She also examines the differences in child allowances between Jews and Arabs throughout the state's history, as well as family-planning programs initiated in 1980 by the minister of health, which focused excessively on Arab families (Kanaaneh 2002: 37).

system. These dynamics contribute to the alienation between the doctor and the patient. Kanaaneh reveals that Palestinians in Israel distrust the healthcare system, because of their deep awareness that their fertility gave rise to Zionist anxiety (Kanaaneh, 2002: 73–75).

This study similarly found that the national identity and citizenship of Palestinians in Israel amplify Palestinian women's difficulties as they undergo fertility treatments.

Entry into the therapeutic space demarcates a distinct time period for Palestinian women. The tensions between Palestinian inferior citizenship and the Israeli healthcare system's claims to be universal become apparent (Daoud 2007; Khatib 2012). Up until this point, women meet with doctors and medical staff, who are usually Arab, in their place of residence. Making the decision to initiate IVF treatment is effectively a decision to engage with Israeli state institutions.

One key arena of both alienation and difficulty Mastery of the Hebrew language is vital for patients. An extensive study of women's health and welfare in Israel found that the language barrier seriously harms the welfare and health of Palestinian women, primarily because of the importance of clear communication between doctors and patients (Gross and Brammli-Greenberg 2000).

Language played an important role in all of my interviewees' experiences. Shuruk describes her experience with linguistic barriers: "At first, I would stutter. My Hebrew wasn't good. I would ask outside [other women] how to translate a certain word or sentence. Sometimes I would come straight out of the doctor's and ask the women outside if they knew what this medicine was, or what something else was." Hiba's description is similar: "Language was a problem for me many times. I didn't always understand, and many times, I was embarrassed to ask."

Yet language was not the only source of alienation for Palestinians navigating Israeli space. Many felt the medical staff did not understand their needs and approached them with a set of presumptions. Some interpreted the nurses' attitude as a racist. Abir said: "Listen, I speak Hebrew fine, I have no problem. But I don't always feel comfortable. You can't express feelings in a language that isn't yours. And not only that, they don't understand our mentality. My mother-in-law and my sister-in-law and all those. How can they understand the pressures I live with? The nurse keeps saying to me: 'relax, you're stressed.' She doesn't understand and will never understand why and how stressed I am."

Ruba also noted a discrepancy in treatments: "The doctor yelled at me because I was five minutes late. He was rude, so I decided to leave this specific hospital. The nurses were also racist and spoke to Arabs disrespectfully. They didn't treat us as well as they treated Jewish women."

In response to these less-than-friendly encounters with Israeli space and services, some women chose Arab doctors. But this choice did not always safeguard them from difficult encounters. Hiba recounts: "Moving to an Arab doctor didn't help that much. You are in contact with the staff, the nurses in particular. And there wasn't always an Arabic-speaking nurse there." Mariam was similarly disappointed: "I wanted an Arab doctor. I thought it would solve some of the difficulties. I got an Arab doctor, and it helped a little, but did not get rid of the problems. You have no control over the staff."

Access to clinics was another barrier to entering Israeli space. Judith Shuval and Ofra Anson argue that despite the universality of the National Health Insurance Law, discrepancies in access to health services in Israel between Arabs and Jews, in favor of Jews, preclude equality (Shuval and Anson 2000). Fertility clinics are located in hospitals at large distances from Arab villages and cities. Women often become dependent on others for transportation and mobility. Usually, this dependence entails courting favor from their husbands' side of the family, since they usually reside closer to them. Here again we find the very intimate struggle and daily interactions with fertility become a subject of public knowledge. Areej describes: "compared with having to ask someone to take me to the hospital for checkups all the time, the physical pain was bearable. How was I supposed to get to the hospital? I had to be driven there by car. My husband leaves for work early, and we couldn't afford for him to take a day off every time I had a checkup." Shada explains the difficulties having to do with distances: "I leave the house at five, five thirty in the morning. I have to make it there by seven. And I have to make it back to work on time. I have to be in class at eight. Eight is late as it is, but the school is considerate."

Despite these difficulties in both accessing and experiencing exclusionary and often unfriendly Israeli spaces and staff, interviewees focused on their desire for a child and on social expectations. They tended to follow treatment instructions carefully (without necessarily understanding them) as a means of fulfilling their own expectations, as well as those of the surrounding environment. They developed coping strategies that rendered their interactions with Israeli therapeutic space as a means to an end. These coping strategies were multifaceted and complex and thoroughly complicate our understanding of women conforming to and confronting social expectations and citizenship, as well as shed light on their strategies of survival and resistance.

Coping Strategies

Conventional scholarship in Israel depicts Palestinian women in general and Palestinian women in Israel in particular primarily as victims of oppression (Zu'bi 2007) and objects of both social pressure and political marginalization. However, my interviewees molded creative and dynamic strategies to cope with the paradox of being a Palestinian woman who is at once subject and object of Israeli treatment and suspicion.

To deal with the challenges of the doctor–patient relationship, some chose to be what Greil calls "infertility contractors" (2002). Abir, Nuhad, and Ruba challenged classic doctor–patient relations, which assume the patient passively accepts and follows the doctor's orders. All three turned to alternative sources of knowledge to play an active role in and attain some measure of control over their treatment.

Abir explains: "I had no choice. I have to understand, to be part of what is happening to me. It's true that I don't control many things in the treatment, but at least I try to understand, even just a little." Ruba reinforces this rationale: "I looked for information that would help me understand a little what was going on. It's true that I didn't totally understand, or that it didn't totally help, but at least I felt that I was doing something. I could be a partner in something, even if just a little."

In light of the invisibility, the loss of control, and loss of self-worth that the women experienced in the therapeutic space, most exercised agency (Greil 2002). They changed doctors, despite their obedience to doctors' orders. Some left their doctors in protest of their harsh or negligent treatment. Maissa describes one such decision: "I didn't like the doctor's attitude. I'll never forget how she spoke to me: her attitude was very inhuman. . . . I was disappointed and cried all the way home. . . . And then I decided to go to a doctor I had met accidentally in the past, even though I wasn't his patient. He gave me advice and was very nice to me. I liked his attitude."

For other women, this strategy was an additional means of establishing their responsibility and control. Mariam describes one of the times she changed doctors: "I went through so many treatment cycles, and they were all unsuccessful. The doctors said there was no problem, so why wasn't it working? I don't know. . . . I decided I needed to take action, so I decided to try my luck with another doctor. . . . Maybe this time it would succeed." As noted, some chose to switch to an Arab doctor to alleviate alienation and language barriers, but this solution too was usually only partial.

Turning to traditional medicine was another strategy. Turning to a traditional therapy and women healers has long been a source of empowerment for women in various contexts (Popper-Giveon and Al-Krenawi 2010). Popper-Giveon and Al-Krenawi's study of Palestinian women's use of traditional healers finds that these healers increase patients' sense of control and self-esteem, as well as enabling their performance of social roles (2010: 74). Half of my interviewees underwent traditional folk medical treatments. Education, length of marriage, and occupation did not correlate in any way with the choice to try this treatment.

However, some women turned to traditional healers as a result of social pressure rather than a search for empowerment. Inas, for example, said: "I decided to take a break from treatments for a period of six months, during which I was talked into trying a natural treatment by a Bedouin woman who uses herbs. I had heard about this woman before, and said to myself: 'So what? Why not try? If it doesn't help, it certainly won't do any harm.'"

For most women, traditional treatments responded to their need for control over a process of waiting and uncertainty. Areej explains: "It seemed at first, and in the end too, that it was inappropriate [going to a traditional folk healer]. I didn't believe in it.

But, you know, I thought, 'What have I got to lose?' The hospital treatment wasn't working anyway, and I felt stuck. So at least you feel as if you're doing something. You try something new. Worse comes to worse, it won't work. You keep his family quiet on the one hand, and on the other hand you feel as if you are doing something."

Women also adapted strategies to cope with the disappointment of a failed treatment and prepare to embark on another. Faith was a core mechanism for bridging failure and continuing the intrusive treatments once again. All interviewees enlisted God, regardless of their varying degree of religiosity. Ruba says: "It's in the hands of God. He is the source of my strength." In answer to the question "How long will you keep trying?" Inas replied: "Until God says to me 'enough.' But I believe that God is on my side."

For most women, spouses were an additional source of support. Conventional perceptions hold that infertility ultimately leads to divorce in Arab social contexts. Yet often bonds of love and partnership can outweigh these gendered expectations (Inhorn 2007: 5). Each of my interviewees took refuge in the love and support of her spouse. Husbands accompanied most of my interviewees to all of their treatments. Abir described her experience: "My husband supports me the most. He takes care of me all the time. Even in the toughest time, for example, the period between the extraction and the implantation, he does everything he can to make things easier for me." Mariam also takes pride in the fact that her husband will not give her up, even if they never have children: "'I want you, with or without children. I love you.' That is what he says to me all the time."

The couples' financial independence, and even more so, the financial dependence of their families on them, works to contain familial meddling and pressure. Indications of this nascent process of transformation in Arab Palestinian family structures in Israel are found in the case of Maissa, who explained why her husband's family did not intervene when she did not become pregnant: "I felt that they – his family – were talking about the fact that I wasn't getting pregnant, but they didn't talk about it in front of me ... they were deferring to my husband. They didn't want to make us angry. It wasn't like that in the case of my sister-in-law, who also didn't get pregnant immediately. It took her two years, and after just a few months they were already driving her crazy. Her husband is weak; he doesn't have status in the family, unlike mine."

In some cases, couples presented a united front in the face of familial curiosity and interventions. Inas's choices and desires drove her and her spouse's united and independent decision: "We didn't want children. I wanted to complete my studies. I was in my third year when I got married. We used condoms for five months and then we stopped, just like that, for no reason. We agreed that we would be careful, but it didn't help and I became pregnant. I had an abortion in the sixth week." This case complicates our binary understandings of Arab social and familial life, and reveals spaces for adaptation and resistance.

Another example of experiences that challenge both social conservatism and knowledge production on it, is that of Abir and her husband. She explains: "We lived together for four years before our wedding. We got married only when we both felt that we wanted children. It's still not accepted in our society to have children out of wedlock. Still, we got married in a civil wedding even though we both belong to the same religion." Abir and her husband's case, while rare, is further suggestive of change in the Arab-Palestinian family in Israel in general, and in marital life in particular. These transformations seem to indicate the formation of space for changes in the structure of Arab family.

CONCLUSION

Palestinian women undergoing fertility treatments in Israel navigate a plethora of obstacles. Infertility presents Palestinian women living in a pro-natal conservative society with many emotional challenges. Living without children is almost unacceptable; women seek out all possible solutions to their problem. Palestinian women have internalized the social discourses that enshrine their bodies as sites for the reproduction of the family and the nation. Motherhood and childbearing take shape as women's highest value. Consequently, these women are subject to a wide array of affective registers: responsibility, guilt, faith, hope, and disappointment. Often their success or failure to conceive is directly tied to their self-worth.

A far-reaching pro-natal policy marks Israeli life. This policy responds to both ideological and religious imperatives to build and fortify a Jewish state. It medicalizes and disciplines the bodies of women, both Jewish and Palestinian. However, principles driving Israeli pro-natal policies position the Palestinian uterus and Palestinian reproduction as a threat to the state. Palestinian women who are citizens in Israel thus have access to a system their compatriots in the West Bank and Gaza can only dream of. At the same time, they become subject to a system that is structured around their very exclusion.

New reproductive technologies take shape as an overarching solution to personal, familial, and social pressures. Women "choose" to employ new reproductive technologies in order to fulfill social expectations. They enter the therapeutic space to achieve one goal, having a child to strengthen their control and position in the family. While uncritically obeying medical instructions, they strategically navigate their discrimination and marginalization in the health care system. In the process, these women, whose fertility treatments entail intense physical interventions, repress both their bodily and emotional pain.

As a Palestinian woman manages this tapestry of pain and emotion, she must also engage her subject position as a demographic threat. Her access to Israeli health care is contingent on her historical and contemporary position as Zionism's penultimate other. The daily articulations of this othering takes shape in linguistic barriers and racist undertones in the therapeutic space. The space itself is often at far distances that render national health insurance less "universal" than it claims to be.

Yet women were not silent objects in this process. Their repertoire of coping strategies was complex and diverse. Some challenged traditional doctor–patient roles and attempted to actively participate by using alternative sources of information. Some turned to traditional medicine.

In addition, a close look at Palestinian fertility treatments reveals an array of affective experiences that challenge our conventional understanding of Palestinian social life. Spouses were sources of love, support, and comfort for all interviewees. Indeed, in many cases, men and women consolidate a united front to contain social pressure and carve their own timelines for childbearing. The partnership and financial independence of the couple were crucial to coping with infertility.

References

Amir, D. and O. Benjamin (1997). Defining Encounter: Who Are the Women Entitled to Join the Israeli Collective? *Women's Studies International Forum* 20 (5–6): 639–651.

Barakat, H. (1993). *The Arab World: Society, Culture, and State*. Berkeley: University of California Press.

Barakat, H. (2000). *Arab Society in the Twentieth Century*. Beirut: Center for Arab Unity Studies (Arabic).

Benjamin, O. and H. Haelyon (2002). Rewriting Fertilization: Trust, Pain and Exit Points. *Women's Studies International Forum* 25 (6): 667–678.

Berkovitch, N. (1997). Motherhood as a National Mission: The Construction of Womanhood in the Legal Discourse of Israel. *Women's Studies International Forum* 20 (5–6): 605–619.

Birenbaum-Carmeli, D. (2003). Reproductive Policy in Context: Implications on the Rights of Jewish Women in Israel, 1945–2000. *Policy Studies* 24 (2): 101–114.

Birenbaum-Carmeli, D. (2004). "Cheaper than a Newcomer": On the Political Economy of IVF in Israel. *The Sociology of Health and Illness*, 26 (7): 897–924.

Birenbaum-Carmeli, D. and M. Dirnfeld (2008). In-Vitro Fertilization Policy in Israel and Women's Perspectives: The More the Better? *Reproductive Health Matter* 16 (31): 181–191.

Boivin, J. and J. E. Takefman (1996). Impact of the In-Vitro Fertilization Process on Emotional, Physical and Relational Variables. *Human Reproduction* 11: 903–907.

Daoud, N. (2007). Patriarchy and the Political-Economic Situation in the Health Narratives of Palestinian Women in Israel, in N. Shalhoub-Kevorkian (ed.), *Palestinian Feminist Writing: Between Oppression and Resistance*. Pp. 276–310 Haifa: Mada-al-Carmel (Arabic).

Callan, V. J. and J. F. Hennessey (1988). Emotional Aspects and Support in In-Vitro Fertilization and Embryo Transfer Programs. *Journal of In-Vitro Fertilization and Embryo Transfer* 5: 290–295.

Enloe, C. (2004). *The Curious Feminist: Searching for Women in the New Age of Empire*. Berkeley and London: University of California Press.

Foucault, M. (1980). *Power/Knowledge: Selected Interviews and Other Writings 1972–1977*, C. Gordon (ed.). New York: Pantheon Books.
Gooldin, S. (2008). Technologies of Happiness: Fertility Management in a Pro-natal Context, in A. Kemp and Y. Yona (eds.), *Citizenship Gaps: Migration, Fertility and Identity*. Pp. 265–302. Jerusalem: Van Leer/Hakibutz Hameuchad (Hebrew).
Gooldin, S. (2013). "Emotional Rights," Moral Reasoning, and Jewish–Arab Alliances in the Regulation of In-Vitro-Fertilization in Israel: Theorizing the Unexpected Consequences of Assisted Reproductive Technologies. *Social Science & Medicine* 83: 90–98.
Greil, A. L. (2002). Infertile Bodies: Medicalization, Metaphor, and Agency, in M. C. Inhorn and F. van Balen (eds.), *Infertility around the Globe: New Thinking on Childlessness, Gender and Reproduction Technologies*. Pp. 101–118. Berkeley, Los Angeles and London: University of California Press.
Gross, R. and S. Brammli-Greenberg (2000). *Women's Health and Welfare in Israel: Results of a National Survey*. Jerusalem: Myers-JDC-Brookdale Institute (Hebrew).
Haelyon, H. (2004). Experiences of Israeli Women with New Reproductive Technologies: A Sociological Discussion Combined with Body-Identity-Emotion Interrelations. PhD Dissertation. Ramat-Gan: Bar-Ilan University (Hebrew).
Haelyon, H. (2006). "Longing for a Child," Perceptions of Motherhood among Israeli-Jewish Women Undergoing In-Vitro Fertilization Treatments. *Nashim: A Journal of Jewish Women's Studies and Gender* Issues 12 (fall): 177–202.
Haelyon, H. (2007). *Gan Na'ul: Bodily Experiences, Identity and Emotion of Women Undergoing Fertility Treatments in Israel*. Haifa: Pardes (Hebrew).
Hammarberg, K., J. Astbury, and H. W. G. Baker (2001). Women's Experience of IVF: Follow up Study. *Human Reproduction* 16 (2): 374–383.
Hashiloni-Dolev, Y. (2004). *Searching for the Perfect Child*. PhD Dissertation. Ramat Aviv: Tel Aviv University (Hebrew).
Inhorn, M. C. (1994). *Quest for Conception: Gender, Infertility, and Egyptian Medical Traditions*. Philadelphia: University of Pennsylvania Press.
Inhorn, M. C. (1996). *Infertility and Patriarchy: The Cultural Politics of Gender and Family Life in Egypt*. Philadelphia: University of Pennsylvania Press.
Inhorn, M. C. (2002). Sexuality, Masculinity and Infertility in Egypt: Potent Troubles in the Material and Medical Encounters. *Journal of Men's Studies* 10: 343–359.
Inhorn, M. C. (2003). *Local Babies, Global Science: Gender, Religion, and In Vitro Fertilization in Egypt*. New York: Routledge.
Inhorn, M. C. (2006). Making Muslim Babies: IVF and Gamete Donation in Sunni versus Shi'a Islam. *Culture Medicine and Psychiatry* 30 (4): 427–450.
Inhorn, M. C. (2007). Masculinity, Reproduction and Male Infertility Surgery in the Middle East. *Journal of Middle East Women's Studies* 3 (3): 1–20.
Inhorn, M. C. and D. Birenbaum-Carmeli (2008). Assisted Reproductive Technologies and Culture Change. *Annual Review of Anthropology* 37: 177–196.

Inhorn, M. C. and F. van Balen (eds.) (2002). *Infertility around the Globe: New Thinking on Childlessness, Gender, and Reproductive Technologies*. Berkeley: University of California Press.

Jamal, A. (2007). Strategies of Minority Struggle for Equality in Ethnic States: Arab Politics in Israel. *Citizenship Studies* 11 (3): 263–282.

Joseph, S. (1993a). Connectivity and Patriarchy among Urban Working Class Arab Families in Lebanon. *Ethos* 21 (4): 465–484.

Joseph, S. (1993b). Women, War and History: Debates in Middle East Women's Studies. *Journal of the History of Sexuality* 4 (1): 128–136.

Joseph, S. (2000). *Gender and Citizenship in the Middle East*. Syracuse, NY: Syracuse University Press.

Kahn, S. M. (2000). *Reproducing Jews: A Cultural Account of Assisted Conception in Israel*. Durham, NC: Duke University Press.

Kanaaneh, R. A. (2002). *Birthing the Nation: Strategies of Palestinian Women in Israel*. Berkeley: University of California Press.

Khalidi, W. (1992). *All That Remains: The Palestinian Villages Occupied and Depopulated by Israel in 1948*. Washington, DC: Institute for Palestine Studies.

Khatib, M. (2012). *Health of Arab Women in Israel: Policy Paper*. Shefa-'Amr: The Galilee Society – The Arab National Society for Health, Research and Services (Arabic).

Moghadam, V. M. (1993). *Modernizing Women: Gender and Social Change in the Middle East*. Boulder, CO: Lynne Rienner Publishers (chapter 3).

Popper-Giveon, A. and A. Al-Krenawi (2010). An Empowering Encounter between Traditional Arab Healers in Israel and Their Clients, in S. Abu-Rabia-Queder and N. Weiner-Levy (eds.), *Palestinian Women in Israel: Identity, Power Relations and Coping Strategies*. Jerusalem and Tel Aviv: Van Leer Jerusalem Institute and Hakibutz Hameuchad (Hebrew).

Portugese, J. (1998). *Fertility Policy in Israel: The Politics of Religion, Gender, and Nation*. Westport, CT: Praeger.

Remennick, L. (2000). Childless in the Land of Imperative Motherhood: Stigma and Coping among Infertile Israeli Women. *Sex Roles* 43 (11–12): 821–841.

Remennick, L. (2008). Contested Motherhood in the Ethnic State: Voices from an Israeli Postpartum Ward. *Ethnicities* 8 (2): 199–226.

Robinson, S. (2013). *Citizen Strangers: Palestinians and the Birth of Israel's Liberal Settler State*. Stanford, CA: Stanford University Press.

Rouhana, N. N. (1997). *Palestinian Citizens in an Ethnic Jewish State: Identities in Conflict*. New Haven, CT: Yale University Press.

Shalev, C. (1998). Halakha and Patriarchal Motherhood – An Anatomy of the New Israeli Surrogacy Law. *Israeli Law Review* 32 (1): 51–80.

Shalev, C. and S. Goldin (2006). The Uses and Misuses of In-Vitro Fertilization in Israel: Some Sociological and Ethical Considerations. *Nashim: A Journal of Jewish Women's Studies and Gender Issues* 12 (fall): 151–176.

Shalhoub-Kevorkian, N., S. Ihmoud, and S. Dahir-Nashif (2014). Sexual Violence, Women's Bodies, and Israeli Settler Colonialism. *Jadaliyya* www.jadaliyya.com

/pages/index/19992/sexual-violence-women%E2%80%99s-bodies-and-israeli-settler.

Shuval, J. T. and O. Anson (eds.) (2000). *Health Is What Matters: Social Structure and Health in Israel*. Jerusalem: Hebrew University Magnes Press (Hebrew).

Van Balen, F. and M. C. Inhorn (eds.) (2002). Introduction: Interpreting Infertility. A View from the Social Sciences, in *Infertility around the Globe: New Thinking on Childlessness, Gender and Reproduction Technologies*. Pp. 3–32. Berkeley, Los Angeles and London: University of California Press.

Yuval Davis, N. (1996). Women and the Biological Reproduction of "the Nation." *Women's Studies International Forum* 19 (1–2): 17–24.

Zaatari, Z. 2003. Women Activists of South Lebanon. Dissertation. Davis: University of California at Davis.

Zu'bi, H. (2007). *Palestinian Women in Israel: A Bibliography of Academic Literature 1948–2006*. Haifa: Mada-al-Carmel (Arabic).

9

Childbirth in Israel: Home Birth and Newborn Screening

Margherita Brusa and Yechiel Michael Barilan
In memory of Dr. Daniela Gobber

1 INTRODUCTION

Demographic transitions accompany economic success. This is borne out by marked changes in health indices, especially infant and maternal mortality rates. The poorer the community, the higher its infant mortality rates. From the eighteenth century throughout the first decades of the twentieth century, infant mortality in the West ranged above 20 percent, sometimes 30 percent (Klaus 1993: ch. 1; Ross 1993: 183; Rose 1986: 7). Even though the Jews were poorer than their non-Jewish neighbors, wherever records survive, contrary to expectations, infant mortality among the Jews was significantly lower. Demographers who study this paradox hypothesize that lower levels of alcohol use and abuse, as well as a "pro-active mentality" among the Jews in relation to the protection of babies' health, accounts for the gap (Derosas 2003).[1]

The story of the Jewish community of Palestine is especially impressive. Not only was infant mortality among the Jews lower relative to the local population, but it also stood at the level of technologically advanced nations. Already in 1939, Jewish infant mortality in Palestine was on par with U.S. and UK levels.[2]

In this chapter, we explore two periods and two practices of neonatal health care. The episodes are the first attempt at neonatal public health in traditional Jewish society in Palestine, during the first half of the twentieth century, and the corresponding high-tech regulation and practices of contemporary Israel. The practices are elective home birth and newborn screening.

The proactive and "life-saving" mentality of the traditional Jewish communities was part of a cultural ethos and a psychosocial makeup – a *mentalité* – that is irreducible to communal institutions and laws (Barilan 2014; Derosas 2003). In

---

[1] Other, potentially relevant factors are "baby farming," single-parent families, maternal age, and the treatment of out-of-wedlock children.
[2] It was less than 3 percent. Government of Palestine, Department of Health's annual report. Infant mortality among the non-Jewish Palestinians was three times higher.

this chapter, we argue that the Zionist vision of breaking away from the traditional ways of life has remained loyal to the communal refrainment from enforcement, especially when it expanded the proactive mentality into the spheres of public health law and practice. It seems that the Jews have always been open to novel technologies. Large-scale public services, from unionized work to school chains and health care and health insurances, have always been part of political Zionism. Israeli public health especially relies on information technologies (IT). The Israeli public is already used to certain levels of infringements into private life, in contexts such as universal conscription and homeland security measures.

While this chapter tells the story of the "Jewish life-saving mentality," in a broader context, it also asks "which kind of life counts" in the Jewish-Israeli psychosocial mindset. Michael Gross has pointed out that the Israeli practice of very aggressive and vitalistic neonatal care does not square well logically with Israel's very liberal law and practices in relation to elective abortion, especially late-term abortion (2000). Moreover, whereas Israeli national health care insurance provides full coverage for all elective abortions motivated by a medical consideration, however remote, Israel's Ministry of Health vigorously opposes any state coverage for elective home birth. The state's supreme efforts to screen – and potentially save – every newborn should be evaluated in light of the state's support and widespread practice of prenatal screening that leads to a very high rate of abortion. This chapter offers a comparative social history of key themes in perinatal public health in Israel, with the aim of shedding light on the bioethical discourse.

2 THE HISTORY OF BABY AND NEWBORN SCREENING

At the turn of the twentieth century, women gave birth at home, tended by a midwife and a few lay attendants. The affluent benefited from the presence of a licensed physician as well. Few of them mastered the eighteenth-century art of forceps delivery, which was handy in difficult labor. The very poor and the unwed gave birth in public hospitals (Ross 1993: 111–127; Walzer-Leavitt 1988: 73–74). Because the novelties of anesthesia and obstetric surgery were available in hospitals, in the middle of the twentieth century, most women in affluent nations gave birth in hospitals (Declercq et al. 2001; Shorter 1982: 156–157). The opposition to modern training of midwives in the United States accelerated the process (Klaus 1993: 224–227). Although the shift to hospital birth did not correlate with lower mortality, the improved survival, which had begun earlier, accelerated with the introduction of antibiotics and safe surgical techniques.

Toward the end of the nineteenth century, infant mortality among the poor was a major social and political concern in industrialized nations. Eugenics developed as a scientifically informed response to the perceived crisis of degeneration in population health. Another response was the humanitarian "baby health movement." It beheld motherhood as a health practice, promoting the "education" of poor and "ignorant" mothers as well as state regulation of fresh milk (Klaus 1993; Sealander 2003: 294–299).

In the late nineteenth century, the infant welfare movement launched mass efforts at weighing infants to detect sick and needy babies. In the second decade of the twentieth century, registration of babies' weights became widespread. Unluckily, despite a huge success in the implementation and popularization of weight charts, the screening terminated due to lack of statistically valid standards (Brosco 2001).

This laborious screening initiative established some revolutionary conceptions. The first is the notion that some apparently healthy babies may actually be "sick" or "at risk"; second, that it was not advisable anymore to wait until symptoms appeared to solicit medical attention. Indeed, in the 1920s, the American Medical Association promoted a novel recommendation to perform a periodical medical exam of "those supposedly at health," with the aim of finding latent and undiagnosed conditions (Starr 1982: 195). The third revolutionary conception is that "healthy" and "responsible" childcare entails compliance of the intimate sphere of the home with public health instruments of surveillance, among which were numerical spreadsheets and Cartesian graphs associated with business and engineering. The fourth is that the emergent network of pediatricians and other "experts" coordinates services and arbiters on questions of children's health and welfare. These experts must review "abnormal" screening results and make the final diagnosis of a "child at risk."[3] The weight chart movement sought nonspecific signs covering as many pathologies as possible. The second wave of screening was about a specific sign to a serious disease.

In 1958, the authors of the first publication on a successful treatment of phenylketonuria (PKU) – a rare inborn error of metabolism responsible for mental retardation – suggested that a screening test be applied to every neonate at the age of three weeks (Woolf et al. 1958: 43).

A reliable and more practical screening method was introduced in 1961 in Massachusetts. The method entailed testing a tiny blood sample taken at the third day of life, the Guthrie method. It allowed testing before discharge from the hospital. Because Guthrie's invention almost concurred with the FDA's approval in 1958 of a commercial dietary formula for PKU (Paul and Brosco 2013: 42), the canonization of the diagnostic test coincided with the canonization of the treatment. For the first time, it was possible to apply a standardized scientific test to an apparently healthy newborn child and preempt an imminent but preventable catastrophic disease (Holt-Koch 1997). These events also coincided with the completion of the transition

---

[3] Other landmark interventions were laws of registration such as the 1907 UK Birth Notification Act, salt enrichment with iodine, discussed later, removal of lead-based wall paint, vaccination, promotion of breastfeeding among populations without access to clean water, and improved product safety and the medicalization of child abuse under the title "battered child syndrome." State and NGO activity for the sake of disaster-stricken children and rehabilitation of millions of World War II orphans contributed much to the buildup of state responsibility for children's welfare and its bureaucratization. The first nationwide screening program took place in Italy in the 1950s. All the population of certain areas was screened for thalassemia with the intention of instituting premarital counseling. It was not about detection of preclinical diseases.

to hospital birth, and with the peak of institutionalization of people with mental deficiencies and illnesses. In the United States, more than half a million people lived permanently in such institutions, posing a heavy toll on public coffers (Harcourt 2011: 53). Less than 1 percent of this inmate population suffered from PKU (Jervis 1939). However, the enthusiasm over the prospect of a preventive scientific solution to neuropsychiatric social problems was great.[4]

In 1973, when screening for PKU was already an established practice, Canadian researchers developed a diagnostic test for congenital hypothyroidism, another treatable condition that if left untreated, results in severe and irreversible retardation. Attempts to expand biochemical screening programs failed to meet the combined target of severe conditions, whose preclinical detection by means of cheap, accurate, and acceptable tests was a precondition to successful treatment.[5] In the 1990s, tandem mass spectrometry (MS/MS) enabled the testing of numerous metabolites in the few drops of blood soaked by the Guthrie cards. By the late 2000s, most countries that deployed MS/MS technology expanded their NBS programs significantly.

Nowadays, the transition to mass population screening by means of DNA analysis seems imminent. It will allow direct access to genetic knowledge and the testing of thousands of genetic markers in a single swath (Dhanda and Reily 2003; Goldberg and Sharp 2012).

3 NEWBORN SCREENING AND HOME BIRTH

Nothing in the nature of newborn screening predicated a universal and hospital-based coverage. Indeed, in 1958, public health authorities mailed do-it-yourself kits of urine tests for PKU to all women who had given birth in Cardiff. The compliance rate was more than 70 percent (Gibbs and Wolf 1959). At the same time, most health departments in California ran a similar pilot of PKU screening (Centerwall and Centerwall 1958). Because abnormal levels of PKU appear in the urine only in the second week of life, some have suggested attaching screening to the first session of vaccination (Centerwall et al. 1960). In 1960, experts considered reduced medicalization of screening instrumental to its universalization:

> To place the mechanics of testing into the hands of the parents so that even the least suspicious patient is tested. (Allen 1960)

---

[4] A similar wave of interest followed the 1965 publication of the now defunct "XYY" hypothesis, which employed a different lab test (karyotyping) to the diagnosis of another medicalized problem of mass institutionalization – violent crime (mental institutes and prisons) (Re and Birkhoff 2015). Israel was quick to follow on this theory as well, hosting in May 1969 a conference on its forensic aspects. Publications of the Institute of Criminology, Jerusalem, #16.
[5] This framework fit the WHO criteria for screening programs (Committee for the Study of Inborn Errors of Metabolism 1975; WHO 1968; Wilson and Jungner 1968).

A factor that may account for this universalist approach, rather than screening babies "at risk" only (e.g., family history), was the unprecedented success of universal enrichment of table salt with iodine as a preventive measure against hypothyroidism (Freyer, Politi, and Weil 2010; Merke 1984, 234–250). However, the introduction of the Guthrie method entailed a step that had always been a medical skill – drawing blood. Additionally, the grassroots activists responsible for the transition of the Guthrie method from a laboratory technology into a policy-guided public health service – NARC – did not even entrust screening to the hands of family doctors and pediatricians. They sought the efficient and universal coverage of the modern hospital (Paul 2008).

The association between hospital birth and the practice of newborn screening seems to have gained more currency with the passing of time, to the point that nowadays, birth is not "completed" until newborn screening has been performed. The first clue comes from the recent tendency to cut on health care costs. Contemporary standards of coverage for maternity hospital stays range between thirty-six and seventy-two hours, coinciding with the window time for screening. Indeed, the actual hospital stay for birthing mothers worldwide is 1.4 days in the average (Campbell et al. 2016). The second clue comes from a simple calculation. Once removed from the hospital, the costs of screening might tip the balance against the practice. Newborn screening is cheap only because it is an externality accrued by the heavy costs of hospital birth. The third clue comes from a comparison of the United States and the United Kingdom. In many states of the United States, home birth is either illegal or grudgingly tolerated. Birth centers and midwifery (as a profession separate from specialized nursing) are nonexistent. Newborn screening policies are expansive – they typically cover numerous conditions and are compulsory and payable by the mother (with variations among states). In the United Kingdom, home birth services are available to every woman who wants them, provided by publicly funded midwives. UK midwifery is independent from nursing; childbirth is not conceived of as a "medical" but a "natural" event. The average hospital stay for birthing mothers is the shortest among developed countries, not reaching the screening threshold (Campbell et al. 2016). Newborn screening is limited to nine conditions, compared to more than fifty conditions in some U.S. states, and thirteen in Israel. The NHS defined newborn screening as "a free choice."[6]

Indeed, already in 1965, when the rate of hospital birth in America was at its peak, the American Academy of Pediatrics recommended that screening be carried out prior to the baby's discharge from the hospital (Committee on Fetus and Newborn 1965). Undoubtedly, hospital birth is the only way to ensure cheap and universal screening. Moreover, in addition to the facilitation of newborn screening, advocates of late discharge (hospitalization longer than twelve hours) count the opportunity for

---

[6] www.gov.uk/government/uploads/system/uploads/attachment_data/file/440859/STFYAYB_010715_web_ready.pdf.

patient education, assistance in breastfeeding, "infant care techniques," and other activities that were at the core practice of the early twentieth-century visiting nurses and consultation clinics (Braveman et al. 1995).

The key motto of both newborn screening and hospital birth is a unified package of medical surveillance that guarantees protection from rare complications; it is about a pathology-oriented cultural construction of childbirth, of gearing up the intimate event of birth in preparation for the worst, so as to optimize overall protection from catastrophes.

In sum, because of its cultural construction as lifesaving, newborn screening has developed as an extension of the new routine of safe delivery – the hospital childbirth supervised by physicians. Because screening cannot be performed before a day and a half have passed since the moment of birth, the association of newborn screening with childbirth care entails a cultural construction of "childbirth" as an event marked by prevention of extreme pathologies, their rarity notwithstanding.

4 THE DEVELOPMENT OF THE ISRAELI GOVERNANCE OF CHILDBIRTH AND NEWBORN SCREENING

In this section, we survey the Israeli history of the transition of childbirth and infant care from the intimate sphere of the home into a tightly regulated event in a public hospital. Whereas the regulation of pregnancy and the protection of babies' lives was a central and growing theme in premodern European criminal law, the Jewish communities have not tried to regulate issues such as contraceptives, abortion, and dead infants. While non-Jewish European societies were cracking down on independent "wise women" and midwives, the rabbis and Jewish authorities expressed full trust in the clinical judgment and moral probity of these female practitioners, in all matters of "women's health" (Barilan 2014: chs. 6–7).

Jewish philanthropic aid to mothers and babies began in the second half of the nineteenth century, organized by middle-class and prosperous Jews from Western Europe, in the benefit of the poor Jewish community in Jerusalem, whose origins were from Eastern Europe and the Orient. Two local women's organizations were established in the 1890s – "Feminine Aid" (עזרת נשים) and "Aid to the Parturient Mother" (עזר ליולדת). These efforts continued a long tradition of Jewish communal assistance to the sick (Barilan 2014: 51–62).

In 1912, a group of urban, progressively educated American Jewish women established an organization called Hadassah.[7] One of its four stated objectives was the promotion of public health institutions in Palestine (Shvarts 1998). Hadassah's first activity was the opening of clinics for mothers and expectant mothers. During the 1880s, consultation clinics on babies' nourishment and health (*consultation de*

---

[7] Hadassah is the biblical figure Esther, whose courageous ingenuity saved the Jewish nation from genocide. For the history of the Hadassah organization, see Shvarts and Shehory-Rubin 2012.

nourissons) were established in France. By the turn of the century, the United Kingdom had more than 1,000 mother-infant consultation clinics (Lane-Claypon 1920: 6). There were 15,000 in the United States, almost exclusively dedicated to "education of mothers" (Schereschewsky 1911). Of special inspiration to Hadassah's women was the "Little Mothers" program devised by public health pioneer Sara Josephine Baker in New York for the instruction of poor mothers (Simmons 2006: 17).

In 1892, Pierre Bodin, chief of obstetrics in a Paris hospital, opened a new kind of clinic. Mothers would bring their babies to the clinic weekly for weighing, and consultation on breastfeeding. The clinic would dispense pasteurized cow milk to those who were not able to breastfeed adequately. These clinics were later named Drop of Milk (Gouttee de Lait), and emphasized the distribution of milk and other basic goods, often on the condition of participation in education programs (Klaus 1993: 62–64). This model was imported to New York as well (Koplik 1914). In 1913, Italy had only one such clinic, thanks to an endowment by King Umberto III to the poor of Bari. Italian infant mortality rates at the time were as high as among the poor Jews of Palestine (Dixon-Whitaker 2000: 89).

Nathan Strauss, a New York Jewish businessperson and philanthropist, was an enthusiastic advocate of pasteurized milk, introducing milk depots to the United States. He was also the chief patron of Hadassah and other public health initiatives in Palestine (Miller 1993).

Hadassah's mission in Palestine, which started with two American nurses in an Ottoman country without any medical and public health services, was incredibly ambitious. Not only were Hadassah women quick to import this novel service from one of the most prosperous metropolitans in the world to a tiny, poor community in the middle of a wobbly and backward empire, but they also devised a concept encompassing both the consultation and drop of clinics. In addition to weighing babies and offering advice on diverse health care issues, Hadassah distributed milk, clean bed sheets, and home calls by nurses and physicians (Adams-Stockler 1977: 34). In emulation of the French model, Hadassah named its clinics Tipat Halav – Drop of Milk. However, the French clinics proliferated with significant state support and were integrated in the 1874 Roussel Law protecting infants, mainly from negligent and abusive wet-nursing (Sussman 1980). Hadassah activists operated in the void, unabashedly relying on their own judgment and material resources.

Hadassah devised a comprehensive medical follow-up plan from the sixth month of pregnancy until the second year of the baby's life. Compliance was a serious concern, because many practices prescribed by the clinic appeared strange and unacceptable. One notable example was opposition to baby weight charts. The devout believed that because God shuns public miracles, knowing and documenting a baby's weight deprives Him of the opportunity to boost the child's weight clandestinely. The program's directors appealed to the leading rabbis, asking for their support of the baby weight charts. Additionally, to secure compliance, the voluntary organizations emulated the French practice and stipulated that material assistance be provided on the condition of full adherence to the medical program. Doctors decided whether the woman should give birth in a hospital or could do so at home. The local community resented these rules as "tyrannical." According to Hadassah's sources, most women accepted the program without resistance (Admon-Rick 2005: 25–51; Shvarts 2000; Shehory-Rubin and Shvarts 2003: ch. 3). In 1919, Hadassah's first hospital opened in Jerusalem. The "drop" of milk nurses had now a whole enveloping hospital system, whose services were a strong incentive for all women to comply with the public health program. Hadassah promoted the concept of the "nurse-midwife," thus medicalizing midwifery, at least in terms of public health ethics (Katvan and Bartal 2010). Hadassah's policy harbingered a few features of future Israeli public health programs. Even though the services were not compulsory, financial incentives were used to overcome cultural and psychological barriers. For the first time, a choice (which was actually the default practice) to give birth at home might be considered unhealthy and worthy of a penalty.[8] Even though Hadassah and affiliated local activists were feminine organizations, they did not try to represent a feminine perspective, but to bring biomedical knowledge to bear on the welfare of mothers and babies. They would first draft a policy and then set out to recruit reception, legitimization, and cooperation.

The secular organization Hadassah was also active in the promotion of the 1929 Midwifery Act, which displaced the traditional "wise women" in favor of biomedically educated midwives. The Act granted the latter limited powers relative to doctors. The Act excluded midwives from performing medical interventions and from issuing death certificates. They were not practitioners of "women's health" anymore, but facilitators of normal, healthy childbirth. This was a break from the trust invested by the rabbis and traditional communities in their midwives.

During the British rule of Palestine (1918–1948), childbirth moved gradually from the home setting to hospitals and medically controlled birth centers. In addition to charitable help to poor women, in the style of Hadassah, the socialist-Zionist movement constructed hospital birth as a social benefit to the working people. During the 1920s and 1930s, a gradual transfer of financial and administrative responsibility for mother and child clinics took place, shifting from the grassroots voluntary organizations to the civil authorities.

When the State of Israel was established, public health approaches to childbirth were conflicting. On one hand, because hospitals were not able to accommodate many parturient women, doctors tried to admit only high-risk and pathological cases (Leissner 2011b, 355–356). The largest insurance fund in Israel covered birth at home only if hygienic conditions were satisfactory. On the other hand, the first committee on national health security, the Kanev Committee, observed that hospital births should be encouraged because of lower mortality rates (1950).

---

[8] The traditional Jewish community in Jerusalem had been living off charities sent from the diaspora. In this context, denial of a charitable benefit was highly punitive.

The mass immigration of Jews, many of whom were refugees, and the responsibility of the young State of Israel to its Arab population posed urgent public health challenges to the fledgling state established in 1948. In the heydays of immigration, when hundreds of thousands lived in temporary shelters, even tents, for many Israelis, "home birth" was not a meaningful choice.

However, in the early years, the hospital system had difficulties coping with the mass immigration. The Jewish Agency tried to encourage home birth and even granted cash benefits to mothers who chose to do so, while relying on the services of local nurses and immigrant traditional midwives (Stoler-Lisa, Shvarts, and Shani 2016, 213–215).

The National Security Law (1953) granted full coverage of birth expenses, as well as a "birth endowment" of cash money given to every parturient woman. Initially, this endowment would cover the cost of a baby cradle. It was considered a gift from the state, but it also symbolized the proper standards for modern infant care. The other communicated standard was hospital birth. The law stipulated the endowment be given only to mothers who check themselves into a hospital. By 1956, more than 90 percent of births in Israel took place in hospitals.[9]

The law tied both benefits to the hospital birth concept. The law stipulated the cash endowment by the presentation of the newborn for a medical exam in a medical center within a day of birth. Out-of-hospital birth was becoming a dissenting, barely tolerated, and expensive practice.

Whereas the young State of Israel preserved the structure and level of services provided by the charitable Hadassah's Drop of Milk clinics, the National Security Law downgraded the services offered to birthing mothers. Private midwives and home birth care, which were part of the patients' fund services (*Kupat Holim*), were not included in the state's coverage of birth care anymore. Although some of the clinic's services are part of the third amendment to the National Insurance Act (1995), Drop of Milk clinics have never been incorporated by state law. Nonetheless, compliance with Drop of Milk schedules of visits and care is very high (Lazarus and Hersh 1977; Shvarts 2000).

The Hadassah strategy of using financial aid to leverage compliance with public health policies in the benefit of children has died hard. In 2011, the Israeli parliament passed a law making financial child support contingent on compliance with vaccination.[10] Ultra-Orthodox circles protested the "tyrannical" public health measures (Cohen 2015). In a way, this episode reenacts the early twentieth-century conditioning of material assistance on compliance with public health, and it reenacts the Israeli National Insurance Law from the 1950s, granting childbirth benefits only to babies who are either hospital born or brought to a hospital within hours from birth.

---

[9] State Archives ISA-health-health-000z9az. The major impact, however, was on the Arab population, whose hospital birth rate had been less than 10 percent.

[10] The Israeli Supreme Court upheld the law as constitutional. However, later modifications of the National Security Law have rendered it irrelevant.

A small circle of ultra-Orthodox and anti-Zionist women in Israel opts for home birth as the traditional and femininely modest choice (Fuchs 2016). In our interviews with midwives and the NBS lab, we learned that an even tinier locus of conscientious resistance to screening thrives among anarchist, "new-age"-oriented Orthodox circles as well. Both groups gainsay the secular Zionist ethos in favor of alternative conceptualization of the "pure" and old ways of life.

Not only was the Zionist Jewish community in Israel an early adopter of public health policies in the benefit of mothers and their babies (prenatal follow up, hospital birth, and Drop of Milk clinics), but in 1964, Israel was among the first countries to implement the hospital-based universal newborn screening for PKU (Cohen et al. 1966). Israelis were the first to publish a screening program outside of the United States, thus stimulating the practice worldwide (e.g., Chahalane 1968).

In the beginning, screening started in Israel's largest hospital, Tel HaShomer, fast expanding to cover all Israeli neonates. This unprecedented success led to the hosting of the second international conference on PKU in Tel HaShomer in 1969. The infrastructure and health care ethos of preventive baby care and the screening lab in Tel HaShomer contributed to the early expansion of screening for hypothyroidism (Sack et al. 1985). Tel HaShomer also established the first and only dedicated PKU and hyperphenylalaninemia clinic in Israel. Until this very day, it is not clear whether hyperphenylalaninemia is associated with any sort of morbidity (Campistol et al. 2011). Hyperphenylalaninemia means above normal blood levels of phenylalanine, which are short of the high levels indicative of PKU. Most infants whose screening test is positive do not suffer from PKU, but have hyperphenylalaninemia, which is an artificial construct of newborn screening. The still independent PKU clinic in Tel HaShomer is an artificial construct of Israel's early adoption of PKU screening, which antedated the era of clinics dedicated to metabolic and genetic disorders.

In very detailed historical research, Ommi Leissner argues that the intensification of medicalization of childbirth in Israel contributed to the growing pressure toward home birth and toward increased consumption of hospital-based services (Leissner 2011). We hypothesize that newborn screening has been the key conceptual as well as administrative foundation for the solidification of birth as a hospital-based, public health service.

In the early 2000s, anonymized blood samples from Israeli babies were sent to the United States for analysis in order to map out the incidence of metabolic diseases in the Israeli population. When it became evident that Israeli babies could have been diagnosed in due course, the motivation to expand the screening program grew. Alas, in 2002–2005, Israel suffered from an economic crisis. The right-wing government tried to privatize the Tipat Halav clinics and cut public health expenditures.[11]

---

[11] See Supreme Court Ruling 3453/04 (צ"ב). A public committee (the Mann Committee) deliberated this service in 2006. The State Audit issued a report on the 1,000-strong clinics service in 2014. Budget is not the only factor behind a lapse in Israel "early adaptor" policies in neonatal and perinatal health care during the 1990s–2000s. Another example is the relatively late promotion of folic acid as a

Luckily, in 2005, a geneticist from Tel HaShomer secured a donation from an American Jewish benefactor for purchasing the MS/MS technology in the benefit of expanded newborn screening in Israel.[12] On one hand, the state represents newborn screening as "lifesaving"; on the other hand, it had waited for an American Jewish charity to fund its expanded program.

Responsibility for screening remained in the jurisdiction of the Department of Community Genetics, but the screening itself was centralized and placed in a dedicated MS/MS lab in Tel HaShomer. The Ministry of Health nominated a professional advisory committee to oversee the expansion and decide which conditions were to be included. The advisory committee has no official status. No nomination writ was issued; minutes are not taken down from its deliberations.[13] In professional meetings, committee members profess to include screening tests whose results show clear beneficial promise to the screened person, compared with much broader conceptualizations of "benefit" in screening, such as benefit to the family and society.

The expanded screening program, initiated in 2007 as a pilot, has been operating routinely from 2009, covering thirteen conditions, two of which serve as a pilot.[14] Whereas almost all blood samples are collected in hospitals, and a few by home birth midwives, it is also possible to bring infants for screening to Drop of Milk clinics. Thus, these clinics preserve the parent-centered, voluntary, and outpatient face of infant care in Israel.

Screening remains concentrated in the central, national lab, furnished with advanced IT technology. The center stores samples up to two years for the sake of "quality control." The center's computer automatically synchronizes with all Israeli hospitals' registries of births, matching the data with the arrival of blood samples. The center's computer also compares data with the Ministry of the Interior's registry of births. Even though screening is not compulsory, the center reports to the public health authorities every case of an unscreened newborn that is not accompanied by a

preventive measure against birth defects. The Ministry of Health issued a policy ordinance on the matter in 2000, eight years after the CDC issued its guidelines on the matter. While the courts are still deliberating a few malpractice lawsuits in relation to folic acid, a regional court set very high standards of accountability in relation to another incident in which vitamin deficiency caused severe retardation to babies. This incident from 2003 involved an imported baby formula from which thiamine (Vitamin B1) was absent. Even though such an omission had never occurred, the food safety regulators in the Ministry of Health made a plea deal to the offense of "an act that might disseminate disease" (Shamir 2012). This particular clause referred to people suffering from contagious diseases. Its adaptation to unexpected failures and very low-risk incidents in infant nutrition underscores Israel's integration of infant feeding in the ambit of public health and state regulation.

[12] We thank the Center's director, Dr. Almashanu, and the former vice deputy of Tel HaShomer Hospital, Prof. Boleslav Goldman, for telling us the story. See also Zuckerman 2009.

[13] The members are the chief of the NBS lab, the chief of the Department of Community Genetics, the chair of the Israeli Society for Pediatric Endocrinology, the chair of the Israeli Society for Metabolic Diseases, and the heads of three large metabolic clinics.

[14] This section focuses on biochemical screening, even though hearing and other screening tests are also performed on every newborn.

signed refusal form. In case of suspicious screening results, the center calls the mothers and refers them to a metabolic clinic. The center dispatches public health officers to trace out unreachable babies. Some such expeditions require military protection in case they need to enter hostile Palestinian neighborhoods.

The melding of newborn screening with innovative information technology and the center's undertaking to reach every "baby at risk" (rather than pass on the data) have created a locus that holds the most comprehensive information on births, which is also accompanied by data, and tissue banking – the newborn screening operation. This panoptical locus is biomedical; the universal test is the new token of safety.

5 ISRAELI FORMAL GOVERNANCE OF CHILDBIRTH

In this section, we focus on some bureaucratic-regulatory issues that shed much light on the contemporary biopolitics of childbirth and on the peculiarities of the Israeli ethos of the state's duty to protect life and respect liberty. Ordinary, hospital birth is subject to legal regulation, but to indirect professional standards. The government does not tell physicians when to connect a woman to a monitor and which blood tests to draw. However, when patients express choices that deviate from the clinical standards, official policies come into relief in the form of convoluted ordinances, whose aim is to balance the state's professionals' conceptions of medical responsibility with respect for liberal values. In the case of childbirth, this balance appears as an Apollonian responsibility restraining Dionysian women.

Suppose a mother wishes to leave the hospital twenty-four hours after birth. This is virtually a risk-free choice. However, because the neonate's blood for screening is sampled thirty-six hours post-partum, the Medical Management's Ordinance (02/2009) (חוזר מנהל רפואה) decrees:

> 5.3 A birthing mother who wishes to leave the hospital prior to 36 hours.
> 5.3.1. The Chair of Obstetrics or a person on his or her behalf will explain to the birthing woman that early discharge means forgoing and / or refusal to perform newborn screening. The mother/parents is required to sign the refusal form along with the signature of the person giving explanation. The latter will present the option of going at her own initiative to the Drop of Milk Clinic in order to perform the screening test.
> 5.3. In case of early discharge, a newborn screening card should be sent to the [national newborn screening] lab with the identifying info, without a blood sample and with the words "refusal to test."

These words seal the official construction of "childbirth" as an event that terminates a day and a half to three days post-partum, with the act of newborn screening. The Ministry of Health labels and frames early discharge in ways that induce mothers to stay in the hospital more than is clinically necessary. These mothers are already nudged to give birth in the hospital by the financial penalties imposed by the National Security Law and by the hostile language and attitude of the Ministry of Health to home birth. The state portrays the wish to go home early as refusal of "lifesaving" care for one's own newborn child.

Indeed, in order to understand better the present-day governance of childbirth, we turn our attention to elective home birth. In the past fifteen years, and especially following the closure of the last birthing center in Israel, elective home births have been gaining currency, reaching a rate of more than 0.5 percent of live births. After the exclusion of high-risk deliveries, which are medically inappropriate for the home setting, the relative number of women who choose to give birth at home is evidently higher. Because Israeli Arabs (~20 percent of the population) have not joined yet the home birth movement, the relevant rate of elective home births is even higher. Loyal to the 1929 Midwifery Act, the Jewish tradition, and to Israel's commitment to liberty of choice, and in response to a few accidents that took place during home birth, the Ministry of Health has passed a special ordinance regulating home birth (Medical Management Ordinance 1/2008, replaced by 17/2012). The ordinance's attitude of tolerance is explicit, stating that the preferred setting for childbirth is a licensed hospital, and that the ordinance addresses those who, nevertheless, ignore expert opinion and insist on planned home birth. This is a controversial issue, debated by professional bodies, with marked cultural variation (Snowden 2015; *Journal of Clinical Ethics*, issue of fall 2013). The UK Ministry of Health officially recommends home birth and midwife-run birthing centers for low-risk pregnancies (about half of birthing mothers).[15] In the Netherlands, about one-third of children are born at home (De Vries 1996). WHO also supports planned home birth.[16]

A hallmark of the contemporary home birth or "alternative childbirth" movement (initiated in the 1970s) is the credo that childbirth is a natural, not medical event, and that it should remain a private experience controlled by the woman and her chosen circle of support (DeVries 1996: preface). This motto appears on the website of the Israeli Organization of Homebirth Midwives and on the website of the Israeli advocacy group in promotion of home birth.[17] Ironically, within the reality of Israeli law, every childbirth is carried out within a hospital. Even if the actual setting might be a private home, the formal context remains a hospital governed by a nurse-midwife. The Newborn Screening Ordinance (2/2009) places the responsibility for screening on the hospital director (3.1). In case of home birth,

> The attendant's responsibilities are equal to those of a hospital director as specifies this directive and all of its sections. Additionally, the responsibility of the [attending] physician / nurse / midwife at home is even broader, as it includes repeat home visits

---

[15] www.nice.org.uk/news/press-and-media/midwife-care-during-labour-safest-women-straightforward-pregnancies.

[16] http://apps.who.int/iris/bitstream/10665/63167/1/WHO_FRH_MSM_96.24.pdf.

[17] www.imahi.co.il; http://www.leida.co.il/nashimko/. See also Idelman 2016.

in case of an abnormal result, which the lab deems necessary to carry out a second time. (clause 3.3)

The state's efforts to direct women and practitioners away from home birth brings forth the paradoxical arrangement according to which a single midwife assisting at home has more responsibilities than the director of a big hospital. This clause is even more perplexing in light of clause 6.7, Ordinance 12/2012, which regulates home birth. According to clause 6.7, one of the midwives' duties is "to inform the mother that the baby must be seen by a pediatrician within 24 hours post-partum." If a pediatrician sees the baby within a day, it would make sense to have that doctor instruct the mother about screening and monitor compliance.

Official publications of health information serve as a complementary view on the state's efforts to delineate and regulate "good" and "responsible" choices. A case in point is an official brochure, "Towards Birth" (לקראת לידה), issued in 2008 by the Department of Health Promotion in the Ministry of Health, with the intention of disseminating it among all expectant mothers. The subtitle of the brochure reads, "including screening tests to healthy neonates." The brochure discusses thirteen different topics, ranging from financial benefits and symptom control to safety measures:

- Pain control during childbirth
- Episiotomy
- Medical examination
- Breastfeeding
- Smoking in the company of the baby
- Medical examination of the baby
- Administration of vitamin K and antibacterial eye drops
- Vaccination against hepatitis B
- Newborn screening
- Birth-related financial benefits from the National Security Agency
- Guidance program on baby care
- Use of safety seats in the car
- Drop of Milk clinics

Not only does the brochure situate newborn screening at its heart, thus granting the expanded newborn screening program normalcy and legitimacy equal to breastfeeding, refrainment from smoking, and road safety, but it also receives a by far larger proportion of text. It is also the only section containing a URL reference to a dedicated website. The text narrates the lifesaving nature of screening for PKU and hypothyroidism. Then, it informs the reader about the expanded panel, not reporting that these conditions are much rarer and that their early diagnosis has less evident clinical benefit. Most notable, perhaps, is the complete silence of the official health-promoting brochure with regard to the possibility of home birth and all other personalized options of childbirth, some available in public Israeli hospitals.

Another effort to reach out to the public is a dedicated webpage on the Ministry of Health's website that allows mothers to insert their own ID numbers along with their infants' and receive the results of the screening.[18] The website publishes only negative (=healthy) results. In case of a positive finding, there is a statement asking mothers to bring their babies to a clinic.

Israeli regulation contains strong unilateral avenues of information, which include a duty to inform the expectant mother, campaigns of patient education, and a website with personalized results. However, while most Western countries increase public participation in newborn screening, the Israeli policy and practice offer a very shallow one (Arnstein 1969; Hiller, Landenburger, and Natowicz 1997). Information flows in a top-down manner, with no structures for public participation, feedback, and recognition of personal choice. Choices such as elective home birth, early discharge, and refusal to screen are a matter of toleration rather than respect, of manipulation rather than patient education. Choices of partial screening (e.g., PKU and hypothyroidism only) are not available at all.[19] The Israeli Ministry of Health constructs personalized care in childbirth as risky defection. In the era of neoliberal state policies, the minute attention to state regulation of childbirth and "educating" mothers by means of nudges and financial penalties brings into relief the marginalization of issues that are much more associated with health care indices, such as poverty, long hours of parental absence, and similar social issues. Israel's legal rights of birthing mothers lag behind many EU countries.

6 INTEGRATIVE DISCUSSION

From a comparative historical perspective, in this chapter, we have surveyed three phases of the medicalization of childbirth in Israel. The first is the network of voluntary charitable clinics and social services provided by an organization of progressive, secular American women to the poor and ultra-Orthodox "old community" (היישוב הישן) of Palestine. The second is the state's construction of its responsibility for mothers' and babies' health as a socialist service to working women, and during the waves of mass immigration into the young State of Israel. The third is newborn screening as a case study of Israel as an early adopter and bold innovator in public health.

Functionalist approaches (e.g., Marxist, structuralism, actor-network theory) coax metanarratives of power interactions among diverse stakeholders and loci of interests. In such a spirit, contemporary home birth activists in Israel point at the revenues hospitals generate from childbirth services as the "real" motivation behind the establishment's hostility to home birth (e.g., Leissner 2011a, 2011b). This might be so. Nonetheless, such conclusions do not take into account alternative historical pathways that childbirth in Israel could have taken. Had the English friendliness to

---

[18] www.old.health.gov.il/yelod/.   [19] This is the situation all over the world.

home birth and independent midwifery taken root in Palestine, midwifery and neonatal outpatient services would have become similarly powerful, resisting transition of services into the inpatient settings, and promoting an expansion, rather than disappearance, of birth centers. Had Josephine Baker's initiative to establish scientific training for midwives succeeded, the midwifery (rather than medical) paradigm might have prevailed in both the United States and Israel. In the midst of the First World War, an all-men committee commissioned by the Council for National Defense rejected this model, and led to the prohibition of independent midwifery in America (Klaus 1993: 226). One wonders to what extent the military background of the top echelon of the Israeli Ministry of Health plays a role in the adamant and official hostility to home birth. The chain of ordinances regulating childbirth appears similar to military orders in terms of comprehensiveness, specific delegation of responsibilities, and level of details. No other area of medical care is so thoroughly covered by secondary legislation, tying together medical, nursing, administrative, and public health services.

We propose that perceptions of "responsibility" and effective public health measures in the benefit of the infant predicated the governance of childbirth more than gender-related factors and the financial and professional interests of specific actors. The promise of simple, well-disciplined, yet affordable interventions acting as the panacea of children's health has been irresistible, the costs of the disciplinary measures notwithstanding. The traditional, poor, and disperse Jewish communities had very little public health institutions, even awareness. However, secular nationalist Zionism easily latched onto the traditional sense of responsibility for childcare and moved the Jewish settlement, and the young state of Israel, toward unprecedented actions and successes in terms of infant mortality. The traditional Jewish communities did not belong to the European census and registries of population. They did not even keep their own registries. However, Israel's instruments of national security spilled over fast to the mobilization of IT based universal registries and neonatal public health.

The centralization and penetration of the Israeli biochemical NBS program does not appear more aggressive than the military and homeland security's. Beginning in 2002, DNA is sampled from all Israeli conscripts and stored in a special databank to enable future identification of human remains.[20] The Ministry of Health's plan to launch DNA-based newborn screening is a very similar undertaking. "Saving babies" is no less exigent than the identification of the dead.

Our linear and comparative two-pronged case study (location of birth and systematic screening of babies) challenges gender-oriented explanations as well. For example, the Jewish communities have never participated in the struggle between male surgeons and female folk midwives. Remarkably, the Jewish

---

[20] Similar to NBS, the legal framework of this enterprise is an internal executive document, accompanied by a law proposal, which is still pending. For a hypothesis on the impact of the conscription mentality in Israel on home birth, see Morgenstern-Leissner 2006.

communities did not police women's health, including family planning, abortion care, and obstetrics (Barilan 2009: 152–158). The medicalization of childbirth in Israel was the product of a secular feminist organization, in line with the Zionist embrace of the suffrage (1926) and even the paramilitary and military service of women. The secular and messianic Zionist ethos contributed to the confidence in structural and technological innovations, as well as ambitious social reforms. Infant mortality among the Jews was not high by a comparative scale, but was unacceptable to the utopist Zionist mindset. The dispersed Jewish people had not been preoccupied by demography, "degeneration," and similar themes that were central to nineteen-century European social thinking. In line with their tradition, the Jewish activists defaulted to non-coercive efforts to save babies' lives. Pregnant women and birthing mothers were a target for care, paternalistic notwithstanding, but not discipline.

Indeed, in the early twentieth century, the secular activists and professionals found infant health standards in the traditional community "appalling" (e.g., Simmons 2006: 19), even though, when comparatively taken, infant mortality among the poor Jewish communities was lower than among the poor non-Jewish ones. Hadassah's integrative construction of the competing English and French strategies of service was as novel and bold as the Israeli newborn screening database and its quasi-universal outreach program. In Israel, an infant is "at risk" until the agents of the state trace him or her personally and clear his or her biochemical status. Whereas, especially in the United States, NBS has been expanding in terms of the number of conditions tested, the Israeli commitment to the paradigm of "saving lives" has led to unprecedented expansion in terms of coverage of targeted populations. The law proposal on genetic screening harbingers the professionals' wish to stretch the number of conditions tested to the maximum recommended by an international professional body.

In developed countries, there is much controversy about data and tissue banking by expanded newborn screening programs (Carmichael 2011; Lewis et al. 2011).[21] It is not clear whether the Israeli public's indifference to the law proposal authorizing genetic newborn screening reflects habituation to state surveillance, usually in the name of national security, or a genuine difference of values, as is probably the case regarding embryonic stem cell research (Barilan 2014: ch. 7). Even the "alternative" voice in Israel's birth scene, the home birth midwives, in their interviews with us, expressed support of the expanded newborn screening program. A few of them stated that, whereas childbirth is a "natural, healthy and feminine event," screening is about "diseases of children" and falls under the full jurisdiction of medical doctors.[22]

---

[21] For other main loci of controversy, see Timmermans and Buchbinder 2013.
[22] The authors' interviews with Israeli home birth midwives.

The tiny group of Hadassah volunteer nurses and the high-tech bureaucracy of the Israeli Ministry of Health exercise a high level of self-confidence, not shunning away from attempts to outperform the standards of the most affluent and technologically sophisticated societies. This is especially borne out by the incorporation of IT, by the clinical approach to undetermined cases, and by longish, intricate, and overbearing bylaws regulating every conceivable aspect of safety in childbirth.

The story of the Zionist movement is also a story of a health transition accompanying a socioeconomic leap. At least in the context of neonatal care, this story has its unique cultural features in terms of the social construction of "risk," the state's responsibility for this risk, and the power invested in professionals in relation to the perception of risk. Childbirth in Israel is marked by a high level of what Derosas refers to as "pro-active" mentalities. Israel's reputation regarding its achievements in terms of obstetric and infant mortality are widely acknowledged. Yet, today, this pro-activism verges on little marginal utility. It is based on extensive IT surveillance of all neonates, and it constrains maternal choice by means of an intricate bureaucracy whose technical jargon bullies mothers who seek their own pathway along the road of healthy childbirth, and suppresses old Jewish habits of informal and trust-based practices of childbearing.

A subtler subtext narrates the Jewish and Israeli construction of "life" that stands for saving. Israel's high natality rate stands on top of a very liberal practice of elective abortion. The state is an active partner to this situation by financing and legitimizing extensive prenatal testing and elective abortion. The positive liberty given in Israel to infertility treatments, abortion care, and newborn screening for extremely rare conditions comes in stark contrast to the cold, negative liberty granted to elective home birth.

If "saving lives" was a calculus of babies saved and lost, the impact of Israel's policies on home birth and newborn screening would be negligible relative to those lost to elective abortion. If respect for personal choice and "pro-active mentality" reign high in women's health, it is very difficult to incorporate Israel's practices of elective abortion and home birth. Israel's health care services related to childbirth demonstrate that in Israel, "chosen babies," which are pregnancies endorsed by the mothers, count as life worth saving even at the cost of paternalistic state control, that is uncompromising in its efforts to capture every "life at risk." This pattern might echo Zionism's focus on a selected population and outreach to every single Jew "at risk," and every person "at risk" in the Jewish state.

ACKNOWLEDGMENTS

This project was supported in part by a grant from the Israeli Ministry of Science and by a research program, Department of Pediatrics, University Hospital, Padua. "We also wish to thank Dr. Almashanu for hours of interviews and painstaking explanations. We have been much inspired by his sincere, conscientious, and professional dedication to infant public health.

References

Adams-Stockler, R. 1977. *Development of Public Health Nursing Practice as Related to the Health Needs of the Jewish Population in Palestine, 1913–1948*. Tel Aviv: Tel Aviv University.

Allen, R. J. 1960. The Detection and Diagnosis of Phenylketonuria. *American Journal of Public Health* 50: 1662–1666.

Arnstein, S. R. 1969. A Ladder of Citizen Participation. *AIP Journal*, July: 216–224.

Barilan, Y. M. 2009. Her Pain Prevails and Her Judgment Is Respected – Abortion in Judaism. *Journal of Law and Religion* 25: 97–186.

Barilan, Y. M. 2014. *Jewish Bioethics: Rabbinic Law and Theology in Their Social and Historical Perspectives*. Cambridge: Cambridge University Press.

Braveman, P., S. Egerter, M. Pearl, and K. Marchi. 1995. Early Discharge of Newborns and Mothers: A Critical Review of the Literature. *Pediatrics* 96: 716–726.

Brosco, J. P. 2001. Weight Charts and Well-Child Care: How the Pediatricians Became the Expert in Child Care. *Archives of Pediatric and Adolescent Medicine* 155: 1385–1389.

Brusa, M. and Y. M. Barilan. 2009. Cultural Circumcision in EU Public Hospitals: An Ethical Discussion. *Bioethics* 23: 470–482.

Campbell, O. M. R., L. Cegolon, D. Macleod, and L. Benova 2016. Length of Stay after Childbirth in 92 Countries and Associated Factors in 30 Low- and Middle Income Countries. *Plos Med* 13(3): e1001972.

Campistol, J., R. Gassió, R. Artuch, and M. A. Vilaseca. 2011. Neurocognitive Function in Mild Hyperphenylalaninemia. *Developmental Medicine and Child Neurology* 53: 405–408.

Carmichael, M. 2011. A Spot of Trouble. *Nature* 475: 156–158.

Centerwall, W. R. and S. A. Centerwall. 1958. *Early Diagnosis and Management of Phenylketonuria*. San Francisco, CA: American Medical Association Annual Meeting.

Centerwall, W. R., R. F. Chinnock, and A. Pusavat. 1960. Phenylketonuria: Screening Programs and Testing Methods. *American Journal of Public Health and Nations Health* 50: 1667–1677.

Chahalane, S. F. 1968. Phenylketonuria: Mass Screening of Newborns in Ireland. *Archives of Diseases of Childhood* 43: 141–144.

Cohen, B. E., A. Szeinberg, I. Peled, B. Szeinberg, and R. Bar-Or. 1966. Screening Program for Early Detection of Phenylketonuria in the Newborn in Israel. *Israeli Journal of Medical Science* 2: 156–164.

Cohen, Y. 2015. Children Benefits Will Be Given Only to Parents Who Vaccinate Their Children. *Kikkar Hashabat* news website, May 6 (Hebrew). www.kikar.co.il/170260.html#.

Committee on Fetus and Newborn, American Academy of Pediatrics. 1965. Screening of Newborn Infants for Metabolic Disease. *Pediatrics* 35: 499–501.

Committee for the Study of Inborn Errors of Metabolism, Division of Medical Sciences, Assembly of Life Sciences, National Research Council. 1975. *Genetic Screening. Programs, Principles, and Research*. Washington, DC: National Academy of Science.

Committee for the Study of Inborn Errors of Metabolism. 1975. *Genetic Screening: Programs, Principles, and Research*. Washington, DC: National Academy of Science.

Declercq, E., R. DeVries, K. Viisainen, H. B. Salvesen, and S. A. Werde. 2001. Where to Give Birth? Politics and the Place of Birth. In R. DeVries, S. Werde, E. van Teijlngen, and C. Benoit (eds.) *Birth by Design: Pregnancy, Maternity Care and Midwifery in North America and Europe*. 7–27. New York: Routledge.

Derosas, R. 2003. Watch the Children! Differential Infant Mortality of Jews and Catholics in nineteenth-Century Venice. *Historical Methods* 36:109–130.

De Vries, R. 1996. *Making Midwives Legal: Childbirth, Medicine and the Law*. 2nd ed. Colombus: Ohio State University Press.

Dhanda, R. K. and P. R. Reilly. 2003. Legal and Ethical Issues of Newborn Screening. *Pediatric Annals* 32: 540–546.

Dixon-Whitaker, E. 2000. *Measuring Mamma's Milk: Fascism and the Medicalization of Maternity in Italy*. Ann Arbor: University of Michigan Press.

Freyer, J. D., D. N. Politi, and N. Weil. 2010. The Economic Effects of Micronutrient Deficiency: Evidence from Salt Iodization on the United States. *Sire Discussion Papers* SIRE-2010–10.

Fuchs, T. S. 2016. "This Time I was a Person": Orthodox Jewish Home Birthers' Conceptualizations of (Home)Birth in Israel. MA Thesis (4758683), Free University of Berlin.

Gibbs, N. K. and L. I. Wollf. 1959. Test for Phenylketonuria. *British Medical Journal* 26: 532–535.

Goldberg, A. J. and R. R. Sharp. 2012. The Ethical Hazards of Programmatic Challenges of Genomic Newborn Screening. *Journal of The American Medical Association* 307: 461–462.

Gross, M. L. 2000. Abortion and Neonaticide: Ethics, Practice and Policy in Four Nations. *Bioethics* 16: 202–230.

Harcourt, B. 2011. An Institutionalization Effect: The Impact of Mental Hospitalization and Imprisonment on Homicide in the US, 1934–2001. *Journal of Legal Studies* 40: 39–82.

Hiller, E. H., G. Landenburger, and M. R. Natowicz. 1997. Public Participation in Medical Policy-Making and the Status of Consumer Autonomy: The Example of Newborn-Screening Programs in the United States. *American Journal of Public Health* 87: 1280–1288.

Holt Koch, J. 1997. *Robert Guthrie: The PKU Story*. Pasadena: Hope.

Idelman, O. 2016. Ezrat Nashim: Midwives Establish an Independent Structure for Pregnancy Care. *Haaretz* February 12 (Hebrew).

Jervis, G. A. 1939. The Genetics of Phenylpyruvate Oligophrenia. *Journal of Mental Science* 85: 719–762.
Kanev, I. 1950. *An Outline for Social Security in Israel*. Jerusalem: Ministry of Labor (Hebrew).
Katvan, E. and N. Bartal. 2010. A Law Is Born: The Midwives Ordinance, Gender and Professional Regulation during the British Mandate. In E. Katvan, M. Shilo, and R. Halperin-Kadari (eds.) *One Law for Men and Women: Women and Law during the British Mandate*. Ramat Gan: Bar Ilan University.
Klaus, A. 1993. *Every Child a Lion: The Origins of Maternal and Infant Health Policy in the United States and France, 1890–1920*. Ithaca, NY: Cornell University Press.
Koplik, A. 1914. The History of the First Milk Depot or *Gouttee de Lait* with Consultations in America. *JAMA* 68(18): 1574–1575.
Lane-Claypon, J. E. 1920. *The Child Welfare Movement*. London: Bell.
Lazarus, W. and A. Hersh. 1977. Tipat Halav: Linking Families to Health Services in Israel. *Child Today* 6: 22–25.
Leissner, O. 2011a. The Birth industry in Israel. *Ha'Mishpat* 615–646 (Hebrew).
Leissner, O. 2011b. Sure, Give Birth! ‎ללדת ועוד איך!‎ In M. Shiloh and G. Katz (eds.) *Studies in the Rejuvenation of Israel – Gender*. ‎עיונים בתקומת ישראל - מגדר‎. Beer Sheva: Ben Gurion University Press.
Lewis, M. H. et al. 2011. State Laws Regarding the Retention and Use of Residual Newborn Screening Blood Samples. *Pediatrics* 127: 703–712.
Merke, F. 1984. *History and Iconography of Endemic Goiter and Cretinism*. Berne: Hans Huber.
Miller, J. 1993. To Stop the Slaughter of the Babies: Nathan Straus and the Drive for Pasteurized Milk, 1893–1920. *New York History* 74: 158–184.
Morgenstern-Leissner, O. 2006. Hospital Birth, Military Service and the Ties That Bind Them: The Case of Israel. *Nashim* 12:203–441 (Hebrew).
NHS. 2015. *Health Professional Handbook: A Guide to Newborn Blood Spot Screening for Healthcare Professionals* (revised version). London: NHS.
Paul, D. B. 2008. Patient Advocacy in Newborn Screening: Continuities and Discontinuities. *American Journal of Medical Genetics, Part C Semin Med Genet* 148C: 8–14.
Paul, D. B. and J. P. Brosco. 2013. *The PKU Paradox: A Short History of Newborn Screening*. Baltimore, MD: Johns Hopkins University Press.
Re, L. and J. M. Birkhoff. 2015. The 47,XYY Syndrome, 50 Years of Certainties and Doubts: A Systematic Review. *Aggression and Violent Behavior* 22: 9–17.
Rose, L. 1986. *Massacre of the Innocents. Infanticide in Great Britain 1800–1939*. London: Routledge & Kegan Paul.
Ross, E. 1993. *Love and Toil: Motherhood in Outcast London 1870–1918*. Oxford: Oxford University Press.
Sack, J., G. Kletter, O. Amado, and E. Astein. 1985. Screening for Neonatal Hypothyroidism in Israel during a 4-Year Period. *Israel Journal of Medical Science* 21: 485–489.

Schereschewsky, J. W. 1911. The Present Status of Infant Welfare Work in the United States. *Transactions of the American Association for the Study and Prevention of Infant Mortality* 2: 40–43.

Sealander, J. 2003. *The Failed Century of the Child: Governing America's Young in the Twentieth Century*. Cambridge: Cambridge University Press.

Shamir, R. 2012. Thiamine-Deficient Infant Formula: What Happened and What Have We Learned? *Annals of Nutrition and Metabolism* 60: 185–187.

Shorter, E. 1982. *A History of Women's Bodies*. New York: Basic Books.

Simmons, E. B. 2006. *Hadassah and the Zionist Project*. Lanham, MD: Rowman & Littlefield.

Snowden, J. M. et al. 2015. Planned Out-of-Hospital Birth and Birth Outcomes. *New England Journal of Medicine* 373: 2642–2653.

Shvarts, S. 1998. Women Organizations in the Benefit of Jewish Mothers in Palestine. *Bitahon Sociali* 51: 57–81 (Hebrew).

Shvarts, S. 2000. The Development of Mother and Infant Welfare Centers in Israel 1854–1954. *Journal of the History of Medicine and Allied Sciences* 55: 398–425.

Shvarts, S. and Z. Shehory-Rubin. 2012. *Hadassah for the Health of the People: The Health Education Mission of Hadassah – The American Zionist Women in the Holy Land*. Monterey, CA: Samuel Wachtman's Sons.

Starr, P. 1982. *The Social Transformation of American Medicine: The Rise of a Sovereign Profession and the Making of a Vast Industry*. New York: Basic Books.

Stoler-Lisz, S., S. Shvarts, and M. Shani. 2016. *To Be a Health Nation: Massive Immigration and Public Health in Israel*. Beer Sheva: Ben Gurion University Press.

Sussman, G. D. 1980. The End of the Wet-Nursing Business in France, 1874–1914. In R. Wheaton and T. K. Hareven (eds.) *Family and Sexuality in French History*. Philadelphia: University of Pennsylvania Press.

Timmermans, S. and M. Buchbinder. 2013. *Saving Babies? The Consequences of Newborn Genetic Screening*. Chicago: University of Chicago Press.

Walzer-Leavitt, J. 1988. *Brought to Bed: Childbearing in America 1750–1950*. Oxford: Oxford University Press.

Wilson, J. M. G. and G. Jungner. 1968. Principles and Practice of Screening for Disease. *Public Health Papers* 34. Geneva: World Health Organization.

Woolf, L. I., R. Griffiths, A. Moncrieff, S. Coates, and F. Dillistone. 1958. The Dietary Treatment of Phenylketonuria. *Archives Diseases of Childhood* 33: 31–45.

Zuckerman, S. 2009. The Expansion of Newborn Screening in Israel: Ethical and Social Dimensions. PhD dissertation. Case Western University.

10

"Life after Death": The Israeli Approach to Posthumous Reproduction

Vardit Ravitsky and Ya'arit Bokek-Cohen

This chapter addresses posthumous assisted reproduction (PAR) in the context of Israeli sociocultural norms and biopolitics. PAR involves the conception and birth of a baby after the death of one of its genetic progenitors.[1] The ability of freezing and storing sperm, eggs, and embryos, without an expiration date for using them to produce healthy babies (Côté et al. 2014), has opened up the possibility of conceiving or transferring an embryo after the death of one or both progenitors. While the loss of a father during pregnancy is a tragedy that has always been possible, the intentional initiation of a parental project after death is a novel possibility that assisted reproductive technologies have enabled.

This chapter first presents the Israeli approach to reproduction in general and then zooms in to explore the Israeli approach to PAR. While this approach is undergoing changes over the years, some distinct features emerge when it is being explored against the backdrop of the sociocultural and historical context in which it evolves. This chapter then presents research findings regarding the willingness of soldiers serving in the Israeli Defense Forces (IDF) and parents of combat soldiers to use sperm for PAR. We supplement these findings with an overview of some Jewish halakhic approaches to PAR. We aim to shed light on certain aspects of the Israeli approach by exploring PAR in a context that links reproduction to social attitudes, cultural values, biopolitical ethos, and military service.

1 THE ISRAELI APPROACH TO REPRODUCTION

The Israeli approach to reproduction is considered unique and has been amply documented as heavily pro-natalist when compared to other Western countries (Portugese

---

[1] An interesting terminological issue is the use of "parent" in the case of PAR, since such use of the term implies that a mere genetic connection is sufficient for the establishment of a parental relationship. While this is indeed the case in other contexts (such as the possible legal obligation of a man to pay child support based on a paternity test even if he was unaware of the pregnancy and is estranged from the child), the case of PAR differs significantly. It may be more appropriate to refrain from the use of "father" or "mother" in the case of PAR and adopt a term that more accurately reflects the pure genetic link. This, however, may also be controversial, considering that the motivation of the surviving partner is inherently linked to the desire of having an enduring link to the deceased loved one through a sense that he or she is the parent of the conceived child.

1998; Kahn 2000; Birenbaum-Carmeli and Carmeli 2010; Donath 2015). The crucial importance of the role parenthood plays is grounded in some key features of Israeli society and has been explored in various empirical studies (Kahn 2000; Remennick 2000; Birenbaum-Carmeli 2004). Israeli culture is imbued with Jewish traditional values that center on the family and on genetic parenthood. From the first imperative in the book of Genesis – "be fruitful and multiply" – to the societal view of childlessness as a tragedy, these prevalent traditional views lead the vast majority of Israelis to perceive parenthood as unquestionable (Kahn 2000). Beyond being perceived as an obvious personal choice, parenthood is linked in the Israeli collective consciousness to a host of national narratives. It expresses to some degree a "national duty" to contribute to the physical survival of the Jewish people in the shadow of the Holocaust and to assist in demographic efforts to maintain the Jewish character of the state by sustaining a Jewish majority (Birenbaum-Carmeli 2010). The Israeli birthrate is 3.11 children per family (CBS 2015), approximately double that of other Western countries (Katz and Lavee 2004), which is explained by the factors listed previously, as well as a constant sense of threat and an implicit concern of losing a child in war or a terror attack.

These cultural themes translate into unique policies and case law surrounding assisted reproductive technologies (ART) in general. Since the 1980s, Israel has become a world leader in IVF research and practice. Its eligibility criteria for publicly funded IVF are some of the most liberal and generous worldwide. Universal health care insurance covers fertility treatments, including costly procedures such as IVF, for all Israeli women, including single women and lesbian couples, up to the birth of two children from the current relationship. Partial support is provided by private health insurance for achieving pregnancy for a third child or more, as well as for IVF treatments in private clinics (Gonen 2016).

In Israel, having children is considered a "cultural imperative," and voluntary childlessness receives no societal legitimacy. Nearly 60 percent of Israelis believe that life without children is "empty," and about 80 percent consider childrearing the greatest joy of life (Steier et al. 1998). Moreover, Israeli culture – in line with Jewish traditional values – is centered on the creation and the protection of human life and consequently exhibits a strong tendency to facilitate research and embrace technologies aimed at enhancing reproduction (Ben-Or and Ravitsky 2010). In this context of the Israeli approach to reproduction, PAR should be understood as one practice among others aimed at fulfilling the cultural imperative of promoting procreation and parenthood, even after death.

2 POSTHUMOUS ASSISTED REPRODUCTION: ETHICAL, SOCIAL, AND POLICY LANDSCAPE

Similarly to other innovative uses of ART, e.g., human reproductive cloning, PAR raises complex ethical and social issues. Much ink has been spilled in the bioethics literature regarding the ethical debate surrounding this practice, with arguments for and against being developed and refined over the years (Corvalan 1996; Batzer, Hurwitz, and Caplan 2003; Stechschulte 2014; Young 2014; Lawson, Zweifel, and Klock 2016). The main arguments in favor of PAR address the reproductive autonomy of the surviving partner and his/her rights with regard to the deceased's genetic material; the notion of respect for the wishes of the deceased; the idea that genetic continuity is inherently valuable; and the cultural or symbolic importance of continuing the familial heritage through the physical existence of genetically related offspring.

The main arguments against it address the well-being of the prospective child, which some have dubbed a "planned orphan," (Landau 1999) a loaded term with a negative connotation. Specifically, Landau contends that "an adult's desire to give birth to an orphan should not have priority over the child's basic right to two living parents, at least at the time of its conception" (2004: 1953). Other arguments focus on the potential pressure that the deceased's relatives may exert on the surviving partner to make this reproductive choice in order to honor or commemorate the deceased loved one. Finally, there is a general sense of unease regarding unconventional reproductive practices and the consequent diversity of family structures that is perceived by conservative social agents as threatening.

In light of the complex issues raised by PAR, various jurisdictions have differing approaches toward this practice. Some countries ban it completely (for example, Germany, Italy, France, and Norway), while others regulate it in a variety of ways (for example, the United Kingdom, Australia, and some U.S. states). The legal regulation of PAR entails a complex host of issues as well, from the determination of parentage to the entitlement of the prospective child to inherit or to be eligible for social benefits (Batzer et al. 2003; Sperling 2008; Young 2014).

To make sense of the complex international landscape of PAR, a few key distinctions must be taken into consideration. First, the implications of PAR for men and women are different. While reproductive technology has recently advanced to the point that eggs can be efficiently frozen, the use of sperm for PAR remains much simpler and much more prevalent. A woman wishing to use the sperm of her deceased partner or to transfer a frozen embryo conceived with her former partner before he died can become pregnant and carry her own future child. However, a man wishing to use reproductive material from his deceased female partner would require a surrogate to carry a pregnancy or to involve in the process a current partner who would be carrying a future child that is genetically unrelated to her, an emotionally complex relationship that could have an impact on family members. Scenarios of PAR by men using frozen eggs entail the involvement of a third party and are therefore inherently more complex.

Second, the reproductive material used for PAR can be obtained prior to death, as in the scenario of embryos created from eggs and sperm that were frozen prior to the death of the parents, frozen sperm for fertility preservation for cancer patients (Finnerty et al. 2001), frozen sperm from soldiers taken prior to deployment, or eggs frozen for medical or social fertility preservation (Mertes and Pennings 2011). However, it can also be obtained after death in the case of postmortem sperm extraction or egg harvesting (Bahadur 2004). The extraction of sperm after death raises ethical issues in addition to the actual use of this sperm for reproduction, such as respect for the body of the deceased. The first recorded posthumous sperm extraction was conducted in 1976 by Dr. Rothman, who later called attention to the urgency of this decision due to the relatively brief window (of about seventy-two hours) in which the procedure is biologically possible (1999).

Third, PAR can be requested by the partner or the parents of the deceased. Parents' requests raise more complex issues than the request of a partner. In the case that the deceased had a partner, such a request can reflect the genuine wishes of the partner, but it may also come as a response to pressures that she is experiencing from the deceased partner's family, most likely his parents, to "honor" her beloved partner's memory and/or to guarantee his genetic continuity through PAR. In the case that the deceased did not have a partner, PAR would require a donated egg and a surrogate and then the child would be raised by his or her grandparents, a scenario that has recently reached an Israeli court (Barkan 2016) and that raises a host of issues. Alternatively, PAR could involve a woman who wishes to carry and rear the child, a scenario discussed later in this chapter. While most countries that allow PAR limit the request to a partner, in Israel, the courts have acknowledged the requests of parents, as described later.

Finally, PAR can be performed with or without prior consent of the deceased. Cases where the possibility of PAR has been explicitly discussed prior to death and a written consent has been signed are considered less controversial from an ethical standpoint, and as a consequence are seen as more acceptable by decision makers. In most cases, however, the deceased has not provided explicit documented consent for PAR, which complicates the matter. Most countries that allow PAR require explicit consent, but another possibility is the reliance on "inferred consent" (i.e., testimonials regarding the will of the deceased to become a parent) or "presumed consent" (i.e., assuming that genetic continuity is a universal human desire and has inherent value). The ethical challenge of inferred consent is that most such testimonials refer to the desire of the deceased to become a parent while alive, i.e., to have a parental relationship with a child, and rarely do they refer to the desire of the deceased to become a genetic progenitor posthumously. The ethical challenge of presumed consent is that it is currently not based on empirical data showing that the majority indeed holds this view, and is it thus pure conjecture based on one possible approach among others.

3 PAR IN THE CONTEXT OF MILITARY SERVICE: AN ISRAELI PERSPECTIVE

While much has been written about the ethical and legal aspects of PAR, not many empirical studies have assessed public opinion on the matter or the views of specific relevant populations, such as soldiers freezing sperm, IVF patients freezing embryos, or widows or widowers who have access to reproductive material of their deceased partners. The studies that have been conducted paint a complex picture of the views, values, preferences, and concerns of various populations. In a series of studies, Hans (2008) and Hans and Yelland (2013) examined the effect of the circumstances of death on public attitudes toward posthumous gamete procurement. They found that PAR following death as a military casualty was perceived as slightly more "justifiable" than following death caused by bungee-jumping (Hans and Yelland 2013). Respondents' level of religiosity also had an impact on attitudes, with more religious individuals tending to be less supportive of PAR.

Another study examined the effect of contextual factors on attitudes toward PAR and found that they were more favorable when the surviving partner was female, the marital bond was relatively long, the deceased expressed wishes to become a parent in the future, the death was not the result of suicide, but rather caused by a car accident, and when the deceased's parents had positive attitudes toward the procedure (Hans and Frey 2013). A more recent study also revealed that attitudes toward PAR are more positive when the surviving partner is a woman, and researchers suggested that this gender bias stems from the common belief that women have better parenting skills (Hans and Dooley 2014).

These studies were conducted on healthy civilians, for whom PAR is a hypothetical issue that does not directly impact their daily life. Empirical studies on populations directly touched by PAR are scant. In this chapter, we present research designed to address this gap by surveying two populations for whom PAR is not solely a hypothetical issue: soldiers serving in active duty, half of which were combat soldiers, and parents of combat soldiers (to be clear: not of those soldiers surveyed). The surveys aimed to assess attitudes toward PAR and willingness to conduct it. Because participating combat soldiers often experience life-threatening circumstances, of which their parents are well aware, the external validity of the results of these surveys can be assumed to be higher than that of civilians living in relatively peaceful environments.

The use of PAR in the case of soldiers who died in battle or during military service raises unique challenges in the Israeli context,[2] due to a complex set of historical and sociocultural factors. Israel has a well-established "militaristic" social fabric (Lomsky-Feder and Ben-Ari 2012). Historically founded in the shadow of the

---

[2] To the best of our knowledge, no army worldwide is currently running a program for gamete cryopreservation to allow PAR. The IDF has been discussing this issue, but currently no agreement has been reached. The Pentagon launched a pilot program for freezing soldiers' gametes at the beginning of 2016 with the aim of retaining young troops by covering the cost of fertility preservation. Note, however, that cryopreserved gametes are meant to be used by soldiers in case of injury that would lead to loss of fertility, and not posthumously. See www.militarytimes.com/story/military/benefits/health-care/2016/01/29/militarys-new-fertility-benefit-let-troops-freeze-their-sperm-and-eggs/79511918/ and www.nytimes.com/2016/02/04/us/politics/pentagon-to-offer-plan-to-store-eggs-and-sperm-to-retain-young-troops.html?_r=1.

Holocaust as a place meant to protect the Jewish people and to ensure its security, the Israeli state is embedded in a sense of an ongoing threat and consequently a fight for survival. Moreover, a universal and obligatory enlistment policy means that every eighteen-year-old, Jewish or Druze, male or female (excluding those who are medically unfit as well as Arabs and ultra-Orthodox Jews), serves two (for women) or three (for men) years in the IDF. This turns Israel into a "nation in arms" (as Israelis often say). Finally, due to a real and constant threat of violent attacks of various kinds, combat soldiers tend to be glorified as the defenders of the nation. Many who start off as senior commanders in the IDF move on after early retirement to senior careers in politics, educational institutions, or business, in which they successfully apply their military knowledge, skills, and experience. Some even become leaders, opinion-shapers, or parliament members, making their mark on Israeli society.

In line with these cultural norms and trends, two recent studies have shown that Israeli women on the search for sperm to conceive prefer donors who are or have been combat soldiers in the IDF (Bokek-Cohen 2016a, 2016b). The official policy of Israeli sperm banks is to exclude men who did not serve in the army as donors, and only use sperm from men who enlisted. Generally speaking, sperm has been symbolically imbued with cultural beliefs and attributes beyond its heritable genetic material (Martin 1991; Haimes 1993; Konrad 1998; Edwards 2004; Nash 2004; Daniels 2006). More specifically, these studies have shown that in the Israeli context, sperm donated by former or current combat soldiers is considered of higher quality than that donated by noncombatants (Bokek-Cohen 2016a, 2016b). These studies have shown that sperm recipients tend to use the information about the donor's military service as a clue to his personality. While military service in itself attests to the mental and physical health of the soldier, combat soldiers are perceived as devoted citizens who are willing to contribute to their country and nation. A senior sperm bank manager explains that the policy of excluding men who did not serve has nothing to do with political ideology, but rather serves to facilitate the screening process and ensure donors' mental and physical fitness (Bokek-Cohen 2016b).

In light of the central role that the IDF plays in Israeli society and culture, and the large number of casualties that occur continuously and not necessarily in times of war, the issue of PAR for parents of soldiers who died during military service is particularly sensitive and unfortunately relevant to many Israeli citizens.

IDF Soldiers' Willingness to Preserve Sperm for PAR

In light of the unique sociocultural features of Jewish Israeli society, it is therefore of particular interest to empirically assess the willingness of soldiers to conduct PAR. The findings described here relate to the willingness of *living* soldiers to freeze sperm for the purpose of PAR if they die. They thus supplement existing scholarship referring to the *presumed will* of *dead* men (Hashiloni-Dolev and Triger 2016), which Israeli courts consider when there is no way of tracing the actual, explicit preferences of the deceased in this matter.

Based on an extensive literature review on posthumous sperm extraction, sperm cryopreservation, and PAR, a questionnaire was developed by the second author of this chapter to explore soldiers' willingness to conduct PAR. The questionnaire was piloted on eight soldiers recruited through the second author's personal networks, clarified and refined based on their comments, and piloted again on twelve different soldiers recruited through personal networks and snowballing. Based on these two pilots, the final version of the questionnaire was prepared. Recruitment was based on the snowball method: each of the soldiers who participated in the pilot stage was requested to provide names and contact details of other soldiers with whom he was acquainted. Recruitment ended when the sample size arrived at 245. Some soldiers declined participation in the study, and the final sample consisted of 212 soldiers; the mean age was 19.72 ($SD = 0.85$). Respondents were all male, Jewish, and never married; about half of them were from combat units and the other half from noncombat units.

Results show that overall, soldiers are willing to preserve sperm and consider PAR. Religious soldiers expressed the lowest level of willingness, traditional soldiers were more supportive, and secular soldiers expressed the highest level of willingness to conduct PAR. The findings regarding the low inclination of religious soldiers to preserve sperm for PAR are in line with the fact that religious Jews are committed to *halakha* (the collective body of Jewish religious laws derived from the written and oral Torah), which forbids masturbation. Sperm collection in living men requires the ejaculation of semen outside the context of intercourse, which is seen by Jewish law as *hotza'at zera levatalah* (extracting sperm in vain). This prohibition is based on the view that wasting sperm is sinful since it jeopardizes the fulfillment of the first commandment of Torah: "be fruitful and multiply" (Genesis 1:21) (Jakobovits 2005). These findings align with research conducted in the United States showing that religious Christian respondents also tend to have less favorable attitudes toward PAR (Hans and Yelland 2013).

Soldiers were presented with six scenarios of familial circumstances and were asked to mark those scenarios in which they would be willing to conduct PAR. Note that these scenarios were based on the notion that the sperm will be used posthumously by a woman who would be the genetic and rearing mother of the child, with the parents of the deceased playing the role of grandparents. The most frequently selected scenario was "if my parents would ask me to allow them to have a grandchild after I die." The second most frequent was "if at the time of my death I do not have any children and my parents do not have any grandchildren." The expected support by the woman's parents in taking care of the prospective posthumous child was preferable over geographic proximity of the place of residence to the soldiers' parents (i.e., the prospective child's paternal grandparents). This demonstrates the practical orientation of the respondents, who assume the mother of their posthumously conceived child would prefer to be assisted by her own parents (i.e., the maternal grandparents).

Respondents were also asked questions regarding the sociodemographic profile of the potential mother of their posthumously conceived child. They attached high importance to the economic status of the woman (e.g., owns a house, works in a steady/tenured job). When presented with several profiles of women that differed in relation to marital status, sexual orientation, and gendered stereotyped occupation, they preferred that their posthumous child be raised by a heterosexual couple in which the male partner is infertile. They tended to recoil from profiles of women holding senior and time-consuming jobs or lacking stability and security and preferred those working in jobs perceived as traditionally feminine.

Attitudes of Combat IDF Soldiers' Parents toward PAR

To shed more light on the Israeli attitude toward PAR, a second study explored the attitudes of parents of combat soldiers in active compulsory duty toward the option of having a posthumous grandchild in case their son dies during his military service. Only secular parents were recruited, in order to get a clearer picture regarding attitudes toward PAR in the absence of religious constraints.

An original questionnaire was developed and included statements on a ten-point Likert scale ranging from "absolutely disagree" to "absolutely agree." It also included scenarios that differed in two dimensions: (a) the son's stated will regarding posthumous use of his sperm; (b) monetary cost of the procedure (sperm extraction and cryopreservation) and of child support for the future grandchild. Respondents were asked to mark in what scenario they would consider conducting PAR from their son's sperm.

Recruitment was based on the snowball method: members of the second author's personal networks were asked to provide the names and contact details of parents of combat soldiers in active duty with whom they were acquainted until a sample of 348 was obtained. Of these potential respondents, forty parents declined participation, yielding a compliance rate of 88.5 percent. The surveyed sample thus consisted of 308 parents. All respondents were Jewish and had sons who were combat soldiers in active duty and childless at the time of the data collection. Their mean age was 44.78 (SD = 7.85). 58 percent of them were mothers and 42 percent were fathers. Male and female respondents were not marital partners.

Results show that combat soldiers' fathers are more willing to conduct PAR, as compared to mothers. This was also reflected in the willingness of fathers to pay a significantly larger sum of money than mothers for this procedure. The son's will prior to death had a major impact on the inclination of parents of both genders to consider PAR. When presented with three different scenarios regarding the son's will (unknown, explicitly asked his parents to conduct PAR, explicitly opposed the possibility of PAR), parents attached great importance to their son's will.

Accordingly, they showed a lower tendency to consider PAR when presented with the scenario of a son who explicitly opposed PAR. It was also found that the number of children parents have had almost no impact on the tendency to consider PAR. This finding may imply that PAR is not considered to be based on "egocentric" interests of parents who have only one or two children, but rather that they see the continuity of the dead as the crucial factor in considering PAR. By "egocentric," we mean either the parents' interest in genetic continuity, or their interests in grandchildren who may care for them in their old age.

Interestingly, both soldiers and their parents were more inclined to consider PAR if the other party expressed explicit desire to do so. Soldiers indicated that they would be willing to preserve sperm and conduct PAR if they knew their parents wanted it, or if this were their parents' only chance of having grandchildren; parents indicated that they would be more inclined to initiate PAR if their son had expressed explicit desire to conduct PAR out of his preserved sperm. This means that each party tended to be considerate and agree to what seemed to be in the best interest of the other party. This also leads to an interesting challenge of a cyclic approach, in which cultural values push both parties to pursue PAR and then each party's desire feeds into that of the other.

4 JEWISH LAW (HALAKHIC) APPROACHES TOWARD POSTHUMOUS ASSISTED REPRODUCTION

Halakhic approaches toward PAR are not monolithic, as is the case regarding numerous novel reproductive technologies. In this section, we present the views of three prominent Israeli rabbis regarding PAR, in order to demonstrate the diversity of approaches on this matter. The views of Rabbi Dr. Halperin, who was for years in charge of ethics at the Israeli Ministry of Health, were gleaned from an article he published in 2006. The views of Rabbis Katz and Sharlo are presented based on interviews conducted with them and then analyzed based on Hsieh and Shannon's method of "directed content analysis" (Hsieh and Shannon 2005). Each interview lasted about two hours and took place at the rabbi's office. Each was presented with the same set of questions addressing different aspects of PAR.

Rabbi Dr. Halperin cites Rabbi Goldberg's halakhic decision (*psak*) that posthumous sperm extraction from a married man would be allowed if the deceased gave explicit consent or based on presumed consent. He stresses that as a general rule, halakhic prohibitions require a rationale, in the absence of which the default position is to permit the act. A relevant consideration in this respect is the fact that the Torah attaches great significance to the human will to leave a name and a trace after death, as can be learned from the law of levirate marriage, according to which an unmarried man must marry his dead brother's widow, in order to procreate with her and pass on his brother's name. Rabbi Dr. Halperin's position is thus that if there is no reason to forbid PAR, then fulfilling the deceased's will is considered a religious imperative (*mitzvah*), since it would be considered an act of lovingkindness (*gemilut hasadim*).

Rabbi Sharlo expresses a diametrically opposed approach to PAR. His negative view regarding this practice is based on two main reasons. The first relates to the finality of human life, which he sees as the prevalent notion among halakhic authorities. Just as a grave is impure and death is a final concept, it is not recommended to leave "residues" after a man dies. Bringing a posthumous child into the world is considered in his eyes a senseless act. A deceased man's request for PAR should not be fulfilled and his relatives are not expected to fulfill it. The second reason is the absence of halakhic discussions regarding PAR, and in particular the lack of halakhic attitude regarding the rights of a posthumously conceived child. In Sharlo's opinion, PAR poses a dilemma of whether to give birth to a child that would be disadvantaged by the fact of being an orphan at birth, or not to bring it into the world at all. He also relates to potential tensions between the widow and the deceased's parents, and raises a scenario where the parents want to bring a posthumous child into the world, but the widow refuses or recoils. He further argues that such a child would require resources that a single mother may find difficult to obtain, and that the child may as a result fall as a burden on society, which would be unjust.

Rabbi Katz from the Puah Institute[3] holds a nuanced position regarding the impact of consent to PAR. He contends that if the deceased did not explicitly express his will for PAR, then posthumous extraction of sperm would be forbidden and thus PAR would not be possible. However, if a man did explicitly express a will for PAR, then it would be allowed. He further recommends that a widow should not conceive the child of her deceased husband posthumously in order to ease her separation from him and lessen the sorrow caused by his death. He believes that the religious imperative of "be fruitful and multiply" relates only to living men. Since the dead are exempt from observing all religious imperatives, PAR is irrelevant from that perspective. Regarding PAR for soldiers, he argues that their morale may be impaired if they freeze sperm before deployment.

These three rabbis convey three different attitudes toward PAR. Rabbi Halperin expresses a more permissive and favorable attitude, Rabbi Sharlo opposes PAR, and Rabbi Katz proposes a refined approach. We ascribe these differences to divergent views regarding the meaning of death: death as the ultimate finality of life versus death as a merely physical phenomenon while commemoration and genetic continuation of the dead is valued. Furthermore, the attitudes stem from a contrast regarding the focal figure: the dead person versus his living relatives, i.e., widow, future posthumous child, and/or the extended family and community.

---

[3] The Puah Institute is devoted to helping couples with fertility problems and women in all stages of life fulfill their dreams of building a family without violating halakhic laws. Counselors at the Puah Institute embody a unique synthesis of rabbinical knowledge and specialized training in modern reproductive medicine. www.puahonline.org/images/stories/P-Brochure-3-6-09.pdf.

The narrative of Rabbi Halperin is in accord with the view that the dead should be commemorated through genetic continuity. He sees the deceased as the focal figure to be considered while deciding whether to allow PAR. In contrast to Rabbi Halperin, Rabbi Sharlo expresses the view of death as the final state of a person, which leads him to forbid the fulfilling of an explicit request for PAR. The focal figure(s) to be considered are the living and not the dead, hence the well-being of the widow is highlighted, as well as potential conflicts with her in-law parents. The posthumous child is perceived as a fatherless victim who may become a burden on society. Rabbi Katz presents a middle ground. On one hand, he stresses that the finality of life means that the *mitzvah* requiring men to procreate no longer applies. On the other hand, he argues that if the deceased explicitly asked for PAR, then his request should be respected, while nevertheless remaining concerned about the well-being of the widow and the posthumous child.

5 THE ISRAELI APPROACH TO POSTHUMOUS ASSISTED REPRODUCTION

In light of the sociocultural context, as well as the pluralistic halakhic approaches we described, it is no surprise that when it comes to PAR, the Israeli approach is an outlier compared with the rest of the world. Going back to the distinctions described previously, Israel has a unique approach regarding what type of consent is required for PAR and who has the right to request it.

In the early 2000s, the Israeli Ministry of Justice started receiving calls from hospitals faced with requests for urgent posthumous extraction of sperm following tragic deaths of young men. Hospitals did not have any regulatory or legal guidance in this novel matter and did not know how to respond. In line with the general approach of "erring on the side of life," the reaction of the Ministry of Justice was to first allow the procedure of sperm extraction, in order not to miss the relatively brief biological window during which this is possible, then to freeze the sperm and consider the next steps.

The Ministry of Justice then convened professionals from various disciplinary backgrounds, including medical, legal, bioethics, and Jewish law experts, to discuss a possible coherent Israeli approach in the face of a growing demand for PAR.[4] Based on these consultations, the Israeli attorney general issued in 2003 Guidelines (Guidelines of the Attorney General 2003) allowing posthumous sperm extraction even in the absence of explicit consent from the deceased, and instructed Israeli courts to allow the use of this sperm for PAR by a female partner of the deceased, following an assessment of his inferred will, i.e., what would have been the will of the deceased based on his behavior prior to death (e.g., being involved in fertility

---

[4] Disclosure: the first author of this chapter was among these experts and participated in a number of meetings discussing this issue prior to the publication of the Guidelines.

treatments) and based on the testimonials of family and friends (e.g., having said that he wishes to become a father) (Ravitsky 2004).

By allowing PAR without the explicit consent of the deceased, these Guidelines made Israel an outlier compared with other jurisdictions that do require explicit written consent to allow the practice. The rationale underlying the attorney general's Guidelines was complex and reflected a mix of traditional Jewish values; assumptions about a universal desire for genetic continuity that translates into a notion of "presumed consent" for PAR; a prioritization of the desires of the surviving partner in relation to the unknown wishes of the deceased; and a view of the deceased as "unharmed" by PAR since "even in case of a mistake in evaluating the deceased's will, parenthood is not being forced upon him," as "he will not be coerced into fulfilling the obligations that a parent usually has vis-à-vis his child" (Ravitsky 2004). The Guidelines also instruct the courts in the case of PAR to mandate the state to register the resulting child as the legal child of the deceased.

As emphasized by Hashiloni-Dolev (2015), these Guidelines reflect an "expertocratic" approach, as they are based on a consultation process with experts (Shalev and Hashiloni-Dolev 2011), rather than a public consultation of the sort that has been employed in other countries prior to policymaking in relation to novel assisted reproductive technologies, for instance, by the Human Fertilisation and Embryology Authority in the United Kingdom. Hashiloni-Dolev's (2015) recent qualitative study, which involved interviews with thirteen Jewish Israeli couples, demonstrates that this approach may not necessarily reflect public views on the matter, as participants in her study highlighted the counterargument stating that a desire for PAR cannot be inferred from one's desire to become a parent in life.

While the 2003 Guidelines are very permissive in terms of consent, they did limit the request for PAR to the deceased's female partner (although not requiring legal marriage for the acknowledgment of partnership status). They explicitly excluded the parents of the deceased as possible initiators of PAR, arguing that their interest cannot be recognized since they would not have had a say in the matter if their son had been alive. The exclusion of parents from reproductive decisions regarding their deceased sons remains the official Israeli position, and has been reaffirmed more recently in 2012 by the Public Committee for the Examination of a Legal Regulation of Fertility and Reproduction in Israel (Recommendations 2012), which did not recommend expanding PAR to include parents' requests.

Despite this consistent formal approach, the Israeli PAR landscape has been shifting based on case law. Parents who wish to use their deceased son's sperm to conceive a genetic grandchild have been supported by the NGO New Family (New Family website), led by attorney Irit Rosenblum, who invented in 2011 the legal tool of the Biological Will^{TM} (Danya 2013). New Family has played an important role in opening up the door to parents' requests, by "matching up" interested parents of deceased men with women who are interested in becoming single mothers and who intended to use donated sperm for this purpose in any case. For certain women, the possibility of using identifiable sperm from a known deceased man is seen as a preferable alternative to the use of anonymously donated sperm (which is to date a legal requirement for sperm donation in Israel). Some of these agreements between single women and parents of deceased men have already been approved by Israeli courts and babies have been born as a result of these "matches."

While in most of these approved cases, the death did not occur in the context of military service, the connection between PAR and the military is present in the Israeli consciousness. Debates have been ongoing about a potential program that would offer soldiers the possibility of freezing sperm (at the expense of the army) as a part of compulsory enlistment. New Family has been promoting the idea of allowing soldiers to sign the Biological Will^{TM} document, in order to obtain explicit written consent for PAR by parents in case they are killed during their military service. While such programs are not currently in place, it remains to be seen how receptive the Israeli public would be to such a policy in years to come, as PAR potentially becomes more routine in civilian cases. In a meeting of the Science and Technology Committee of the Israeli Knesset[5] in the early 2000s, a bereaved father who lost his son while he was serving as a soldier in the IDF pleaded Knesset members with tears in his eyes to allow soldiers' parents to request posthumous sperm extraction, arguing that parents "give their children to the state" and this is the least that the "state can do for them in return." This emotional plea resonated with some Knesset members present at the meeting, who seemed to agree that an approach that only allows a partner to request PAR may be too limiting. The notion that the state may "owe" parents access to PAR in the case of deceased soldiers because the state mandates military service may be a uniquely Israeli perspective, stemming from the idiosyncratic set of sociopolitical circumstances that shape Israeli bioethics. This notion may eventually pave the way to a shift in the Israeli regulatory approach to allow PAR based on parents' requests.

The first case in which parents requested PAR with the use of their deceased son's sperm was the case of an Israeli soldier named Keivan Cohen, who was killed during his military service in the Gaza Strip in 2002. He was nineteen years old, unmarried, and did not have a partner. His parents turned to the court to approve sperm procurement a few hours after he died. The parents looked for a woman who would agree to conceive and raise a child with their support. They published an ad and received 200 answers within the first hour of publication. After a period of screening potential mothers, they chose their preferred candidate and turned together to the hospital where the material was preserved. However, when they asked to release the sperm, the hospital refused. Consequently, the family turned to obtain court approval. Their request was declined at first because Cohen was not the woman's partner. The attorney general opposed the request because, as stated

---

[5] In which the first author of this chapter participated.

earlier, the Israeli Guidelines allowed PAR only for the surviving spouse of a deceased person, and not his parents.

The prospective mother then turned to attorney Irit Rosenblum, the founder of New Family. Rosenblum achieved a legal precedent that allowed the parents to initiate PAR and receive the sperm for use by the woman they selected. Eleven years after Cohen's death, a baby girl was born from his sperm. Kindregan (2015) points to the fact that the request was approved only after the judges were convinced that the woman had agreed to the arrangement out of her free will and that she intended to raise the future child herself and to be a mother in every sense. Since the status of a child born of PAR needs to be clarified in relation to the resolution of various legal conflicts (Kindregan and Snyder 2008), Rosenblum is attempting to promote legislation that would regulate the procedure by approving the legal instrument of the Biological Will^{TM}.

6 CONCLUSION

In Israel, a unique set of cultural and political circumstances leads to what is probably the most liberal approach to posthumous assisted reproduction worldwide. This can be explained by factors related to pro-natalism, and in the case of soldiers, to a sense that the death of a soldier is not just a personal tragedy, but rather a national one, requiring various types of state support. Such support can extend all the way to the courts accepting requests for posthumous use of deceased soldiers' sperm even from parents, and women preferring to use such sperm to become mothers. In addition, the positive view of soldiers' PAR may stem from a cultural inclination to respond to the biblical verse "the more they were afflicted, the more they multiplied and the more they spread" (Exodus 7:12). This verse constitutes the gist of the Jewish collective consciousness, which is also reflected in many holiday traditions that through various symbolic customs express and emphasize the long-standing resilience of the Jewish people.

We argue that against the backdrop of the Israeli cultural context, and in cases where explicit consent of the deceased for PAR has been given prior to death, PAR based on parents' request – in the case of soldiers who died during military service as well as in other cases – may be ethically acceptable. It may result in a win-win-win situation, where all parties benefit from the birth of a posthumously conceived child. The parents and/or the partner of the deceased can be content that they are able to fulfill their loved one's "biological will." The mother may benefit from emotional and even material support from the parents of the deceased, and possibly even from support from his extended family. The child has a paternal personae, in contrast to donor-conceived offspring who may suffer from lack of access to any information regarding the donor (Ravitsky 2010) and possibly from genealogical bewilderment (Bokek-Cohen and Gonen 2016). He or she may benefit from genealogical certainty (Bokek-Cohen and Ravitsky 2017) and also benefit from the love and care of the extended family of both parents, rather than only from the mother's side, as is the case of anonymous sperm recipients.

The significant impact of traditional values and beliefs on the Israeli approach to PAR demonstrates that "one size does not fit all." Policies pertaining to assisted reproductive technologies in general, and regarding PAR in particular, reflect the cultural contexts in which they are embedded. While the traditional emphasis on autonomy and consent led to a requirement for explicit consent to PAR prior to death in any jurisdiction that allows this practice, Israeli regulators chose to allow the practice based on presumed or inferred consent. Although they initially allowed the initiation of PAR only by a partner, Israeli courts are now demonstrating openness to consider requests by parents of deceased men. While both these approaches are controversial from a bioethical perspective, they demonstrate how the Israeli cultural and biopolitical context plays an important role in shaping a unique attitude toward PAR.

ACKNOWLEDGMENTS

The authors would like to thank Yael Hashiloni-Dolev, Shai J. Lavi, and Hagai Boas for their insightful comments on the manuscript, as well as the other editors of this volume and the participants in the workshop leading to this publication organized by the Edmond J. Safra Center for Ethics at Tel Aviv University. We would also like to thank the participants in the studies mentioned in this chapter for sharing their perspectives on such private matters.

References

Bahadur, G. (2004). Ethical Challenges in Reproductive Medicine: Posthumous Reproduction. *International Congress Series*, 1266, 295–302.

Barkan, N. (2016, September 5). The Touching Battle of the Bereaved Parents: Allow Us to Conceive with Our Son's Sperm. *Ynet*. Retrieved September 14, 2016 at www.ynet.co.il/articles/0,7340,L-4850474,00.html (in Hebrew).

Batzer, F. R., Hurwitz, J. M., and Caplan, A. (2003). Postmortem Parenthood and the Need for a Protocol with Posthumous Sperm Procurement. *Fertility & Sterility*, 79(6), 1263–1269.

Ben-Or, G. and Ravitsky, V. (2010). Cultural Values in Action: The Israeli Approach to Human Cloning. In D. Birenbaum-Carmeli and Y. S. Carmeli (Eds.). *Kin, Gene, Community: Reproductive Technology among Jewish Israelis* (pp. 226–251). New-York: Berghahn Books.

Birenbaum-Carmeli, D. (2003). Reproductive Policy in Context: Implications on Women's Rights in Israel, 1945–2000. *Policy Studies Journal*, 24(2/3), 101–113.

Birenbaum-Carmeli, D. (2004). Cheaper than a Newcomer: On the Social Production of IVF Policy in Israel. *Sociology of Health and Illness*, 26(7), 897–924.
Birenbaum-Carmeli, D. and Carmeli, Y. S. (2010). Reproductive Technologies among Jewish Israelis: Setting the Ground. In D. Birenbaum-Carmeli and Y. S. Carmeli (Eds.). *Kin, Gene, Community: Reproductive Technology among Jewish Israelis* (pp. 1–48). New-York: Berghahn Books.
Bokek-Cohen, Y. & Ravitsky, V. (2017, forthcoming) "Soldiers' preferences regarding sperm preservation, posthumous reproduction and attributes of a potential 'posthumous mother'" OMEGA– Journal of Death and Dying.
Bokek-Cohen, Y. (2016a). How Are Marketing Strategies of Genetic Material Used as a Mechanism for Biopolitical Governmentality? *Consumption, Markets & Culture*. 19 (6), 534–554. DOI: 10.1080/10253866.2015.1137897.
Bokek-Cohen, Y. (2016b). Falling in Love With a [Sperm] Warrior: Conscripting Women's Wombs to the Dissemination of a Religio-political Ideology. *Journal of Gender Studies*. DOI: 10.1080/09589236.2016.1155436.
Bokek-Cohen, Y. and Gonen, L. D. (2016). Advocacy for Unborn Sperm Donor Conceived Children and Family Policy. *Social Theory & Health*, 14(2), 207–223. DOI: 10.1057/sth.2015.29.
CBS (Central Bureau of Statistics, Israel) (2015). Selected Data for International Child Day 2015. Retrieved from: http://cbs.gov.il/reader/newhodaot/hodaa_template.html?hodaa=201511312.
Corvalan, A. (1996). Fatherhood after Death: A Legal and Ethical Analysis of Posthumous Reproduction. *Albany Law Journal of Science & Technology*, 7, 336–365.
Côté, S., Affdal, A. O., Kadoch, I. J., Hamet, P., and Ravitsky, V. (2014). Posthumous Reproduction With Surplus Embryos: Exploring User's Choices. *Fertility and Sterility*, 102(5), 1410–1415.
Daniels, C. R. (2006). *Exposing Men: The Science and Politics of Male Reproduction*. Oxford: Oxford University Press.
Danya. (2013, February 25). The Biological Will™ – a New Paradigm in ART? Retrieved September 13, 2016 at www.newfamily.org.il/en/4905/the-biological-will%E2%84%A2-%E2%80%93-a-new-paradigm-in-art/.
Donath, O. (2015). Regretting Motherhood: A Sociopolitical Analysis. *Signs: Journal of Women in Culture and Society*, 40(2), 343–367.
Edwards, J. (2004). Incorporating Incest: Gamete, Body and Relation in Assisted Conception. *Journal of Royal Anthropological Institute*, 10(4), 755–774.
Eshre Task Force on Ethics Law. Pennings, G., de Wert, G., Shenfield, F., Cohen, J., Devroey, P. et al. (2006). ESHRE Task Force on Ethics and Law 11: Posthumous Assisted Reproduction. *Human Reproduction*, 21(12), 3050–3053.
Ethics Committee of the American Society for Reproductive Medicine. (2013). Posthumous Collection and Use of Reproductive Tissue: A Committee Opinion. *Fertility & Sterility*, 99(7), 1842–1845.

Finnerty, J. J., Thomas, T. S., Boyle, R. J., Howards, S. S., and Karns, L. B. (2001). Gamete Retrieval in Terminal Conditions. *American Journal of Obstetrics & Gynecology*, 185(2), 300–307.

Gonen, L. D. (2016). Social and Private Benefits of Assisted Reproductive Technology: A National Survey-Based Evaluation in Israel. *Journal of Comparative Effectiveness Research*, 5(1), 49–63.

Guidelines of the Attorney General of the Government, Guideline Number 1.2202. Ministry of Justice, Jerusalem. October 27, 2003 (in Hebrew).

Haimes, E. (1993). Issues of Gender in Gamete Donation. *Social Science and Medicine*, 36(1), 85–93.

Halperin, M. (2006). Post-Mortem Artificial Insemination – Prohibition and Permission. *Asya*, 20, 113–123 (in Hebrew).

Hans, J. D. (2008). Attitudes toward Posthumous Harvesting and Reproduction. *Death Studies*, 32(9), 837–869. DOI: 10.1080/07481180802359789.

Hans, J. D. and Dooley, B. (2014). Attitudes toward Making Babies ... With a Deceased Partner's Cryopreserved Gametes. *Death Studies*, 38(9), 571–581. DOI: 10.1080/07481187.2013.809033.

Hans, J. D. and Frey, L. M. (2013). American Attitudes in Context: Posthumous Use of Cryopreserved Gametes. *Journal of Clinical Research & Bioethics*, S1: 006. DOI: 10.4172/2155–9627.S1-006.

Hans, J. D. and Yelland, E. L. (2013). American Attitudes in Context: Posthumous Sperm Retrieval and Reproduction. *Journal of Clinical Research & Bioethics*, S1: 008. doi: 10.4172/2155–9627.S1-008.

Hashiloni-Dolev, Y. (2015). Posthumous Reproduction (PHR) in Israel: Policy Rationales versus Lay People's Concerns, a Preliminary Study. *Culture, Medicine & Psychiatry*, 39(4), 634–650.

Hashiloni-Dolev, Y. and Triger, Z. (2016). Between the Deceased's Wish and the Wishes of His Surviving Relatives: Posthumous Children, Patriarchy, Pronatalism, and the Myth of Continuity of the Seed. *Tel-Aviv University Law Review*, 39(3) (in Hebrew).

Hsieh, H. F. and Shannon, S. E. (2005). Three Approaches to Qualitative Content Analysis. *Qualitative Health Research*, 15(9), 1277–1288.

Jakobovits, Y. Assisted Reproduction through the Prism of Jewish Law. Jewish Action. Spring 2005. Retrieved September 14, 2016 at http://ou.org.s3.amazonaws.com/publications/ja/5765/5765spring/Prism.pdf (in Hebrew).

Kahn, S. M. (2000). *Reproducing Jews: A Cultural Account of Assisted Conception in Israel*. Durham, NC, and London: Duke University Press.

Katz, R. and Lavee, Y. (2004). Families in Israel. In B. Adams and J. Trost (Eds.), *Handbook of World Families* (pp. 486–506). Newbury Park, CA: Sage.

Kindregan, C. P., Jr. (2015). Dead Soldiers and Their Posthumously Conceived Children. *Journal of Contemporary Health Law & Policy*, 31, 74–95.

Kindregan, C. P., Jr. and Snyder, S. H. (2008). Clarifying the Law of ART: The New American Bar Association Model Act Governing Assisted Reproductive Technology, *Family Law Quarterly*, 42, 203–229.

Konrad, M. (1998). Ova Donation and the Symbols of Substance: Some Variations on the Theme of Sex, Gender and the Partible Body. *Journal of the Royal Anthropological Institute*, 4(4), 643–667.
Landau, R. (1999). Planned Orphanhood. *Social Science & Medicine*, 49(2), 185–196.
Landau, R. (2004). Posthumous Sperm Retrieval for the Purpose of Later Insemination or IVF in Israel: An Ethical and Psychosocial Critique. *Human Reproduction*, 19(9), 1952–1956.
Lawson, A. K., Zweifel, J. E., and Klock, S. C. (2016) Blurring the Line between Life and Death: A Review of the Psychological and Ethical Concerns Related to Posthumous-Assisted Reproduction. *The European Journal of Contraception & Reproductive Healthcare.* www.tandfonline.com/doi/full/10.1080/13625187.2016.1203892.
Lomsky-Feder, E. and Ben-Ari, E. (2012). *The Military and Militarism in Israeli Society*. Albany: State University of New York Press.
Martin, E. (1991). The Egg and the Sperm: How Science Constructed a Romance Based on Stereotypical Male–Female Roles. *Signs: Journal of Women in Culture and Society*, 16(3), 485–501.
Mertes, H. and Pennings, G. (2011). Social Egg Freezing: For Better, Not for Worse. *Reproductive Biomedicine Online*, 23(7), 824–829.
Nash, C. (2004). Genetic Kinship. *Cultural Studies*, 18(1), 1–33.
Portugese, J. (1998). *Fertility Policy in Israel: The Politics of Religion, Gender and Nation*. Westport, CT: Praeger.
Ravitsky, V. (2004). Posthumous Reproduction Guidelines in Israel. Commentary, *Hastings Center Report*, 34(2), 6–7.
Ravitsky, V. (2010). "Knowing Where You Come From": The Rights of Donor-Conceived Individuals and the Meaning of Genetic Relatedness. *Minnesota Journal of Law Science & Technology*, 11(2), 655–684.
Recommendations of the Public Committee for the Study of Legislative Regulation of Fertility and Reproduction in Israel. (2012). Retrieved September 13, 2016 at www.health.gov.il/publicationsfiles/bap2012.pdf (in Hebrew).
Remennick, L. (2000). Childless in the Land of Imperative Motherhood: Stigma and Coping among Infertile Israeli Women. *Sex Roles*, 43(11/12), 821–841.
Rothman, C. M. (1999). Live Sperm, Dead Bodies. *Journal of Andrology*, 20, 456–457.
Schmidt, M. S. (2016, February 3). Pentagon to Offer Plan to Store Eggs and Sperm to Retain Young Troops. Retrieved from www.nytimes.com/192016/02/04/us/politics/pentagon-to-offer-plan-to-store-eggs-and-sperm-to-retain-young-troops.html?_r=1.
Shalev, C. and Hashiloni-Dolev, Y. (2011). Bioethics Governance in Israel: An Expert Regime. *Indian Journal of Medical Ethics*, 8(3), 157–160.
Sperling, D. (2008). *Posthumous Interests: Legal and Ethical Perspectives*. Cambridge: Cambridge University Press.
Sperling, D. (2010). Commanding the "Be Fruitful and Multiply" Directive: Reproductive Ethics, Law, and Policy in Israel. *Cambridge Quarterly of Healthcare Ethics*, 19(3), 363–371.

Sperling, D. and Simon, Y. (2010). Attitudes and Policies Regarding Access to Fertility Care and Assisted Reproductive Technologies in Israel. *Reproductive Biomedicine Online*, 21(7), 854–861.

Stechschulte, T. (2014). Symposium: The Legal and Ethical Implications of Posthumous Reproduction. *Journal of Law and Health* 27, 1.

Steier, H., Oren, A., Elias, N., and Lewin-Epstein, N. (1998). *Gender Roles, Family, and Women's Participation in the Labor Force: Attitudes of Veteran Israelis and Newcomers in a Comparative Perspective – Research Eeport*. Tel Aviv: The Institute for Social Research (in Hebrew).

Weiss, M. (2002). *The Chosen Body: The Politics of the Body in Israeli Society*. Stanford, CA: Stanford University Press.

Young, H. (2014). Presuming Consent to Posthumous Reproduction. *Journal of Law & Health*, 53, 68–97.

PART III

Is There an Israeli Exceptionalism?

11

Reckless or Pioneering? Public Health Genetics Services in Israel

Aviad E. Raz

This chapter looks at public health genetics services in Israel as a network of people, resources, and institutions whose cooperative activity produces current genetic knowledge and practice. This chapter will situate the production of genetics services within relevant political, cultural, and professional contexts, looking at the social factors that make them possible, indeed desirable, and the dynamics that shape their design and prioritizing. Public health genetics services carry special significance from a sociological and bioethical perspective. When states offer (and sometimes mandate) population-based genetic screening for public health and reproductive purposes, they risk "backdoor eugenics" and the potential compromising of individual autonomy. When ethnicity and religiosity are used as categories in genetic databases and screening programs, this may entail the racial marking of genetic risks or biomarkers, with possible stigmatizing effects on minority communities. When genetic screening becomes part of public health, it usually follows the logic of control and prevention of genetic diseases; this is a top-down "population" approach that is not necessarily attentive to individual needs and preferences (Khoury et al. 2000; Stewart et al. 2007). Leo ten Kate described the problem with a public health approach to genetics services in the following manner:

> Clinical genetics is concerned with individual persons or couples or families who have or fear a health problem. These individuals, couples or families are seen one by one. Public health, on the other hand, is not primarily interested in persons or families who are already aware of a problem, but it focuses on people who may not yet be aware but are at risk of developing a health problem. (2005: 7)

Screening for Down's syndrome provides a striking example. Down's syndrome has been viewed for most of its history as a public health problem, with public (often mandated) prenatal screening aimed at reducing its incidence (Raffle 2001). As Bryant and colleagues (2008) show, only relatively recently have there been efforts to promote reproductive choice rather than test uptake as the preferred measure of public health screening success. While the public health goal is reducing the prevalence of disease, genetic counseling to the parents of a Down's syndrome fetus should ideally be nondirective and conducted in a manner that respects the parents' norms and values. In certain religious communities, this means that selective abortion would not be the preferred option (Raz 2009).

In Israel, public health genetics services appear to be everywhere. The Department of Community Genetics in the Ministry of Health is responsible for a variety of public health genetics services including newborn screening, prenatal diagnosis for women at increased risk for children with Down's syndrome and other genetic diseases, a national program (established in 1980) of carrier screening of adults for genetic diseases such as Tay-Sachs, cystic fibrosis (CF), SMA, and familial dysautonomia, as well as various community-based carrier screening programs targeting particular subpopulations who are at risk for specific genetic diseases (Israeli Department of Community Genetics 2003–2004). Importantly, the title of the major Israeli public health body overseeing genetics services is the Department of "Community Genetics." This is not a standard title. But what does "community genetics" mean in the Israeli context? This question provides a point of departure for the ensuing discussion.

Comparing Israel and other Western countries in terms of public health genetics services can shed light on the interplay of the technological imperative and other "imperatives" – political, social, and personal (Geisler and Heller 1998; Hofmann 2002; McCoyd 2010). The notion of the technological imperative suggests that once genetic technologies are available, countries will inevitably adopt them. Israel is, however, unique in adopting some but not other genetic technologies. In short, public health genetics services provide a window into the unique ways in which the bio-governmentality of health issues has been taking shape in the Israeli setting. Since I cannot cover all genetic engagements in Israel, the focus of this short chapter will be on three major genetic hotspots of public health genomics, namely, genetics services that are organized, administered, and overseen by the state: newborn screening (NBS), the national genetics database, and carrier screening programs.

PUBLIC HEALTH GENETICS SERVICES IN ISRAEL: AN OVERVIEW

A unique combination of factors has turned Israel into a "start-up nation" for innovative genetics services. The socialized medical system and the availability of medical genetics units influence the extensive utilization of genetic services. The Israeli National Health Insurance Law (1995) provides coverage for the national carrier screening program as well as for the more recent community-based carrier screening programs. As we shall see, the religious and ethnic diversity of the population had major implications for the design of screening programs and the use of genetics services under the auspices of the Department of Community Genetics.

In 1964, the first genetic counseling clinic opened in Jerusalem. Today there is in the majority of Israeli hospitals a medical genetics department that includes a genetic counseling clinic and a genetics laboratory. In addition, most health funds have genetic clinics run by medical geneticists that provide genetic consultations. "Outreach" genetic consultations take place in high-risk communities in the northern and southern parts of Israel. Genetic counseling by nonphysicians has been practiced in Israel since the early 1970s, first by graduates of Sarah Lawrence College (United States) who moved to the country and then by graduates from Israel's (currently two) master-level genetic counseling training programs (Sagi and Uhlmann 2013). Genetic counseling and many, but not all genetic tests, are provided free of charge to all residents of Israel as part of its national health insurance.

The initiation in 1971 of a screening program to prevent Tay-Sachs disease among Ashkenazi Jews in the United States (Kaback 2001) led to the establishment of a similar program in Israel under the aegis of the Ministry of Health. The ultra-Orthodox Ashkenazi Jewish community, where selective abortion is banned by many rabbis, has developed and is still operating a special program ("Dor Yeshorim") that prevents the marriage of two carriers (Ekstein and Katzenstein 2001). The ultra-Orthodox carrier screening and matching program is organizationally and financially supported by the State of Israel and served by Israeli genetics labs (Broide et al. 1993). Genetic carrier screening for reproductive choices that was introduced in Israel for Tay-Sachs disease is responsible for its near disappearance among Israeli Jews.

Ever since, national screening has gradually increased in terms of additional diseases and communities. A national carrier screening program for the prevention of β-thalassemia was implemented in Israel for the Arab-Israeli population and some Jewish communities in which the disease is relatively frequent. The National Program for the Detection and Prevention of Birth Defects, established in 1980, covered adult screening of those high-risk populations, newborn screening, and prenatal genetic diagnosis (in the form of amniocentesis offered to women older than thirty-five). Today, the national carrier screening program also includes CF, fragile X syndrome (FXS), and spinal muscular atrophy (SMA). The screening is performed either before or during a pregnancy. It is targeted to couples, usually with the woman tested first and if she is found to be a carrier, her partner is also tested (Zlotogora et al. 2015). The tests are performed either in medical genetic units or in community clinics, and patients with a positive result receive genetic counseling. More extensive prenatal genetic testing is offered with coverage shared between the patient and the supplementary health insurance. Since 2002, targeted carrier screening is also offered free of charge to additional, smaller ethnic communities in which well-established, severe genetic diseases are present with a frequency higher than 1/1000 live births, namely, Arab, Druze, and Bedouin populations who live mostly in villages and have a high rate of consanguinity. Multiple founder mutations have been documented in these various ethnic populations, often down to the level of specific villages or tribes.

The Israeli national genetics database, launched in 2006, provides to genetics professionals information on disorders and mutations according to religious, ethnic, and geographic categories. While in many Western countries, such "barcoding" of ethnicity and religion may be subject to debate or rejection, in Israel, it has been well accepted or at least has not raised any public debate. A few international examples should illustrate the uniqueness of the Israeli situation. Even when carrier screening is being recommended by American medical associations, as in the case of CF screening to Caucasian couples, U.S. governmental bodies avoid using the term "program" in this context and emphasize its voluntary, individual, and "pan-ethnic" nature (Raz 2009). In the Netherlands, initiatives of pre-conception carrier screening for CF and hemoglobinopathies are being promoted, but usually without directly labeling the targeted ethnic communities (such as immigrants from Surinam and the Netherlands Antilles, or from Turkey and Morocco), even though members of such ethnic communities have a higher risk of being carriers (Lakeman et al. 2008, 2009). Furthermore, many of the immigrant or indigenous ethnic communities who are at higher risk for recessive genetic diseases are also characterized by high frequencies of consanguinity; however, education and genetic counseling aimed at such communities are restricted by sensitive politics, for example, in the case of British Pakistanis (Shaw 2008). In the United States and Europe, ethnic identification might be considered an illegitimate part of risk assessment in the physician–patient encounter. In Israel, it is standard practice. Details about ethnicity and religion are routinely used in clinical genetics encounters either for Jews, Arabs, or Druzes without any debate or questions about discrimination or stigmatization either within the medical community or the general public.

The construction of the "Jewish gene pool" by health professionals as especially prone to inherited disorders has boosted "genetic anxiety" (or "responsibility," depending on one's perspective) – creating a collective sense of risk in which the uptake of genetic screening and testing is exceptionally high and seen by many as a moral *duty* (Raz and Schicktanz 2009a, 2009b; Remennick 2006). The duty to test and share the information with your relatives also matches Israel's Genetic Information Law (2000), which, quite uniquely compared to international regulation, prescribes that genetic information could be transmitted to third parties if it is "required for the maintenance of the health of a relative or to improve such person's health, and for the prevention of death, illness or serious disability of such relative, including an unborn relative."

COMPARATIVE PERSPECTIVE ON PUBLIC HEALTH GENETICS SERVICES

Table 11.1 highlights the unique contours of the Israeli public health genetics services by comparing its major practices to those of California. It would be fruitless to compare the entire United States to Israel since the United States is too varied to

TABLE 11.1 *A Comparison of Israel and California in the Context of State-Administered, Public Health Genetics Services*[1]

	Israel	California
Central governmental authority	The Department of Community Genetics in the Ministry of Health	The California Department of Public Health – Genetic Disease Screening Program
Prenatal genetic diagnosis	Women with screening results indicating a high risk for a birth defect are offered follow-up diagnostic services including genetic counseling and amniocentesis, whose uptake is voluntary	Women with screening results indicating a high risk for a birth defect are offered follow-up diagnostic services including genetic counseling and amniocentesis, whose uptake is voluntary
Newborn screening (NBS)	Twelve genetic and metabolic conditions screened	More than eighty genetic, metabolic, and congenital disorders screened
Pan-ethnic carrier screening programs	A national program (established in 1980) of carrier screening of adults for Tay-Sachs, CF, SMA, and familial dysautonomia	N/A
Community-based carrier screening programs	Since 2003, the Department of Community Genetics administers various community-based carrier screening programs targeting particular Arab and Bedouin subpopulations at risk for specific genetic diseases.	N/A
State-administered DNA databases	The Israeli national genetic database, launched in 2006, provides to genetics professionals information on disorders and mutations according to religious, ethnic, and geographic categories.	The California Biobank Program, launched in 2014, provides to researchers anonymous leftover DNA specimens (dried blood spots) from newborn screening.

be a unit of comparison. California was selected for this comparison because both California and Israel are acknowledged hotspots of genetics research where innovative genetics technologies have a short time-to-market. The collective health care

---

[1] Based on data collected from the websites of the Israeli Department of Community Genetics (www.health.gov.il/UnitsOffice/HD/PH/Genetics/Pages/default.aspx), and the California Department of Public Health – Genetic Disease Screening Program (www.cdph.ca.gov/programs/gdsp/pages/default.aspx) last accessed March 2, 2016.

system in Israel is evidently different from California's managed care system; however, this difference also helps to highlight the unique features of the Israeli case. Of note, both California and Israel administer public health prenatal screening programs providing pregnant women with a risk assessment for open neural tube defects, Down's syndrome (trisomy 21), trisomy 18, and Smith-Lemli-Opitz Syndrome (SLOS) through biochemical blood tests and nuchal translucency ultrasound. For women with screening results indicating a high risk for a birth defect, both California and Israel offer follow-up diagnostic services, including genetic counseling and amniocentesis, whose uptake is voluntary. However, this is where the similarities basically end. Both Israel and California also offer newborn screening – but the similarity here is superficial as the range of tests offered varies greatly between the countries. Only Israel has instituted national carrier screening programs (for the entire public as well as for particular religious and ethnic communities). And only Israel has instituted a national genetic database that provides to genetics professionals information on disorders and mutations according to religious, ethnic, and geographic categories. Here the closest Californian equivalent would be the Biobank Program that provides to researchers anonymous leftover DNA specimens (dried blood spots) from newborn screening. However, the latter is used only for research and is free of ethnic and religious denominators, while the former is used for practical genetic counseling that highlights ethnic and religious denominators as health risk predictors. The following analysis focuses on the genetics services that are unique to Israel, further highlighting their interconnectedness.

FROM NEWBORN SCREENING TO CARRIER SCREENING

The original basis of newborn screening (NBS) was the detection of phenylketonuria (PKU) and congenital hypothyroidism (CH). These two conditions were also the basis for the Israeli NBS program, which started in 1964, only a few years after it started in the United States (Cohen et al. 1966). In Europe, Germany expanded its NBS in 2004, but decided to limit screening to eight conditions. The Netherlands added fourteen conditions in 2007. Austria screens for twenty disorders. In the United Kingdom, the National Screening Committee recently recommended that the National Health Service expand the number of screened conditions from five to nine rare genetic conditions. The difference between Israel and California is striking: in 2006, California (as well as many other states) expanded newborn screening to more than fifty conditions, while in Israel, its expansion (using the same technology) was limited to eleven conditions. At the same time, in Israel, health care providers screen prenatally for some of the conditions that are part of newborn screening in California, and community-based programs for carrier screening of adults test for some of the conditions that are part of newborn screening in California. Hemoglobin diseases and cystic fibrosis (CF) are part of NBS in California, but not in Israel, where CF is nationally screened as part of adult carrier diagnosis and thalassemia is screened in community-based programs (Zlotogora and Israeli 2009; Zlotogora and colleagues 2009). Disease incidence, and the cost-effectiveness of new tests, are not the issue – the cost of running additional tests is overall similar. It could be anticipated that, once the new technology was in place, more tests would be added to the existing NBS panel in Israel.

In the United States, patient advocacy organizations lobbied various statehouses to expand NBS (Paul 2008). But Israeli patient organizations that had an active role in promoting prenatal genetic testing (Raz 2004) have been silent in regard to NBS, reflecting a preference for prenatal prevention alongside postnatal care. The North American political sensitivity regarding abortion has hindered the public administration of any genetic screening linked to reproductive decisions. Yet in Israel, abortion is legally constructed since 1977 as a public issue formally regulated by the official medical authorities.[2]

Screening for CF prenatally (as part of adult carrier screening and fetal diagnosis), rather than postnatally in NBS, may be disdained or promoted depending on one's perspective regarding prevention or care. CF is nowadays largely a manageable chronic disease. How should we prioritize the when and how of its screening? Importantly, while bioethicists will consider the various screening systems separately and according to abstract principles, for affected people, all these screening systems become interconnected. A by-product of newborn screening would be the identification of the affected infant's parents as carriers. These carriers are healthy and usually unaware of their carrier status. Being identified as carriers of CF (or another disease), parents will inevitably reconsider their reproductive choices for subsequent pregnancies. Some of these parents will inevitably ask why they had to wait until a CF baby was born. Why not "offer pre-conception carrier testing to parents-to-be that would reduce the frequency of CF in newborns?" (Massie et al. 2007: 722). Indeed, this question has already been positively answered in Israel. Such a question may be regarded as provocative by many as it blurs the boundaries between care and prevention, as well as between old (state-coercive) and new (liberal) eugenics. When the state "offers" genetic testing "to reduce the frequency of CF in newborns," this is blatantly preventive (whereas others would emphasize the importance of those born with CF, which is often a manageable chronic disease). It is also blatantly eugenic, even though the choice is

---

[2] The Israeli penal law concerning the interruption of pregnancy (1977) provides a flexible legal framework. On one hand, it sends out an ideological message delegitimizing "abortion on demand" and prohibiting abortion due to financial distress. On the other hand, it provides elbow room for the hospital committees to accept applications for abortion on the basis of medical reasons (to do with the mother, the fetus, or both) or in cases of underage or unwed mothers, or of adultery, rape, or incest.

presumably individual. Reckless or pioneering? According to an Australian physician, the Israeli approach is much better, since waiting for couples to have a baby with CF before they are identified as carriers denies them choice (Massie et al. 2007). Israel is thus leading the way for countries that are considering a national policy on CF carrier screening, such as Australia. This is an example of how political contests regarding care vs. prevention and eugenics vs. choice are "naturalized" in Israel and effectively compromised.

Even when adult carrier screening is offered, the majority of adults will choose to undergo screening during pregnancy – in Israel, this involves about 60–70 percent of those screened in the national carrier screening program, usually husbands undergoing "stepwise" screening when their wives are pregnant (Joel Zlotogora, personal communication). Carrier testing of the parents during pregnancy is relatively problematic in terms of the time constraints and having fewer options. The practical goal then is to get more people to take the test earlier, before they become actually involved with pregnancy, thus providing them with more reproductive options – in line with the motto of the national Israeli carrier screening program, which is "to know in time" (cited in the Department's instructional film, www.health.gov.il/pages/default.asp?maincat=42&catId=655&PageId=3627). As a result of the Israeli carrier screening program, Tay-Sachs disease has almost disappeared among Jews in Israel. Also in the case of thalassemia, screened for as part of the national program for at-risk populations, a dramatic reduction in the prevalence of the disease has been observed (Zlotogora et al. 2009).

COMMUNITY-BASED SCREENING AND GENETIC DATABASES

Some Israeli ethnic communities are targeted for particular diseases (e.g., Ashkenazi Jews for Tay-Sachs, Arab-Israelis for hemoglobinopathies), while in other cases, particular ethnic communities are excluded from screening (e.g., screening for CF is done in most of the population, excluding Jews from Ethiopia and most of the Bedouin of the Negev; see Zlotogora et al. 2015). This routinization is described in the following manner by the previous director of the Department of Community Genetics:

> Population screening for Tay Sachs disease among Ashkenazi Jews was the first community oriented screening. Thereafter, the community of origin has been routinely used in medical genetics either for Jews, Arabs or Druzes without any debate either within the medical community or the general public. The availability of these data is very important for genetic counselling since it enables clinicians to offer patients more accurate and accessible information and genetic testing as needed. (Zlotogora 2015: 183)

In Israel, such use has been accepted without any public debate whatsoever, and by doing this, political contestation was replaced by an apparent compromise. This may be surprising given that when such distinctions (between Jews and non-Jews, Ashkenazi and Sephardi) are made in the public sphere, they are often emotionally and politically loaded and met with antagonism. For medical purposes, these distinctions have been reinforced by differences existing in the frequency of genetic diseases between communities.

The U.S. cultural sensitivity concerning ethnic profiling, especially in the context of the national trauma of sickle cell screening in the 1970s (Wailoo 2001), has arguably limited community-based carrier screening, for better or worse. The controversies that erupted over sickle cell carrier screening continued to have a negative impact even after this program had disappeared. In the United States, "the notion of a program that targets a specific ethnic group is frowned upon because it would focus on minorities and advocate measures that are expected to be culturally unacceptable" (Bornik and Dowlatabadia 2008: 92). In their critical commentary on Zlotogora (2015), Clayton and Brothers neatly sum up the point:

> Ethnicity, religious affiliation, and location of origin are already imperfect surrogates for genetic diversity and will become even more so with increasing admixture. In addition, targeted screening runs the risk of reifying socially defined categories, while at the same time missing important genetic variation. Ultimately, targeted newborn screening simply became politically unacceptable in the United States, a topic other countries struggle with as well. (2015: 1)

Of note, a community-based program that was later established in the United States in the context of sickle cell disease (SCD) represented a grassroots initiative rather than a federal or state program; and a focus on care and treatment rather than on prevention. This program, entitled "Sickle Cell Sabbath," was established in 1999 to increase awareness about SCD and the importance of blood donations (required for the routine transfusions needed by SCD patients) within the "African American faith community." Church involvement in the program included a five-minute scripted educational session regarding the importance of blood donations for SCD treatment, followed by a blood donor drive hosted by the church. The program more than quadrupled the rate of expected first-time blood donors in relation to the general population (Price et al. 2008).

Ethnic and religious categorization of genetic data underpins, in Israel, not just carrier screening programs, but also genetic databases. A database including the entire Israeli population (available at http://server.goldenhelix.org/israeli/) allows consulting online about genetic disorders in the Israeli population according to ethnicity and religion (Zlotogora et al. 2009). The database includes all the available data about genetic diseases among Jews according to their communities of origin and among Arabs and Druzes according to the localities where they are living. In order to protect the privacy of the patients and ensure anonymity, access to data on diseases according to locality is provided only to Israeli geneticists on the basis of a username and password. This feature allows a list to be obtained of the disorders and their frequencies in each locality. This part of the database includes all the known monogenic disorders among Arabs and Druzes in each locality, as well as molecular data if available. Clinicians working in the localities are encouraged to add to the database as more genetic information is gathered. While reports on the database mention its utility ("in 18 of those localities there were data on 15 or more different diseases," Zlotogora 2015: 183), it is not mentioned whether and how community consent was provided. The national genetic database has to comply with the regulations issued by the Ministry of Health on "the establishment and utilization of genetic samples banks" (2005), which aim to protect the "security" of the samples and to avoid harming a certain public or ethnic community. Particular attention is given to the issue of transferring samples from Israeli collections to abroad, which requires approval from the Supreme Helsinki Committee and must not contain any names of individuals (Israeli Ministry of Health 2005).

Before and in parallel with the national genetic database, other genetic databases were also active in Israel, including commercial databases (the disease-based DNA collection of IDgene Pharmaceuticals), community-owned databases (the Dor Yesharim's repository targeting ultra-Orthodox Ashkenazi Jews), and research databases (the National Laboratory of the Genetics of Israeli Populations at Tel-Aviv University comprising the DNA of several "isolated populations"). In all of these genetic databases, ethnic and religious categories feature prominently and without public criticism (Prainsack 2007). The national genetics database perpetuates this paradigm and amplifies it. From a sociological perspective, the "taken-for-granted" characterization of these ethnic categories as closed genetic entities is intriguing. It reflects the prioritizing of what can be termed as "community exceptionalism." As Kirsh has shown in her study on population genetics in Israel in the 1950s, "Israeli researchers preferred to see the Jewish subject population as closed, unaffected genetically by non-Jewish neighbors" (2003: 646).

Genetic databases are evidently not unique to Israel. What is unique to Israel is its blatant, either reckless or pioneering (depending on one's perspective) highlighting of the ethnic and religious communities with which the DNA is associated. To begin to understand why the Israeli paradigm is so unique, consider the most famous U.S.-based genetic database – the Human Genome Project, completed in 2003 – which drew on the genes of a few individuals to map a universal: human genome, one that does not exist in the body of any specific person. The Human Genome Project was interested in representing humanity in general. When other geneticists reacted by launching the Human Genome Diversity Project (HGDP), which records the genetic profiles of indigenous populations, they were criticized for contributing to racism. Critics claimed that when governments are armed with genetic data linked to certain racial groups, those governments might deny human rights based on those genetic data. In 1993, the World Council of Indigenous Peoples in Guatemala repudiated the HGDP for racism (Marks 2002).

The use of ethnicity and religion in genetic databases and screening programs continues to be a subject of international debate as Western social scientists and liberal bioethicists rail against the racial marking of genetic risks or biomarkers because of possible stigmatizing effects on minority subjects (Juengst 1998; Reardon 2004). These political contests have been largely silenced and naturalized in the Israeli public discourse on genetic databases. But today, more than ever, Israel may become a pioneering model in this context. Racialized genomes or "the molecularization of race" is at the cutting edge of personalized medicine, where race or ethnicity becomes a "barcode" for gauging genetic susceptibilities (Fullwiley 2007). As DNA databases in Iceland and Singapore are competing for commercial value and return-on-investment, the ethnic dimension is becoming highlighted as a merit rather than a liability. Thus, the new Singapore-based Asian DNA database ("biopolis") is marketed as better because while the Icelandic database managed by deCODE Genetics was narrowly focused on a few Caucasian groups, the Singapore database boasts representation of the three major Asian races (Malays, Chinese, and Indians), linking ethnic/racial differences to disease susceptibility, thus anticipating a value-magnifying effect from using the ethnic heuristic to correlate Asian ethnicities to genetic variants and disease development (Ong 2015).

Finally, it should be mentioned that the "community genetics" approach is dynamic and subject to change as admixture increases. Differential screening of Israeli Jews is expected to be replaced by a single test that includes all the mutations ubiquitous in that population since there has been a steady increase in the mixing of Jews of different ethnic origins. Nevertheless, some ethnic communities will probably remain endogamous for a longer time than others, and they will continue to be targeted for specific screening and testing.

CONCLUDING REMARKS

This chapter examined public health genetics services in "bio-Israel" as embedding a script (Bowker and Star 1999) that is the result of political contests and compromises that are forgotten (naturalized) once the technology is implemented but still may exert an important influence on the ongoing implementation of the technology. The cross-cultural comparison enabled the addition of the necessary social component to the technological imperative in health care (McCoyd 2010), suggesting a more nuanced view that technologies embed political, social, and personal decisions (Geisler and Heller 1998; Hofmann 2002; McCoyd 2010). The analysis presented here showed that the technological imperative does not work alone. It is already entangled within social, economic, and political "imperatives." Furthermore, all the genetic hotspots examined could not be understood on their own but in relation to each other, as components of a broader network of relations of production and consumption. For example, to understand why NBS has not expanded in Israel, we need to consider NBS in relation to carrier screening and prenatal and genetic diagnosis; and to understand the expansion of the Israeli national genetic database, we need to locate it in the context of state-administered community-based programs.

"Community genetics" has been highlighted here as a hallmark of Israeli public health genetics services. The community approach in genetics services is part of a broader historical approach that has characterized the development of "community medicine" in Israel, for example, the community-oriented primary care approach Sidney Kark initiated at the Hebrew University-Hadassah School of Public Health and Community Medicine in Jerusalem (Epstein et al. 2002; Kark 1981). Community genetics was a derivative of the community medicine approach and it followed earlier implementations in the 1960s of community control of hemoglobinopathies in nearby Cyprus, for example (Angastiniotis et al. 1986). While the community genetics approach features prominently in the design and implementation of targeted community programs for carrier screening and in the Israeli national DNA database, it also underpins and explains the unique effort in Israel to reach out for, test, and offer medical follow-up to each and every newborn as part of NBS. This is yet another link between the public and the clinical. In California, NBS is formally offered to all newborns, however many of these newborns may not have a health plan that pays for post-testing follow-ups and treatments (Timmermans and Buchbinder 2013).

I described in the introduction the "community approach" as different from the public health approach. However, the Israeli case shows how the two can be complementary. Public health professionals in the United States, too, are recently acknowledging the importance of working out how to respect and involve the community perspectives in genetic research and testing. Writing in the *American Journal of Public Health*, Gollust and colleagues describe this belated realization in the following manner:

> The notion that *community perspectives* should be given special attention in genetics research is the result of research findings within the last decade, in response to research that indicated Ashkenazi Jews have a higher carrier frequency of genes that predispose them to breast and ovarian cancer. ... While *community* can evoke a range of group characteristics, our discussion is focused on the involvement of communities *affected* by genetic conditions. There are fundamental conceptual challenges associated with defining the community, the legitimacy of community representation, and deciding which community voices should be solicited – those who have a given condition, those who have a family history of a given condition, or representatives of the general public (original emphasis). (2005: 96)

This chapter has shown that Israel is both reckless and pioneering – depending on one's perspective. There has been criticism of Israel for its recklessness and for not looking before leaping, for example, in the context of its expanded prenatal panel of genetic tests (Borry et al. 2008). While this criticism is sometimes true, we have also seen how for some countries and in the context of other genetics services, Israel is leading the way – examples discussed are CF population screening in Australia and the ethnic DNA database in Singapore. What started in Israel as part of its community medicine approach is now being increasingly discussed and reconsidered around the world.

Is there one, all-encompassing factor that can explain why did Israeli health professionals develop and embrace these public health genetics services? Despite the temptation to look for parsimonious models (especially in the context of Jewish nationalism), the answer is more complicated. In her excellent series of studies that touch on many of the genetics services discussed here, their policies and regulation, Barbara Prainsack (Prainsack 2006a, 2006b, 2007; Prainsack and Firestine 2006; Prainsack and Hashiloni-Dolev 2008; Prainsack and Siegal 2006) concluded that Israeli genomic policies are underpinned by:

> the existence of a noncontroversy: all narratives, religious and political ones, serve the same goal, maintaining the continuity of the collective body which is in danger. The permissive attitude towards genomics and advanced medical technologies in general in Israel should not be explained by the absence of a moral discourse in this field, but rather by a different discursive framing of risk. (Prainsack 2006a: 244)

Prainsack locates this "different discursive framing of risk" in the context of biopolitics: a collective Jewish-Israeli risk that reflects a continuing demographic and militaristic threat to the Jewish-Israeli nation-state.

The analysis presented here hopefully complicates this picture by showing how Israeli public health genetics services have been shaped by an ongoing pragmatic concern of public health policymakers with religious and ethnic distinctions within Israeli society. While Prainsack (and other scholars) have persuasively focused on the dominant role of the Jewish-Israeli community, the Israeli gene world includes many other ethnic and religious communities. It was the dominant Jewish-Israeli medical establishment that continuously promoted the targeting and servicing of these ethnic and religious communities as being "at risk." This is apparent in the various genetic hotspots described, from the national carrier screening programs to the national DNA database. In addition, the hotspots of newborn screening and prenatal testing – where patient associations replace ethnic communities – demonstrate how the "risk" constructed by and for individuals is embedded in social paradigms of care and prevention. The framing of "genetic risk" is thus being conducted and constructed on several levels, not just in the context of the Jewish–Palestinian conflict. It is by looking at the production of genetics services within relevant political, financial, and professional contexts that we can discern more fully the upstream factors that make them possible, and the downstream dynamics that shape their uses and meanings and make them actionable. In doing so, the distinction between "reckless" and "pioneering" becomes inevitably blurred, for there can be no true pioneering without, arguably, at least some recklessness.

References

Akrich, M. 1992. The Description of Technical Objects, in Bijker, W. and Law, J. (eds.) *Shaping Technology/Building Society: Studies in Sociotechnical Change.* Cambridge, MA: MIT Press, pp. 205–224.

American College of Medical Genetics (ACMG). 2005. Newborn Screening: Toward a Uniform Screening Panel and System. Available at http://mchb.hrsa.gov/screening.

Angastiniotis, M. A., Kyriakidou, S., and Hadjiminas, M. 1986. How Thalassaemia Was Controlled in Cyprus. *World Health Forum* 7: 291–297.

Bowker, G. and Star, S. L. 1999. *Sorting Things Out.* Cambridge: MIT Press.

Bornik, Z. B. and Dowlatabadia, H. 2008. Genomics in Cyprus: Challenging the Social Norms. *Technology in Society* 30(1): 84–93.

Borry, P., Clarke, A., and Dierickx, K. 2008. Carrier Screening: Look before You Leap. Carrier Screening for Type 1 Gaucher Disease: Difficult Questions. *European Journal of Human Genetics* 16(2): 139–140.

Broide, E., Zeigler, M., Eckstein, J., and Bach, G. 1993. Screening for Carriers of Tay-Sachs Disease in the Ultraorthodox Ashkenazi Jewish Community in Israel. *American Journal of Medical Genetics* 47: 21–35.

Bryant, L., Ahmed, S., and Hewison, J. 2008. Conveying Information about Screening, in Rodeck, C. and Whittle, M. (eds.) *Fetal Medicine: Basic Science and Clinical Practice* Edinburgh: Elsevier, pp. 225–234.

Clayton, E. and Brothers, K. B. 2015. State-Offered Ethnically Targeted Reproductive Genetic Testing. *Genetics in Medicine* DOI: 10.1038/gim.2015.74.

Cohen, B. E., Szeinberg, A., Peled, I., Szeinberg, B., Bar-Or, R. 1966. Screening Program for Early Detection of Phenylketonuria in the Newborn in Israel. *Israel Journal of Medical Science* 2(2): 156–164.

Ekstein, J. and Katzenstein, H. 2001. The Dor Yeshorim Story: Community-Based Carrier Screening for Tay-Sachs Disease. *Advances in Genetics* 44: 297–310.

Epstein, L., Gofin, J., Gofin, R., and Neumark, Y. 2002. The Jerusalem Experience: Three Decades of Services, Research, and Training in Community-Oriented Primary Care. *American Journal of Public Health* 92(11): 1717–21.

Fullwiley, D. 2007. The Molecularization of Race: Institutionalizing Racial Difference in Pharmacogenetics Practice. *Science as Culture* 16(1): 1–30.

Geisler, E. and Heller, O. 1998. *Management of Medical Technology: Theory, Practice and Cases.* Berlin: Springer.

Gollust, S. E., Apse, K., Fuller, B. P., Miller, P. S., and Biesecker, B. B. 2005. Community Involvement in Developing Policies for Genetic Testing: Assessing the Interests and Experiences of Individuals Affected by Genetic Conditions. *American Journal of Public Health* 95(1): 35–41.

Hashiloni-Dolev, Y. 2007. *A Life (Un)Worthy of Living: Reproductive Genetics in Israel and Germany.* Berlin: Springer-Kluwer.

Hofmann, B. 2002. Is There a Technological Imperative in Health Care? *International Journal of Technology Assessment in Health Care* 18(3): 675–689.

Israeli Ministry of Health 2005. General Manager's Publication Regarding Instructions of the Supreme Committee on Experiments on Human Beings Regarding the Establishment and Utilization of Genetic Samples Banks, No. 01/05, January 2, 2005 (in Hebrew).

Israeli Ministry of Health. Expecting Birth (Including Screening for Healthy Newborns). Public Health Services (leaflet). May 2009. Jerusalem: The Government's Publication Agency (in Hebrew).

Juengst, E. T. 1998. Groups as Gatekeepers to Genomic Research: Conceptually Confusing, Morally Hazardous, and Practically Useless. *Kennedy Institute of Ethics Journal* 8(2): 183–200.

Kaback, M. M. 2001. Screening and Prevention in Tay-Sachs Disease: Origins, Update, and Impact. *Advanced Genetics* 44: 253–265.

Kark, S. L. 1981. *The Practice of Community-Oriented Primary Care*. New York: Appleton-Century-Crofts.

Khoury, M. I., Burke, W., and Thomson, E. I. 2000. *Genetics and Public Health in the 21st Century*. Oxford: Oxford University Press.

Kirsh, N. 2003. Population Genetics in Israel in the 1950s: The Unconscious Internalization of Ideology. *Isis*, 94: 631–655.

Lakeman, P., Plass, A. M. C., Henneman, L., Bezemer, P. D., Cornel, M. C., and ten Kate, L. P. 2008. Three-Month Follow-Up of Western and Non-Western Participants in a Study on Preconceptional Ancestry-Based Carrier Couple Screening for Cystic Fibrosis and Hemoglobinopathies in the Netherlands. *Genetics in Medicine* 10: 820–830.

Lakeman, P., Plass, A. M. C., Henneman, L., Bezemer, P. D., Cornel, M. C., and ten Kate, L. P. 2009. Preconceptional Ancestry-Based Carrier Couple Screening for Cystic Fibrosis and Haemoglobinopathies: What Determines the Intention to Participate or Not and Actual Participation? *European Journal of Human Genetics* 17(8): 999–1009.

Marks, J. 2002. *What It Means to Be 98% Chimpanzee*. Berkeley: University of California Press.

Massie, J., Forbes, R., duSart, D., Bankier, A., and Delatycki, M. B. 2007. Community-wide Screening for Cystic Fibrosis Carriers Could Replace Newborn Screening for the Diagnosis of Cystic Fibrosis. *Journal of Paediatrics and Child Health* 43(11): 721–723.

McCoyd, J. 2010. Authoritative Knowledge, the Technological Imperative and Women's Responses to Prenatal Diagnostic Technologies. *Culture, Medicine & Psychiatry* 34(4): 590–614.

Ong, A. 2015. Why Singapore Trumps Iceland. *Journal of Cultural Economy*, online first DOI: 10.1080/17530350.2015.1009149.

Paul, D. 2008. Patient Advocacy in Newborn Screening: Continuities and Discontinuities. *American Journal of Medical Genetics*, Part C 148C: 8–14.

Prainsack, B. 2006a. "Natural Forces": The Regulation and Discourse of Genomics and Advanced Medical Technologies in Israel, in Glasner, P., Atkinson, P., and Greenslade, H. (eds.) *New Genetics, New Social Formations*. New York: Routledge, pp. 231–253.

Prainsack, B. 2006b. Negotiating Life: The Regulation of Embryonic Stem Cell Research and Human Cloning in Israel. *Social Studies of Science* 36(2): 173–205.

Prainsack, B. 2007. Research Populations: Biobanks in Israel. *New Genetics and Society* 26(1): 85–103.

Prainsack, B. and Firestine, O. 2006. Science for Survival: Biotechnology Regulation in Israel. *Science and Public Policy* 33(1): 33–46.

Prainsack, B. and Hashiloni-Dolev, Y. 2008. Faith and Nationhood, in Atkinson, P. Glasner, P., and Lock, M. (eds.) *Handbook of Genetics and Society: Mapping the New Genomic Era*. London: Routledge, chapter 28.

Prainsack, B. and Siegal, G. 2006. The Rise of Genetic Couplehood: A Comparative View of Pre-marital Genetic Screening. *Biosocieties* 1: 17–36.

Price, C. L., Johnson, M. T., Lindsay, T., Dalton, D., and DeBaun, M. R. 2008, November 25. The Sickle Cell Sabbath: A Community Program Increases First-Time Blood Donors in the African-American Faith Community. *Transfusion*. http://dx.doi.org/10.1111/j.1537-2995.2008.02009.x.

Raffle, A. E. 2001. Information about Screening: Is It to Achieve High Uptake or to Ensure Informed Choice? *Health Expectations* 4(2): 92–98.

Raz, A. 2004. Important to Test, Important to Support: Attitudes toward Disability Rights and Prenatal Diagnosis among Leaders of Support Groups for Genetic Disorders in Israel. *Social Science and Medicine* 59: 1857–1866.

Raz, A. 2009. *Community Genetics and Genetic Alliances: Eugenics, Carrier Testing, and Networks of Risk*. New York and London: Routledge.

Raz, A. and Schicktanz, S. 2009a. Lay Perceptions of Genetic Testing in Germany and Israel: The Interplay of National Culture and Individual Experience. *New Genetics and Society* 28(4): 401–414.

Raz, A. and Schicktanz, S. 2009b. Diversity and Uniformity in Genetic Responsibility: Moral Attitudes of Patients, Relatives and Lay People in Germany and Israel. *Medicine, Healthcare and Philosophy* 12(4): 433–442.

Reardon, J. 2004. *Race to the Finish: Identity and Governance in an Age of Genomics*. Princeton, NJ: Princeton University Press.

Remennick, L. 2006. The Quest after the Perfect Baby: Why Do Israeli Women Seek Prenatal Genetic Testing? *Sociology of Health and Illness* 28(1): 21–53.

Sagi, M. and Uhlmann, W. R. 2013. Genetic Counseling Services and Training of Genetic Counselors in Israel: An Overview. *Journal of Genetic Counseling* 22: 890–896.

Shaw, A. 2008. *Negotiating Risk: British Pakistani Experiences of Genetics*. Oxford: Berghan.

Stewart, A., Brice, P., Burton, H., Pharao, P., Sanderson, S., and Zimmern, R. 2007. *Genetics, Health Care and Public Policy: An Introduction to Public Health Genetics*. Cambridge: Cambridge University Press.

ten Kate, L. P. 2005. Community Genetics: A Bridge between Clinical Genetics and Public Health *Community Genetics* 8(1): 7–11.

Timmermans, S. and Buchbinder, M. 2013. *Saving Babies? The Consequences of Newborn Genetic Screening*. Chicago, IL: University of Chicago Press.

Timmermans, S. and Shostak, S. 2016. Gene Worlds. *Health* 20(1): 33–48.
Wailoo, K. 2001. *Dying in the City of the Blues: Sickle Cell Anemia and the Politics of Race and Health*. Chapel Hill: University of North Carolina Press.
Zlotogora, J. 2009. Population Programs for the Detection of Couples at Risk for Severe Monogenic Genetic Diseases. *Human Genetics* 126(2): 247–253.
Zlotogora, J. 2014. Genetics and Genomic Medicine in Israel. *Molecular Genetics & Genomic Medicine* 2(2): 85–94.
Zlotogora, J. 2015. Using Community Genetics for Healthy Consanguinity, in Shaw, A. and Raz, A. (eds.) *Cousin Marriages: Between Tradition, Genetic Risk and Cultural Change*. London: Berghahn, pp. 175–185.
Zlotogora, J. R., Carmi, B. L., and Shalev, A. 2009. A Targeted Population Carrier Screening Program for Severe and Frequent Genetic Diseases in Israel. *European Journal of Human Genetics* 17(5): 591–597.
Zlotogora, J. and Israeli, A. 2009. A Comprehensive Screening Program for Cystic Fibrosis. *The Israel Medical Association Journal* 11(9): 555–557.
Zlotogora, J., and Leventhal, A. 2000. Screening for Genetic Disorders among Jews: How Should the Tay-Sachs Screening Be Continued? *Israel Medical Association Journal* 2(9), September: 665–667.
Zlotogora, J. et al. 2015. The Israeli National Population Program of Genetic Carrier Screening for Reproductive Purposes. *Genetics in Medicine* advance online publication. DOI:10.1038/gim.2015.55.

12

The End-of-Life Decision-Making Process in Israel: Bioethics, Law, and the Practice of Doctors

Nili Karako-Eyal and Roy Gilbar

1 INTRODUCTION

Making decisions for patients at the end of life is a delicate process that involves moral values, bioethical principles, personal beliefs, and legal rules. This is particularly true for Israeli society, which comprises various communities with different cultural backgrounds. This heterogenic aspect of Israeli society is reflected in different approaches to life-prolonging treatments that have yielded an ongoing public debate on the subject. A seminal point in this debate was the enactment of the Dying Patient Act (2005) by the Israeli Parliament (The Dying Patient Act 2005).

Despite the ongoing debate on this issue in academic and public discourse and the time that has passed since the enactment of the Act, the impact the Act has on medical practice has scarcely been examined.[1]

In light of this background, and in view of the scope of this book, the purpose of this chapter is to examine how the legal framework set in Israeli law influences the practice of doctors who face – together with dying patients and their relatives – decisions about life-prolonging treatments. To fulfill this purpose, findings from an empirical study conducted among Israeli doctors are presented and analyzed vis-à-vis the relevant legal rules and ethical principles.

The structure of this chapter is as follows. To appreciate the differences and similarities between the law and doctors' practice, we first provide a short review of the current position of Israeli law. We then provide a description of the study, including its findings. This is followed by a discussion about the findings' legal and bioethical implications. We conclude by asking whether Israeli legal and bioethical position in this area tells a unique story.

---

[1] We found two studies that examined how doctors apply the legal rules set in the Act, and two more studies that examined doctors' views about the Act (Shaulov, Lahat-Streichman, and Bentur 2008; Doron 2013).

2 THE LEGAL FRAMEWORK

A Background

Prior to the Act, there were several attempts to regulate end-of-life decision-making through specific legislation, but none of them was successful. In the absence of a specific piece of legislation, this area was regulated by general legal rules that still apply today. For example, hastening the death of a dying patient or assisting her to die are prohibited by the penal code (The Penal Code 1977, Articles 302, 309(4)). Furthermore, a patient has, to a considerable extent, a right to refuse treatment (The Patient Rights Act 1996, Article 15(2)). Finally, the Basic Law: Human Dignity and Liberty (1992), which has gained constitutional status over the years, secures one's right to life, human dignity, and autonomy (Human Dignity and Liberty 1992, Articles 2, 3). Although these general legal rules are relevant to end-of-life decision making, they did not set specific guidelines for doctors who treat dying patients.[2]

Consequently, the task of setting specific rules in this area was left to the courts, which made clear that active euthanasia and physician-assisted suicide are prohibited (CA 506/88 *Shefer v. The State of Israel* 1993). However, the district courts upheld dying patients' explicit requests not to receive artificial ventilation, and to stop it once it has already been started, provided the patient is in the final stage of her terminal illness (Gilbar 2015). The justification for this line of decisions was twofold: the patient's right to autonomy and the perception of withholding and withdrawal of life-prolonging treatment as passive euthanasia or as an omission rather than an act (CA 506/88 *Shefer v. The State of Israel* 1993).

In light of this background, the Ministry of Health appointed a national committee in 2000 to propose a bill that would regulate the treatment of dying patients. The committee, known as the Steinberg Committee, included clergymen (rabbis, kadis), different professionals (e.g., doctors, nurses, social workers), and scholars from various disciplines (law, philosophy) (The Steinberg Committee 2002). Despite the different views held by its members, the aim was to reach a wide agreement on the central issues at hand (Steinberg 2007). This aim was by and large achieved, though several members provided a minority opinion. The Committee's final report was presented to the minister of health in 2002. A governmental bill was then drafted (The Dying Patient Bill 2004) and in 2005, the Act received the assent of the Israeli Parliament (The Steinberg Committee 2002).

The drafters of the Act faced the difficult task of finding a bridge between the proponents of two opposing approaches (The Joint Meeting of the Work, Welfare and Health Committee and the Constitution, Law and Justice Committee on the Issue of Prolonging Life 2004). On one side stood those who supported a liberal position that highlights the dying patient's right to make autonomous end-of-life

---

[2] The Ministry of Health published guidelines for clinicians in 1996 regarding the decision-making process at the end of life (Circular 2/96, Treating the Dying Patient, 1996).

decisions. On the other side stood those who presented a religious-based approach, emphasizing the importance of sanctity of life (Steinberg 2008). Interestingly, doctors' views, though cited in the Committee's report, did not gain substantial attention in the parliamentary discussion. In an effort to receive the approval of supporters of both approaches, the drafters of the Act argued that it reflects a compromise between the values of the liberal tradition and those of Jewish law (The Steinberg Committee 2002).

B *The Dying Patient Act (2005)*

The Act determines three principles that guide its interpretation and implementation. First, in regulating the treatment of dying patients, a balance should be struck between sanctity of life, patient autonomy, and quality of life. Second, the Act is based on democratic and Jewish religious values, as well as on fundamental principles of morality, ethics, and religion. Third, the patient's medical condition, her wishes, and degree of suffering are the only considerations that should guide the provision of treatment to the dying patient (The Dying Patient Act 2008, Articles 1 and 2).

The Act prescribes a detailed decision-making process. First, the patient has to be diagnosed as a dying patient or as a dying patient in the final stage (The Dying Patient Act 2008, Articles 3 and 8).[3] Second, the patient's mental capacity to make decisions has to be determined (The Dying Patient Act 2008, Articles 3 and 6). Third, the patient should be notified that she is defined as a dying patient.[4] Fourth, the doctor has to find out what the patient's preferences are regarding life-prolonging treatment (The Dying Patient Act 2008, Articles 5, 13–15). This can be achieved by asking the patient about her preferences. If the patient has already lost her mental capacity to make decisions, her preferences can be ascertained by advance directives or by a relative with a power-of-attorney. If none exists, the doctor can make a decision after obtaining a declaration from a close relative about the wishes the patient expressed before losing her mental capacity (The Dying Patient Act 2008, Article 5). Last, once the patient's wishes are known, treatment decisions can be made, subject to the limitations set in the Act.

When making decisions about treatment, the Act determines that a patient's refusal to life-prolonging treatments should be respected under certain conditions (The Dying Patient Act 2008, Articles 15(a) and 16(a)). If the patient has mental capacity to make decisions, reasonable efforts should be made to persuade her to

---

[3] According to Articles 3 and 8, a patient is dying if she suffers from a terminal illness and is expected to die within six months even when medical treatment is provided to her. A dying patient in the *final stage* is defined as a patient with a life expectancy of less than two weeks.

[4] This is not set explicitly in the Act. It derives from Articles 4, 5, 12, and 41. The Ministry of Health's guidelines impose on doctors a duty to inform the patient explicitly that she is dying (Circular 7/08 Applying the Dying Patient Act 2008, section D 1.1.5).

receive oxygen, nutrition, and fluids, as well as routine treatments for her background diseases and palliative care, but she should not be coerced to receive these treatments (The Dying Patient Act 2008, 15 (b)). If the patient has already lost her mental capacity to make decisions, withholding the provision of nutrition, fluids, routine treatments, and palliative care is not permitted, regardless of her wishes (The Dying Patient Act 2008, Article 16(b)).[5]

Furthermore, the Act declares that while withholding life-prolonging treatments is generally permitted, deliberate killing, assisted suicide, and any other action that intentionally and actively shortens the patient's life are prohibited, even if it is in accordance with the patient's will or motivated by mercy and compassion (The Dying Patient Act 2008, Articles 19–20).

In addition, stopping continuous medical treatment that is likely to prolong life (e.g., disconnecting a dying patient from a ventilator) is prohibited, regardless of the patient's wishes. However, if a continuous medical treatment was unintentionally or "not unlawfully" stopped (e.g., due to a power failure), it is lawful to avoid its renewal (The Dying Patient Act 2008, Articles 3, 21). Finally, the Act permits to discontinue a cyclic life-prolonging treatment (such as radiotherapy, chemotherapy, or dialysis) if the patient so wishes. Interestingly, this legal rule also applies to treatments that are essentially continuous, such as ventilation, but were planned in advance, through technological means, as a cyclic treatment. This would be the case, for example, if a timer is installed on a ventilator and is programmed to stop intermittently.[6]

The legal rule that distinguishes between continuous and cyclic treatments is based on a distinction between withholding and withdrawal of treatment. This rule is considered the most significant change the Act produces. Recall that the district courts in cases brought to them before the Act came into force approved dying patients' requests for withdrawal of ventilation. Note also that there was no legal rule or a governmental policy prior to the Act that prohibited withdrawal of ventilation. Arguably, to obtain the support of the religious parties in the Israeli Parliament, it was necessary to create this distinction. We will address this issue further.

C The Critique

Since it came into force, the Act has been subject to academic criticism. Among the various critiques, it is worth mentioning the argument that bioethically the Act tilts heavily toward Jewish values at the expense of liberal principles, as it provides precedence to the halachic principle of sanctity of life over the right of dying patients to autonomy (Shapira 2006; Shalev 2009). Implicitly, scholars expressed discomfort with a situation where a minority in a democratic society imposes its values on the majority. Furthermore, it was also argued that the Act creates uncertainty about the

---

[5] Different rules apply to dying patients in the final stage. See Article 17.
[6] These timers are, however, not yet in use.

rights of patients with terminal illnesses, such as Alzheimer's disease, who do not meet the definition of a dying patient in the Act (Doron and Shalev 2011). Since the Act does not apply to patients with terminal illnesses who have more than six months to live, the Act was criticized for denying these patients their right to refuse life-prolonging treatments (Edelstein 2010; Ticho 2008).

A different criticism related to the distinction between withholding and withdrawing of life-prolonging treatment. It was argued that such a distinction cannot be morally justified (Asiag 2008; Gilbar 2015). In addition, it was argued that the prohibition on withdrawal of continuous life-prolonging treatment regardless of the patient's wish is an infringement of her right to autonomy (Shapira 2006). This was followed by the argument that the Act contradicts past decisions of the district courts that had approved dying patients' requests to be disconnected from ventilators (Asiag 2008; Gilbar 2015). Finally, critics expressed a concern that a prohibition on withdrawal of continuous life-prolonging treatment might cause patients to refuse desirable treatments, knowing that its withdrawal later on would be impossible (Ticho 2008; Asiag 2008).

Since its enactment, the Act has been addressed by the courts on three occasions. All cases involved patients who did not meet the definition of a dying patient set in the Act. In two cases, the patients' requests were declined partly because the patients did not meet the definition of a dying patient set by the Act (Case number 28450/09 (Rishon L'ezion) *General Attorney v. B.V.V* 2009; Case number 24638–02-14 (Jerusalem) *Shaare Zedek Medical Center v. A.H.* 2014). The third case was significant. Although it addresses the same question of what rules apply when a patient is not defined as a dying patient by the Act, it nevertheless resulted in a different outcome. In the *John Doe* case, a competent patient with amyotrophic lateral sclerosis (ALS) wished to be disconnected from a ventilator (Case number 16813–11-14 *John Doe v. Attorney General of Israel* 2014). Medical opinions indicated that if given appropriate treatment, the patient might continue living for many years. Therefore, he did not meet the definition of a dying patient set in the Act. That being the case, the court had to decide which rules applied to the patient: the legal prohibition on withdrawal of ventilation set in the Act, or past district courts decisions that had approved dying patients' requests to be disconnected from a ventilator. Eventually, the court did not address this issue, due to the declaration given by the attorney general (A-G). The A-G stated that based on the "spirit of the Act" and the special circumstances of the case, a gradual reduction of the level of oxygen the ventilator produces to the level of oxygen in the open air is legally permitted. The A-G explained that this solution strikes an appropriate balance between the prohibition on withdrawal of ventilation and the right to autonomy. Moreover, it appears that the A-G believed that a gradual reduction of the level of oxygen the ventilator produces is different from withdrawing life-prolonging treatment, and thus can be legally permitted. Without directly addressing the complex questions the patient's petition raised, the judge fully accepted the A-G's position and adopted the suggested solution. It follows that the court approved the use of a procedure that, in fact, enables doctors to stop a continuous life-prolonging treatment when the patient is dying, regardless of the legal prohibition.

3 THE STUDY: AIMS AND METHODS

The central aim of the study was to examine whether the rules set by the Act are applied by doctors who provide daily treatment to dying patients. The study focuses on the following questions: (1) Does the different stages set in the Act regarding the decision-making process and the provision of treatment accord with the daily practice of doctors? (2) How do doctors determine in practice the wishes of their patients? (3) What is the level of influence doctors and relatives have on the decision-making process? (4) What do doctors think about central moral issues such as withholding and withdrawal of life-prolonging treatment? Answers to these questions would be used as the grounds for examining the relationships between practice and law in Israel in this area.

The study was based on qualitative and quantitative methods. The quantitative part of the study was based on a questionnaire developed for this study. Some questions were adopted from the questionnaire developed by Lavat-Streichman (2012) particularly regarding the doctors' methods of conduct. The questionnaire consists of several parts. The first includes demographic data. The second addresses the methods of conduct employed by doctors regarding, for example, the conversations they have with the patient and her family. In the third part, the participants were asked about their views regarding central principles in this context (i.e., patient autonomy, sanctity of life). The qualitative part of the study was based on in-depth semi-structured interviews conducted with twenty-two doctors, who were asked about the decision-making process they conduct with dying patients and their relatives. The interviews were based on an interview guide developed for the study.

The study was conducted in four different hospitals across Israel. The participants came from various specialties and professional ranks. They treated dying patients on a daily basis. Data were collected once an institutional ethics approval for the study was granted. Data analysis included several stages and was based on a framework approach that suits a study whose aims are selected in advance, and its research questions are specific and relatively narrow (Ritchie and Spencer 2009; Srivastava and Thomson 2009).

4 THE FINDINGS

The findings reported in this part refer to three issues: communication with the patient, family involvement in the decision-making process, and the provision of life-prolonging treatment.

A Demographic Background

The quantitative part of the study was based on a convenience sample of 109 participants, of which 64% were males and 36% were females. Their age ranged from 26 to 69. Most of the participants were Jews (65%), define themselves as secular (76%), and were born in Israel (64%). Most of the participants work in internal medicine wards (49%), and most of the dying patients they treat suffer from cancer (39%), Alzheimer's disease/dementia (26%), or heart diseases (16%). The study participants treated, on average, nine dying patients in the three months prior the study. In the qualitative part, the study included interviews with 22 doctors from different specialties and ranks. Twelve participants were males and 10 were females.

B Communication with the Dying Patient

According to the Act, the doctor has to tell the patient that she is defined as a dying patient, namely, that she has less than six months to live. Yet the interviews reveal that many doctors do not tell the patient explicitly that she has six months or less to live. This was echoed, for example, in the interview with K, a female hematologist: "Interviewer: Do you tell them . . . ? K: That they have only six months [to live]? No, I don't tell them that. Interviewer: Does somebody in the hospital tell them? Perhaps the social worker? K: No, she does not say six months." Furthermore, participants stated that they do not initiate a conversation about the patient's prognosis. F, a female oncologist, stated: "I usually do not talk about prognosis if they do not ask me. . . . I do not impose this information on them, 'you have this and that.'"

One of the reasons for the doctors' reluctance to inform patients that they are dying relates to the professional conviction that the doctors' role is to heal and not to manage death. For example, F, a female oncologist, stated that "the atmosphere in the health care system is not one which discusses death." Another reason is the emotional difficulty involved in telling patients they are dying. P, a female specialist in internal medicine, stated: "I won't lie to you, I am a bit afraid of having these conversations, it is not easy for me at all." Yet another reason relates to the doctors' belief in the bliss of ignorance. K, a female hematologist, stated: "My patients arrive with a sense of optimism. We bring optimism with us. I would not give [a patient] a proposal of how to die because it contradicts the entire job I do." This belief led doctors to state that "most people do not want to know that they are dying" (A, a female specialist in internal medicine). Another clinician, U, a male cardiologist, explained that patients deny the severity of their condition.

However, the interviews also reveal that the doctors try to raise patients' awareness about their prognosis. One of the methods used is asking patients what they know about their illness. This method is employed by T, a female oncologist: "I do not tell the patient bluntly, 'listen, you are going to die,' [but] I try to use open questions [like] 'what do you know about your illness,' 'what did they tell you,' [and] 'what do you think?'" Another method is informing the patient or the relatives implicitly that the prognosis is poor. F, a female oncologist, tells patients that "we exhausted all conventional treatment options." However, as L, a male oncologist, admits, there is no guarantee that the patient understands this implicit information: "there are situations when I tell them that I do not have a standard option at this stage. There is an option of stopping treatment and focusing on palliative care." Interviewer: "And do they know what it means?" L: "I am not sure; I do not know. Some do, some don't."

Moving on, according to the Act, the next stage in the decision-making process is to elicit the patient's preferences regarding life-prolonging treatment. The study's quantitative findings reveal that 32% of the doctors did not conduct conversations with the dying patient about her wishes in the three months prior the study. In addition, 46% conducted this kind of conversation a few times in this period. Only 18% conducted such a conversation in a high number of cases.

Similarly, in the qualitative part of the study, doctors stated that in their practice there are hardly any talks with patients about their preferences. D, a female cardiologist, stated: "I do not see here talks with patients about their death. I do not see it, do not see it here." P, a female specialist in internal medicine stated: "We do not ask the patient exactly ... that we think that it is time to make decisions and what does he think about his end of life."

On the other hand, there are doctors who reported that they have conversations about life-prolonging treatment with their patients, with whom they have close relationships. T, a female oncologist who works in the community and in a hospital, emphasized that her work in the community enables her to talk with her patients about their wishes at the end of life: "Since the relationship is closer, then from the start, when I talk to a patient, and it can be in the first meeting, I ask what the patient would want at the end of life." Moreover, there are hospital wards where the ongoing relationship between the doctor and the patient enables them to talk about end-of-life decisions. H, a male neurologist, stated: "There are veteran patients, and you know them ... and this subject is discussed [with them] all the time."

C The Relationships with the Family

Notably, the Act does not provide relatives an independent role. If the patient has mental capacity to make decisions, the decisions should be made by the doctor and the patient alone. When the patient has already lost her mental capacity and not left advance directives or nominated a relative with a power-of-attorney, the doctor has the authority to make decisions about life-prolonging treatment provided she receives a statement from a close relative about the patient's expressed wishes.

In practice, however, the picture is more complex. The study's quantitative findings reveal that 30% of the participants had a conversation with relatives about the preferences of the dying patient regarding life-prolonging treatment in all or most cases they had in the three months prior the study. In addition, 56% of the participants conducted these conversations a few times in this period. Only 13% did not conduct such a conversation at all. Furthermore, 40% of the doctors stated that they ask the relatives about *their* preferences regarding the provision of life-prolonging treatment in all or most of the cases they had three months prior to the study. In addition, 48% conducted such a conversation a few times. Only 12% of the participants had not conducted such a conversation in the three months prior to the study. These questions were not limited to patients who have no mental capacity to make decisions.

These findings, which suggest that relatives have a dominate role in making end-of-life decisions, accord with the qualitative interviews. First, when the patient has the mental capacity to make decisions, the doctors are aware that in most cases, the patients do not make decisions on their own and that their preferences are influenced by relatives' views. M, a female specialist in internal medicine, stated: "If the patient is lucid, the patient decides on his own. [But], it is [never] on his own. The patient usually consults his family." She added that as far as decision-making goes, "there are patients who talk to their family, asking them [what to do]." Furthermore, there are cases where the patient delegates the authority to make a decision to a relative. L, a male oncologist, stated: "[The patient] sits in front of me and says, 'my wife will make the decisions.' His wife accepts this. I do not see any reason to intervene in this dynamic."

Second, when the patient's physical and mental capacity is diminished or nonexistent, the involvement of the relatives in the decisions about life-prolonging treatment becomes substantial. A, a female specialist in internal medicine, states: "Usually, the patients ... even if they are lucid, they do not always have the resilience. They do not have the strength to deal with [decisions], so they direct me to the family – 'my son will come; talk to him.'" Similarly, H, a male neurologist, addressed a situation where the patient has already lost her mental capacity: "The [patient] is unconscious, and you need to resuscitate him and leave him unconscious, so it is only the family, so you are interested in knowing what the [patient] thought, and what the family thinks. This is not written in any book. You know that actually, according to the law, the family has nothing, but ... here [in this ward] we listen to the family's view. So, if there is a family who wants, if the [patient] is in coma and is going to die and the family says 'treat him,' we treat him."

H's statement indicates that the family is influential not only throughout the decision-making process, where the patient's condition is assessed, treatment options are considered, and information between the parties is communicated, but it is also very influential where a decision is actually made. This is echoed, for example, in the statement provided by A, a female specialist in internal medicine, who reported that she gives independent weight to relatives' views, and follows their wishes when a decision has to be made, unless there is "a real strong opposition" from the patient.

Yet, a different approach was presented by other doctors who acknowledged the involvement of the family, but thought that its place in the decision-making process should be limited when the dying patient is lucid. For example, V, a male cardiologist, who supports the involvement of the family in the decision-making process, believes that the patient's wishes should be the determining factor: "I work for the benefit of the patient, and not for the family's benefit. The patient came to me, and the relation between us is between me and him."

The findings from the interviews about the dominant role of the family receive support from the quantitative findings. It was found that 62% of the participants agreed that when the dying patient cannot express her wishes, the relatives, who present a united front, are the ones who should decide whether to provide life-prolonging treatments. In addition, 70% agreed that the view of the patient's family should be preferred to the principle of sanctity of life. This suggests that if the family prefers that treatment would be withheld or withdrawn, its wishes should be followed.

D Provision of Life-Prolonging Treatment

The Act recognizes the dying patient's right not to receive life-prolonging treatment, provided her wishes can be clearly determined by the doctor. Accordingly, the Act allows doctors to withhold life-prolonging treatment such as artificial ventilation, if this is the patient's wish. However, it prohibits doctors from stopping a life-prolonging treatment that continuously keeps the patient alive regardless of the patient's request. This was a central change in the Israeli legal position.

Examining the doctors' views suggests that they express a more liberal approach than the Act. Generally, 85% of the doctors agreed that a dying patient has the right, in any situation, to decide whether to receive life-prolonging treatment. Sixty-two percent fully agreed with this statement and an additional 23% slightly agreed with it. These findings accord with the doctors' attitudes toward the tension between patient autonomy and sanctity of life. Seventy-eight percent of the participants agreed with the statement that the wishes of the dying patient should supersede the principle of sanctity of life. Similarly, 74% of the doctors did not agree with the statement that the principle of sanctity of life should supersede the principle of respecting the wishes of the dying patient. More specifically, most of the participants were of the view that the wishes of the dying patient to stop ventilation should be respected: 57% fully agreed with this view, and an additional 15% slightly agreed with it. Only 28% disagreed.

These findings are interesting because the participants in the qualitative part of the study distinguished between withholding of ventilation and its withdrawal. A, a female specialist in internal medicine, said: "From my perspective ... I cannot do something which intentionally and unequivocally ends [the patient's] life." When asked whether she perceives disconnecting the patient from the ventilator as an act and a DNR order as an omission, A agreed and said: "It may seem like fine lines with no real difference but at least in my view ... I do something which is really active. I take out the tube and he dies because he cannot breathe on his own. I have not yet crossed this line." F, a female oncologist, echoed this, stating that there is a difference between not connecting a patient to a ventilator and disconnecting her from it, explaining that the latter is "active" and "similar to killing someone." This was echoed in the quantitative findings. Sixty-five percent of the participants disagreed with the statement that there is no difference between connecting a dying patient to a ventilator and disconnecting her from it.

Yet, despite this distinction, the interviews indicate that the participants preferred not to have the legal prohibition on withdrawal of continuous life-prolonging treatment. O, a female intern in an oncology department, said that "I think that I would have wanted the option of disconnecting patients." S, a male nephrologist, commented that "I would have preferred that this prohibition would not exist." The reasons for this preference are doctors' wishes to respect patients' autonomous decisions and the knowledge that being connected to a ventilator is painful. This preference relates to situations when the patient was connected to a ventilator contrary to her wishes (usually because the doctor could not ascertain the patient's wishes when facing an emergency situation that required a quick decision). It also addresses situations where patients whose requests to receive ventilation were respected, later on expressed a wish to be disconnected from it (e.g., ALS patients).

Regardless of their personal preferences, the doctors admitted that they provide futile life-prolonging treatments, such as artificial ventilation, to dying patients in the final stage. In the quantitative part of the study, 49% stated that they provide a futile treatment to patients in a low number of cases, and 25% stated that they provide such a treatment in a high number of cases. In addition, 49% stated that they provided treatment they would not want to receive had they been in the same situation in a low number of cases, whereas 26% stated that they provided such a treatment in a high number of cases.

These findings are supported by the results from the qualitative part of the study. For example, C, a male nephrologist, commented: "I think it happens every day in Israel. Interviewer: That they connect [a patient to a ventilator] without a purpose? C: I do not like the words 'without a purpose.' Interviewer: That [the treatment] is futile? C: Yes, that it is futile." A central reason that explains the provision of futile treatment in this area is the family's request. O, a female intern in an oncology center, admitted that "ultimately, if there is a situation where [the family] insists on ventilation, the patient would receive ventilation." L, a male oncologist, added that "there were cases where we administered artificial ventilation to the patient due to the family's pressure. There were such cases."

5 DISCUSSION

The study reveals gaps between the legal framework created by the Act and the practice of doctors in three areas: doctor–patient communication, family involvement, and the provision of life-prolonging treatment.

A Doctor–Patient Communication

From a bioethical perspective, Israeli law and doctors adopt different approaches. This is shown in the weight given to the central bioethical principles of autonomy, non-maleficence, and beneficence and in the perception of patient autonomy that Israeli law and doctors adopt.

As for the weight given to central bioethical principles, the Act – subject to its prohibition on withdrawal of continuous life-prolonging treatment – emphasizes the importance of patient autonomy. The decision of whether to provide treatment depends ultimately on the patient's wishes, whether she expresses it when a decision has to be made, or in the past, before she lost her mental capacity. Although the principles of non-maleficence (not to cause the patient harm) and beneficence (to benefit the patient) appear in the Act, they are not determining factors. For example, the Act provides the patient the authority to determine the level of suffering she is willing to tolerate.

Alternatively, the doctors highlight non-maleficence and beneficence as dominant principles, believing, for example, that informing the patient that she is dying may upset her and cause more harm than good. Furthermore, the doctors' belief that delivering distressful news to the dying patient may steal the sense of hope she has suggests that beneficence is high on the doctors' agenda. Arguably, this, as indicated in the findings, leads doctors to act paternalistically, by not telling the patient she is dying, or by not telling the family that there is an option of connecting the patient to a ventilator.

As for the particular perception of patient autonomy, the doctors' belief that the autonomy of the dying patient should be respected accords with the position reflected in the Act. However, the study indicates that there are differences between the law and doctors' practice concerning the need to find out the patient's preferences. The law requires the doctors to find out the patient's preferences about end-of-life treatment, but many doctors refrain from doing so. From a bioethical perspective, while the Act reflects a liberal approach that secures the patient's independence and her right to determine how she leads the last period of her life, some doctors, in light of their emotional difficulties, may act paternalistically and provide treatments not knowing exactly what the patient really wants. However, as the findings about family involvement show, the doctors do not act extremely paternalistically, namely, they do not make the decisions alone, but they conduct the process of communication and decision making with the patient's family whether the patient is lucid and can legally make decisions or not. As the analysis that follows shows, the doctors thus adopt a relational approach to autonomy, perceiving the patient and her autonomy in a context of social relationships.

Moreover, different approaches arise regarding the weight given to disclosure of information as a component of autonomy. First, the Act requires doctors to inform patients that they are dying, but in practice they refrain from explicitly doing so.

Second, the Act perceives disclosure of information to patients as an essential component of autonomy. However, the doctors reflect a different approach that recognizes both a general interest of the patient in not receiving the full picture, and also, more specifically, an interest in not having *distressful* information. Although the Act allows doctors to refrain from communicating information which may cause harm to patients,[7] the difference between the Act and medical practice, from a bioethical perspective, is as follows: on one hand, the doctors' general assumption and default position is that telling patients that they are dying probably causes more (psychological) harm than good, whereas the Act presumes, on the other hand, that the patients would be benefited if informed. In addition, whereas the Act allows doctors not to inform patients if it can cause serious harm to them, the findings suggest that doctors refrain from doing so because they do not want to upset the patients. This shows that, for doctors, the bar that morally justifies nondisclosure is lower than the one set in the Act.

Another difference between the bioethical approach to autonomy adopted by the Act and the one held by the study's doctors relates to the patient's general right to control the flow of information she chooses to receive. Our analysis reveals that while Israeli legislator and courts adhere to wide disclosure, particularly regarding the risks involved in a proposed treatment, doctors acknowledge a patient's interest in not receiving the full picture.

This issue of the scope of disclosure is discussed in the bioethical literature. There are bioethicists from various streams of thought who doubt whether the capacity to exercise autonomy indeed requires a comprehensive disclosure of information (Walker 2013). They argue that to exercise autonomy, the patient's particular preferences regarding the scope of information communicated to her should be respected, so if she wishes to avoid a particular piece of information and not to receive all type of information available to her, her wish should be respected. This leads to the contention that what is essential is not the information per se, but rather the ability to control its flow. Thus, the patient is autonomous if she controls the amount of available information communicated to her and understand it (Dodds 2000; Maclean 2009).

This bioethical approach reflects the views and practice of doctors in our study. They perceive the patient as an autonomous individual whose interest in not receiving all types of information available to her should be recognized. Although it is possible to argue that Israeli law respects a patient's right not to know, such a right is not explicitly recognized in the Act or in other pieces of legislation in Israeli

---

[7] Article 41 of the Act states that once the doctor determines that the patient is defined as a dying patient and is legally competent to make decisions, she must inform him that he can draft advance directives or nominate someone as a power-of-attorney. However, Article 41 incorporates Article 13(d) of the Patient Rights Act (1996), which allows the doctor to obtain the approval of an institutional ethics committee and refrain from communicating information that may cause the patient serious physical or psychological harm.

medical law. Thus, while recognizing the patient's right not to know generally fits with her right to autonomy, the problem with the doctors' view is that they assume that generally patients prefer not to receive distressful information, without specifically asking them whether this is indeed the case. Thus, it seems that the patient's right to decide the amount of information delivered to her is not recognized either by the Act or by the doctors.

B Family Involvement

The discussion about autonomy leads to another area where a gap between law and practice is detected. This concerns family involvement. Although the Act does not provide the patient's relatives an independent formal status in the decision-making process when the patient has the mental capacity to make decisions, the findings clearly indicate that not only do doctors believe that the family should be involved, they involve the family in practice. In addition, although according to the Act the family has an instrumental role in the decision-making process when the patient has already lost her mental capacity in identifying the patient's wishes, in practice many doctors give the relatives the final say.

From a bioethical perspective, the reason for these gaps lies in different approaches to autonomy. The Act sends the message that autonomy is an individualistic conception. According to the Act, when a dying patient has mental capacity to make decisions, she should make decisions about life-prolonging treatments on her own, with the doctors' help. The relatives have no legal status. In finding out what she wants, legally, the doctors have to direct their attention to the patient, as if no relative accompanies the patient in the various junctions she meets toward her end of life.

However, the doctors expressed a relational approach to autonomy. This approach has been gaining influence in the bioethical literature (Mackenzie and Stoljar 2000). It highlights the positive contribution of the individual's close relationships to the decisions she makes and executes recently (Herring 2013). Feminist and communitarian scholars argue that the patient's relatives and close friends nurture her capacity to make independent decisions recently (Nedelsky 1989). They contend that, ultimately, making decisions is a collaborative project. Furthermore, they claim that since the patient's relatives influence the decisions she makes and are influenced by them, their interests should be taken into account (Donchin 2000).

Undoubtedly, the doctors in the study adopted a relational approach to autonomy. Not only did they consider the views and interests of the relatives, and involve them in the decision-making process, in some situations, they provided the relatives the final say. Moreover, the different approaches to relational autonomy that one can find within the scholarly discourse can also be found in the attitudes and conduct of the doctors in the study. Thus, in the bioethical literature, there are scholars who provide the relatives an independent voice in the decision-making process (Hardwig

2000), while others perceive the involvement of the family as a source of empowerment for the patient but give her the final say in the decision (Lindemann-Nelson 1995). Last, there are those who acknowledge the negative aspects of family involvement especially when the relationships are inherently dominated by the relatives, but they nevertheless promote a relational approach subject to minimal conditions, arguing that distancing the family from the patient leads to loss of the patient's identity (Bell 1993).

Similarly, the study shows that doctors hold different conceptions of relational autonomy. Some doctors perceive the patient in a social context, acknowledging the fact that she consults her relatives before making decisions, but hold the view that the final say belongs to her. Others provide the family an independent and dominant status not only in the decision-making process, but also when the decision is actually made regardless of whether the patient has lost her mental capacity or not.

C Provision of Life-Prolonging Treatment

A third area where gaps between law and practice are detected relates to the provision of life-prolonging treatment, or more specifically to withdrawal of a continuous treatment that keeps the dying patient alive. In this context, the Act prohibits withdrawal of continuous life-prolonging treatment. The doctors, in contrast, present a liberal approach and believe that in principle the right of the patient to be disconnected from a ventilator should be respected.

Yet the doctors' view is not one-dimensional. They distinguish between withholding of treatment that they see as morally acceptable and its withdrawal, which, in their eyes, is not. Some also admit that they never switched off ventilators and have no intention of doing so in the future. It follows that when it comes to actual conduct, doctors follow the Act. At the same time, doctors prefer that the legal prohibition on withdrawal of ventilation would be abolished because it restricts their practice, thus challenging the prohibition set in the Act.

The doctors also admit that at times – due to families' requests – they provide futile treatment such as ventilation to a dying patient in the final stage. When the patient is already connected to a ventilator, this practice corresponds with the legal prohibition on withdrawal of treatment. However, when the patient has not yet been connected to a ventilator, this practice stands in contrast with the legal rule that a patient's request not to be connected to a ventilator should be respected.

From a bioethical perspective, the doctors' views and practice reflect an approach that highlights respect for the right to self-determination, non-maleficence, and a relational approach to autonomy. As for the right to self-determination, the doctors' preference of abolishing the prohibition on withdrawal of ventilation reflects a support of the patient's right to make her own decisions. Yet their emotional difficulties in stopping ventilation because it results in the patient's death reflect a commitment to non-maleficence and to the obligation of not causing harm to the patient. Finally, the provision of futile treatment to patients following families' requests suggests that the doctors adopt a relational approach to autonomy.

Furthermore, in our view, the views and conduct of doctors, particularly in the context of withdrawal of ventilation, reflect the inherent tension in Israeli society between the religious-based approach, which gives precedence to sanctity of life, and the liberal approach, which gives precedence to patient autonomy. As noted earlier, the Act, which allows withholding of continuous life-prolonging treatment but prohibits its withdrawal, was a result of a compromise reached in Parliament between the religious camp, who believes that life-prolonging treatment should not be stopped once it has been initiated, and the liberal camp, who believes that patients' right to make end-of-life decisions should not be limited.

Interestingly, the Steinberg Committee employed the views of doctors to justify the prohibition on continuous life-prolonging treatment it proposed. The report stated that doctors distinguish between withholding and withdrawal of treatment and find it emotionally and professionally more difficult to stop ventilation than to withhold it. The report added that from a professional perspective, doctors' role is to save lives and therefore physically withdrawing life-prolonging treatment contradicts their professional ethics (The Steinberg Committee 2002).

Our findings accord with these statements of the Committee's report. However, our findings present a more nuanced picture than the one stated in the report. Indeed, the doctors distinguish between withholding and withdrawal of treatment, but, essentially, they support the patient's right not only to make autonomous decisions generally, but also to stop a continuous life-prolonging treatment that has already been started particularly. Thus, the Committee's contention that the legal prohibition on withdrawal of ventilation accords with doctors' views and therefore justified is not – to say the least – accurate. This, in our view, should lead policy- and lawmakers to reconsider the prohibition on withdrawal of treatment.

6 CONCLUSIONS

This chapter shows that there are differences between the legal framework that regulates end-of-life decision making in Israel and the views and conduct of doctors in practice. The findings from our study show that the differences between law and practice relate to different approaches to bioethical principles such as autonomy, sanctity of life, and non-maleficence. It seems to us that the actual views and conduct of doctors in this area have so far not received proper consideration in the legislative process. Finally, the lesson to be learned from this study is that the law, with the particular bioethical view it adopts, operates in a social context and consequently has only limited influence on the medical practice it aims to regulate. Lawmakers have to consider this and take into account the moral views and practices of those who are involved in the decision-making process if they want to create an effective and workable legal framework in a diverse society.

References

Asiag, E. (2008). Observing the Prohibition on Withdrawal of Continuous Medical Treatment in the Dying Patient Act. *Medical Law and Bioethics*, 1: 160–182.
Bell, D. (1993). *Communitarianism and Its Critics*. Oxford: Clarendon Press.
Bentur, N. (2008). The Attitudes of Physicians towards the New "Dying Patient Act" Enacted in Israel. *American Journal of Hospice & Palliative Medicine*, 25(5): 361–365.
Dodds, S. (2000). Choice and Control in Feminist Bioethics, in Mackenzie, C. and Stoljar, N. (eds.). *Relational Autonomy: Feminist Perspectives on Autonomy, Agency and the Social Self*. Oxford: Oxford University Press, pp. 213–235.
Donchin, A. (2000). Autonomy and Interdependence: Quandaries in Genetic Decision-Making, in Mackenzie, C. and Stoljar, N. (eds.). *Relational Autonomy: Feminist Perspectives on Autonomy, Agency and the Social Self*. Oxford: Oxford University Press, pp. 236–258.
Doron, I. and Shalev, C. (2011). Between the Patient Rights Act and the Dying Patient Act: A Progress or Walking Backwards? *Medicine and Law*, 43: 25–34.
Doron, D. et al. (2014). Israeli Dying Patient Act – Physician Knowledge and Attitudes. *American Journal of Clinical Oncology*, 37(6): 597–602.
Edelstein, Y. (2010). The Dying Patient Act 2005 in Israel as a Jewish and Democratic State. *Medicine and Law*, 42: 51–64.
Gilbar, R. (2015). Breathless: On [the] Israeli District Court's Decision to Allow Doctors to Switch Off a Terminal Patient's Ventilator. *The Law on the Net: Human Rights*. 42: 35–69.
Hardwig, J. (2000). *Is There a Duty to Die? And Other Essays in Medical Ethics*. London: Routledge. pp. 29–44.
Herring, J. (2013). *Caring and the Law*. Oxford: Hart.
Lahat-Streichman, Y. (2012). *Is Shared Medical Decision Making Possible at the End of Life?* www.hadassah-med.com/media/2014577/issharedmedical.pdf.
Lindemann-Nelson, H. & Lindemann-Nelson, J. (1995). *The Patient in the Family*. London: Routledge. pp. 114–117.
Mackenzie, C. and Stoljar, N. (eds.). *Relational Autonomy: Feminist Perspectives on Autonomy, Agency and the Social Self*. Oxford: Oxford University Press.
Maclean, A. (2009). *Autonomy, Informed Consent and Medical Law: A Relational Challenge*. Cambridge: Cambridge University Press.
Ritchie, J. and Spencer, L. J. (1994). Qualitative Data Analysis for Applied Policy Research, in Bryman A. and Burgess R. G. (eds.). *Analysing Qualitative Data*. London: Routledge, pp. 173–194.
Shalev, C. (2009) End of Life Care in Israel – The Dying Patient Law 2005. *Israel Law Review*, 42: 279–305.

Shaulov, A. (2011). *Arranging End-of-Life in Geriatric Institutions in the Jerusalem District*. www.hadassah-med.com/media/2014580/eol.pdf.
Shapira, A. (2006) Law and Bioethics in Israel: Between Liberal Ethical Values and Jewish Religious Norms. *Journal International de Bioéthique*, 117: 115–123.
Srivastava, A. and Thomson, S. B. (2009). Framework Analysis: A Qualitative Methodology for Applied Policy Research. *Journal of Administration and Governance*, 4(2): 72–79.
Steinberg, A. (2008). The Halachic Basis of the Dying Patient Law. *Assia – Jewish Medical Ethics*, 6(2): 30–40.
Steinberg, A. and Sprung, C. (2007). The Dying Patient Act 2005: Israeli Innovative Legislation. *ISMJ*, 9: 550–552.
Ticho, A. (2008). The Dying Patient Act, 2005 – The Impact of Jewish Religion on Euthanasia According to Israeli Law *Medical Law and Bioethics*, 1: 107–159.
Walker, T. (2013). Respecting Autonomy Without Disclosing Information. *Bioethics*, 27(7): 388–394.

Cited Laws

Basic Law: Human Dignity and Liberty, 1992.
The Dying Patient Bill, 2004.
The Dying Patient Act, 2005.
The Patient Rights Act, 1996.
The Penal Code, 1977.

Cited Court Rulings

CA 506/88 *Shefer v. The State of Israel*, PD 48(1) 87 (1993).
Case number 28450/09 (Rishon L'ezion) *General Attorney v. B.V.V* (13/9/2009).
Case number 24638–02-14 (Jerusalem) Shaare Zedek *Medical Center v. A.H.* (February 19, 2014).
Case number 16813–11-14 *John Doe v. Attorney General of Israel* (December 9, 2014).

Cited Circulars

Circular 2/96, Treating the Dying Patient (Ministry of Health, 1996).
Circular 7/08 Applying the Dying Patient Act 2005 (Ministry of Health, 2008).

Cited Reports

Ministry of Health, The National Committee Report on the Dying Patient (January 2002), Appendix B, www.health.gov.il/PublicationsFiles/steinberg_committee.pdf.
The Joint Meeting of the Work, Welfare and Health Committee and the Constitution, Law and Justice Committee on the Issue of Prolonging Life, Protocol no. 1, October 12, 2004, the 3rd Parliamentary Session of the 16th Knesset, 8–14, 23.

13

Organ Donation, Brain Death, and the Limits of Liberal Bioethics

Hagai Boas and Shai J. Lavi

INTRODUCTION

Is the regulation of bioethics in Israel exceptional? Does Israeli law regulate questions of life and death differently than in other Western societies, to which Israel proudly compares itself? Scholars who have studied this question have often noted the distinct role Jewish law has played in shaping Israeli bioethics. Hardly any new bill or regulation passes without the approval of leading Orthodox Jewish rabbis. The distinct approach of Jewish law to questions of natality and mortality has reinforced the belief, prevalent among scholars and laypeople alike, that religion is a key element (albeit not exclusive) in understanding Israeli bioethics, and that many bioethical controversies can be understood as reflecting a tension between religious commitments and secular liberal values.

The following chapter offers a critique of this line of analysis. Taking the brain death (BD) and organ donation (OD) controversy as our point of departure, we wish to think of Israeli bioethics not as an exception that lies outside of Western liberal bioethics, but rather as a vantage point that allows critical reflection on Western liberal bioethics. Israeli bioethics makes manifest and thus challenges aspects of liberal bioethics that are often hidden or taken for granted in more mainstream bioethics.

Specifically, we contend here that the Israeli case of BD and OD exposes two fallacies of bioethics: liberal bioethics seeks to clearly separate science, ethics, and politics whereas such separations are prone to fail, and second, liberal bioethics clearly separates the rights and privileges of individuals and those of groups to which individuals belong, especially family and state. The first divide places scientific judgment as the producer of truth claims independent from ethical considerations and power relations. Thus, for example, determining whether a woman is pregnant is a truth claim of a technological and scientific judgment independent of the normative readings of what are the implications of this pregnancy. The second divide sets the individual as the prime frame of reference. Autonomy and consent are the pillars upon which liberal bioethics promotes the working assumption that individual rights trump the interest of family members and the state. Following

Bruno Latour (2012), we will refer to these strategies of separation as "practices of purification."

In the BD and OD controversies in Israel, as we shall see, such purifications practices hardly exist. In fact, Israeli politicians, Israeli law, and the Israeli public tie together science, ethics, and politics in what we term here as "crisscrossing." Whereas most liberal democracies seek to erect a clear wall of separation between the science of BD and the ethics and politics of OD, in Israel, these lines of demarcation are blurred. Furthermore, the Israeli case illustrates that the rights and dignities of the individual are indistinguishable from those of the family, as guardian of individual interests, whether or not the individual expressed this as his wish.

Tracking the history of BD and OD in Israel enables us to engage in a critical analysis of liberal bioethics and its attempts to purify distinct spheres of mores for the two questions at hand. Whereas liberal bioethics instructs policymakers to strictly preserve a well-defined system of classification that separates BD from OD, in Israel, this purification project collapses into different modes of mixtures bringing together science, ethics, and politics. However, we contend that Israel is not an exception to liberal bioethics, nor a less perfected form, but rather an epitome of the tensions, dissonances, and incommensurability inherent in the liberal bioethics approach to BD and OD. In this sense, the specific features of the Israeli case are not evidence for Israeli exceptionalism, but rather amplify existing tensions that could not be sublimated in Israel as they were in more liberal contexts.

Our analysis starts with the introduction of BD and OD in Israel. The first section departs from the controversy surrounding the first heart transplant in Israel in 1968. Whereas the ethical rules of BD and OD were not clear in many places during those times, in Israel, this ethical ambiguity was not translated to a clear ethical guidance, but rather to a political debate. The second part details the history of this debate from 1968 to 2008. The third part introduces the transplantation act and the brain-respiratory act of 2008 as a package deal in which BD definition would be inscribed into the law in return for rabbis' support of OD. The fourth part discusses the failure of the 2008 package deal and its political ramifications and the fifth part discusses our argument of the Israeli case as an amplifier of inherent tensions of OD and BD. We conclude by arguing that although the politics of OD and BD, from its beginning, was portrayed in the colors of a religious–secular divide, such an account is a way of marginalizing Israeli bioethics and ignoring the lessons it may teach us about liberal bioethics. In fact, the Israeli case, we argue, is a paradigmatic one for studying the limits of liberal bioethics in the regulation of BD and OD.

THE SADGAT CASE AND THE FAILURE OF THE DEAD DONOR RULE

Israel was one of the first countries to perform a heart transplantation worldwide. The operation took place in December 1968, in almost parallel timing to the introduction of the BD criterion in the United States and only a year after the first operation of this kind was ever performed. The medical team at the Beilinson Medical Center, a hospital at the outskirts of Tel Aviv, found a suitable donor, Avraham Sadgat, who died from a stroke. According to the Israeli Anatomy and Pathology Act (1953), no consent was needed to harvest Sadgat's heart for transplant. The hospital did not even think it would be advisable to inform Sadgat's family in advance. It was only through the media celebration of the first Israeli transplant that the family was able to connect the dots and realized that the transplanted heart came from their beloved one. In fact, the hospital refused to share with the family members any information as to the source of the transplanted heart and only after applying to the health minister, demanding full disclosure, did they discover the truth. Although the hospital followed the law and did not need to obtain informed consent, hiding the heart's source ignited a public debate that overshadowed the celebration of the first transplant. A compromise in court settled the issue with the hospital admitting that the transplanted heart was the heart of Avraham Sadgat (Weiler-Pollack 2008).

The Sadgat scandal was a result of an ethical ambiguity that often envelopes new technologies. It raised to the surface the blurred demarcation lines between the science, the ethics, and the politics of the new BD criterion. It also presented the connection between BD and OD in its most naked manifestation. BD is a condition *sine qua non* for the transplantation of viable organs such as heart and liver. Indeed, the main reason for introducing the new criterion of BD was the desire to provide organs for burgeoning transplant medicine (Giacomini 1997). The first heart transplant, which was performed a few months prior to the publication of the BD criterion, could not have been developed into a full-scale medical industry without establishing, some would say inventing, the medical condition of the "living cadaver" or of the "brain-dead patient" (Giacomini 1997; Belkin 2003; Bishop 2011; Belkin 2014).

The development of ventilators, artificial activation of the heart muscle, and brain-wave detection led in 1968 to the introduction of the BD criterion that, in turn, made OD possible. The historical proximity between the emergence of transplant medicine during the 1960s and the ad hoc committee at Harvard University that first introduced the BD criterion in 1968 raised the concern that BD and OD are instrumentally linked, with the former introduced to meet the requirements of the latter. Furthermore, with the transformation of transplant medicine into routine medical care since the 1980s, the need for replaceable organs has only become more urgent. The desire to reduce the acute shortage of organs has further enhanced the interconnectedness of BD and OD as a practical necessity.

While the link between OD and BD is a practical necessity, it became highly questionable in liberal bioethics. Since the new criterion of determining death was first published by the ad hoc committee at Harvard University in 1968, ethicists demanded more normative clarity. They were concerned by the morally repugnant possibility that patients would be declared dead, only because doctors would want to procure their vital organs. The solution that the Harvard committee and following bioethicists promoted was drawing a clear boundary between determining death and organ donation. Doctors were expected to provide the new neurological death a scientific certainty similar to that of cardiac death, banning any pragmatic consideration to affect the brain death criterion and its application in individual cases. This separating logic is epitomized in the "dead donor rule" (Robertson 1999) that clearly demarcates the science of the BD criterion from the ethics and OD. Declaring death was to become a scientifically verifiable factual question, conceptually, chronologically, and institutionally separable from organ procurement.

The Sadgat scandal could have become the "zero point" of a new liberal bioethical framework for regulating BD and OD in Israel. Israel could have adopted the liberal bioethics purification system in which medical teams would have exclusive authority in determining death on scientific grounds, and organ donations would be an ethical decision based on the scientific validity of BD. Instead, the Sadgat case became the "ground zero" of the crisscrossing of BD and OD in Israel. The scandal erupted precisely because there was uncertainty about the authority of the medical profession to pronounce a brain-dead patient dead, and the legislator did not regulate the necessary consent process for organ donation. Consequently, both the science of BD and the ethics of OD became politicized. Whereas in other countries, liberal bioethics has managed to push politics to the background and hide the science-ethics-politics nexus, in Israel, politics has been in the foreground from the outset.[1] Rather than becoming a turning point, the Sadgat scandal became the rule. Whereas liberal bioethics managed to bring to relief an inherent moral tension between science and politics, between individual rights and social interests, and between BD and OD, Israeli bioethics took a different route. In the Israeli setting, the efforts to create distinct ethical spheres for BD and OD collapsed into mixtures and hybrids that only entangled further the interconnections between the two, creating a distinct sphere of end-of-life biopolitics.[2]

---

[1] Controversies over the definition of brain death exist worldwide. Opposition to brain death definition can be found within the medical profession (Youngner et al. 1999; Capron 2001; Youngner and Arnold 2001) and in general public opinion (Siminoff and Bloch 1999; Siminoff et al 2004). Debating the implications of defining death is led mostly by bioethicists whose leading voice since the early 1970s was Robert Veatch (1972, 1982, 2004). In Germany and Denmark, for example, brain death was mainly debated by ethicists and theologians (Haupt and Rudolph 1999; Schone-Seifert 1999; see also Penrick (1999) for more on the cultural setting of defining death). The ethical opposition to brain death definition is mainly about the medicalization of a death and against the dominance of medicine in defining such a contested concept as death. This opposition, however, runs along what we term here as "purification strategies" in separating the sphere of medical science, which is responsible for defining death, from the sphere of ethics, which is responsible for accepting/rejecting this definition.

[2] Japan is perhaps a close example to the Israeli case where the opposition to BD was promoted by different actors in the cultural and the political spheres and delayed the enactment of a BD rule (Lock 1996, 2002). The state of New Jersey is even a closer example as its brain death act (1991) enables individuals whose religious values are in opposition with the definition of brain death to be exempt

A BRIEF HISTORY OF BRAIN DEATH AND ORGAN DONATION IN ISRAEL: 1968–2008

The Sadgat scandal led to a complete halt of transplant medicine in Israel and to the lingering understanding that the definition of death is a political question. In the 1970s, transplant medicine was still in its infancy and the medical establishment felt there was little to gain from advocating the practice. The invention of immunosuppressive treatments that enable long, durable life quality for organ recipients in the early 1980s brought back transplant medicine to the front of medical care in Israel as well as in many developed countries.

Once organ transplants became a feasible medical possibility, the question of brain death reentered the public scene. In Israel, the criterion of brain death suggested by the Harvard committee faced public suspicion and encountered political resistance. Religious politicians and rabbinic authorities took the lead in voicing these concerns. Traditionally, the Jewish law criterion for death was the cessation of aerobic activity (Halperin 2015; Offer-Stark 2015).

Along with the questioning of the validity of the BD criterion emerged the issue of OD consent. Organ shortage became the omnipresent reality of transplant medicine worldwide, and Israel was no exception. Limited number of organs and long waiting lists became the hallmark of the shortage problem wherever transplant medicine was practiced. In Israel, following the death of a young person waiting for a kidney donation in 1978, organ shortage led to the foundation of ADI, an association devoted to promoting public awareness to OD and donor cards.

The foundation of ADI marked the introduction of transplantation ethics to Israel. Israel, in this sense, was not unique. Across the developed world, donor cards became a mark of liberal bioethics and part of a purification system setting apart science from politics and individual rights from societal interests. In most countries, donor cards were about individual consent to the donation of organs after brain death was established as an unquestionable fact. In Israel, as soon became clear, donor cards became a token of belief in the brain death criterion.

Whereas in other countries, the response to the BD-OD controversy was an attempt at purification, the developments in Israel took an alternative path. Rather than separating science and politics and individual from the family and other collectivities, there was much more toleration of the crossover of politics and medicine. There was no use of the liberal bioethics toolbox to erect walls of separation and the stage was set for a variety of social actors to step in. Against this background, it is no wonder then that the Chief Rabbinate – a state apparatus – appeared as a mediating agency. From

---

from the application of neurological definition of death by mandating a uniform detailed protocol of defining death. Unlike the Israeli law – as we shall see – the New Jersey law does not grant the individual's relative any status and it recognizes the need for periodically reviewing the medical protocol of determining death in order to keep in pace with science and technology (Olick 1991).

this perspective, the Chief Rabbinate's involvement and more generally Jewish law influence was less a cause of politicization and more its outcome.

In 1987, the Israeli Chief Rabbinate endorsed a compromise that recognized the total, irreversible, destruction of the brain stem – responsible for respiration – as an additional death criterion. The intervention of a religious body in medical decision making was abhorrent to many among the medical profession (Boas 2008). From this point onward, much of the debate about BD led to challenging the very scientific fact of brain death. Both sides – supporters and opponents of BD – openly combined scientific arguments with political agendas to promote their cause.

During the 1980s, transplantation units were open, first in Beilinson and then in other medical centers. Israeli national insurance schemes cover transplantations as well as postoperative care, making organ transplantations economically accessible to all Israeli citizens. Economic accessibility and existing biomedical expertise, however, only underscored the problem of organ shortage; the medical system was set to operate and yet there were too few donors to operate on. Israel's organ shortage gave her a low mark even among developing countries (Abadie and Gay 2006). Even the fact that the Israeli Ministry of Health formally adopted ADI, turning it to the Israeli Transplant Center in 1993, did not lead to a dramatic breakthrough in procuring cadaveric organs. Indeed, the Center invested much effort in boosting awareness and raised the number of donor card holders. Over the years, the Ministry of Health increased the rate of organ procurement and family consent, but together with the increase in demand for organs, these achievements remained unsatisfactory and are still low today. This led to a new phenomenon of organ trafficking.

For renal patients (composing around 80 percent of all patients on waiting lists), the alternative of a living donor alleviated the problem of organ shortage. Progress in tissue matching and advances in post-transplant treatments enlarged the potential pool of living donors beyond the circle of close genetic proximity. These developments, coupled with the exacerbating limited pools of organs taken from BD patients, gave rise during the 1990s to an organ black market. The emergence of organ trafficking is closely connected to the political economy trends of globalization and unleashed neoliberalism. In Israel, the availability of state-sponsored post-transplant treatments and high-level follow-ups made organ trafficking even more tempting for Israeli patients. During the 1990s, Israeli patients, mainly patients waiting for kidney transplants, traveled to South Africa, Eastern Europe, South America, and neighboring Arab countries to obtain a kidney through networks of organ trafficking, mainly from living vendors (Mor and Boas 2005; Budiani-Saberi and Delmonico 2008).

During the first decade of the 2000s Israel became notoriously associated with organ trafficking. Reports on organ trafficking, published during the beginning of the 2000s, have emphasized the role of Israelis in leading organ trafficking networks. Between 2002 and 2008, the number of Israelis who underwent organ transplantations outside Israel reached 781, whereas only 459 Israelis underwent transplantation in Israel (Broder 2013). Transplantations abroad took place in black or gray markets without a confirmation of the organ source. According to Rosenfeld (2013), one leading insurance company approved 445 requests of reimbursing transplant outside Israel out of 628 applications. Israeli public providers, the national insurance funds, reimbursed these procedures in the thousands of dollars,[3] turning a blind eye to ethical misgivings.

Side by side with the rise of global trafficking emerged a global liberal bioethics. International health agencies, such as the WHO, condemned Israel and Israeli health services as a hot spot of organ trafficking. Notably, during these years, Israel was also targeted as a hot spot of international human trafficking of sex workers by the U.S. foreign ministry. The spread of organ trafficking followed the routes of human trafficking in the emerging "new economy" of the globalized world. Organ trafficking, like human trafficking, has become the epitome of the exploitations chains of this new economy (Scheper-Hughes 2000, 2001). Although Israel was never officially condemned as fostering organ trafficking (as China was and still is), Israel was heavily criticized in international professional forums of transplants as a gray zone for organ trafficking.

Combating organ trafficking became in the first decade of the 2000s an international effort, resulting in the Declaration of Istanbul (2008) signed by transplant associations from seventy-eight countries underscoring the unrewarded donation as the ethical gold standard of OD worldwide (Danovitch et al. 2013). The combat against organ trafficking focused the ethical concern on the political economy of organs for transplantations rather than on the brain death criterion. The question of the brain death criterion was matched with the pressing problem of organ shortage and organ trafficking.

The Israeli government and legislator were determined to remove Israel from the black list of human law violators and to adopt a regulatory scheme that would be in accordance with liberal values. As we shall see, however, pursuing this end required, in the Israeli context, unorthodox measures that would seem very strange in most Western countries. Whereas the solution in other countries was to create a "firewall" between BD and OD, in Israel, the chosen path to resolve the problem was to bring this tension into the open, politicizing the scientific criterion for determining death and connecting BD and OD regulation. Under external international pressure, Israel sided with an emerging global liberal bioethics prohibiting organ trafficking, and sought new ways to resolve the organ shortage challenge. The solution was to create a self-sustaining organ economy in which the supply for organs would be met by solving the problem of BD. This could only be achieved by repacking together BD and OD.

---

[3] Costs of transplantations vary between countries: during the mid-1990s, transplantation in Turkey cost $40,000 and reached $220,000 a decade later. In China, the costs ranged between $60,000 and $70,000 and in the Philippines, they ranged between $80,000 and $110,000 (Rosenfeld 2013).

2008 – THE PACKAGE DEAL

The Transplantation Law and the Brain-Respiratory Act ls were enacted on the same day, March 24, 2008, as one legal package coupling BD and OD in an unprecedented manner. Up until 2008, OD was regulated by ad hoc guidelines from the Ministry of Health rather than by state law. Similarly, BD was determined by hospital committees and, due to the ongoing controversy about the legitimacy of BD, no universal code was issued. The aim of the laws was to simultaneously bring an end to organ trafficking and to compensate for the inevitable drop in organ supply by mainstreaming the BD criterion. The new BD law was dubbed, somewhat oxymoronically, "the Brain-Respiratory Law." The initiator of the new legislation, then a member of the Knesset, Otniel Schneller, openly admitted that his motivation was to solve the problem of organ scarcity. Schneller, who self-identified as "a Zionist religious Jew," and a member of the ruling party at the time "Kadima," wished to solve the problem by finding a solution that would resolve the opposition to BD as well as alleviate the organ shortage. The conjoining of the two did not take place behind the scenes, but was rather openly discussed.[4] Schneller recalled a meeting with his neighbor, an end-stage hepatic patient waiting for a liver transplant (Levi 8-3-2010 ynet). It was after this meeting that he became determined to change the BD law so as to allow for organ procurement. The utilitarian aspect, naked of any liberal bioethical sublimations, surfaced – in the same fashion as it appeared in 1968 – in its most direct form. For Schneller, the BD-OD connection was not an obstacle to be avoided, but rather an objective that must be achieved through political negotiation. This did not require a mastery of liberal bioethics, but rather an understanding of the local political culture of Israel and of its sociology.

The Brain-Respiratory Law

While the Chief Rabbinate agreed to a compromise already in 1987, the 2008 law added some important nuances. The new law adopted the 1987 resolution that death could be determined when the total irreversible loss of the brain stem, responsible for respiration, could be confirmed. This way the neurological test could be adopted without forsaking the traditional aerobic criterion. Interestingly, the title of the law itself implies the political creativity; it inscribed the political compromise onto the body of the brain-dead patient. Furthermore, the law required a combination of clinical and machine-generated tests. By doing so, the law transgressed the separation between the medical and the political, ordering in details the medical protocol necessary to determine brain-respiratory death.

Further, the law was at odds with liberal bioethics by placing the family as the final arbitrator of patient consent. The law, openly and without hesitation, turned

---

[4] See Offer-Stark (2015: 357–358) for MP Schneller's declaration at the Knesset that clearly tied BD and OD.

the medical determination of death into a matter of ethical decision and choice. Article 8 subsection (d) states: "Notwithstanding what is stated in this Law, if brain-respiratory death is determined, and such determination is contrary to the religion or worldview of the patient based on the information obtained from his family members, the patient will not be removed from life support and medical care that directly supports his respiratory treatment shall not be terminated until the heart ceases to function." Subsection (d) changed the situation completely. This leads to rather a strange situation: the medical record, including all the data from the diagnostic equipment used to determine death, is subject to the family's interpretation. The law can be viewed as a "gentle" way of determining death, in concert with family representatives, but it can also be read as limiting the influence of the medical establishment in determining death. Ultimately, even after the physicians exercise their professional discretion and declare "a state of brain ... death," to use the language of the law, the medical implications of such determination are at the discretion of the family.

Thus we encounter two definitions of death and two sets of interpretations and actions: the medical definition and the family definition. These definitions may, of course, converge, but a conflict between the two exposes an alternative, non-liberal bioethics in Israel. Echoing the 1980 amendment of the Anatomy and Pathology Law, the deceased's family is granted the power to determine the implications of determining BD. Whereas in the 1980 modification, the family was given the option to refuse organ removal and the value judgment was separated from the actual definition of death, in this law, the family is involved in the very definition of death, provided with the power to order the continuation of life support therapy even when there is a medical consensus that BD has occurred.

The Brain-Respiratory Death Law deviated from liberal bioethics in two major points: first by the politicization of scientific truth about death, and second, by placing the family as the final authority on organ donation. Thus the science of death becomes an ethical call. The de-medicalization of death through politics and ethics runs counter to fundamental principles of liberal bioethics and individual autonomy is replaced by family interests. The purification system of liberal bioethics is nakedly exposed in the Israeli version of BD-OD regulation.

The Transplantation Law

The amalgamation of science, ethics, and politics in the Brain-Respiratory Death Act leads us back to our package deal. The medical establishment, policymakers, and liberal bioethicists conceded to the politicization of BD because they believed it would boost OD rates in Israel. This was not a far-fetched hope. In fact, only by creating a link between BD and OD in one legislative package could they hope to resolve the decades-old political impasse.

Indeed, the Ministry of Health tried to enact the transplantation bill in 2003, and the Israeli Parliament debated the bill for years until its enactment together with the brain-respiratory death law in 2008. Its importance lies in combating organ trafficking by criminalizing involvement of Israeli citizens (aside from the patients and vendors) in such an activity with a penalty of up to three years in prison. The law followed international legislation that excludes any materialistic incentive for OD as legitimate. Further, the law forbade sick funds, insurance companies, and any other institution to reimburse patients for organ transplants outside Israel (with few exceptions). Noteworthy is the timely proximity of the law with the publication of the Istanbul Declaration – also on 2008 – that set the international standard against global organ trafficking (Green 2015).

The law is decisive in its battle against organ trafficking. It seeks to abolish any ambiguity on the matter and bring to an end the flourish of organ trafficking in Israel and the quiet collaboration of formal institutions in sponsoring questionable transplantations outside Israel. Indeed, data indicate a dramatic decrease after 2008 in Israeli patients who return to Israel after having organ transplantation abroad. Between 2009 and 2012, only 130 Israelis underwent transplantation abroad (in comparison to 387 between 2006 and 2008). Furthermore, soon after the law was enacted, the number of transplants performed in Israel reached 266, more than double the incidence of transplants outside the country (Broder 2013).

Closing the door on organ tourism, however, implied an even worse local organ shortage. The trade-off between conforming to the international ethical standard and exacerbating organ shortage could only be mitigated if the National Transplant Center could enlarge the pool of deceased donations in what can be termed as a self-sustained organ economy. In fact, the national transplant center, as a state apparatus, could exercise its procurement techniques only on cadavers. The center could regulate living donations as well as control them, but it could not order someone to become a living organ donor. This left the sole option of deceased donations as the main field of such a self-sustained organ economy. Balancing the trade-offs between combating organ trafficking and enlarging the potential pool of donors could only be – for the state – by increasing consents for OD.

An agreement regarding BD was needed in order to serve as a guarantee against exacerbating organ shortage. The two laws were to act in tandem to bring Israeli transplant medicine closer to the organ supply standards of developed countries. The transplantation law was supposed to provide an ethical certification for Israeli transplant medicine. The goal of eliminating organ trafficking and raising organ supply led the medical establishment and liberal bioethicists to accept a compromise that would resolve the political tensions and depoliticize the BD-OD controversy. But the politicization of the controversy seems to have been more endemic to the Israeli scene than they had expected.

UNPACKING THE DEAL – REFIGURING NEW FORMS OF ETHICS

Schneller, the MP who initiated the two-law compromise, hoped to boost OD by politicizing the BD criterion, but ultimately he failed. It did not yield a dramatic change in actual OD rates. In fact, the politicization of the BD criterion enabled opting out of the donors' pool even if the deceased held a donor card. The story of Avi Cohen, a public figure and former captain of the Israeli national soccer team, illustrates how the politicization of the law led precisely to mistrust, making the 2008 deal fragile. In late 2010, Cohen suffered a critical head injury as the result of a motorcycle accident and was rushed to the hospital, where his condition deteriorated. Eight days later, he was declared brain dead. According to the media (Channel 2 News, December 29, 2010), Cohen had signed a donor card and upon his death became a candidate for OD. Following the determination of BD, a transplant coordinator appealed to Cohen's family for consent to donate his organs. The family agreed, and even received the approval of the chief rabbi of Israel, Rabbi Shlomo Amar, but after further consultation, the family retracted its permission and – following section 8(d) in the Brain-Respiratory Death Act – did not allow the life support to be disconnected until Cohen's heart stopped beating for a period of nine hours. The family's refusal was described in the media as resulting from "pressure by rabbis" (ynet, December 30, 2010). News channels reported that a former soccer player, who had become religiously observant, called the family while the consent forms were being prepared and convinced them not to withdraw their consent and refuse to donate Cohen's organs.

The case shows how Israeli bioethics continues to be marked by the same fusions of science and politics, and individual and familial hybrids. Further, it emphasizes the distance between Israeli regulation of BD and OD and liberal ethics. Not only was determining Cohen's death finalized by the family and not by scientific experts, but also the expressed wishes of Cohen to become an organ donor were not respected.

The media framed the debate as religious superstition versus progressive and enlightened medicine. This framing of the affair of the debate is misleading. It was a leading rabbinic figure who authorized the donation to begin with, and it is the family and not any rabbi, who had the final say on the matter. Framing the debate as a religious/secular tension is highly characteristic of Israeli public debate, and both sides of the debate are often happy to adopt these labels, but the truth of the matter is more complicated, as we shall see.

The politicization of BD has led to other instances where brain-dead patients were kept under artificial life support by family members against medical decision. Only a few years earlier, Chief Rabbi Lau blocked the donation of organs from a young girl who had suffered BD. And in 2009, not long after taking up his post as deputy health minister, Yaakov Litzman hurried to Schneider Children's Medical Center to stand by the parents of a girl diagnosed as brain dead and support their decision not to disconnect her from life support. This and similar incidents emphasize the de-medicalization of death that runs counter to liberal bioethics.

The failure of the two new laws to boost donation rates led to a counter-reaction of unpacking the deal. Proponents of the BD criterion decided to take measures against individuals who refused to donate organs. Specifically, they introduced the policy of according priority in waiting lists to donor card holders and actual donors that represents a shift toward an approach that converges utilitarianism and narrow social solidarity in linking again BD and OD. The principle is simple: those who sign an organ donor card, as well as their family members, gain an additional point on the waiting list to receive an organ (Quigley et al. 2012, Lavee et al. 2013). Living donors who donate to family members or acquaintances are also granted another point. Instead of reaching out for those who find difficulties in accepting the BD criterion, the move of policymakers was to fortify an in-group sentiment of narrow solidarity among those who carried a donor card.

The legal background for the measure is section 9(b) of the Organ Transplant Law, which stipulates that one of the functions of the steering committee of the National Transplant Center is to advise the health minister in formulating policy. The steering committee, led by Prof. Jacob (Jay) Lavee, a cardiologist and heart transplant specialist at Sheba Medical Center-Tel Hashomer, proposed the new regulation giving priority to donor card holders. Prof. Lavee recounts his immediate motivation for creating the priority regulations:

> A case that shocked me, and that made me decide that we had to change the approach to OD from the ground up, involved a heart transplant candidate who was hospitalized in my department for a long time in serious condition and, as a result, was placed at the head of the waiting list. He turned to me one day and confessed in all honesty that if, God forbid, the situation were reversed, and he was asked to give his agreement to donate the organs of his loved one who had died, he would refuse to grant this consent based on his beliefs and the advice of his rabbi. Even though I appreciated his honesty, the basic injustice and immorality of his words infuriated me and would not let me rest. As much as I respected this man's right to adhere to his belief against recognizing BD as the death of a person – and thus to also oppose the donation of his organs – I could not reconcile myself with his decision to abandon this belief when it came to saving his own life. If his faith did not permit him to donate organs after death since he did not recognize BD, he should have adopted this same moral stance and refused to be a candidate for a heart transplant. A person does not have the right to expect someone else to save his life without agreeing to pay him back in kind if the situation were reversed.

We quote Dr. Lavee at length not only because of his central role in setting the process in motion, but also because his words bring together a number of points discussed previously: to begin with, OD and the definition of BD are presented as a continuum, mirroring again the linkage between the two as the working assumption of Israeli bioethics. But in contrast to "the package deal," this time the assumption led in the opposite direction: instead of aiming at fostering consensus, the prioritization policy bases OD on a narrow solidarity among those who consented to opt in.

Lavee justified his prioritization policy using the secular-religious split lexicon:

> Despite the legitimate criticism, I fought stubbornly for the idea [of priority for donor card holders], since in my eyes it had the potential to provide a suitable answer to the widespread phenomenon in Israel of "free riders" – the large number of people who openly declare that they are opposed to OD but who do not shy away from accepting organs from others in time of need. Following lengthy discussions, it was decided to adopt my proposal, but to condition its implementation on primary legislation in the Knesset that would mandate the addition of the non-medical criterion of signing an OD card to the list of medical criteria based on which transplant organs are allocated. (2013)

In the collective Israeli imagination, the label of "free rider" or "parasite" carries additional implications that once again feed into the religious–secular tension and into the question of "sharing the burden," to use the current Israeli term. The conflict over equality in meeting one's civic obligations is immediate. In the context of organ donor cards, the criterion of "burden sharing" is universally applied: any citizen – secular, religious, ultra-Orthodox, Jew, or non-Jew – who is not signed on an organ donor card does not receive an additional point. However, in practice, the assumption of universality is mistaken, not only due to questions of accessibility that discriminate against weaker groups in society (like models of presumed consent), but also because it relates to an autonomous model of the individual.

The "if you sign, move up the line" measure reflects the image of an individualistic society, of people who act based on independent will, pure calculation, and with full and comprehensive information available to them. In other words, it is a move in which the liberal-secular ideology of utilitarian individualism presents its hierarchy of values and relates to it as an ethical agenda. It is an act of protest in the face of the politics of accommodation, which has failed repeatedly to find a broad consensus in the matter of determining BD.

Furthermore, implementing the prioritization policy required an ethical compromise. According to a long and respected medical tradition, the only criteria for granting medical treatment are medical standards. Doctors do not distinguish between patients on the basis of their altruistic virtues, and a terrorist should receive the same medical treatment as a soldier. The prioritization diverts from these rules in the name of a liberal bioethics, but simultaneously undermines this stance in the name of Israeli secularism.

The prioritization policy was read as a direct confrontation with those parts of the population who cannot donate postmortem organs due to their objection to BD criterion. The counter-reaction came in 2012. As if no law had been enacted only four years earlier, the Chief Rabbinate sought to establish a committee to oversee the determination of BD – an advisory body of sorts that would offer guidance to families at the moment of truth. This proposal, which ultimately was not acted upon, was coupled with additional attempts to institute rabbinic oversight in the determination of death. Chief among these was the founding of the Arevim organization and the nonprofit Bilvavi organization, whose focus is a donor card that ensures that the determination of death is legal, that is, in accordance with the prescribed sequence of actions and the belief system of the patient.

The argument of the Arevim and Bilvavi organizations is directed precisely against this shift. In their view, the Bilvavi card ensures OD by religious people and should therefore be accepted as a donor card for all intents and purposes (the Ministry of Health and the National Transplant Center do not recognize it). By granting priority points, they argue, it is the ADI (National Transplant Center) card and not the Bilvavi card that can encourage deception. A person who does not believe in BD will sign an ADI card in order to receive preferential status, but in the moment of truth will not donate. Signing a card directed and organized by rabbinic authorities will make it harder, they claim, to evade the obligation to donate.

With Arevim and Bilvavi on one side and the prioritization policy on the other, it seems as if nothing had significantly changed since the Sadgat case in 1968. The history of OD and BD in Israel appear as repeated rounds of boxing between the same players. Once and again claims on the illegitimacy of BD and organ salvaging are countered with allegations of undermining transplant medicine and the saving of life. Although these debates are framed within the political culture of the religious–secular tensions in Israel, we claim that this political culture serves only as an amplifier – absent in parallel controversies outside Israel – of an inherent set of dissonances and contradiction embedded in the bioethics of OD and BD. In the next section, we explain why and how the Israeli case is not an exemption explained by "the religious factor," but rather a reflection of bioethics' liberal limits.

IS THE ISRAELI CASE AN EXCEPTION OR THE RULE OF THE OD-BD CONTROVERSY?

The dead donor rule became the ethical standard in policymaking regarding OD and BD in almost all developed countries. Generally, it includes three sets of purification mechanisms. The first separates BD from OD conceptually; the brain death criterion is a truth claim (whether or not the patient is dead), whereas organ procurement entails the ethical and pragmatic determination to donate the organ. The second separates the scientific from the ethical chronologically. The determination of death must precede the procurement of organs. The third isolates the scientific from the ethical institutionally. Different medical persons compose the teams responsible for determining brain death (at the ICU) and those responsible for obtaining consents for OD. The teams are also separated spatially, each in its own unit. The dead donor rule as a comprehensive ethical code introduced a buffer between BD and OD so that no utilitarian linkage could be directly drawn between the two. This ethical buffer became the golden rule in worldwide policymaking.

This was not the case in the history of BD and OD in Israel. The crisscrossing of science and ethics became a prominent feature since the politicization of the controversy seemed to be its solution. Indeed, the dead donor rule is a problematic standard to follow not only in Israel. The three-tier separation mechanism encounters difficulties elsewhere. Yet, whereas the shortcomings of the dead donor rule remain an ethical difficulty discussed within professional and academic forums, in Israel, it has become a political issue transgressing the fundamentals of liberal bioethics. Thus, the Brain-Respiratory Law runs against the standard in which declaring death is a medical fact and a truth claim that is fully within the prerogative of the medical profession. Under liberal bioethics, physicians can and will declare death whether or not the patient or his family approves or disapproves this call.[5] Liberal bioethics draws another clear divide between individual rights and supra-individual interests, including interests of family, community, and state. The interests of the individual, even after his or her death, cannot be sacrificed for the better benefit of society without prior consent. Under liberal bioethics, the family does not have a say in determining organ donation. The decision lies fully in the hands of the deceased, hence the great reliance on the expression of consent in living wills and donor cards.

Although ADI cards express the consent of the individual, it is not the individual who has the final authority to donate organs, as seen with the Avi Cohen case. Indeed, as early as 1980, the Israeli Parliament amended the Anatomy and Pathology Act so that a family could refuse the donation of organs. Whereas in most liberal countries, the issuing of donor cards paved the road for respecting individual postmortem wishes, the Israeli legislature blocked this road by providing the family with the option to veto individual discretion. It is important to emphasize that Israel does not fall short of some liberal ideal, but rather that the Israeli case does not use similar purification mechanisms and consequently reveals what other countries keep under cover. Israel in this sense is not as distinct as it may first seem. Many countries, for example, allow families to veto OD decisions, but this veto is not inscribed into the law the way it is in Israel. It is rather an informal arrangement that does not undermine the appearance of the liberal standard.

Given the different path the OD-BD controversy took in Israel, is the Israeli case an exemption of liberal bioethics? We argue that the Israeli case is rather an instructive case for learning about the limits of liberal bioethics in regulating the OD-BD controversy. Furthermore, although it is tempting to depict the history of OD and BD in Israel as another case where the double definition of Israel as a Jewish and democratic state leads to an alternative regulation of end-of-life biopolitics, we

---

[5] It is noteworthy that in this sense, brain death differs greatly from other end-of-life decisions in which the patient's will plays an important role. Consent, living wills, and advanced directives – or in our case, donor cards – are a variety of ways that liberal bioethics provides to individuals to express their distinct postmortem wishes. These wishes usually trump other considerations (Hacker, Hashiloni-Dolev, and Boas 2014).

argue that this framing overlooks the underpinnings of the problem. The failure of the "package deal" was precisely since understanding the OD-BD problem within the lens of the religious–secular tension is at least a partial understanding of what is at stake.

The negotiations from their inception in 1968 were about the science of BD. Unlike their counterparts in the Western liberal societies, the opponents of BD in Israel did not care about the medicalization or the instrumentalization of death. In fact, the opposition to brain death has raised counter-scientific perspectives and technological measurements that only further instrumentalize death in order to challenge the definition of BD (Gross and Lavi 2015). Creating the respiratory-brain death definition as a legal fact protected by legally inscribed scientific protocols is no less than the politicization of science. The firewall separating the science of defining death from the politics of BD was never erected in the Israeli case. The dead donor rule, therefore, was never even an option in the Israeli case.

Indeed, Israel is different from other Western liberal democracies that have by and large accepted the brain death criterion and have created a functioning system of organ allocation and distribution. However, it would be more accurate to say that purification mechanisms such as the dead donor rule have mitigated tensions to the point where they remain the occupation of theoretical bioethicists. The failure of such mechanisms in the Israeli case does not single out Israel as an outlier, but rather as a vantage point for delineating the so called ordinary case in which BD and OD have been consensually adopted into the legal and medical system and allegedly cleared the tensions inherent in these medical technologies.

Israel, so to speak, wears these tensions on its sleeve. It does not try to hide the fact that brain death is not simply a matter of medical expertise, but is a highly controversial question that combines ethics and politics as much as truth. Furthermore, it does not continue the cult of the individual and the bioethical tactics of informed consent beyond death. The family, which plays an informal role in many countries, receives in Israel a formal standing under the law.

CONCLUSIONS

Different societies have different ways of framing bioethical dilemmas. Bioethical cultures offer frameworks to resolve tensions and provide conceptual frameworks for making sense of tensions and providing opponents with a social script to voice their positions. Israeli bioethics has its own way of making sense of the controversy. Framing the dissonances of OD and BD within the religious–secular debate easily conformed to many other bioethical problems from birth and abortion to death and burial in Israel. In fact, these labels are probably as ideological as the ones liberal bioethics offers. While in other Western countries, the BD-OD controversy is dismantled through the purifying mechanisms of liberal bioethics, in Israel, they are overly extenuated due to their ordering as a secular–religious tension. In this sense, the political culture of the religious–secular split in Israel exposed, loudly and publicly, the dissonances of BD and OD. The Israeli politicization of bioethics did not resolve the controversy. It exposed, however, the naked roots of BD and OD bioethics.

References

Abadie, A. and S. Gay (2006). The Impact of Presumed Consent Legislation on Cadaveric Organ Donation: A Cross-Country Study. *Journal of Health Economics* 25(4): 599–620.

Belkin, G. (2003). Brain Death and the Historical Understanding of Bioethics. *Journal of the History of Medicine and Allied Sciences* 58(3): 325–361.

Belkin, G. (2014). *Death before Dying: History, Medicine, and Brain Death*. Oxford University Press.

Bishop, J. P. (2011). *The Anticipatory Corpse*. University of Notre Dame Press.

Boas, H. (2008). The Struggle over the Last Minute. *Israeli Sociology* 11(1): 219–241.

Boas, H. (2009). The Value of Altruism – The Political Economy of Organ Supply, PhD Dissertation submitted to the department of sociology and anthropology, Tel Aviv University.

Budiani-Saberi, D. A. and F. L. Delmonico (2008). Organ Trafficking and Transplant Tourism: A Commentary on the Global Realities. *American Journal of Transplantation* 8(5): 925–929.

Capron, A. M. (2001). Brain Death – Well Settled Yet Still Unresolved. *New England Journal of Medicine* 344(16): 1244–1246.

Danovitch, G. M., et al. (2013). Organ Trafficking and Transplant Tourism: The Role of Global Professional Ethical Standards – The 2008 Declaration of Istanbul. *Transplantation* 95(11): 1306–1312.

Giacomini, M. (1997). A Change of Heart and a Change of Mind? Technology and the Redefinition of Death in 1968. *Social Science & Medicine* 44(10): 1465–1482.

Green, Y. (2015). *Organ Transplantations – Legislation, Rulings and Practice*. Resling.

Gross, S. and S. Lavi (2015). Visibly Dead: On Making Brain Death Believable. *Leonardo*.

Hacker, D., Y. Hashiloni-Dolev, and H. Boas. (2014). The Deceased Will – Three Israeli Case Studies. *Israeli Sociology* 16(3):31–56.

Halperin, M. (2015). *Determining Brain Death – Essays Collection*. Schlesinger.

Haupt, W. F. and J. Rudolf (1999). European Brain Death Codes: A Comparison of National Guidelines. *Journal of Neurology* 246(6): 432–437.

Latour, B. (2012). *We Have Never Been Modern*. Harvard University Press.

Lavee, J., et al. (2013). Preliminary Marked Increase in the National Organ Donation Rate in Israel Following Implementation of a New Organ Transplantation Law. *American Journal of Transplantation* 13(3): 780–785.

Lock, M. (1996). Death in Technological Time: Locating the End of Meaningful Life. *Medical Anthropology Quarterly* 10(4): 575–600.

Lock, M. (2002). *Twice Dead: Organ Transplants and the Reinvention of Death*. University of California Press.
Martinez, J. M. et al. (2001). Organ Donation and Family Decision-Making within the Spanish Donation System. *Social Science & Medicine* 53(4): 405–421.
Mor, E. and H. Boas (2005). Organ Trafficking: Scope and Ethical Dilemma. *Current Diabetes Reports* 5(4): 294–299.
Offer-Stark, I. (2015). Philosophical Justifications for Brain-Death Criteria According to the Jewish Law. PhD dissertation submitted to the department of Jewish thought, Bar-Ilan University.
Olick, R.K. (1991). Brain Death, Religious Freedom, and Public Policy: New Jersey's Landmark Legislative Initiative. *Kennedy Journal of Ethics* 1(4):275–288.
Pernick, M. S. (1999). Brain Death in a Cultural Context. In *The Definition of Death: Contemporary Controversies*, 3–33.
Quigley, M., et al. (2012). Organ Donation and Priority Points in Israel: An Ethical Analysis. *Transplantation* 93(10): 970–973.
Robertson, J. A. (1999). Delimiting the Donor: The Dead Donor Rule. *Hastings Center Report* 29(6): 6–14.
Scheper-Hughes, N. (2000). The Global Traffic in Human Organs. *Current Anthropology* 41(2): 191–224.
Scheper-Hughes, N. (2001). Commodity Fetishism in Organs Trafficking. *Body & Society* 7(2–3): 31–62.
Schöne-Seifert, B. (1999). Defining Death in Germany: Brain Death and its Discontents. In *The Definition of Death: Contemporary Controversies*, 257–271.
Siminoff, L. A. and A. Bloch (1999). American Attitudes and Beliefs about Brain Death: The Empirical Literature. In *The Definition of Death: Contemporary Controversies*, 183–194.
Siminoff, L. A., et al. (2001). Factors Influencing Families' Consent for Donation of Solid Organs for Transplantation. *JAMA* 286(1): 71–77.
Siminoff, L. A., et al. (2004). Death and Organ Procurement: Public Beliefs and Attitudes. *Social Science & Medicine* 59(11): 2325–2334.
Veatch, R. M. (1972). Brain Death: Welcome Definition ... or Dangerous Judgment? *Hastings Center Report* 2(5): 10–13.
Veatch, R. M. (1982). Maternal Brain Death: An Ethicist's Thoughts. *JAMA* 248(9): 1102–1103.
Veatch, R. M. (2004). Abandon the Dead Donor Rule or Change the Definition of Death? *Kennedy Institute of Ethics Journal* 14(3): 261–276.
Youngner, S. J., et al. (1999). *The Definition of Death: Contemporary Controversies*, JHU Press.
Youngner, S. J. and R. M. Arnold (2001). Philosophical Debates about the Definition of Death: Who Cares? *Journal of Medicine and Philosophy* 26(5): 527–537.

Newspaper Articles and Reports

Lavee, J. (2013). Justice in Organ Donations. *Haaretz* www.haaretz.co.il/opinions/1.1900034

Levi, T. (2009). The Day When the First Israeli Heart Recipient Fought for His Life. *Haaretz* www.haaretz.co.il/news/health/1.1295321

Weiler-Porat, D. (2008). The Broken Heart behind the First Israeli Heart Transplant. *Haaretz* www.haaretz.co.il/news/health/1.1366768

Conference Presentations

Broder, M. (2013) Organ Transplantation Act 1008 – A Five Years Perspective, Talk at 5 Years to Transplantation Law, March 2013, The Edmond J. Safra Center for Ethics, TAU.

Mandel, Y. (2013). Five Years to the Transplantation Law, Talk at 5 Years to Transplantation Law, March 2013, The Edmond J. Safra Center for Ethics, TAU.

Rosenfeld, F. (2013). Five Years to the Transplantation Law, Talk at 5 Years to Transplantation Law, March 2013, The Edmond J. Safra Center for Ethics, TAU.

14

Toward an Israeli Medical Ethics

Michael Weingarten

This chapter seeks to give an account of clinical ethics in Israel in its social and historical context, and to highlight the challenges that the society and its medical profession face in formulating a locally relevant ethics.[1] The interplay of European, Levantine, American, and religious influences is the environment in which the politics of Israeli medicine is conducted, and which provides the context for the moral reactions of its practitioners. As a basis for proposing possible future directions for Israeli medical ethics, we look back over the seventy-odd years since the foundation of the state.

THE SOCIAL AND HISTORICAL CONTEXT OF CLINICAL ETHICS IN ISRAEL

When faced with ethical dilemmas, Israeli doctors, like everyone else, have moral reactions, and in this chapter, we seek to discover the underpinnings or underlying assumptions of these reactions. Although the overwhelming majority of Israel's physicians are Jewish, this does not mean that they are religious and committed to or knowledgeable of religious law (*halakhah*). So their moral reactions cannot be directly related to the dictates of religious doctrines (Liebman 1999). Their current cultural environment, alongside their Jewish culture, must therefore be considered in understanding these reactions.

Israeli medicine, historically, developed out of Eastern and Central European medicine. Its earliest practitioners were typically Jews who fled from European antisemitism, but whose affinity with the rituals and laws of the Jewish religion was vestigial or nonexistent. They brought with them the liberal enlightenment of Kant embedded in a Bismarckian social bureaucracy. In the mold of Kant, human reasoning gave authority to their opinions, with the dignity of the individual at the moral epicenter. Bismarck contributed policies of social solidarity, including a

---

[1] Reproductive ethics, including genetic ethics, is dealt with elsewhere in this volume and will not be discussed here.

commitment to the maintenance of the health of the productive worker and for the temporarily or permanently disadvantaged, sick, or disabled. This being in the overall economic interest of the employers, it was they and not the government who were deemed responsible for the health care system. This was organized through public "sick fund" insurance, funded jointly by employee and employer premiums. Jewish society in mandatary Palestine and later in the State of Israel was structured around massive public corporations and cooperatives, staffed almost exclusively by unionized labor. At its incorporation within the General Federation of Labour (the *Histadrut*), in 1920, the Clalit sick fund covered the health care of 80% of the insured population, alongside the other major functions of the unions in education, housing, banking, and commerce. In terms of the total population, Clalit covered 5% at its inception, 40% by the time it took its current form in 1937, and 85% in 1948 at the foundation of the state, retaining this predominance until 1995 when the National Health Bill came into effect. Today, it covers 54% (Bin Nun, Berlovitz, and Shani 2002; Seidman 2006; Shvarts 2002).

The national Labour Party's power base was in the unions, and in the communist *kibbutzim*. The Labour movement held the hegemony in the country, so much so that there was no pressure for the government to take direct control of health care as it did in the British NHS, which was founded in 1948, the same year as the State of Israel, and in other countries that followed the same route, most notably the Soviet Union.

A new generation of homegrown doctors was educated in Jerusalem by the pioneer generation and its disciples and imbibed their philosophy as part of the latent "hidden" curriculum in their studies. *Extra murum*, the bedside teacher would say whenever there was a diagnostic discussion on a ward teaching round, so that the patients would be systematically excluded from the deliberations on their clinical care. The patient was assumed to be unfamiliar with Latin. Paternalism was the default.

Doctors held ambiguous status – at one and the same time they were almost all salaried union workers themselves, serving their comrades in a communitarian system of mutual help, but they also formed an elite within this socialist egalitarian society, by virtue of their special professional expertise and the traditionally special status of the doctor in Jewish society (Efron 2001). Increasingly, they capitalized on their status and opened private practices that they operated alongside their public positions, providing their clients with a fast track and personalized side door into the sluggish and often impersonal and bureaucratic public service, otherwise known by its familiar Russian term *protekzia*. What little true power they had, then, was from outside the establishment. Inside, they remained subjugated by the political leadership and relegated to an essentially technical function. There, their social status was worth relatively little.

But other groups were gradually gaining ground in Israeli society – small businesses, nonunionized privately owned industry, the military, the ultra-religious, and the Arab minority. Over the decades, the European pioneer generation was supplemented and, to a great extent, supplanted by new waves of medical immigrants, especially from English-, Spanish-, and Arabic-speaking countries, and from the 1980s on and in massive numbers, from the former Soviet Union, and most recently from France too.

Each group brought its own medical culture, but few had recognizably Jewish elements. The English speakers were perhaps more gentle in their manners but elitist nonetheless. They came either from the NHS with its values of solidarity, equality, and government control, or from the opposite American extreme of private medicine and a large social divide with government salvage for the most vulnerable. The Russians were more brusque but more romantic underneath, bringing with them low expectations of pay and accustomed to complete government control of health. They wore their profession with pride, and were often quite open to bending the rules for the good of their patients – for a price. The Arabic speakers were perhaps more sensitive but less articulate, seeing their medicine as a scientific system rather than as a service profession embedded in a sociopolitical context. The French were mostly second-generation migrants from North Africa, but identified more with their European than their *Maghreb* culture. Unlike the English, Spanish, and French speakers, the Russians and the Arabic speakers clearly formed an inferior underclass within the medical community, reflecting the status of their groups of origin in Israeli society in general.

Indigenous Arab doctors had always been part of the scene, at first few and far between, but as the Israeli Arab population shared in the increasing prosperity, especially among the Christian and Druze communities, more and more studied medicine either in Israel or abroad (Shuval 1992). Often their studies abroad were funded by Communist Russia (Shuval and Anson 2001). An increasing number of Jewish Israelis too studied medicine in Europe, at first in Italy, as the number of places available in Israel was insufficient. Whereas the Jews studying abroad tended to keep to themselves and did not noticeably absorb the ambient culture, the Arabs more often saw their studies abroad as an opportunity to rise above their background and modernize their culture. They returned to work in Israel, often in private practice, feeling closer to their Jewish secular colleagues than to their traditional village culture (Elnekave and Gross 2004).

This new mixed population of doctors challenged the old professional hegemony. Not only did they generally not identify with a traditional Jewish ethos, they also did not identify with the European socialist ideal. Thus were medical ethics thrown into the melting pot.

From the 1970s, young Israeli doctors started traveling abroad to complete their professional education in the subspecialties, almost exclusively to English-speaking countries and especially to the United States, which is where the money to support them was to be found. They returned with experience of the new liberal West, with new fundamental principles such as autonomy, transparency, and patients' rights.

This is not to say that is what they saw universally in practice, but the discourse was distinctly different from the one they recognized in Israel. The accelerated Americanization of Israeli society, dating back to the 1973 war, led to a gradual replacement of the pioneers' socialist ethos with the rule of the free market. Begin's ascendancy in 1977 ended the hegemony of the Ashkenazi labor movement, and competition, personal gain, and social divides became acceptable in the context of a neoliberal monetarist economy.

Within twenty years, the structure of Israeli society changed radically. When the government took control of health care through the 1994 National Health Insurance Law, it seemed at first to go against this individualistic trend, introducing universal tax-funded health care. But it was swiftly put back on course by the 1998 amendment that introduced voluntary supplementary health care insurance. This second tier of health care was incorporated within the public sector, but unlike the basic level, it was not funded by progressive taxation, but by standard individual premiums. The health economy was revolutionized, with the private contribution to health costs rising to 40%, topped only by the United States among Western nations. The doctors' union was given a fixed percentage of the national health tax and became immensely wealthy and used its resources to exercise its influence in national policy; the health research community was given access to unprecedented grant money administered via the Israel Institute for Health Policy Research, also funded by the health tax revenues.

The sick funds survived, funded now by the government and not directly by members' and employers' contributions. The residual few percent of previously uninsured citizens were now covered by the universal government health care coverage, but the price was direct government control of the whole system. Labour Party institutions and their internal politics became totally irrelevant; everything was in the hands of the civil service and its ever-changing political bosses.

Israel's doctors, with their tradition of professional elitism, accommodated well to this new regime, perhaps feeling more comfortable than they had as just another worker in a workers' cooperative. They now commanded a stronger position in the salaried market with their special expertise and control of the vast expenditure that health care involves. Doctors used their power both for consolidating their control of the health care system and for their own personal gain. In the context of the supplementary health insurance schemes, private medicine came out of the closet and was no longer thought to be subversive of the public service. Since most public medicine was still unionized, the doctors were able to mount a series of strikes, which led to significantly improved wages, expressing their new market strength, to levels well above the national average or the earnings of other health care workers in the public system. Their bargaining power was perhaps threatened by the massive influx of Russian doctors, but the effect was mitigated by the low reputation that the local doctors succeeded in attributing to the immigrants. Medically qualified ministers of health and directors general of the ministry, often rotating between senior administrative positions in the public hospitals, the civil service, and the private sector, decided the medical agenda in Israeli medicine. Academia was coopted, with special criteria for professorships for prominent public medical personalities. In order to gain access to clinical teaching facilities in the public hospitals and clinics, local directors also had to be given academic recognition. The practice of clinical research, dependent on time and money provided by these directors, and the authorization of their local Helsinki committees, also became subject to the power structure of the medical establishment. At the Israel Medical Association, medically qualified civil servants, academics, administrators, and trade unionists shared the table, making it a formidable institution in the life of Israeli medicine. Notwithstanding the models of collaborative multidisciplinary care the returning young specialists brought with them, the old guard saw its regained status and power as a chance to entrench the rigidly hierarchical patterns of work it had originally brought from Europe. Power, not service, had become the name of the game in Israeli medicine.

The two most powerful players are the Ministry of Health, which controls the finances, and the Israel Medical Association, which controls the profession. However, neither of them is in a position to provide moral leadership; they both suffer to this day from dual loyalties and deep conflicts of interest. The Ministry is not only the statutory regulatory body, but it also functions as the direct provider of many services – acute hospitals, mental health services, nursing care, and preventive medicine – and here it supervises and regulates itself. The Israel Medical Association is not only the professional union for Israel's doctors, concerned with their pay, their ethics, and the protection of their rights, but it is also the statutory examiner and regulator of the specialist licensing system, thus sitting on the valve of medical manpower supply for the country. It is constituted by a vast variety of parochial interests, from all walks of the profession, many of whom want a strong public sector to provide solid employment opportunities alongside a strong private sector to provide extra income that is often way in excess of the salaries. The internal contradictions are glaring: the public sector is predicated on a solidarity-based commitment to universal and equitable care; the private sector is competitive and exclusive. As such, the IMA is found to promote a public health agenda and at one and the same time to protect and promote private practice (Avni and Filc 2015).

Legislation has reflected the changing mores of society, emphasizing human rights rather than the common good, with the 1992 Basic Law: Human Dignity and Liberty. The Basic Law is as near as Israel gets to a constitution. Its purpose is stated – "to protect human dignity and liberty, in order to establish ... the values of the State of Israel as a Jewish and democratic state," with "fundamental human rights ... founded upon recognition of the value of the human being, the sanctity of human life, and the principle that all persons are free." It is mostly framed in terms of negative liberties. There is to be "no violation of the life, body or dignity of any person as such ... of the property of a person ... of the confidentiality of conversation, or of the writings or records of a person," etc. But positive liberty is also included – "All persons are entitled to protection of their life, body and dignity."

The 1996 Patients' Rights Act details patients' rights in particular, and is phrased mostly in positive terms: "Every person in need of medical care is entitled to receive it. The patient is entitled to obtain, at his own initiative, a second opinion as to his medical care. The clinician ... and all other workers in the medical facility, shall maintain the dignity and privacy of the patient at all stages of his treatment." A central requirement is "No medical care shall be given unless and until the patient has given his informed consent to it." Further clauses relate to medical information, quality of care, and so on.

Fueled by the Patients' Rights Act and the conspicuously increased affluence of doctors, medical litigation is sharply on the rise, leading to an army of lawyers prospering from both sides of the disputes, and to the rapid spread of defensive medicine (Asher and Reuveni 2010).

Everyone has a vested interest in supporting the system – except those citizens who cannot afford supplementary or private health care, and have to make do with a second-rate basic public service, which is overstretched, often brusque in manner, uncomfortable, and slow in comparison. The vestiges of the public service ethos of the old socialized medicine are hard to find. Few doctors speak in terms of duties, but rather they speak the liberal language of rights: patients' rights and, no less, their own rights. This is evident in the publications of the IMA, both academic and professional, as we will see later.

How has medical paternalism survived this transition from bureaucratized socialism to consumerist liberalism? In both socialist and liberal societies there should be no room for paternalism – in the first case because of the equal standing of doctor and patient, and in the second case because of the respect due to the patient. The answer lies in the aberrations of the system in each phase. In the socialist phase, power was centralized in the labor movement institutions that monopolized both the national and the local political machinery, and through the mutual care organizations of the Histadrut. This included most of the medical care in the country, so doctors became functionaries in a politicized professional service. Where everybody was playing the political game, the doctors knew how to use their own advantages of education and professional traditions, and to compensate for their lack of political clout, they used their trump card, their professional pronouncements. A participatory approach to clinical medicine would have undermined their influence within the organization, so they happily continued to be paternalistic. With the transition to liberalism, the doctors found themselves recast as providers of commodified medical services to their clients, as representatives of the service organization. The latter, in the name of financial efficiency, once again bureaucratized the system, but with career managers rather than political appointees at the helm. At first the doctors continued to flaunt their special professional expertise in order to maintain their hard-gained preeminence in the hierarchy, but the managers learned enough about evidence-based medicine to call them to order. So how did the doctors retain a paternalistic attitude?

Until the turn of the twenty-first century, recognition of ethical dilemmas was severely curtailed – the doctors convinced themselves that they had a correct answer for every situation, and this was delivered *ex cathedra*, reflecting either their own personal moral convictions or those they perceived to be the traditional professional reaction. There was rarely any ethical discussion either on the wards or in the medical press. One careful study of the literature on health equalities found that between 1997 and 2010, only 0.43% of papers in the IMA medical journal in Hebrew related in any way to this issue, and five out of the six publications were published after 2008 (Avni, Davidovitch, and Filc 2015). The IMA's ethics committee restricted itself mostly to issues of professional misconduct. The change came slowly as the new managers started to introduce quality measures and medical standards, rather than restricting themselves to issues of economic efficiency. I suggest that it was in order to counter this intrusion on their professional space by managerial dictates and their clinical protocols that the doctors played a new card, the moral argument. This was often phrased in medico-legal terms, for the doctor rather than the manager was legally responsible for clinical outcomes. The argument ran – you can tell me what the best evidence says about clinical management, but you cannot tell me what is the right and the good course to follow in any particular case, all things considered. It is the difference between "What you should do" and "What should I do, now?" In this way the doctors found an arena in which the managers could not muster international medical consensus in order to constrain the doctors to act as they wished. Moral clinical judgment is one's personal responsibility. So grew a new and active field of medical ethics in Israel.

THE CHALLENGE OF DEVELOPING AN ISRAELI MEDICAL ETHICS

We may identify four major foci: the rabbinical world, the legal profession and the legislature, the medical profession, and academe.

Rabbinical. In the same year the milestone rabbinical publication *Jewish Medical Ethics* (Jakobovits 1959) was translated into Hebrew, 1966, the Jerusalem-based Schlesinger Institute for Medicine and Halakhah was established. It greatly expanded its activities in the 1990s in publishing, conferences, education, and Internet services.[2] Its definition of medical ethics was and still is closely identified with *halakhah*. This set a high standard for the ethical debate in Israel, both in terms of the breadth of topics examined and in terms of publication and dissemination. The monumental Encyclopedia of Jewish Medical Ethics by Avraham Steinberg, rabbi, pediatric neurologist, and professor of medical ethics at the Hebrew University of Jerusalem, is perhaps the outstanding example. It is aimed at a wide

---

[2] A smaller initiative based on the Laniado (religious, private) Hospital in Netanya also produced a journal and books on medicine and *halakhah*.

audience and sets medical *halakhah* in a wide cultural and intellectual context. The sanctity of life is a pervasive theme throughout.

This movement has made some significant innovative contributions to contemporary ethics discussions in Israeli medicine, most notably in the fields of brain death/organ transplantation, assisted reproduction, and therapeutic abortion, as well in the field of maintaining ritual law in the context of modern medical technology, in particular over Sabbath observance. While the latter speaks only to the Orthodox observant Jew, the others have influenced legislation, e.g., the brain-respiratory death and organ transplantation laws, and thus affect all Israelis. This influence has sometimes aroused significant resistance, such as the foundation of a network of doctors in all hospitals trained in the rabbinical criteria for brain death, which might be considered more stringent than standard medical practice. This network, Levavi, provided alternative advance directive donation cards to the public, assuring them that in event of death, this would be determined by *halakhic* standards. Though the motivation was shared – to increase the number of donors – the secular organ donation movement perceived this as an unwarranted incursion of rabbinical influence into a field where medicine holds the prerogative. In other cases, the rabbinical position resonated positively with the wider public, in particular over its highly permissive attitudes both to assisted reproductive technologies and to late therapeutic abortions (Steinberg 1981). Israel holds world records in IVF and in late therapeutic abortions, as detailed elsewhere in this volume.

<u>Legal</u>. Meanwhile, in the secular community, the legal profession led the way, with the activities of the Society for Medicine and Law (1972) and its journal (1986), and the UNESCO Chair of Medical Ethics established in the law school in Haifa (2001) with its international conferences. Once again, the framing of the discussion appealed to a narrow, formalized approach to medical ethics, better attuned to more extreme cases where the dilemmas and opinions are clearly defined, but less to the complexity of everyday clinical ethics. A major output of this enterprise is the 2008 UNESCO Bioethics Core Curriculum, led by the chair, Judge Amnon Carmi, which is based on the Universal Declaration on Bioethics and Human Rights and is aimed at an international audience. In sharp contrast to rabbinical attitudes, the liberal creed of individual freedom is at the heart of the legal discourse, and is clearly reflected in the influence of this group on Israeli public life, as intellectual opinion leaders and through legislation, especially the Basic Law: On Dignity and Freedom, and the Patients' Right Law that is in many aspects a derivative of it.[3] The National Council for Bioethics, a statutory body under the National Health Law, was reactivated, and local ethics committees in hospitals were convened,[4] even if often not

---

[3] Halperin (2004) notes that Carmi's sensitivity to traditional Jewish sources alongside his liberalism is notable in his legal as well as in his editorial work.

[4] I am not relating here to the Helsinki research ethics committees, the national genetics research committee, or the animal experimentation committees. Rather I am only dealing here with clinical ethics.

particularly active. Lawyers are statutory members of these bodies and often the most influential in their deliberations (Wietchner 2014).

The Knesset has become increasingly active in clinical ethics legislation, though not always in as liberal a mode. Most prominent are the 2005 Terminal Patient Law, the twin 2008 laws on brain-respiratory death and organ transplantation, and most recently the 2015 Force-Feeding Amendment.

New legislation sometimes aroused widespread discussion in the profession, as well as among the public. The issue of force-feeding political detainee hunger strikers is a case in point. The Amendment mandates force-feeding when there is danger to life and is supported by a group of mainly religious senior physicians concerned with the sanctity of life.[5] The IMA published, unusually, two position papers on this subject, in 2005 and 2013, concerned more with preserving human dignity and freedom, as well as circulating a letter to all its members warning them that force-feeding is torture and forbidding them to collaborate.[6] Both the government's position and the IMA's are beyond the extremes of the opposing poles of international opinion. So far the new regulations have not been implemented or tested in court.

Professional. Over the years the IMA shifted its ethical discourse from professional issues to clinical and public health questions, its ethics committee became an active forum for doctors, and it published a series of statements and ethical guidelines for its members, which are now given a prominent place on the website.

Its 2014 ethical code devotes only two chapters out of eight to the traditional professional issues of the relationships of doctors with their colleagues and with the medical establishment, while all the others relate to patients, society, research, industry, the law, and the media. As expected, the primary focus of all the IMA discourse remains doctor-centered, though less on their duties and more on protecting their interests. The influence of contemporary Western, more specifically American, thought is quite apparent. For example, an expanded paper published in 2014 and edited by the chairman of the ethics committee, on the reciprocal relationships between doctors and patients, stresses human rights and collaborative decision making. In a 2006 paper on "Medicine and Belief in Medical Treatment," the primacy of the principle of the patient's "autonomy over his body" is stressed repeatedly. The analysis in a 2008 paper on mass casualty incidents is structured directly on the Georgetown principles. The Patients' Rights Act is repeatedly referenced in the IMA's official pronouncements on ethics, but notable by their absence are references to the family and the sanctity of life.

Another perspective on the ethics discourse within the medical profession is provided by the papers published in the two academic journals of the IMA (one in English and one in Hebrew). Significantly, recently the IMA found it appropriate to

---

[5] R. Zafrir, Leading Israeli Experts: Hunger-Striking Prisoners Should Be Force-Fed. *Haaretz*. August 23, 2015. www.haaretz.com/israel-news/.premium-1.672587.

[6] L. Edelman and T. Karni. Letter number 0181–2015 to all IMA doctors. July 30, 2015.

publish a compendium of all the ethics papers in these journals between 1999 and 2011 (Theodor and Theodor, eds. 2012). Looking at this material, written by Israeli physicians for the most part, apart from the specifically religious contribution to the debate, we find an active secular discourse. Close reading of this corpus reveals three dominant themes: extrinsic themes, including sociocultural and legal issues; personal issues, including emotional factors and the value of life; professionalism, including decision making and patients' rights.

Sociocultural factors.[7] This category included statements where various contextual factors were seen as ethically relevant to medicine. Examples include culture, family, social stigma, vulnerable populations, environment, history, economics, politics, and medical institutions. Religion was seen more as a constraint, a feature of a particular subculture, rather than as a moral resource.[8]

The Law. Laws, regulations, and guidelines were very common reference points.[9]

Emotional factors were cited as relevant to ethical decisions – coping patterns, the response to suffering, doctor–patient relationships, the patients' relationships, for example.

Life and death. A considerable amount of moral attention was given to various aspects of life and death. The value of life was a constant backdrop to the discussions of issues, including quality of life, control over life, pregnancy, fertility, sexuality, euthanasia, death, end-of-life, prolongation of life, and transplantation.

Doctors were seen as members of a *profession* concerned with issues of medical education, application of skills, new technologies, interdisciplinary and team work, professionalism, safety, support, and professionally privileged information. As members of the profession, doctors have not only a special set of responsibilities, but also a special level of responsibility vis à vis society.

Decision making.[10] Several papers showed an awareness of the complexity of clinical decision making, involving considerations of philosophical approaches, balancing ethical principles, ethics committees, a preventive approach, conflicts, priorities, errors, different medical approaches, barriers to care, efficiency of treatment, patient responsibility, physician responsibility, and involvement in research. The general trend was a search for good algorithms or guidelines, rather than leaving decisions to the discretion of the individual doctor.

Patients' rights were frequently referenced as taken for granted, reflecting the rhetoric of the liberal West. Issues that were brought up included confidentiality,

---

[7] "The cultural-sociological structure of Israel differs from that of many western countries" (Theodor 2012: 32).
[8] "A question that arose frequently ... was whether the principle of patient autonomy is valid and operational in the religious orthodox context and within the family" (Theodor 2012: 32).
[9] "The law has given the statutory medical ethics committees no role in deliberating the difficult dilemmas of prolonging or terminating life" (Theodor 2012: 31).
[10] "The dearth of medical knowledge regarding ... traumatic stress ... leaves us professionals with not a few dilemmas" (Theodor 2012: 283).

justice, equality, autonomy, and consent. Some authors did challenge the applicability of some of these concepts in the context of Israeli society.[11]

The content areas covered a wide range: reproduction and gynecology – five papers; end-of-life – six papers; economic considerations – seven papers; patients' rights – five papers; physicians' rights and burnout – four papers; Judaism and *halakhah* – six papers; complementary medicine – three papers. The other nine papers were overviews or individual chapters on specific issues.

Academic. Appointments in medical ethics have been made in the universities, with undergraduate and masters courses and research programs. Important centers have also developed in community colleges of higher education, such as Ono and Zefat. More recently major research institutes have entered the field, with the Van Leer Institute in Jerusalem running a medical ethics track of research, workshops, conferences, public lectures, and publications. The multidisciplinary Safra Center in Tel-Aviv University is doing similar work in several areas of applied ethics, including health care.

The universities have provided a home to an ever-expanding group of academics from various disciplines who research many aspects of medical ethics, keeping close contact with the international academic community. Special note may be made of two fields that reflect and highlight domestic concerns, the Holocaust and military medicine. Among the manifold activity in Holocaust medicine studies, high profile is provided by the annual national multidisciplinary conferences in Nahariya, headed by Professor Saul Shasha, now in their sixteenth year. Constant referral to the Holocaust serves a political identity-confirming function for many Jews, especially Ashkenazim, as well as underpinning the survivalism motif of much else in Israeli medical ethics, such as the unprecedentedly high rate of long-term ventilation in terminal care. Survivalism resonates too with the value-of-life ethic in rabbinical thought. Leading academic thinkers have made central contributions to Israeli military medical ethics, including philosopher Professor Asa Kasher, who composed the first ethical covenant for the IDF, and Professor Eran Dolev, a former surgeon-general and chair of the IMA Ethics Committee. Alongside the republicanism of this security-focused school there is a vocal radical humanist group of academics, many of whom are identified with the NGO Physicians for Human Rights – Israel. As it should, the Israeli academic scene maintains a vital tension among all the various trends and philosophies that comprise Israeli medical ethics.

SYNTHESIS

In order to remain congruent with the moral reactions of present-day Israeli patients and doctors, a culturally appropriate contemporary Israeli medical ethics is one that

---

[11] "Despite the passing of 'Rules Concerning Ethical Conduct of Physicians' at the 38th general assembly of the Israel Medical Association (1995), no impetus was forthcoming from the physicians regarding the Israeli Patient's Bill of Rights 1996" (Theodor 2012: 31).

is more nuanced than a straightforward human rights-based account resting on Kantian notions of autonomy. It may at times be framed in the language of virtues, of consequences, of relationships, or of religious dogma, but it develops dialectically in a highly specific sociohistorical context. To sum up, we may survey some of the most salient themes that our review has highlighted.

Critical thinking. Over history, Jews and Judaism have been constantly redefined in a dialectical process. However, the growing regulation and legalization of Israeli medicine seems to be affecting the medical ethical discourse too, expressed as a preoccupation with abiding by the law. The highly centralized Israeli establishment does not encourage independent critical thinking, so prominent in the diaspora, and Israeli doctors seem to comply with this and replace it with a respect for and fear of rules and the law. This is in contrast to the critical thinking that has always been a central feature of the fabric of the Jewish story, from the time that the Bible depicts Abraham challenging God himself over the justice of the destruction of Sodom and Gomorrah, through the literary structure of the Talmudic debates, the great medieval disputations, and down to some of the greatest innovators of modern times, Freud, Marx, and Einstein. All of the latter were assimilated enlightened people of Jewish origin, but none of them was committed to or even knew much about *halakhah*. In Yiddish, questions are typically not answered by answers but by a further question. Argument and protest typify the Israeli High Street to this day. Critical thinking is a strong candidate to be seen as *the* Jewish disposition. Critical thinking implies confronting one's fallibility. A current research initiative in the United States situates fallibility within the wider virtue of humility: "Intellectual humility is an intellectual virtue, a character trait that allows the intellectually humble person to think and reason well. It is plausibly related to open-mindedness, a sense of one's own fallibility, and a healthy recognition of one's intellectual debts to others. If intellectual humility marks a mean between extremes, then related vices (on the one side) would be intellectual arrogance, closed-mindedness, and overconfidence in one's own opinions and intellectual powers, and (on the other side) undue timidity in one's intellectual life, or even intellectual cowardice" (Greco and Stump 2013). If some Israeli doctors are frankly imperious, the neglect of the traditionally Jewish stance of critical thinking may be having serious repercussions, which abiding by the rules cannot counterbalance when the good of the patient is at stake. At least in this regard, Israel is proving quite un-Jewish.

Survivalism. We have seen that the local academic and professional debate in secular Israeli medical ethics reflects a major concern with life-and-death issues that parallels the social reality of Israeli society with its emphasis on the production and preservation of life, as seen in the preoccupation with IVF and prolonging life at all costs. Survivalism, if we may denote the preoccupation with the preservation of life as such, has been part of the Jewish historical narrative, from accounts of the biblical exodus from Egypt, through the Babylonian exile from the Land of Israel, the Roman diaspora, the Spanish Inquisition, the European Holocaust, and down to the struggle for the survival of the State of Israel in our day. True, there is a powerful moral and legal articulation of survival in rabbinic sources, but you do not have to be a rabbinic Jew to be part of the Jewish survival narrative. The rabbinic account indeed espouses a religious metaphysics to ground its valuation of human life, but this may be seen as just one side of a cultural coin, the other side of which is a shared historical memory. It seems, then, that contemporary Israeli medicine expresses the traditional religious emphasis on the value of life and its reinforcement by the historical experience of the Jewish people's and the State of Israel's survival in the face of repeated threats of extinction. The emphasis on a duty to preserve life is also identifiable as characteristic of a profession relating to its own history and ethos, over and above the general cultural context.

Social accountability. Traditional duty-driven professional ethics is fast losing ground in the Israeli discourse on medical ethics, with at least equal emphasis placed on patients' rights. Biblical Judaism was definitely preoccupied with social solidarity, from the Decalogue – honor your parents – and the Golden Rule – love your neighbor as yourself, down to tithes, laws of charity, and inheritance. We may identify here both dignity (Barilan 2012) and intimacy themes (Zoloth 1999). Sociologically, structures of solidarity are critically important to groups struggling for survival (Greene 2013). So it is neither surprising nor exceptional to find a strong sense of community among Jews through history. However, the strongly communitarian society that evolved in the Jewish diaspora, though still evident in Israel today, is eroding, especially in the large cities. In its place, the modern state is expected to respect the positive rights of individual citizens and to provide for them. This is the way contemporary Israeli medical ethics writing tends to frame the context of its debates.

Family. One arena of social intercourse remains paramount in Israeli society, the family. The impact of family on medical care is clearly recognizable in Israeli practice, even if this is not always well reflected in its academic or professional writings. The crisis in organ supply for transplants is due in part to the very common situation of the family vetoing postmortem organ donations even where the patient had given prior authorization (Lavee et al. 2010). The family's wishes are respected over and above the patient's. Revealing the diagnosis of terminal illness to the family but not to the patient is widespread and socially acceptable, despite its being in infringement of the Patients' Rights Law. In a study of staff attitudes to seemingly futile chronic respiratory support given to patients with dementia in Jerusalem's long-stay facilities, many nurses claimed that the families demanded it (Shaulov et al. 2015). Perhaps the family as an institution is less challenged in Israel than in the Western world, and Israeli doctors take it for granted that families are routinely and intimately involved in medical decisions. The family context has been seen through the generations as the vehicle of transmission of the shared memories of the Jews. The almost universally observed central family ritual of the *Seder* meal on Passover serves to confirm the mutuality of families with shared histories. It provides even more than that – it provides identity through relationships.

Religion. To a large extent, the arena of ethical debate in Israeli medicine was initially appropriated by *halakhah*, leaving the non-*halakhic* majority disenfranchised and bereft of a moral voice (Wietchner 1998). The Steinberg National Commission's discussion on withdrawal of life support exemplifies this situation, where the opinion of secular ethicists, where it differed from *halakhah*, was noted but rejected (Steinberg 2002). A subsequent Ministry of Health committee appointed to propose revisions to the law ten years later was disbanded by the next minister of health, a rabbi belonging to a religious political party (Linder-Ganz 2016).

Contemporary Western ethics has grown from Christian soil, and as such may not necessarily fit Israel's needs. In the United States in particular, Protestant ideas that stress individual achievement (Weber, Baehr, and Wells 1905), Catholic teachings on redemptive suffering, and a Thomist emphasis on developing virtues (McIntyre 1984) are all identifiable. Certainly Western ethics is more inclusive than that, and in contemporary secular society, its Christian content is latent rather than overt, but nonetheless a misfit with Jewish culture may be surmised. Just as the West has been secularized in recent generations, so too has Israel. So we are not talking here about medical *halakhah*, which only speaks to its adherents, but rather to an underlying set of moral reactions that have over the generations become a part of the heritage of general Jewish culture, as a result of a shared history and the ongoing dialectic of Jewish identity (Zohar 1997). Whether the religious heritage is seen as a residue or as a distillate of a long history, its presence is felt in everyday interactions with patients, religious or not. In particular, religious sensibilities tend to surface when people are challenged by potentially fatal illness. The special import of preserving life is one example where the religious heritage dovetails with the story of national survival. Another example would be the involvement of children in the medical care of their parents, where traditional rabbinical notions of filial piety are congruent with a social history of communal solidarity.

Tolerance. One quarter of the population of Israel is not Jewish, but predominantly Moslem, so that any local ethic must accommodate some sort of pluralism. This may take the form of tolerant relativism, accepting the coexistence of different values, or some sort of universalist humanism, aiming to find the commonalities. The historical tolerant side of Judaism, suppressed so long by the ordeals of survival under oppression, suddenly becomes relevant again in Israel, where the majority group is Jewish. The recurrent biblical injunctions to "love the stranger," as a positive reaction to the national experience of the sojourn in Egypt as strangers, takes on new meaning and normative force when Jews are in the majority. However much Israeli medical ethics might incorporate diaspora rabbinic attitudes, it also needs to give expression to this earlier and no less Jewish position. Despite the incorporation of Western humanistic values, there seems to be no evidence yet of a specific trend toward a fusion of Jewish and Moslem ethical modes.

While on the subject of inclusivism, a final note on gender is appropriate here. The orthodox rabbinical world sees women differently from men, and it is orthodoxy that is the preeminent and the establishment form of religious Judaism in Israel. Formally excluded from the requirement to study Jewish law as a religious precept, historically their access to the traditional textual sources has been severely curtailed, up to the present day. Most Jewish women traditionally gain knowledge of Jewish law and lore either at second-hand via men or by means of folk narratives and other informal forms of literature. Only in the past decade or so has the religious feminist movement in Israel made the first inroads toward equality of access to religious knowledge for women, with the corresponding social power that special knowledge gives its possessor (Zoloth 1999). These efforts are strenuously resisted by the vast majority of the rabbinical establishment, attesting to the central importance of this issue in Jewish life. In the medical world, many of the daily clinical ethical encounters are managed by nurses, in the absence of doctors from the ward, and increasingly, medicine itself is numerically becoming dominated by women doctors.[12] Nursing, as a predominantly female profession, and as such even further from the sphere of influence of rabbinic *halakhah* than nonreligious male society, needs to be considered separately. Under the influence of feminism, nursing as a profession has developed quite distinct approaches to medical ethics, often identified with "care ethics."[13] Israeli nursing literature and practice may well show different characteristics in this respect from those we find among physicians, and may indeed indicate a route to an appropriate contemporary Israeli medical ethics that medicine has not yet managed to formulate with sufficient conviction.

CONCLUSION

This, then, is the profile of Israeli Jewish medical ethics today, displaying universal as well as local factors, both spatially and temporally (Kasher 2015). Our analysis of the historical heritage suggests that some of the ethical preoccupations of today's Israeli doctors are at least partly grounded in a specific and local culture – first and foremost, the preservation of life and the centrality of family. Other aspects bear the signs of exposure to modernity – the respect for patients' rights, along with a dilution of the sense of personal professional duty. We may reasonably detect the inroads of Western liberalism and republicanism. The local social and political milieu makes abiding by the law the moral path of least resistance, in preference to independent

---

[12] I thank Jane Day of Lady Margaret Hall, Oxford for encouraging me to think about the role of nurses. Empirical study has demonstrated some systematic differences between doctors and nurses in their ethical perspectives, e.g., Robertson (1996).

[13] Care ethics is generally associated with Carol Gilligan (1983). For a recent anthology, see T. Kohn and R. McKechnie, eds. (1999). For a good description of the differences in the roles of doctors and nurses in patient care, see Levasseur (1993).

critical thinking. Local context also dictates how religion has reasserted its role in Israeli medicine, even for the secular majority.

These tensions are detectable in Israeli ethical publications, many of whose authors adopt a critical stance, some of them toward the recalcitrant Israeli practitioners who are slow to adopt commonly accepted Western values, such as patients' rights, and others toward those values themselves, claiming that Israeli culture is not the same as Western culture and should not be expected to ape the West at the cost of relinquishing its own values. Many of the papers remain as a call for debate rather than an attempt at a resolution, confirming our initial contention that medical ethics in Israel is still in search of a local ethos.

Israeli medicine today stands at the confluence of its local context and culture, and the Western, especially the American, view of medicine. Acknowledging the local value of survivalism, a traditional concern for family and relationships, consideration of religious sensibilities, and a contemporary respect for patients' rights, should resonate with the local culture and its values and mollify the pressure to align completely with value systems that have developed in other places and circumstances.[14]

References

Asher, E. and Reuveni, H. 2010. Defensive Medicine – The Phenomena and Its Impact on the Israeli Healthcare System. In Bin Nun, G. and Magnezi, R. eds. *Economic and Social Aspects of Israelis Healthcare System*. Hebrew, self-published, 110–120.

Avni, S., Davidovitch, N., and Filc, D. 2015. The Israel Medical Association's Discourse on Health Inequity. *Social Science and Medicine* 144: 119–126.

Barilan, Y. M. 2012. *Human Dignity, Human Rights and Responsibility. The New Language of Global Bioethics and Biolaw*. Cambridge, MA: MIT Press.

Bin Nun, G., Berlovitz, Y., and Shani, M. 2002. *The Health Care System in Israel – An Historical Perspective, Ministry of Foreign Affairs: The Health System in Israel*, 23 www.mfa.gov.il/mfa/aboutisrael/israelat50/pages/the%20health%20care%20system%20in%20israel-%20an%20historical%20pe.aspx.

Efron, J. M. 2001. *Medicine and the German Jews: A History*. New Haven, CT: Yale University Press. 42.

Elnekave, E. and Gross, R. 2004. The Healthcare Experience of Arab-Israeli Women in a Reformed Healthcare System. *Health Policy* 69: 101–116.

---

[14] I acknowledge in particular the respective contributions to the development of this chapter of Charles Foster, Nadav Davidovitch, the members of the Safra workshop, and members of the ETHOX seminars, as well as Galia Shoffman, who was actively involved in analyzing the Israeli literature. This chapter was written while on sabbatical leave from Bar-Ilan University, at the ETHOX Centre for Ethics in Healthcare and Green-Templeton College, Oxford University. I thank Bar-Ilan University for the leave of absence and Oxford University for its hospitality.

Gilligan, C. 1983. *In a Different Voice: Psychological Theory and Women's Development.* Cambridge, MA: Harvard University Press.

Greco, P. and Stump, E. 2013. http://humility.slu.edu/about.html accessed March 15, 2016.

Greene, J. 2013. *Moral Tribes: Emotion, Reason and the Gap Between Us and Them.* New York: Penguin.

Halperin, M. 2004. Milestones in Jewish Medical Ethics: Medical-Halachic Literature in Israel, 1948–1998. *ASSIA – Jewish Medical Ethics* 6(2): 4–19.

Hsieh, H.-F. and Shannon, S. E. 2005. Three Approaches to Qualitative Content Analysis. *Qualitative Health Research* 15: 1277–1288.

Jakobovits, I. 1959. *Jewish Medical Ethics: A Comparative and Historical Study of the Jewish Religious Attitude to Medicine and Its Practice.* New York: Bloch.

Jakobovits, I. 1966. *HaRefuah veHayahadut.* Mosad Harav Kook. Hebrew, trans. G. Bat Yehuda.

Kasher, A. 2015. The Values of Israeli Bio-ethics. In Siegal G., ed. *Bio-ethics Blue and White: On Israeli Bio-ethics.* Tel-Aviv: Mosad Bialik, Hakkibutz Hameuchad (Hebrew). pp. 36–68

Kohn, T. and McKechnie, R., eds. 1999. *Extending the Boundaries of Care: Medical Ethics and Caring Practices.* Oxford: Berg Press.

Lavee, J., Ashkenazi, T., Gurman, G., and Steinberg, D. 2010. A New Law for Allocation of Donor Organs in Israel. *Lancet* 375: 1131–1133.

Levasseur, J. and Vance, D. R. 1993. Doctors, Nurses, and Empathy. In Spiro, H. M., McCrea Curnen, M. G., Peschel, E., and St James, D., eds. *Empathy and the Practice of Medicine: Beyond Pills and the Scalpel.* New Haven, CT: Yale University Press. 76–173.

Liebman, C. S. 1999. Secular Judaism and its Prospects. In Urian, D. and Karsh, E., eds. *Search of Identity: Jewish Aspects in Israeli Culture.* London: Frank Cass. 29–48.

Linder-Ganz, R. 2016. *The Marker.* February 16, 2016 www.themarker.com/news/health/1.2852505 accessed March 14, 2016.

MacIntyre, A. 1984. *After Virtue: A Study in Moral Theory.* Notre Dame IN, University of Notre Dame Press, 2nd edn.

Robertson, D. W. 1996. Ethical Theory, Ethnography, and Differences between Doctors and Nurses in Approaches to Patient Care. *Journal of Medical Ethics* 22: 292–299.

Seidman, G. I. 2006. Regulating Life and Death: The Case of Israel's "Health Basket" Committee. *Journal of Contemporary Health Law & Policy* 23:18, footnote 41.

Shaulov, A., Frankel, M., Rubinov, A., Maaravi, Y., and Brezis, M. 2015. Preparedness for End of Life – a Survey of Jerusalem District Nursing Homes. *Journal American Geriatrics Society* 63: 2114–2119.

Shuval, J. 1992. *Social Dimensions of Health: The Israeli Experience.* Westport, CT: Praeger.

Shuval, J. and Anson, O. 2001. *Social Structure and Health in Israel.* Jerusalem: Magnes Press (Hebrew).

Shvarts, S. 2002. The Workers' Health Fund in Eretz Israel. The University of Rochester, NY, p. 298 – translated from Hebrew *Kupat-Holim Ha-Clalit 1911–1937*, 1997.

Steinberg, A. 1981. Induced Abortion According to Jewish Law. *Journal of Halacha and Contemporary Society* 1: 29–52.

Steinberg, A. 2002. Report of the Public Committee Concerning Terminal Care. www.health.gov.il/PublicationsFiles/steinberg_committtee.pdf accessed March 14, 2016.

Steinberg, A. 2003. Encyclopedia of Jewish Medical Ethics. Jerusalem, Feldheim, translated from the Hebrew edition first published in 1988–1989.

Theodor, I. and Theodor, E., eds. 2012. *Medical Ethics in Israel: A Collection of Articles Published in the Periodicals of the Israeli Medical Association in the Years 1999–2011*. Tel-Aviv: Israel Medical Association.

Weber, M., Baehr, P. R., and Wells, G. C. 1905–2002. *The Protestant Ethic and the "Spirit" of Capitalism and Other Writings*. Penguin. German, translated into English, T. Parsons 1930.

Weingarten, M. A. 2004. Sanctity of Life: A Critical Reassessment of Jewish Medical Ethics. In Twohig, P. and Kalitzkus, V., eds. *Interdisciplinary Perspectives on Health, Illness and Disease*. Amsterdam/New York: Rodopi. 9–20.

Wietchner, N. 1998. The Influence of Religious Values on Medical Ethics in Israel. *Journal International de Bioethique* 9: 117–126.

Wietchner, N. 2014. Healthcare Ethics Committees under Israel's Patients' Rights Law. Ethics, Law and Reality. PhD Thesis Submitted to the Senate of Bar-Ilan University Ramat-Gan, Israel.

Zohar, N. 1997. *Alternatives in Jewish Bioethics*. Albany: State University of New York Press.

Zoloth, L. 1999. *Health Care and the Ethics of Encounter: A Jewish Discussion of Social Justice*. Chapel Hill/London, University of North Carolina Press.

15

Tilting the Frame: Israeli Suicide as an Alternative to Suicide in Israel

Haim Hazan and Raquel Romberg

INTRODUCTION: TILTING THE FRAME OF SUICIDOLOGY

Suicidology and its mother disciplines of public policy, public health, psychiatry, and psychology have taken over both global and national/local discourses of suicide in the past four decades. Global approaches to suicide, in general, and the design of national suicide prevention programs, in particular – have been both led by the World Health Organization (WHO),[1] revealing subjacent yet forceful global bioethical forms of governance. These are driven by mental health and public policy conceptions of suicide, showing the prevalence of the so-called therapeutic society in Israel and the rest of the world. It involves, Brunner and Amrami argue (2016: 7), a sweeping work of "translation" of disparate social fields to the conceptual and applied frameworks of mental health in ways that appear as "legitimate and central to define, manage, and express the modern self" (p. 8). The "triumph of the therapeutic," in Rieff's apt phrase (1966), is evident in the "hijacking" of suicidology research and its bioethical significance, which circumscribes global and local bioethical understandings of suicide to mental health models aimed at the early detection, treatment, and prevention of suicide (see Lester and Rogers 2013).

The marketing of scientific knowledge based solely on standardized, quantifiable methods was critiqued extensively by Porter (1996, 2012). This critique also informs the recent alerts about suicidology monopolizing the study of suicide through positivist, medicalizing forms of knowledge (Brancaccio et al. 2013; Fitzpatrick et al. 2014; Marsh 2015; White et al. 2015). "By relying so heavily on such a narrow range of (positivist) methodologies, the knowledge produced within the field of suicidology can only take us so far, and many interesting and important research questions that are worth asking are not being explored. This includes, for example, questions that pertain to meaning, values, morality, contexts, language, culture, power, relations and discourse" (Marsh

---

Acknowledgments: Parts of this research were supported by the Minerva Foundation through a grant from the Minerva Center for Interdisciplinary Studies of the End of Life at Tel-Aviv University. We wish to thank our research assistants Hila Sharon and Tomer Haruv for their dedicated contributions.

[1] See the reports by the World Health Organization (WHO 2001, 2002, 2012a, 2012b, 2013) and the replication of most of these ideas within psychiatric discourse in Hawton and Heeringen (2009).

and White 2014: 73–74; cf. also Farberow 1975). Particularly disturbing is the technocratic demand for "evidence-based" research (Pringle et al. 2013; Rodgers et al. 2007; Widger 2015; Yip 2011) that guide "audit cultures" (Strathern 2000) such as those administered by modern states, thus reducing suicide research and its ensuing public understanding to mentalist and medicalizing models driven by standard quantifiable methodologies (Bowker and Star 1999). Health policy and bioethical interpretations of suicide produced under these constraints ignore or flatten, to say the least, local conditions, judgments, and sentiments.

This global trend, promoted by the World Health Organization (WHO), has been embedded in Israel's National Program for the Prevention of Suicidality and Suicide (2013). As will be shown, it follows the WHO's blueprint almost to the letter, leaving out locally anchored idiographic bioethical identifications of suicidality. In doing so, it surrenders to the global governance of the global bioethics of suicidology. A brief chronological and thematic account regarding its initiation and establishment will illustrate the local application of a universalist bioethics of suicide.

Against this backdrop, our tridimensional contextual framework considers the interplay of society, morality, and affect as a key for assessing the public dramas emerging around suicide events at different periods in Israeli cultural history. The resulting local diachronic bioethics of suicide considers notions of individual and social injustice, systems of accountability and responsibility that seemingly trigger such extreme responses to personal distress and its ensuing suicide. Not unlike those well-documented discussions of suicide in small-scale societies (Billaud 2012; Macdonald 2007; Staples 2012; Staples and Widger 2012; Widger 2012), the sets of moral predicaments, pronouncements, and judgments expressed about suicide in the public sphere are "folk explanations" (Bohannan 1960) voiced in "emic" lay idioms and images (cf. Bähr 2013). In this manner, rather than building on global bioethical assumptions such as those driving the aforementioned National Program for Suicide Prevention in Israel and governing suicide in Israel, we offer a unique insight on the idiosyncratic bioethical terms of *Israeli suicide*, and their underlying "structures of feeling" (Williams 1977) in a temporal perspective. Guided by the premises of cultural sociology (Alexander 2004; Alexander, Geisen, and Mast 2006; Alexander and Smith 2001), our inquiry focuses on "suicide events" (cf. Katz 1980), rather than on statistical figures, to identify "limit-situations" (Jaspers 1970) or "moral breakdowns" (Zigon 2007, 2009) projected in the media as stirring the social dramas (Turner 1974) of memorable suicides in Israel. We argue that such unspoken ethical conflicts are thrown into public relief when the very historically changing tacit social codes of morality in society cease to provide cues for individuals to being-in and being-with the world.

Our corpus, far from aiming to cover all statistically significant suicide cases in Israel, is composed of thirty-eight suicide cases that have become "suicide events" because of the intense moral judgments and affect invested in them in the public sphere spanning years from the 1950s until today.[2] Problematized in this manner, our exploration of suicide in Israel is temporally contextual and interpretative of latent moral and existential dilemmas about suicide, personhood, and society.[3] Thematically, the social dramas of our corpus revolve around conceptions of the citizen, the nation, and the state, which emerge in the discourses of suicide events alongside a complex continuum stretching between modes of shame and shaming.

In many societies, shame or dishonor (Stewart 1994) refers to critically denied rights for respect that explain the upholding as well as the breaking of social relations. In many cases, shame and shaming involve processes related to two major principles determining suicide: reciprocity and assertion (Berndt 1962: 181), when by virtue of the first, suicide may be a balancing of wrongdoing, and by virtue of the second, suicide may be a "hot belly" response to humiliation that sets up the condition for inflicting harm on the offender – "even if this takes the extreme form of an act of aggression against the self" (Berndt 1962: 204). Extensive cross-cultural examples regarding the connection between shame, shaming, and suicide partly illuminate the complexities that might tie individuals, collectivity, and suicide, reminding us that suicide "cannot be accounted for in any given society without explaining how that society functions" (Macdonald 2007: 4). Indeed, our corpus revealed that shame and shaming, albeit perhaps raising similar reactions of anger and revenge as in ethnographic accounts of simple societies, were bound, in contrast, to changing conceptions of the citizen, the nation, and the state. Indeed, if, according to Durkheim's taxonomy of suicide (1951) – be it anomic, egoistic, or altruistic – the defining variables are the levels of institutionalization of society and the integration of individuals, the suicide events we examine require, in contrast, the assessment of the social representations staged in the open courtroom of the public sphere as variables. Hence, the assumption guiding our thematic typology is that in the course of time different kinds of social relations and discourses inform the affect conveyed in the various media engaged in reporting and construing suicide events. This move involves divergent, yet interconnected sets of local and diachronic moral economies that construe the presumed breakdowns that goad individuals to end their lives. In other words, the moral ruptures lurking in the interstices between mainstream mores (pertaining to Durkheim's levels of institutionalization) – particular to a place in time – and their effective realization by individuals (according to their levels of integration) appear in public discussions of suicide events in Israel. Our corpus lends support to the revolutionary critique anthropologist Dorothy

---

[2] In contrast, suicides, suicide attempts, and threats of suicide directly related to structural racism and powerlessness have been relegated to news stories published only on social networks, reporting, for instance, about self-immolation attempts of people threatened by evacuation from public housing (Ephraim and Morag 2013) and the suicide of a young Israeli of Ethiopian origin following his harassment by the police (Hashmonai 2014).

[3] As media studies in general have shown, the public relevance of suicide acts is socially, culturally, and historically constructed regardless of their statistical figurations. This is the reason for the omission of suicide cases among Israeli Arabs and Israelis of Ethiopian or Russian origin in this corpus.

A. Counts made in the 1980s about the cultural significance and legal use of the term "suicide," which in many cases could be relabeled as "social homicide" – e.g., "They killed her with talk" (1984: 87, 1980, 1987) – which might be a more adequate term than "suicide" (killed herself). In many ethnographic studies of suicide in simple societies, suicide may be an expression of power by otherwise powerless people, but in our corpus, most of the suicide events involve relatively powerful individuals who became powerless either in fulfilling their mainstream values and roles or in defending themselves against public dishonor, as in, but not limited to, cases of cyberbullying or social-network-based impeachments. These are cases in which individuals are left without recourse to confronting or correcting malicious or incriminating allegations, which could be likened to the experience of social death inflicted on someone without due trial or a chance for making amends, as some suicide notes and reports in our corpus show. Thus, expressions such as *mishpat sade* ("field trial") and "character assassination" were used to convey the conceived personal injury resulting from unjust collective indictment without due process.

We have grouped the major shifts in public discussions of suicide events and thematically identified them over the span of sixty years along a continuum extending from shame to shaming. This analysis yielded a total of twelve inductively grounded categories that reflect macro-sociocultural processes related to degrees of nation-state and personal accountability, and to the modes in which the individual and the collectivity figure in various sociocultural contexts. Against prevalent arguments as to the privatization of Israeli collectivity, a diachronic exploration of suicide events shows that the face of the collectivity has not disappeared, but rather has lately taken on a mediatized complexion, as a form of "distant solidarity" – inspired by Boltanski's "distant suffering" (1999) – which explains the recent shift in the agency of the imagined community from a state-controlled edifice to a mediatized yet no less compelling form of governmentality. Overall, the diachronic social dramas of suicide events point to temporally contextualized and biased bioethical interpretations of suicide, where individual and collective shame and shaming rather than mental health issues emerge as the common culprits of communal peace.

In the following sections, after briefly situating the governance of the WHO's global bioethics of suicide, in general, and on Israel's Suicide Prevention Program, in particular, we present our analysis of the idiosyncratic bioethical interpretations of suicide events in Israel within the continuum between shame and shaming in more detail.

GLOBAL BIOETHICS OF SUICIDE: GOVERNING THE LOCAL ON A GLOBAL SCALE

In 2012 the World Health Organization (WHO) published a quick, practical, step-by-step guide for the constitution of national suicide prevention programs, steered by "THE NEED FOR TAKING ACTION." It specifies a stepwise approach for "Developing A SUICIDE PREVENTION STRATEGY" for the purpose of "Identifying stakeholders; Undertaking a situation analysis; Assessing the requirement and availability of resources; Achieving political commitment; Addressing stigma, and Increasing awareness." And then it stipulates the "Key Components of a National Suicide Prevention Strategy" that includes "Clear objectives; Relevant risk and protective factors; Effective interventions; Prevention strategies at the general population level; Prevention strategies for vulnerable subpopulations at risk; Prevention strategies at the individual level; Improving case registration and conducting research; Monitoring and evaluation" (WHO 2012b).

For the purposes of showing how the World Health Organization indirectly acts as a governing instrument on national levels (cf. De Leo et al. 2013), we now zoom in on what the WHO understands as "Undertaking a situation analysis," that is, getting what it deems contextual, local elements:

> A meticulous situation analysis that identifies the extent of the problem in a *particular geographical area* (whether an entire country or a specific subregion in a country) is a vital step. It should include *an estimate of the annual incidence of suicide and suicide attempts* in an area and point to relevant sociodemographic, structural and clinical factors, thereby *identifying those populations that are especially vulnerable*. Also, it should indicate the *most commonly used methods of suicide* and potential reasons for the same, and *assess the availability, use and quality of services* for those who attempt suicide as well as existing *gaps in the health system*, in responses from other sectors, and in intersectoral mechanisms. A comprehensive analysis should identify the presence of a *policy to reduce the harmful use of alcohol*, audit the quality of media reporting on suicide, consider the quality of statistics on suicide and suicide attempts, assess the quality of existing surveillance systems, and identify any gaps that exist in data collection.
>
> Additionally, it should identify *key "hotspots,"* which include bridges or high-rise buildings with low fences or roof walls, or other areas associated with previous suicides. The analysis of *barriers to implementation* is an important part of the situation analysis in which all the barriers are listed and solutions are suggested to remove them one by one. Without barrier identification, strategies may not move from paper to action. (WHO 2012, 9, our emphasis)

It is evident that, while this new program aims at including local diversity, it falls squarely within the universalizing and globalizing agenda of the WHO: to promote standardized blueprints of national prevention programs that – once implemented – could be easily comparable statistically (cf. Jansson 2013).

Paradoxically, though, driven by the need to *locally curtail* suicide within their own societies, nations are increasingly being *governed* and *domesticated* by the bioethical conventions and agendas of global organizations such as the WHO, and Israel is no exception (cf. WHO 2012a).

GLOBAL BIOETHICS WITHIN THE NATIONAL SUICIDE PROGRAM FOR SUICIDE PREVENTION IN ISRAEL

Following the directives of the WHO, several government initiatives led to the establishment of the National Suicide Prevention Program in Israel in 2013. As early as 2000, thirteen parliamentary discussions about "suicide" were held in the Knesset (Israeli Parliament) about the future setting up of the National Suicide Prevention Program.[4] In 2005, the first suicide prevention program was introduced in the army, which reduced the number of suicides from thirty-five in 2005 to fourteen in 2012. It included the modification of the procedures for keeping weapons, the training of officers, seminars for soldiers, and computerized suicide alerts for soldiers at risk (Israeli Knesset 2013). A second program was introduced in the Prison Service, which reduced the number of prisoners' suicides by 70 percent (Israeli Knesset 2013). It entailed changes in the layout of cells and the addition of electronic surveillance in cells and lavatories (Ministry of Public Security, June 3, 2013). By 2007, Knesset debates included suicide attempts and suicidal behavior under the label of "suicidality." In addition to special yearly debates scheduled around the "International Day for the Prevention of Suicide," all others were prompted by "systemic" triggers of suicide, such as "Judge suicide following overload," "Disengagement – Suicide threats of residents close to being evacuated," "Suicide of immigrant after her children were taken for adoption by social services." Responding to the medicalized notion of "risk populations," half of all parliamentary discussions were dedicated to the suicide of youngsters and immigrants, and special sessions were devoted to suicide in the army and its disclosure (Cohen 2013). Following the recommendations of the WHO, guardrails were placed next to bridges (Krauss, November 25, 2013), and restrictions imposed on the sale of analgesics to the general public (Beit-Or, December 3, 2014).

Between 2008 and 2012, a pilot study was conducted in three towns – Rehovot, Ramla, and Kfar Cana – that included major "risk populations," in preparation for the implementation of a national suicide prevention program (The Joint and the Israeli Government 2013a). It assessed, in complete agreement with WHO studies, proactive detection, care systems, telephone helplines, the training of professionals, and public awareness (The Joint and the Israeli Government 2013a). A parallel pilot program that assessed the support of families whose loved ones killed themselves was also conducted. Finally, in December 2013, the government approved the gradual operation of the National Suicide Prevention Program for the entire country, with an investment of 55 million shekels (approx. 15.5 million dollars) for three years. Following the identification of risk groups by the WHO, it would focus on "those who attempted suicide, who are suffering from a psychiatric disorder and clinical

---

[4] The name given finally to this program in 2013 is "National Program for the Prevention of Suicidality and Suicide." But here we refer to it with a shortened name, National Suicide Prevention Program.

depression, immigrants, family members of a person who committed suicide, consumers of alcohol and drugs, and separated and divorced men" (The Joint and the Israeli Government 2013b).

Concomitantly, the guiding parameters of the WHO informed the founding and operation of several nongovernmental organizations in Israel dedicated to the prevention and treatment of suicidality, and support and helplines for suicidal individuals and their families. For example, For Life (Bishvil Ha'haim) was founded in 2000 for the support of families whose loved ones committed suicide, becoming an important player shaping both policy and government initiatives and the form and content of contemporary discourse on suicide in Israel. Members of the organization are often interviewed in the media, telling their personal experiences, especially around international days for suicide prevention. In addition, the association sponsors, once a year, peaceful marches aimed at raising public awareness, humanizing the phenomenon and making it visible. Another important activity of this nonprofit is the organization of academic conferences once or twice a year, gathering professionals, family members of people who committed suicide, and the general public in debating and disseminating current issues and research related to suicide prevention, paralleling those promoted by the WHO.

The general message of the WHO, that suicide is preventable and there are signs for early detection, is embedded in the activities suggested for national programs for suicide prevention, which need to involve all sectors of the population and increase the visibility and publicity of suicide prevention efforts. Indeed, social visibility has become a crucial building block of the current discourse of suicide prevention in Israel and its politics. Some rhetorical devices are employed in this process; among them is the presentation of statistical evidence showing the decreasing numbers of suicide rates as a testimony to the success of suicide prevention programs; another builds on the ethical message of "*arvut hadadit*" ("mutual accountability") to boost government funding for the prevention of suicide. New anti-cyberbullying and social media alert technologies have been adopted and concerted with special units of the police dedicated to the prevention of suicide, in cooperation with operators at support organizations such as Sahar (Online Emotional Assistance) and Eran (Emotional First Aid by Phone & Internet).

As these practices show, the global bioethics of suicide promoted by the WHO not only dominates national health policies, the content of nongovernmental organizations, and public discourse about suicide prevention and populations at risk, but also the ethical standing of the "therapeutic" society. A unique insight into it could be gained from the personal perspective offered by three social workers, members of the Israel National Suicide Prevention Project since 2009, who jointly authored a paper entitled "The Israeli National Project of Suicide Prevention – Thoughts from Within" (2012). They frame the ethical mores of the therapeutic standing of this national agenda by means of two Jewish ethical maxims from the Bible: the value of life as God-given,[5] and to save one person is to save the whole world.[6] They set out to demonstrate the compatibility of the Jewish ethos with the underlying premises guiding the WHO's global bioethics of suicide prevention and their professional calling, arguing that these maxims reflect "those deep perceptions [that] permeate our collective unconscious and identity as a nation, and as part of this nation we, as individuals, and as therapists, are also influenced." A very different take on local culture and its role in shaping the idiosyncratic bioethics of Israeli suicide in a temporal perspective appears in the next section, where social dramas emerging in the public sphere are characterized along the continuum of shame and shaming.

SHAME AND SHAMING: LOCAL BIOETHICAL DRAMAS OF "ISRAELI SUICIDE"

The following account identifies and illustrates the twelve categories that emerged inductively in our research. **(a) Personal heroic shame** and **(b) antiheroic shame** arise in suicide events with regard to the nation and to state bureaucracy, respectively. In the early decades after independence, shame was associated with the impossibility of fully realizing the values of ideally committed citizenship, and thus can be seen as tied to an a priori nation-building process whereby individuals are crafted as hologram-like instances of the collective. Suicide is thus but one option for citizens who fail to withhold that high standard of being an embodiment of the nation. Such were the cases of Uri Ilan (1955) and Nehemia Argov (1957). Uri Ilan committed suicide in a Syrian military jail after being captured together with four other soldiers without showing any resistance. The other four were released, returned to Israel, and were tried. Scraps of Uri Ilan's various suicide notes, hidden and stashed away in the folds of his clothes, became national mantras after military and political leader Moshe Dayan quoted from them in public: "I didn't betray; I killed myself." Col. Nehemia Argov, military aid and close friend of Prime Minister Ben Gurion, killed himself out of utter shame, as his suicide note read, after accidentally hitting and fatally injuring a bicycle rider with his car. Both the suicide events of Uri Ilan and Nehemia Argov bring up the accomplished incarnation of the individual subject within the nation, where the person is engulfed and incorporated into the collective persona of the nation in all its entirety and totality. In contrast, within the category of **(b) antiheroic shame**, the suicide events of Israel Sinai (1954), a "Jerusalem confectioner and alleged tax evader" and of "a factory owner" (1966), put into evidence the yet-unfinished, bureaucratic, tax-related normalization of the new state and the failure and shame of some of its citizens not only to obey the laws without a full-fledged system of legal sanctions, but also withstanding the collective shame it entailed.

---

[5] "Behold, I have placed before you: Life and Goodness, and Death and Evil; and you should choose Life" (Deuteronomy 30:15–16).

[6] "He who saves one soul is the savior of a whole world" (Mishnah Sanhedrin 4:5).

Economic-related suicide events that occurred in the decades after the consolidation of state bureaucracy and finance regulations, between the 1970s and 1980s, are collectively sanctioned as "shameful" for their lack of (c) **civic shame** – even when the guilt of public figures in mishandling public funds was not proved categorically. This category includes suicide events marked by public debates concerning the misconduct of public finance and business figures such as Avraham Ofer (1977), Yaacov Levinson (1984), and Miki Albin (1985). Avraham Ofer, a minister who was suspected of economic corruption, killed himself with a gunshot, leaving a note saying *"shofhim et dami"* ("They're spilling my blood"). He was later vindicated in the public sphere; his case was never brought to the courts. This constitutive social drama was the harbinger of a spate of corruption that triggered suicides by renowned public figures. Corruption charges in a nascent nation-state denote a sense of betrayal committed on the body politic by one of its organs, a thoroughly Durkheimean perspective. The suicide event of Yaakov Levinson, the director of Bank Hapoalim (owned by the national trade-unions organization), involved public accusations of economic fraud, which he described as "character assassination," and ended with his suicide. Beginning in the 2000s, economic and financial mismanaging of funds leading to suicide were debated as cases of personal, not collective debacle. Such (d) **privatized shame** debates marked, for instance, the suicide events involving national sports-team managers Robi Shapira (2001) and Simon Moni Fanan (2009), both accused of the personal mismanagement of communal funds, leading to bankruptcy.

Suicide events debated around the (e) **systemic shaming** of public figures are marked by unsurmountable personal dilemmas related to their specific positions, emerging out of systemic conflicts of interests in which they are caught more as victims of the system than as perpetrators. Such are the discussions around David Weiner (2005) and Ephraim Bracha (2015). The personal shame unjustly suffered by one of the agents of the state while fulfilling his duties was raised by the suicide event of public defender David Weiner, who had been caught, according to his suicide letter, "as a pawn" of two state prosecutors. After the suicide, Attorney General Menachem Mazuz said that "nobody in Weiner's situation can be blamed," and Shendar, one of the state prosecutors involved, said that "it was a tragedy in which each side did its professional best – with tragic consequences" (Yoaz 2005). Another suicide event that was often referred to as a "field trial" is that of National Fraud Squad Head Dep.-Ch. Ephraim Bracha. He did not leave a note before he shot himself in the heart on July 5, 2015, but public debates about mounting suspicions of his alleged compromised loyalty as a senior police commander highlight the moral breakdown that might have led to his suicide. "In 2012, Bracha caused a public stir when he corroborated the case against Rabbi Yoshiyahu Pinto after he recorded the celebrity rabbi offering him a $200,000 bribe in return for information about an investigation against the Hazon Yeshaya foundation he ran" (Hartman and Yonah 2015). From the time he turned the rabbi in, in spite of being one of his followers, many of the rabbi's supporters publicly attacked Bracha. Many allegations of corruption and improper conduct in several other cases were aired against Bracha, but the Ministry of Justice rejected them. Bracha appears in these debates not only as the representative of the state, but also as a religious man, a follower of Pinto. "[When] he learned that the rabbi was accusing him of corrupt dealings with the Israeli mafia ... Bracha became disillusioned and exploded: 'You are no rabbi,' he snapped at Pinto. This fueled an entire industry of fatal, unbridled rumors" (Hartman and Yonah 2015). Whether he was guilty and thus committed suicide, or was innocent and thus committed suicide are both plausible explanations, both of which remain unresolved. What remains are the dilemmas surrounding conflicting loyalties to the state and to religion that this suicide event exposed and the intense debates that it promoted as to the collective media impeachment of a public figure who has been denied due process.

The state and its inability to assure the well-being of its citizens in devastating situations in life and when confronting illness and death figure in suicide events that intentionally or implicitly perform its own shaming. In some cases, which fall under **(f) shaming of the state I**, suicide events are debated publicly in relation to economic and personal hardships related, for instance, to unemployment, homelessness, and legal troubles, which state agencies should have been able to attend to and solve but didn't. Such are the cases of Moshe Silman (2012) and Joseph Ethel (2015). Both were marked by public performative suicidal acts, the first by self-immolation at a rally, and the second by jumping to his death from an unemployment agency. In the case of Moshe Silman's self-immolation at a social rally, the shaming of the state was performed in an overt and dramatic vengeance-accusation of self-execution. Similarly to what Berndt (1962: 204) characterized as "hot belly" reactions, Silman's suicide event was portrayed as an aggressive response to the humiliation that the state, by not being accountable to the compact of the Israeli welfare society, had inflicted on him; his publicly performed self-immolation was perceived as inflicting shame on the government, even if in the process it entailed an extreme, public, aggressive act of sacrificial self-effacement. The suicide event of Moshe Silman appears as the most compellingly iconic suicide event to this day, not only because it represents the downfall of a typical middle-class entrepreneur, but because his suicide was the most violent, public, and performative of all others. The agency and resonance of his letter and self-immolation during a demonstration immediately turned this suicide into a memorable one in the collective memory of the majority of Israelis. His pleas appealed directly to the concerns of many middle-class Israelis who are potentially threatened by similar structural processes of disenfranchisement and self-identify with the politics of the social protest movement that took place at the time. His suicide note leaves no doubt as to who the real culprit of his suicide is: the state. Note that notwithstanding the litany about the fragmentizing and individualization of Israeli culture, Silman demonstrated a deeply seated allegiance to the state, a bond that was betrayed and broken. The state also appears as the culprit in the suicide event of Joseph Ethel. Against the social-moral principles of the welfare state, the state is presented as exacerbating rather than aiding and abetting in the slipping into socioeconomic marginality. Reports stress that he was unemployed for twenty years with a long history of unsuccessful dealings with medical and welfare bureaucratic state agencies when he jumped to his death on the site of the unemployment office in 2015. The family charged state agencies with utter failure in attending to the needs of citizens in dire straits such as Joseph Ethel.

A second type, **(g) shaming the state II**, refers to the failure of the state and its laws to provide adequate protection and dignity to citizens facing the debilitating effects of illness and old age. In the 1990s, a series of suicide events involving aging couples, such as the Avrahamis (1995), the Yaaris (1995), the Bertals (1997), the Arads (1998), the Tanais (1999), and the Sterns (2000), raised the existential dramas of aging Israelis who are confronted by the dilemmas of overstretching their demands on family bonds in view of the poor or no support provided by the state. The suicide event of media personality Adi Talmor (2011), a death tourist to Switzerland, has become iconic due to his detailed documentation of the terminal illness from which he suffered and the futile pleas he made for dying with dignity in his own country. In this category suicide events concerned the protection of human dignity, the avoidance of being a burden to kith and kin, and the shame of being disenfranchised of both their civility and their civic right to preserve their self-respect. Within the category **(h) shaming of the state III** are suicide events that, like the previous two categories, relate to the state's inability to protect its more fragile citizens; but in this case, it encompasses suicide cases that have been saved from utter anonymity, becoming suicide events only after they had been adopted as a poster case by social activists fighting, for example, against prostitution, and for the rights of disabled individuals ("Elderly Couple Kill Son," 2015; "Jessica," 2015; "School Girl," 2015).

With the advent of social media and the pervasiveness of personal communication technologies, suicide events related to **(i) peer shaming** (David El-Mizrahi, 2011; thirteen-year-old boy, 2015), and **(j) professional shaming** (Ariel Runis, 2015) make their appearance in the twenty-first century. Beginning in 2011, suicide events around cyberbullying raised crucial issues about online shaming and accountability when fifteen-year-old David El-Mizrahi hanged himself (Ozen 2013) and then when an even younger boy killed himself after being bullied by his peers. The debates around these cases have focused on the insurmountable shame these youngsters felt, their impotence to change portrayals of themselves and the lack of protection they must have felt, particularly the responsibility of schools, teachers, peers, and ultimately the education system for securing their safety and protecting their rights. In those events, state agencies are deemed accountable for the occurrence of the tragic deaths of helpless children. In addition to children, the most dramatic, affective cases of suicide events are based on the suicide of public figures, who for all matters – except for the suicide itself – have complied with mainstream moral, social, and ethnonational codes through their life.

Suicide events related to **(j) professional shaming** highlight the fact that some form of sudden social, interpersonal, or political situation destabilizes an entirely exemplary social life. The alleged "crisis" appears in the public sphere as unsurmountable to the point of becoming so unbearable that it annihilates the persona of the individual even before the actual suicide occurs. The following emotional excerpts from the note of Ariel Runis (2015) illustrate this:

> Until two days ago, my life seemed to follow a rose-garden scenario. At age 47 I've been a retired officer of the Israeli Intelligence Agency (ISA) after twenty years of exciting, challenging, satisfying service. I earned three academic titles (two in Political Science and one in Law). I've seen half the world. After my retirement, I completed my degree in Law, did my specialization at the Prosecutor's Office of Tel-Aviv, passed my habilitating exams, and was hired as the director of the Department of Immigration and Population, Tel Aviv. All that I wanted – I had. Two days ago, a woman came to the bureau for a certain service. At that time, I was helping other people. She demanded an immediate service and began shouting that the failure to attend to her requests is racist.

Making a strong case for the injustice committed against him by one person and the shaming expanded in social networks, he details his life and career against the very racism he was accused of.

While some of the memorable suicides of artists and popular culture icons (fiction writers, singers, and comedians) were usually framed within typical global scripts of artists who crumble under the pressures of success or artistic anguish, sometimes also accompanied by drug use (Mike Brandt, 1975; Tirza Atar, 1977; Inbal Perlmuter, 1997; Dalia Rabikovich, 2005), the most debated ones are those suicide events that implicate or shame some or all aspects of the Israeli "nation." **(k) Shaming the nation I** refers to cases in which the nation's universal civil rights – conceived as equally applicable to a plurality of publics – failed to represent and defend the rights of specific publics (Esti Weinstein, 2016), and **(l) shaming the nation II** refers to cases in which the nation appears as a community that unjustly rejected or turned its back on some of its members. The suicide events of singers Zohar Argov (1987) and Gaby Shooshan (2016) and entertainer Dudu Topaz (2009) are very different and yet share some crucial elements in regard to legitimate, illegitimate, and anachronistic demands for ethnonational recognition. The first two were debated on account of their ethnic origin and artistry, and the third for his illegitimate racist humor, which positioned him on the margins of mainstream media and eventually excommunicated him. Whereas Zohar Argov is revered today as the sacrificial Mizrahi victim of cultural discrimination of the 1970s, Gaby Shooshan appears as desperately trying to ride on that collective guilt – outdated by the 2010s – for the racial exclusion of Mizrahi singers. Having failed in his attempted comeback to regain recognition of his artistry, he committed suicide in 2016; his suicide reverberated in the media as a case of unsuccessfully facing the double jeopardy of being old and ethnically underprivileged.

CONCLUDING REMARKS

Considered as suicide events, the highly dramatic media debates around spectacular cases of suicide over the course of nearly six decades have afforded the authors a unique seismographic register of the shifts of the pervading and prevailing moral economies of suicide in Israel. These shifts have been found to correspond to macropolitical and sociocultural transformations informing the modes in which suicide events have been debated in various periods: as embodiments of personal shame in relation to an idealized collective; as forms of shaming state bureaucracies and the ethno-nation for not delivering on social and national compacts; and as mediatized forms of personal shame emerging within systemic governmental structures and new social media technologies. Two corollaries follow. First, the violence (cf. Girard [1972] 1979) of these mechanisms is two-pronged, emerging from and directed to the national subject, on the one hand, and commencing and ending in the collective, on the other. Second, the genealogy of the changing effect and affect of public representations of suicide events in Israel suggests a multifarious yet consistent move from state domination of identity to virtual control of personhood. Pursuant to these transformations in the construction of suicide dramas are changing forms of sovereignty and citizenship. Whereas the media projection of suicide during the period of nation building indicated that the regulating of shame by the state determined the context of the phenomenon, the transfer of legitimacy and social surveillance to the networks turned institutionalized mechanisms of debunking dignity into unrestrained surges of public shaming. This shift in sources of sovereignty from indirect to direct representation also spells recent turns in the tenor of the time. Thus, the specter of globalization coupled with the democratization of information and communication facilitated by nascent technologies alters the moral discourse concerning suicide. From the condonable act of voluntary life-ending by physician-assisted suicide to the glorified spectacles of self-immolation, the mass exposure of the unshrouded theater of taking one's life is free to watch either as a subject for identification stirring public controversies or as an object of distant, disengaged observation that entails neither commitment nor intervention.

The unveiled visibility of suicide renders intimacy public and euphemistic camouflage defunct. This oxymoronic tangle of what Illouz (2007) termed in her discussion of late emotional capitalism as "cold intimacies" resonates with Boltanski's concept of "distant suffering" (1999), which formulates the engrossed indifference of shooting anguish and even tormented death through the lens of safe distance. This contemporary observation, while pertaining to some general properties of places devoid of identity and identification, "non-places" in the age of "supermodernity" as coined by Augé ([1992] 1995), is germane to the proverbial attributes of Israeli society. Notwithstanding sociological disagreements as to the persistence or decline of solidarity in current Israeli culture, it is clear that the discourse of melting pot and multiculturalism occupies a glaring spot in the academic and public arena. In this respect, talking of suicide events is a gauge for this kind of collective self-searching. Thus, looking at suicide in Israel is an edifying mirroring device through which suicide events could be rendered Israeli. The crux of this Israeliness of local suicide is in the spiraling dialectic of personal subject and national subject from complete indivisibility of shame through assumed separation between public shame and individual guilt to the restoration of the fusion of the two in the working of the social as practiced in virtual networks. Suicide events, therefore, are not only signifiers of social processes, but, to an extent, their generator.

References

Abu-Lughod, L. (1990). The Romance of Resistance: Tracing Transformations of Power through Bedouin Women. *American Ethnologist*, 17(1), 41–55.
Ahmed, S. (2004). Affective Economies. *Social Text* 22, 121–139.
Alexander, J. C. (2004). Cultural Pragmatics: Social Performance between Ritual and Strategy. *Sociological Theory*, 22(4), 527–573.
Alexander, J. C., Giesen, B., and Mast, J. (eds.) (2006). *Social Performance: Symbolic Action, Cultural Pragmatics, and Ritual*. Cambridge: Cambridge University Press.
Alexander, J. and Smith, P. (2001). The Strong Program in Cultural Theory: Elements of a Structural Hermeneutics. In J. H. Turner (ed.), *Handbook of Sociological Theory* (pp. 135–150). San Francisco, CA: Springer.
Almog, O. (2000). *The Sabra: The Creation of the New Jew*. Translated by H. Watzman. Berkeley: University of California Press.
Augé, M. ([1992] 1995). *Non-places: Introduction to an Anthropology of Supermodernity*. Translated by J. Howe. London: Verso.
Bähr, A. (2013). Between "Self-Murder" and "Suicide": The Modern Etymology of Self-Killing. *Journal of Social History*, 46(3), 620–632.
Battin, M. (2015). *The Ethics of Suicide: Historical Sources*. Oxford: Oxford University Press.
Berndt, R. M. (1962). *Excess and Restraint: Social Control among a New Guinea Mountain People*. Chicago: University of Chicago Press.
Bhugra, D. (2013). Cultural Values and Self-Harm. *Crisis*, 34(4), 221–222.
Billaud, J. (2012). Suicidal Performances: Voicing Discontent in a Girls' Dormitory in Kabul. *Culture, Medicine, Psychiatry*, 32(2), 264–285.
Bohannan, P. J. (1960). Theories of Homicide and Suicide. In P. J. Bohannan (ed.), *African Homicide and Suicide* (pp. 3–29). Princeton, NJ: Princeton University Press.
Boltanski, L. (1999). *Distant Suffering: Morality, Media and Politics*. Cambridge: Cambridge University Press.
Bowker, G. C. and Star, A. S. (1999). *Sorting Things Out: Classification and Its Consequences*. Cambridge, MA: The MIT Press.
Brancaccio, M. T. (2013). "The Fatal Tendency of Civilized Society": Enrico Morselli's Suicide, Moral Statistics, and Positivism in Italy. *Journal of Social History*, 46(3), 700–715.

Brancaccio, M. T., Engstrom, E. J., and Lederer, D. (2013). The Politics of Suicide: Historical Perspectives on Suicidology before Durkheim. An Introduction. *Journal of Social History*, 46(3), 607–619.

Brunner, J. and Amrami, G. P. (eds.) (2016). *Beyond the Clinic: Psychological Discourse in Contemporary Culture* (in Hebrew). Tel Aviv: Resling.

Cohen, G. (2013, October 6). Discussion between Knesset and Israel Defense Force Researchers about Media Reporting of Suicide (in Hebrew). *Ha'aretz*. Retrieved from www.haaretz.co.il/news/politics/1.2133618.

Counts, D. A. (1980). Fighting Back Is not the Way: Suicide and the Women of Kaliai. *American Ethnologist*, 7, 332–351.

Counts, D. A. (1984). Revenge Suicide by Lusi Women: An Expression of Power. In D. O'Brien and S. Tiffany (eds.), *Rethinking Women's Roles: Perspectives from the Pacific* (pp. 71–93). Berkeley: University of California Press.

Counts, D. A. (1987). Female Suicide and Wife Abuse: A Cross-Cultural Perspective. *Suicide and Life-Threatening Behavior*, 17(3), 194–204.

Coyle, J. and MacWhannell, D. (2002). The Importance of "Morality" in the Social Construction of Suicide in Scottish Newspapers. *Sociology of Health & Illness*, 24, 689–713.

Dayan, D. and Katz, E. (1992). *Media Events: The Live Broadcasting of History*. Cambridge, MA: Harvard University Press.

De Leo, D., Milner, A., Fleischmann, A., Bertolote, J., Collings, S., Amadeo, S., and Wang, X. (2013). The WHO START Study: Suicidal Behaviors across Different Areas of the World. *Crisis*, 34(3), 156–163.

Deleuze, G. and Guattari, F. ([1980] 2004). *A Thousand Plateaus*. Translated by B. Massumi. London: Continuum.

Durkheim, É. (1951). *Suicide: A Study in Sociology*. New York: Simon & Schuster.

Ephraim, O. and Morag, G. (2013, October 14). Elderly and Single Mothers Are Evacuated for a Park (in Hebrew). *YNET*. Retrieved from www.ynet.co.il/articles/0,7340,L-4440614,00.html.

Farberow, N. L. (1975a). Introduction. In N. L. Farberow (ed.), *Suicide in Different Cultures* (pp. ix–xvii). Baltimore, MD: University Park Press.

Farberow, N. L. (1975b). *Suicide in Different Cultures*. Baltimore, MD: University Park Press.

Fekete, S. (2002). The Internet – A New Source of Data on Suicide, Depression and Anxiety: A Preliminary Study. *Archives of Suicide Research*, 6(4), 351–361.

Fitzpatrick, S., Hooker, C., and Kerridge, I. (2014). Suicidology as a Social Practice. *Social Epistemology: A Journal of Knowledge, Culture & Policy*, 29(3), 303–322.

Girard, R. ([1972] 1979). *Violence and the Sacred*. Translated by P. Gregory. Baltimore, MD: Johns Hopkins University Press.

Hartman, B. and Yonah, J. B. (2015, June 7). Top Israel Police Investigator Bracha Commits Suicide. *Jerusalem Post*. Retrieved from www.jpost.com/Israel-News/Top-police-investigator-Bracha-commits-suicide-408026.

Hashmonai, A. (2014, July 7). Yoseph Broke Down after Police Officer Tasered Him (in Hebrew). WALLA. Retrieved from http://news.walla.co.il/item/2762226.

Hawton, K. and Heeringen, A. K. (2009). Suicide. *Lancet*, 373, 1372–1381.

Illouz, E. (2007). *Cold Intimacies: The Making of Emotional Capitalism*. Oxford: Polity Press.

Jansson, Å. (2013). From Statistics to Diagnostics: Medical Certificates, Melancholia, and "Suicidal Propensities" in Victorian Psychiatry. *Journal of Social History*, 46(3), 716–731.

Jaspers, K. (1970). *Philosophy, Volume II*. Translated by E. B. Ashton. Chicago: University of Chicago Press.

Jeffreys, M. D. (1952). Samsonic Suicide or Suicide of Revenge among Africans. *African Studies*, 11, 118–122.

Katz, E. (1980). Media Events: The Sense of Occasion. *Studies in Visual Anthropology*, 6, 84–89.

Krauss, Y. (2013, November 25). Following 11 Suicides: Railing on Highest Bridge in the Country (in Hebrew). *NGR*. Retrieved from www.nrg.co.il/online/54/ART2/525/007.html.

Lester, D. and J. R. Rogers (eds.) (2013). *Suicide: A Global Issue* (Volume I: *Understanding*; Volume II: *Prevention*). Santa Barbara, CA: Praeger.

Macdonald, C. J. (2007). *Uncultural Behavior: An Anthropological Investigation of Suicide in the Southern Philippines*. Honolulu: Hawaii University Press.

Marsh, I. (2015). Critiquing Contemporary Suicidology. In J. White, I. Marsh, M. J. Kral, and J. Morris (eds.), *Critical Suicidology: Transforming Suicide Research and Prevention for the 21st Century* (pp. 15–30). Vancouver: University of British Columbia Press.

Marsh, I. and White, J. (2014). Boundaries, Thresholds, and the Liminal in Youth Suicide Prevention Practice. In H. Scott-Mhyre, V. Pacini-Ketchabaw, and K. G. Scott-Mhyre (eds.), *Youth Work, Early Education, and Psychology* (pp. 69–89). New York: Palgrave.

Massumi, Brian. (1995). The Autonomy of Affect. *Cultural Critique*, 31, 83–109.

Minois, G. (2001). *History of Suicide: Voluntary Death in Western Culture*. Translated by L. G. Cochrane. Baltimore, MD: Johns Hopkins University Press.

Ministry of Public Security. (2013, June 3). Gatekeepers – Modes of Suicide Prevention among the Incarcerated and Convicts (in Hebrew). June 3, 2013. Retrieved from http://mops.gov.il/DetentionAndRehabilitation/Pages/Watchmen.aspx.

Ozen, A. (2013). 15-Year-Old Boy Commits Suicide Because of Facebook Bullying, Peers Post a Song about His Life (in Hebrew). *Nana10*, August 20. Retrieved from http://news.nana10.co.il/Article/?ArticleID=999815.

Porter, Theodore M. (2012). Thin Description: Surface and Depth in Science and Science Studies. *Osiris*, 27 (1): 209–226.

Porter, Theodore M. (1996). *Trust in Numbers: The Pursuit of Objectivity in Science and Public Life*. Princeton, NJ: Princeton University Press.

Pringle, B., Colpe, L. J., Heinssen, R. K., Schoenbaum, M., Sherrill, J. T., Cynthia A. Claassen, C. A., and Pearson, J. L. (2013). A Strategic Approach for Prioritizing Research and Action to Prevent Suicide. *Psychiatric Services*, 64(1): 71–75.

Rieff, Philip. (1966). *The Triumph of the Therapeutic: Uses of Faith after Freud.* New York: Harper & Row.

Rodgers, P. L., Sudak, H. S., Silverman, M. M., and Litts, D. A. (2007). Evidence-Based Practices Project for Suicide Prevention. *Suicide and Life Threatening Behavior,* 37(2), 154–164.

Staples, J. (2012). Introduction: Suicide in South Asia: Ethnographic Perspectives. *Contributions to Indian Sociology,* 46 (Special Issue: Suicide in South Asia: Ethnographic Perspectives, guest editor: James Staples), 1–28.

Staples, J. and Widger, T. (2012). Situating Suicide as an Anthropological Problem: Ethnographic Approaches to Understanding Self-Harm and Self-Inflicted Death. *Culture, Medicine, Psychiatry,* 36(2), 183–203.

Stewart, F. H. (1994). *Honor.* Chicago: University of Chicago Press.

Strathern, M. (1968). Popokl: The Question of Morality. *Mankind,* 6(11), 553–562.

Strathern, M. (1972). *Women in Between: Female Roles in a Male World, Mount Hagen, New Guinea.* London: Seminar Press.

Strathern, M. (ed.) (2000). *Audit Cultures: Anthropological Studies in Accountability, Ethics, and the Academy.* London: Routledge.

The Joint and the Israeli Government. (2013a). *The National Program for Suicide Prevention: Documentation of the Pilot* 2008–2012 (in Hebrew).

The Joint and the Israeli Government. (2013b). *The National Program for Suicide Prevention: Summary and Recommendations for the National Program for Suicide Prevention* (in Hebrew).

Turner, V. W. (1974). *Dramas, Fields, and Metaphors: Symbolic Action in Human Society.* Ithaca, NY: Cornell University Press.

Wasserman, I. M. (1994). Suicide and the Media: The *New York Times*'s Presentation of Front-Page Suicide Stories between 1910 and 1920. *Journal of Communication,* 44(2), 64–83.

Weaver, J. C. (2009). *Sadly Troubled History: The Meanings of Suicide in the Modern Age.* Quebec: McGill-Queen's University Press.

Weaver, J. and Munro, D. (2013). Austerity, Neo-liberal Economics, and Youth Suicide: The Case of New Zealand, 1980–2000. *Journal of Social History,* 46(3), 757–783.

White, J., Marsh, I., Kral, M., and Morris, J. (eds.) (2015). *Critical Suicidology: Transforming Suicide Research and Prevention for the 21st Century.* Vancouver: University of British Columbia Press.

WHO. (2001). Mental Health: New Understanding, New Hope.

WHO. (2002). European Monitoring Survey on National Suicide Prevention Programmes and Strategies. Suicide Prevention in Europe.

WHO. (2010). Western Pacific Region: Towards Evidence-Based Suicide Prevention Programs. Retrieved from www.wpro.who.int/mnh/TowardsEvidencebased SPP.pdf.

WHO. (2012a). Country Reports and Charts. Retrieved from www.who.int/mental _health/prevention/suicide/country_reports/en/index.html.

WHO. (2012b). Public Health Action for the Prevention of Suicide: A Framework.

WHO. (2013). Mental Health Action Plan 2013–2020. Retrieved from http://apps.who.int/iris/bitstream/10665/89966/1/9789241506021_eng.pdf.
Widger, T. (2012). Suffering, Frustration, and Anger: Class, Gender and History in Sri Lankan Suicide Stories. *Culture, Medicine, and Psychiatry*, 36(2), 225–244.
Widger, T. (2015). "Suicidology as a Social Practice": A Reply. *Social Epistemology Review and Reply Collective*, 4(3), 1–4.
Williams, R. (1977). *Marxism and Literature*. Oxford: Oxford University Press.
Yip, P. S. (2011). Towards Evidence-Based Suicide Prevention Programs. *Crisis*, 32(3), 117–120.
Yoaz, Y. (2005, January 12). Mazuz Orders Inquiry into Suicide of Attorney Weiner. *Ha'aretz*.
Zigon, J. (2007). Moral Breakdown and the Ethical Demand: A Theoretical Framework for an Anthropology of Moralities. *Anthropological Theory*, 7(2), 131–150.
Zigon, J. (2009). Within a Range of Possibilities: Morality and Ethics in Social Life. *Ethnos*, 74(2), 251–276.

Index

Abduction of Yemenite, Mizrahi, and Balkan children affair, 79–84
  Ein Shemer camp and, 80
  IMA and, 85–87
  NGOs for, 79–80
  nurses' role in, 84–85
  racism in, 81–82
abortions, selective
  under Catholic doctrine, 125
  ethnic background as factor for, 126
  genetic compatibility and, 125
  under German law, 125–126
  under Israeli law, 124–126, 229
    Efrat-C.R.I.B., 125
  PND and, 124–126
activism. *See* disability activism
ADA. *See* Americans with Disabilities Act
advanced directives, 272
Alaan, Muhammad, 57
alternative childbirth movement, 192–193
Alternative Medicine, development of, 3
altruism, surrogacy and, 145
Amar, Shlomo, 268
American Medical Association, 182
Americans with Disabilities Act (ADA), 101–102
anatomo-politics, 67
Andrews, Peter, 139
antiheroic shame, 302
anti-psychiatry movement, 3
Argov, Nehemia, 302
Argov, Zohar, 306
ART. *See* assisted reproductive technology
Ashkenazi Jewish community, 225–226
assisted reproductive technology (ART)
  individuality and, 121
  in Israel, 142
    cultural influences on, 203
  kinship and, 119, 120–121
  surrogacy and, 140
autonomy principles
  in end-of-life decision-making, 251–252
  radical egalitarian republicanism and, 51–52
Avian influenza (H5N1)
  in Gaza strip, 23
  in Israel, 1, 23
  in Jordan, 23
  WHO response to, 23

baby farming, 180
Baby Health Movement, 181–182
BD. *See* brain death
Ben-Ami, Moshe, 87
beneficence principles, 251–252
bio-capitalism, ethics of, 5
bioethics
  of brain death, 258–259, 268–271
    prioritization policy for, 270–271
  communitarian response to, 5–6
  conservative response to, 5–6
  disabilism and, 6
  disability activism and, 97
  of end-of-life decision-making, 240, 251–252
  in Europe, 49
  feminist response to, 3, 6
  historical development of, 3–8
    academic debates during, 4
    doctor–patient relationships and, 3–4
    global expansion as result of, 4
    liberalism as influence on, 4
  Israel public policy on, 2
    analysis of, 8–10
    exceptionalism of, 9–10
    extension of, 3–8
    historical development of, 9
    scholarly debate on, 9

bioethics (cont.)
  Jewish, 9
    religious tradition as factor in, 41
  during Nazi regime, 3
    Helsinki Declaration as result of, 3
    Nuremberg Code as result of, 3
  neutrality of, 5
  of organ donation, 258–259
  political nature of, 4–5. *See also* biopolitics
    framing of, 6–7
    as political economy, 7
  of posthumous assisted reproduction, 203–205
    with parent of deceased requests, 205
    prior consent of deceased and, 205
  principalist approach to, 7
  radical egalitarian republicanism and, 49–53
    life-prolonging drugs and, 53
  suicide and
    global approaches to, 298–299
    National Suicide Prevention Program and, 300–302
    WHO guidelines for, 298–299, 300–302
  technological determinism and, 10
  Tuskegee syphilis study, 3
biopolitics
  anatomo-politics, 67
  defined, 7
  different discursive framing of risk and, 235
  of inmate hunger strikes, 66–69
    conceptualization in, 69–72
    for force-feeding, 71
  Israel public policy on, 2
birth rates, in Israel, 203
body self-image, for women, 168
Bracha, Ephraim, 303–304
brain death
  bioethics of, 258–259, 268–271
    prioritization policy for, 270–271
  dead donor rule and, 271–273
  definition of, 261
  end-of-life decision-making for, 272
  in Germany, 261
  in Israel
    under Brain-Respiratory Law, 265–266
    introduction of, 259
    from 1968–2008, 262–267
    politicization of, 268–269
    Sadgat scandal, 259–261
  in Japan, 261–262
  organ donation and, 259–261, 271–273
Brain-Respiratory Law, 265–266, 285

care ethics, 291
Carmi, Amnon, 284

carrier screenings, 228–230
Catholic doctrine, selective abortions under, 125
CBRC. *See* Cross-Border Reproductive Care
childbirth. *See also* neonatal care
  Baby Health Movement and, 181–182
  at home, 183–185
  in hospitals, 181
    governance policies on length of hospital stay, 191–192
    under National Security Law, 188
    newborn screenings and, 184–185
    in Palestine, 187
    Zionism and, 187
  in Israel, governance policies for, 185–194
    Hadassah organization and, 185–189
    for home births, 192–193
    for length of hospital stay, 191–192
    through official publications and websites, 193–194
    philanthropic aid as influence on, 185
  in Israel, Hadassah organization and, 185–189
  medicalization of, 194–196
    feminist influences on, 196
    Zionism as influence on, 196
  midwifery and, 186, 195
  under National Insurance Act, 188
  in nineteenth century, 181–183
  pro-active mentality for, 197
children, cultural symbolism of
  in Israel, 203
  in Palestine, 163
citizenship, for Palestinian citizens, 163–166
civic shame, 303
civil rights movement, 3
  disability activism and, 101–102
  disability activism as part of, 101–102
clinical ethics, in Israel. *See also* Jewish medical ethics
  academic influences on, 287
  critical thinking approaches to, 288
  decision-making and, 286
  development of, 283–287
  family ideology as influence on, 289
  halakhah and, 277, 283–284, 290
  historical context of, 277–283
  Israeli medicine and
    doctors and, 278, 279, 280–281
    government control of, 279–280
    historical development of, 277–281
    under National Health Insurance Law, 279–280
    sick fund insurance and, 278, 280

legal influences on, 284–285
  Knesset and, 285
nurses and, 291
patients' rights and, 286–287
professional influences on, 285–287
rabbinical influences on, 283–284
social accountability factors in, 289
social context of, 277–283
socio-cultural influences on, 286
survivalism and, 288–289
synthesis of themes in, 287–291
tolerance and, 290–291
coerced feeding, 63–64
Cohen, Avi, 268, 272
Cohen, Keivan, 214
cold intimacies, 307
collective decision-making, in disability activism, 103, 108–111
  intellectual presence in, 109–110
  physical presence in, 109–110
  through public policy, 110–111
Committee for the Rescue of Israel's Babies. See Efrat-C.R.I.B.
commodification, of human body, 148
common good
  hegemony and, 47
  in republicanism, 46–47, 48–49
communication with dying patient, 246–247
communitarianism
  bioethics and, 5–6
  in Israel, 41–43
community genetics, 224, 234
community-based screenings, 230–233
competitive perspective, on pandemic preparedness, 33
compulsory force-feeding, 63–64
congenital hypothyroidism, newborn screening for, 183, 228–229
conservatism, bioethics and, 5–6
Convention on the Rights of Persons with Disabilities (CRPD), 101–102, 103–104
coping strategies, 172–175
the Correction, 56–58
  criticisms of, 57–58
Cross-Border Reproductive Care (CBRC), 140–141
  in Israel, 140–141
cross-border surrogacy, 145–149, 153, 154
CRPD. See Convention on the Rights of Persons with Disabilities

Daniels, Norman, 49
dead donor rule, 271–273
decision-making. See also end-of-life decision-making

clinical ethics and, 286
in disability activism
  collective, 103, 108–111
  individual, 103–108
Declaration of Istanbul, 264
Depo-Provera affair, 82–84
  IMoH and, 87–88
  racism in, 83–84
    denial of, 83–84
different discursive framing of risk, 235
disability, disabilism and, 6. See also disability theory
  eugenics movement and, 77, 99
  under Legal Capacity and Guardianship Law, 112, 113–114
  social Darwinism and, 99
disability activism, 101–103
  bioethics and, 97
  collective decision-making in, 103, 108–111
    intellectual presence in, 109–110
    physical presence in, 109–110
    through public policy, 110–111
  diversity of disability and, 109–110
  individual decision-making in, 103–108
    access to administrative proceedings and, 105–106
    through informed consent, 103–105
    through legal capacity, 103–105
    limited options in, 106–108
    voice in, 105–106
  nothing about us without us perspective on, 103–108, 113
  rights movement and, 97
    civil rights approach, 101–102
    global aspects of, 101
    human rights approach, 101–102
    in Israel, 102
    language of, development of, 102–103
  voice
    through Disability Rights Commission, 111–113
    in individual decision-making, 105–106
    institutionalization of, 111–113
Disability Rights Commission, 111–113
disability rights movement, 97
  civil rights approach, 101–102
  CRPD and, 101–102, 103–104
  global aspects of, 101
  human rights approach to, 101–102
  in Israel, 102
  language of, development of, 102–103
disability theory
  bioethics and, 97
  critique of, 98–103, 113

disability theory (cont.)
  in Israel, 100
  medicalization of disability, 99–101
  misinformation dimension of, 100
  moral dimension of, 100
  individual-medical approach, 97
disease. *See* emerging infectious disease concept; eradication of disease
dishonor, 297–298
distant suffering concept, 307
diversity of disability, 109–110
doctor–patient relationships
  bioethics and, 3–4
  in end-of-life decision-making, 251–253
  historical development of, 3–4
Dolev, Eran, 287
donor cards, 272
Down Syndrome screening, 223–224
Drop of Milk clinics, 186, 188
Dying Patient Act 2005, 240–245
  background for, 241–242
  criticism of, 243–245
  legal framework for, 241–245
  principles of, 242–243

Efrat-C.R.I.B. (Committee for the Rescue of Israel's Babies), 125
egalitarian republicanism
  defined, 42–43
  freedom as part of, 44–46
  political equality as part of, 44–46
  radical, 47, 48–49
    autonomy and, 51–52
    bioethics and, 49–53
    freedom and, 49, 52
    right to health and, 50–51
EID concept. *See* emerging infectious disease concept
Ein Shemer camp, 80
Embryo Carrying Agreements Act, 142–144, 146
emerging infectious disease (EID) concept, 25–26
  eradication of disease in, 25
  preparedness thinking in, 26
  prevention in, 26
EMT. *See* Epidemic Management Team
end-of-life decision-making
  autonomy principles in, 251–252
  beneficence principles in, 251–252
  bioethics of, 240, 251–252
  for brain death, 272
  consent in, 272
  doctor–patient communications in, 251–253
  family involvement in, 253–254
  during final stage, 242
  methodological study of, 245–250
    communications with dying patient in, 246–247
    demographics in, 246
    family relationships in, 247–249
    findings from, 245–250
    life-prolonging treatment provisions in, 249–250, 254–255
    non-maleficence principles in, 251–252
Epidemic Management Team (EMT), 30–32
Equal Rights for Persons with Disability Law (ERPDL), 102, 106
eradication of disease, 25
ERPDL. *See* Equal Rights for Persons with Disability Law
ethics. *See* bioethics; care ethics; clinical ethics; Jewish medical ethics; reproductive ethics
Ethiopian women, Depo-Provera affair and, 82–84
ethnic profiling, in public health genetic services, 231
ethnicity, in public health genetics services, 231–232, 233
Ettinger, Meir, 65
eugenics movement, 77, 99
Europe, bioethics in, 49
expertocratic approach, to PAR, 213

families, end-of-life decision-making by, 247–249
familism, Israeli, 123
family ideology. *See also* abortions
  clinical ethics influenced by, 289
  in Germany, 127, 131–132
  in Israel, 121–123, 131–132, 203. *See also* Jewish American families
    closeness as part of, 121
    early studies of, 122
    intergenerational conflicts and, 130
    PHR and, 127–128
    PND, 124–127
    in popular culture, 122–123
    Western individualist ideals in, 120
  PGD, 131–132
  PHR and, 127–131
    in Israel, 127–129
    national restrictions on, by nation, 127
    in U.S., 128–129
  PND, 124–127
    abortion and, 124–126
  posthumous grandparenthood, 128
  pronatalism, 123, 124
  racial ideology as part of, 142
  reprogenetics, 126
  responsible motherhood and, 126

family involvement, in end-of-life decision-making, 253–254
Fanan, Simon Moni, 303
feminist movement
　bioethics and, 3, 6
　Isha L'Isha organization, 82
　medicalization of childbirth influenced by, 196
fertility treatments
　in Israel, 1
　IVF, 1
　for Palestinian women, in Israel, 162–163, 164–165
　public policy as factor for, 170–172
force-feeding, of inmates, 50–51, 56–58, 59–66
　biopolitical aspects of, 71
　compulsory, 63–64
　definition of, 63–64
　Foucault on, 66–69
Force-Feeding Amendment, 285
Foucault, Michel
　on force-feeding of inmates, 66–69
　GIP and, 66
France, inmate hunger strikes in, 66
Franklin, Sarah, 140
free speech, hunger strikes as, 60–61

Gamzu, Roni, 87
Gaza strip, H5N1 in, 23
gender. *See also* women
　posthumous assisted reproduction and, 204
genetic compatibility, 125
genetic databases, 226, 230–233
Genetic Information Law, 226
genetics. *See* community genetics; public health genetics services
German, Yael, 87
Germany
　abortion policy in, 125–126
　family ideology in, 127, 131–132
GIP. *See* Prison Information Group
Glick, Shimon, 41, 50–51
Global Public Health Security (GPHS), 25–26, 38–39
　dual use arguments, 27–28
　EID concept, 25–26
　ethical challenges to, 27–28
　IHR and, 26–27
"global war on terror," 69
GPHS. *See* Global Public Health Security

H5N1. *See* Avian influenza
Hadassah organization, 185–189
　Drop of Milk clinics and, 186, 188
　Midwifery Act and, 187

halakhah (religious law)
　clinical ethics influenced by, 277, 283–284, 290
　posthumous assisted reproduction and, 208, 210–212
HaLevi, Jonathan, 93–94
health care systems. *See also* medical community
　in Israel, 52–53
　　under National Health Insurance Law, 161
　　for Palestinian citizens, 161
　　for Palestinian women, 160–163, 173–174
　racism in, 77
health governance systems. *See also* medical community
　in Israel, 28–29
　in Palestine, 28–29
hegemony, common good and, 47
Helsinki Declaration, 3
HGDP. *See* Human Genome Diversity Project
Histadrut, 282
home births, 183–185. *See also* neonatal care
　in alternative childbirth movement, 192–193
　functionalist approaches to, 194–196
　governance policies for, in Israel, 192–193
　midwifery and, 186, 195
hospital births, 181
　government policies on length of stay, 191–192
　under National Security Law, 188
　newborn screenings and, 184–185
　in Palestine, 187
　Zionism and, 187
Human Genome Diversity Project (HGDP), 232
Human Genome Project, 232
human rights, disability activism and, 101–102
hunger strikes, among inmates, 1–2
　biopolitics of, 66–69
　　conceptualization in, 69–72
　　for force-feeding, 71
　under the Correction, 56–58
　　criticism of, 57–58, 71
　definition of, 59–61, 70
　　as free speech, 60–61
　force-feeding and, 50–51, 56–58, 59–66
　　biopolitical aspects of, 71
　　compulsory, 63–64
　　definition of, 63–64
　　Foucault on, 66–69
　in France, 66
　"global war on terror" and, 69
　indefinite detention and, 71–72
　inmates and, defined, 64–66
　in Ireland, 69
　mental state as result of, 61
　under Patient's Rights Law, 53, 58, 62, 65
　as political fetishization of body, 69

hunger strikes, among inmates (cont.)
    treatment of, 62–63
        medical treatment compared to, 62
        type of imprisonment as context for, 65
        welfare institutions and, 70

IAG. *See* Israeli Attorney General
ideology. *See* family ideology
IDF. *See* Israeli Defense Forces
IHR. *See* International Health Regulations
Ilan, Uri, 302
IMA. *See* Israeli Medical Association
IMoA. *See* Israeli Ministry of Agriculture
IMoH. *See* Israeli Ministry of Health
in vitro fertilization (IVF)
    in Israel, 1
    under National Health Insurance Law, 164
    posthumous assisted reproduction through, 204–205
indefinite detention, 71–72
India, surrogacy agencies in, 148, 150
individual decision-making, in disability activism, 103–108
    access to administrative proceedings and, 105–106
    through informed consent, 103–105
    through legal capacity, 103–105
    limited options in, 106–108
    voice in, 105–106
individual-medical approach, to disability, 97
infant mortality rates
    in Italy, 186
    for Jews, 180
    in Palestine, 180
infant welfare movement, 181–182. *See also* neonatal care
infertility, among Palestinian women, in Israel, 162
infertility contractors, 172–173
informed consent
    disability activism and, 103–105
    in end-of-life decision-making, 272
inmates, defined, 64–66
insurance. *See* National Health Insurance Law; National Insurance Act; sick fund insurance
intellectual presence, 109–110
internal colonization, 164–165, 167
International Health Regulations (IHR), 26–27
IPS. *See* Israeli Prison Service
Ireland, inmate hunger strikes in, 69
Isha L'Isha, 82
Israel. *See also* clinical ethics; Knesset; Palestinian citizens, in Israel; securitization; suicide
    ART in, 142
    cultural influences on, 203

bioethics policy in, 2
    analysis of, 8–10
    exceptionalism of, 9–10
    extension of, 3–8
    historical development of, 9
    scholarly debate on, 9
biopolitics policy in, 2
biosecurity in, 28–29
birth rates in, 203
brain death in
    under Brain-Respiratory Law, 265–266
    introduction of, 259
    from 1968–2008, 262–267
    politicization of, 268–269
    Sadgat scandal, 259–261
CBRC in, 140–141
childbirth governance policies in, 185–194
    Hadassah organization and, 185–189
    for home births, 192–193
    for length of hospital stay, 191–192
    through official publications and websites, 193–194
    philanthropic aid as influence on, 185
children as cultural imperative in, 203
disability activism in, 102
disability rights movement in, 102
ERPDL in, 102, 106
family ideology in, 121–123, 131–132, 203. *See also* Jewish American families
    closeness as part of, 121
    early studies of, 122
    intergenerational conflicts and, 130
    PHR and, 127–128
    PND, 124–127
    in popular culture, 122–123
    Western individualist ideals in, 120
fertility treatments in, 1
H5N1 and, government response to, 1, 23
health care system in, 52–53
    for Palestinian citizens, 161
health governance systems in, 28–29
IVF in, 1
liberal egalitarian republicanism in, 53
liberalism in, 41–43
military-cultural complex in, 28
neonatal care in, 181
newborn screenings in, 185–191
    new technologies for, 190–191
    at Tel HaShomer hospital, 189–190
organ donation in
    introduction of, 259
    from 1968–2008, 262–267
    organ trafficking, 263–264

though ADI, 262, 263
under Transplantation Bill, 266–267
pandemic preparedness in, 29–36
civil-military cooperation in, 31–32
EMT in, 30–32
historical development of, 29–31
IMoH and, 29–34
policy frameworks for, interaction of, 33–34
regional cooperation for, 34–36
Patient's Rights Law in, 53, 58, 62, 65
posthumous assisted reproduction in, 205–215, 216
expertocratic approach to, 213
halakhah approaches to, 208, 210–212
IDF and, 206, 207–210
military context for, 205–210
pronatal values and policy in, 139, 163–166
public health genetics services in, 224–233
comparative perspectives on, 224, 226–228
genetic counseling clinics, 224–225
historical development of, 224–226
national genetics database in, 226
under National Health Insurance Law, 224
in screening programs, 225–226
religious communitarianism in, 41–43
selective abortions in, 124–126, 229
Efrat-C.R.I.B., 125
surrogacy in, 142–144
under Embryo Carrying Agreements Act, 142–144, 146
rise in births, 144
Welfare (Treatment of Retarded Persons) Law in, 105–106
Zionism and, 100
Israeli Attorney General (IAG), 127–129
Israeli Defense Forces (IDF), posthumous assisted reproduction and, 206–210
combat soldiers' parents and, 209–210
preservation of sperm, 207–209
Israeli Medical Association (IMA), 57–58
Abduction of Yemenite, Mizrahi, and Balkan children affair and, 85–87
on racial segregation in maternity wards, 88–90
Israeli medicine
doctors and, 278, 279, 280–281
government control of, 279–280
historical development of, 277–281
under National Health Insurance Law, 279–280
sick fund insurance and, 278, 280
Israeli Ministry of Agriculture (IMoA), 23
Israeli Ministry of Health (IMoH)
Depo-Provera affair and, 87–88
pandemic preparedness and, 29–34

Israeli Prison Law, 57
inmates defined under, 64–66
Israeli Prison Service (IPS), 59–60
Israeli Supreme Court. *See* Knesset
Israel-Palestine, geographic definition of, 23
Italy, infant mortality rates in, 186
IVF. *See* in vitro fertilization

Japan, brain death in, 261–262
Jewish American families, early studies of, 122
Jewish bioethics, 9
Jewish gene pool, 226
Jewish life-saving mentality, 180–181
Jewish medical ethics, 9
Jewish Medical Ethics, 283–284
Jordan, H5N1 in, 23

Kamara, Ahiya, 112–113
Kasher, Asa, 287
kinship
ART and, 119, 120–121
relatedness and, 120
Knesset
clinical ethics influenced by, 285
on hunger strikes, among inmates, 1–2
under the Correction, 56–58
force-feeding of, 50–51, 56–58

language
in commercial surrogacy marketing, 145
of disability rights movement, 102–103
Palestinian women and, alienation as result of, 171
Latour, Bruno, 258–259
Lavee, Jacob, 269–270
Law of Return, 170
Legal Capacity and Guardianship Law, 112, 113–114
Levinson, Yaacov, 303
liberal egalitarian republicanism, 53
liberalism
bioethics influenced by, 4
in Israel, 41–43
life-prolonging treatments, 53
in end-of-life decision-making, 249–250, 254–255
Litzman, Yaakov, 268–269
living wills, 272

mainstream bioethics. *See* bioethics
marketing, of commercial surrogacy, 141, 144–153
control procedures, 151–152
framing of cross-border surrogacy, 145–149, 153, 154
language in, 145
surveillance in, 151–152

maternity wards, racial segregation in, 88–94
Mazuz, Menachem, 303–304
MECIDS. *See* Middle Eastern Consortium on Infectious Disease Surveillance
medical authority, 166–168
medical community
  Abduction of Yemenite, Mizrahi, and Balkan children affair and, 79–84
    Ein Shemer camp and, 80
    IMA and, 85–87
    NGOs for, 79–80
    nurses' role in, 84–85
    racism in, 81–82
  Depo-Provera affair and, 82–84
    IMoH and, 87–88
    racism in, 83–84
  public criticism of, 3
  racism and, 77–79
    in Abduction of Yemenite, Mizrahi, and Balkan children affair, 81–82
    denial of, mechanisms for, 84–94
    in Depo-Provera affair, 83–84
    nature of knowing and, 84–88
    PHRI and, 88–90
    public acknowledgment of, 88–94
medicalization of pregnancy, 153
Meir, Joseph, 81–82
Meshulam, Uzzi, 50–51
methodological study
  of end-of-life decision-making, 245–250
    communications with dying patient in, 246–247
    demographics in, 246
    family relationships in, 247–249
    findings from, 245–250
    life-prolonging treatment provisions in, 249–250, 254–255
  for securitization of public health, 24–25
Middle Eastern Consortium on Infectious Disease Surveillance (MECIDS), 23, 29
  pandemic preparedness and, 34–36
midwifery, 186, 195
Midwifery Act, 187
military-cultural complex, in Israel-Palestine, 28
El-Mizrahi, David, 305–306
modern republicanism, 46
motherhood. *See* responsible motherhood
My Sister's Keeper, 132

National Health Insurance Law, 161, 164, 279–280
  IVF under, 164
  public health genetics services under, 224
national identity, for Palestinian citizens, 163–166
National Insurance Act, 188
National Pandemic Planning Committees (NPPCs), 29
National Security Law, 188
National Suicide Prevention Program, 300–302
Nazi regime, bioethics during, 3
  Helsinki Declaration as result of, 3
  Nuremberg Code as result of, 3
neo-Aristotelian republicanism, 43
neonatal care
  Baby Health Movement and, 181–182
  Hadassah organization and, 185–189
    Drop of Milk clinics and, 186, 188
    Midwifery Act and, 187
  in Israel, 181
  screening initiatives for, 182
    for congenital hypothyroidism, 183
    with DNA analysis, 183
    for PKU, 182–183, 189–190
    for XYY hypothesis, 183
  under UK Birth Notification Act, 182
neo-Roman republicanism, 43–44
New Family, 128, 213–214, 215
newborn screenings, 183–185, 196
  community-based screenings, 230–233
  Guthrie method in, 184
  hospital births and, 184–185
  initiatives for, 182
    for congenital hypothyroidism, 183, 228–229
    with DNA analysis, 183
    for PKU, 182–183, 189–190, 228–229
    for XYY hypothesis, 183
  in Israel, 185–191
    new technologies for, 190–191
    at Tel HaShomer hospital, 189–190
  public health genetics services and, 228–230
  universalist approach to, 183–184
  Zionism and, 189–190
non-governmental organizations (NGOs)
  for Abduction of Yemenite, Mizrahi, and Balkan children affair, 79–80
  pandemic preparedness and, 37–38
  for posthumous assisted reproduction, 213–214, 215
non-maleficence principles, 251–252
nothing about us without us perspective, 103–108, 113
NPPCs. *See* National Pandemic Planning Committees
Nuremberg Code, 3
nurses
  Abduction of Yemenite, Mizrahi, and Balkan children affair and, 84–85
  clinical ethics and, 291
nutritional security, 70

OD. *See* organ donation
Ofer, Avraham, 303
OFP. *See* Orange Flame Project
One Way Road, 81
online reproductive marketing, 144–153
    language in, 145
Orange Flame Project (OFP), 31
organ donation (OD)
    bioethics of, 258–259, 268–271
    brain death and, 259–261, 271–273
    dead donor rule and, 271–273
    under Declaration of Istanbul, 264
    in Israel
        introduction of, 259
        from 1968–2008, 262–267
        organ trafficking, 263–264
        though ADI, 262, 263
        under Transplantation Bill, 266–267
    transplantation costs, 264
organ tourism, 267
organ trafficking, 263–264

PA. *See* Palestine Authority
Palestine. *See also* Israel-Palestine
    Hadassah organization in, 185–189
    health governance systems, 28–29
    hospital births in, 187
    infant mortality rates in, 180
    pandemic preparedness in, 36–38
        NGOs and, 37–38
        occupied territory status as factor in, 37–38
        PMoH and, 36–37
        regional cooperation for, 34–36
    pro-natal policies in, 163–166
Palestine Authority (PA), 28
Palestine Ministry of Health (PMoH), pandemic preparedness and, 36–37
Palestinian citizens, in Israel
    citizenship of, 163–166
    health care for, 161
        under National Health Insurance Law, 161
    national identity for, 163–166
    settlement history of, 160–161
Palestinian women, in Israel
    children for, symbolism of, 163
    fertility treatments for, 162–163, 164–165
        Israel policy as factor for, 170–172
    health care for, 160–163
        through traditional healers, 173–174
    infertility among, 162
    internal colonization and, 164–165, 167
    medical authority and, navigation of, 166–168
    in therapeutic space, challenges in, 166–175
        alienation as result of language barriers, 171

        for body self-image, 168
        coping strategies, 172–175
        emotional responses to, 168–169
        medical authority, 166–168
pandemic preparedness
    competitive perspective on, 33
    in Israel, 29–36
        civil-military cooperation in, 31–32
        EMT in, 30–32
        historical development of, 29–31
        IMoH and, 29–34
        policy frameworks for, interaction of, 33–34
        regional cooperation for, 34–36
    MECIDS and, 34–36
    OFP and, 31
    in Palestine, 36–38
        NGOs and, 37–38
        occupied territory status as factor in, 37–38
        PMoH and, 36–37
        regional cooperation for, 34–36
    synergistic perspective on, 33
    WHO guidelines, NPPCs and, 29
PAR. *See* posthumous assisted reproduction
patients' rights, 286–287
Patient's Rights Law, 53, 58, 62, 65, 282
peer shame, 305–306
personal heroic shame, 302
PGD. *See* preimplantation genetic diagnosis
phenylketonuria (PKU), screening for, 182–183, 189–190, 228–229
PHR. *See* posthumous reproduction
PHRI. *See* Physicians for Human Rights-Israel
physical presence, 109–110
Physicians for Human Rights-Israel (PHRI), 76
    racism within medical community and, 88–90
PKU. *See* phenylketonuria
planned orphans, 204
PMoH. *See* Palestine Ministry of Health
PND. *See* prenatal diagnosis
political fetishization of body, 69
Portugese, Jaqueline, 170
posthumous assisted reproduction (PAR), 203–215
    defined, 202
    ethical issues with, 203–205
        for parent of deceased requests, 205
    gender implications for, 204
    in Israel, 205–215, 216
        expertocratic approach to, 213
        halakhic approaches to, 208, 210–212
        IDF and, 206, 207–210
        military context for, 205–210
    through IVF, 204–205
    NGOs for, 213–214, 215
    "parent" in, definition of term, 202

posthumous assisted reproduction (PAR) (cont.)
  planned orphans and, 204
  pronatalism and, 215
  public policy issues for, 203–205
  social issues regarding, 203–205
posthumous grandparenthood, 128
posthumous reproduction (PHR), 127–131
  in Israel, 127–128
    IAG regulations, 127–129
    New Family and, 127–129
  national restrictions on, by nation, 127
  in U.S., 128–129
practices of purification, 258–259
Prainsack, Barbara, 235
pregnancy. *See* medicalization of pregnancy; responsible motherhood
preimplantation genetic diagnosis (PGD), 131–132
prenatal diagnosis (PND), 124–127
  abortion and, 124–126
preparedness thinking, in EID concept, 26
prevention, in EID concept, 26
principalist approach, to bioethics, 7
Prison Information Group (GIP), 66
privatized shame, 303
professional shame, 305–306
pronatalism, 123, 124
  in Israel, 139, 163–166
  in Palestine, 163–166
  posthumous assisted reproduction and, 215
public health. *See also* securitization
  bioethical codes and, 4
  in Israel, 32, 81–82, 180–181
    through newborn screening, 189–190
  in Palestine
    Hadassah and, 185–189
    pandemic preparedness and, 36–38
  pandemic preparedness and, 33–34
    in Palestine, 36–38
  Patient's Rights law and, 53
  politics as separate from, 1
  suicidology and, 295
public health genetics services
  Ashkenazi Jewish community and, 225–226
  for carrier screenings, 228–230
  community genetics, 224, 234
  for community-based screenings, 230–233
  for Down Syndrome screening, 223–224
  ethnic categorization in, 231–232, 233
  expansion of, 224
  for genetic databases, 226, 230–233
  HGDP and, 232
  Human Genome Project and, 232
  in Israel, 224–233
    comparative perspectives on, 224, 226–228
  genetic counseling clinics, 224–225
  historical development of, 224–226
  national genetics database in, 226
  under National Health Insurance Law, 224
  in screening programs, 225–226
  for newborn screenings, 228–230
  religious categorization in, 231–232, 233
  in U.S., 226–228
    ethnic profiling by, 231

racial ideology, surrogacy and, 142
racism
  in health care systems, 77
    institutional denial of, 78–79
  in maternity wards, 88–94
  in medical community, 77–79
    in Abduction of Yemenite, Mizrahi, and Balkan children affair, 81–82
    denial of, mechanisms for, 84–94
    in Depo-Provera affair, 83–84
    nature of knowing and, 84–88
    PHRI and, 88–90
    public acknowledgment of, 88–94
radical egalitarian republicanism, 47, 48–49
  autonomy and, 51–52
  bioethics and, 49–53
    life-prolonging drugs and, 53
  freedom in, 49, 52
  right to health and, 50–51
Radin, Margaret, 148
Rapp, Rayna, 126, 140
relatedness, kinship and, 120
religion, public health genetics services and, 231–232, 233
reproduction, Israeli approach to, 202–203
reproductive ethics, 277
reprogenetics, 126
republicanism
  common good in, 46–47, 48–49
  egalitarian. *See also* radical egalitarian republicanism
  defined, 42–43
  freedom as part of, 44–46
  liberal, 53
  political equality as part of, 44–46
  heterogeneity within, 43
  modern, 46
  neo-Aristotelian, 43
  neo-Roman, 43–44
  solidarity aspects of, 46
    fraternity compared to, 46
responsible motherhood, 126
Reznik, Ran, 147
right to health, 50–51. *See also* patients' rights

risk. *See* different discursive framing of risk
Roberts, Ed, 101
Rose, Nikolas, 152
Rosenblum, Irit, 213–214, 215
Rudrappa, Sharmila, 140

Sadgat scandal, 259–261
sanctity of life, 1–2
SCD. *See* sickle-cell disease
screening programs. *See also* newborn screenings
  carrier, 228–230
  community-based, 230–233
  for Down Syndrome, 223–224
  for PKU, 182–183, 189–190, 228–229
  for SCD, 231
securitization, of public health
  components of, 24
  GPHS and, 25–26, 38–39
    dual use arguments, 27–28
    EID concept, 25–26
    ethical challenges to, 27–28
    IHR and, 26–27
  H5N1 outbreak and, 23
  historical background of, 25–29
  methodology for, 24–25
selective abortions. *See* abortions
shame, suicide and, 297–298, 302–306
  antiheroic, 302
  civic, 303
  of nation, 306
  peer, 305–306
  personal heroic, 302
  privatized, 303
  professional, 305–306
  of State, 304–305
  systemic, 303–304
sick fund insurance, 278, 280
sickle-cell disease (SCD), screening
    for, 231
Sigal, Gil, 41, 51
Silman, Moshe, 304–305
social Darwinism, 99
solidarity, 46
  fraternity compared to, 46
Strauss, Nathan, 186
suicide, in Israel. *See also* shame
  bioethics and
    global approaches to, 298–299
    National Suicide Prevention Program and, 300–302
    WHO guidelines for, 298–299, 300–302
  dishonor and, 297–298
  media studies on, 297
  taxonomy of, 297–298

visibility of, 307–308
WHO on, 295, 296, 298–299, 300–302
suicide prevention programs, 295, 296
suicide terrorism, 1–2
suicidology, 295–298
  folk explanations, 296
  public health and, 295
surrogacy
  agreements and contracts, 149, 153
  altruism and, 145
  ART and, 140
  bodily autonomy and, of surrogates, 152–153
  CBRC and, 140–141
  commissioning parents and surrogate
      relationships, 149–151
  financial necessity as factor in, 154–155
  flexible bureaucracy for, 146
  gifts for, 145
  historical development of, 140–141
  in Israel, 142–144
    under Embryo Carrying Agreements Act, 142–144, 146
    rise in births, 144
    state comparisons in, 147
  marketing of, 141, 144–153
    control procedures, 151–152
    framing of cross-border surrogacy, 145–149, 153, 154
    language in, 145
    surveillance in, 151–152
  medical procedures with, 152–153
  medicalization of pregnancy, 153
  racial ideology and, 142
  in Ukraine, 147, 149
surrogacy agencies, 139, 154
  brokers in, 153–154
  in India, 148, 150
  intermediaries within, 153–154
  in Thailand, 150
survivalism, 288–289
synergistic perspective, on pandemic
    preparedness, 33
systemic shame, 303–304

Talmor, Adi, 305
technological determinism, 10
Tel HaShomer hospital, newborn screenings at, 189–190
Terminal Patient law, 285
terrorism. *See* suicide terrorism
Thailand, surrogacy agencies in, 150
therapeutic space, Palestinian women and, 166–175
  alienation as result of language barriers, 171

therapeutic space, Palestinian women and (cont.)
  for body self-image, 168
  coping strategies, 172–175
  emotional responses to, 168–169
  medical authority, 166–168
tolerance, 290–291
Topaz, Dudu, 306
traditional healers, 173–174
Transplantation Bill, 266–267
transplantation costs, of OD, 264
Tuskegee syphilis study, 3

UK Birth Notification Act, 182
Ukraine, surrogacy in, 147
  commissioning parents and, 149
United States (U.S.)
  Jewish American families in, early studies on, 122
  PHR in, 128–129
  public health genetics services in, 226–228
    ethnic profiling by, 231

Veatch, Robert, 261
Virshubski, Mordechai, 112–113
voice, in disability activism
  through Disability Rights Commission, 111–113
  in individual decision-making, 105–106
  institutionalization of, 111–113

Weiner, David, 303–304
welfare institutions, inmate hunger strikes and, 70
Welfare (Treatment of Retarded Persons) Law, 105–106

WHO. *See* World Health Organization
Winfrey, Oprah, 139
WMA. *See* World Medical Association
women. *See also* Palestinian women
  body self-image for, 168
  Ethiopian, in Depo-Provera affair, 82–84
Woods, Fiona, 139
World Health Organization (WHO)
  GPHS and, 25–26, 38–39
    dual use arguments, 27–28
    EID concept, 25–26
    ethical challenges to, 27–28
    IHR and, 26–27
  H5N1 response and, 23
  NPPCs and, 29
  pandemic preparedness guidelines, 29
  suicide and, 295, 296, 298–299, 300–302
  suicide prevention programs and, 295, 296
World Medical Association (WMA), 57–58, 63–64
wrongful life claims, 112

XYY hypothesis, 183

Yated v. Ministry of Education, 107

Zionism, 100
  hospital births and, 187
  medicalization of childbirth influenced by, 196
  newborn screenings and, 189–190
Zuckerberg, Mark, 139

For EU product safety concerns, contact us at Calle de José Abascal, 56–1°, 28003 Madrid, Spain or eugpsr@cambridge.org.

www.ingramcontent.com/pod-product-compliance
Ingram Content Group UK Ltd.
Pitfield, Milton Keynes, MK11 3LW, UK
UKHW022240220326
469255UK00018B/279